Sherlock Bones 7

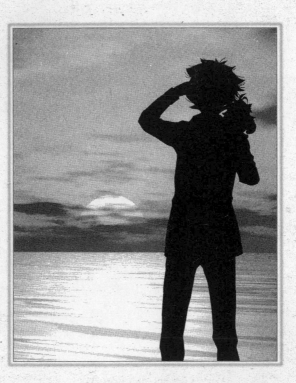

Sherdog & Takeru

Story: Yuma Ando   Art: Yuki Sato

CHARACTERS

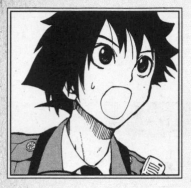

Takeru Wajima

A nineteen-year-old rookie police officer. He is Sherdog's owner and the one person who can understand him. He made a name for himself early in his career, and a special exception was made to transfer him to the detective department.

Sherdog

The mixed-breed puppy that Takeru adopted. His true identity is that of the world-famous detective, Sherlock Holmes. When he has the Wajima family's heirloom pipe in his mouth, he can speak to Takeru. He solves crimes with Takeru, learning about the modern world in the process.

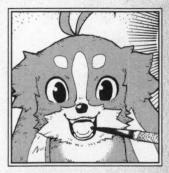

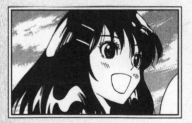

Miki Arisaka

Takeru's friend since childhood and currently a freshman at college. An aspiring journalist, she works part-time at a newspaper company.

Nanami Akane

Takeru and Miki's classmate from high school. Her reputation was once saved by Takeru. She became a police officer, possibly to be with Takeru.

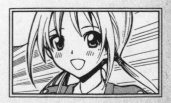

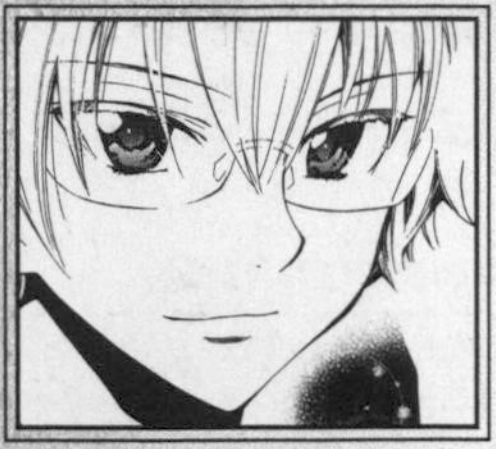

Kento Munakata

A career detective at the London Police Department, the same age as Takeru. An elite freshly back from New York, he boasts of his experience whenever he gets the chance.

Members of the Wajima Family

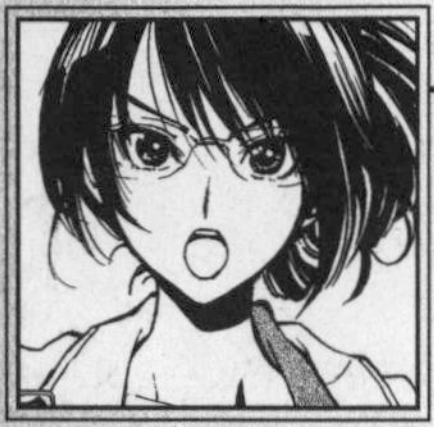

Airin Wajima

Takeru's sister, an inspector in the Violent Crimes Division, and a rather sexy woman. Sherdog calls her Irene.

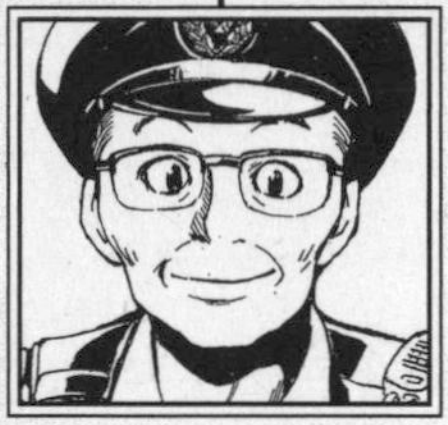

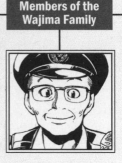

Kōsuke Wajima

Takeru's father. A sergeant in the police force.

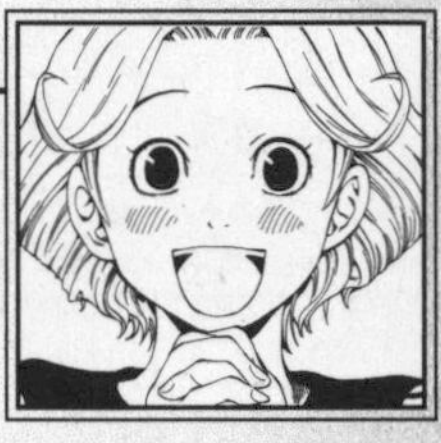

Satoko Wajima

Takeru's mother. She really hates it when Sherdog sits in her favorite rocking chair.

THE STORY SO FAR

STORY

The puppy Sherdog—reincarnation of Sherlock Holmes—and his owner Takeru Wajima team up to solve tough cases!! Soon after Takeru is transferred to the London PD's detective division, a woman is found hanging by her neck from the water tower of her apartment building. The death is believed to be a suicide spurred on by a failed cosmetic surgery operation, but as Takeru delves into the case, he is convinced that it is murder. He suspects the doctor at the woman's former beauty clinic and begins to investigate!

CONTENTS

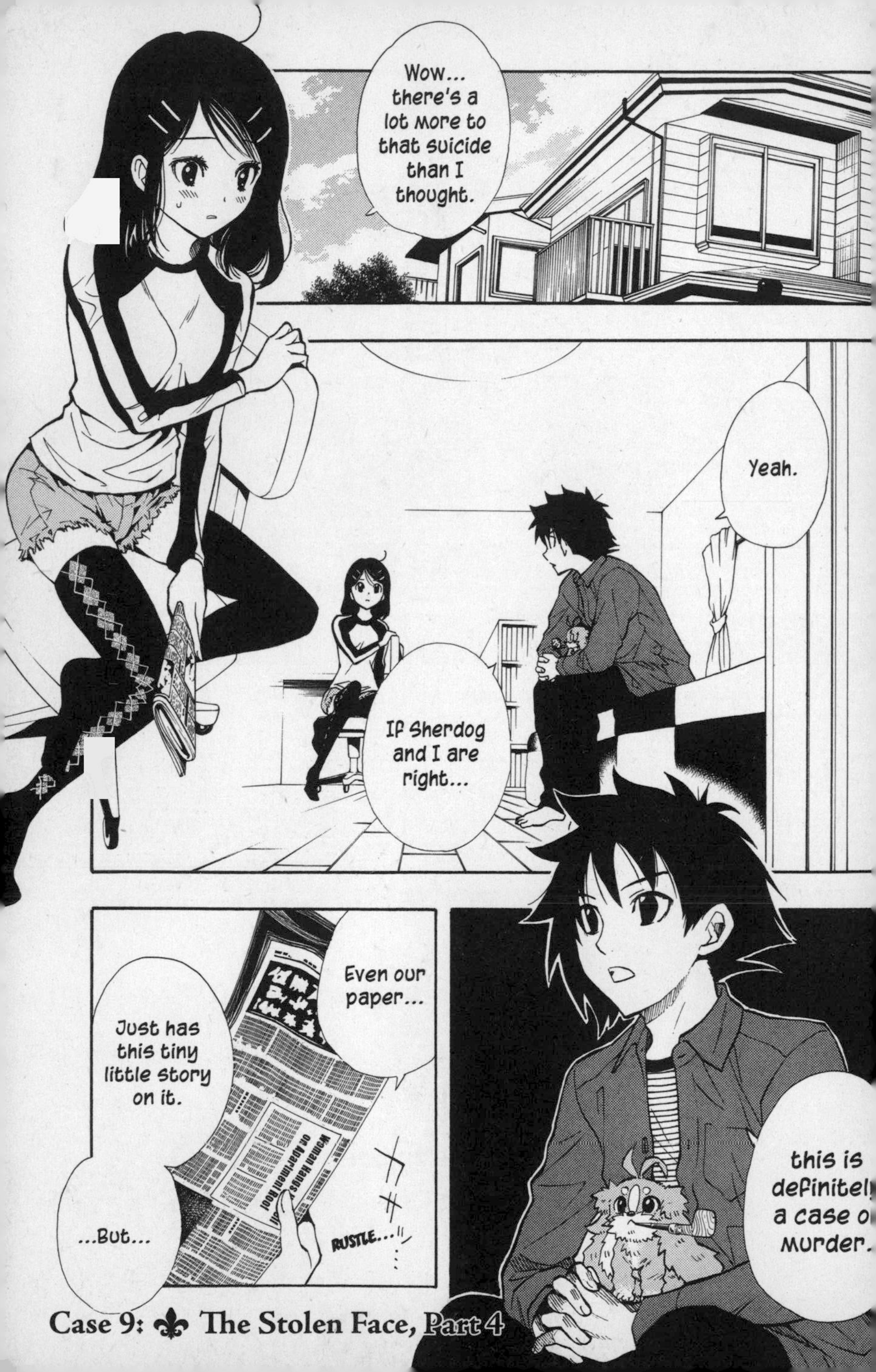
Wow... there's a lot more to that suicide than I thought.
Yeah.
If Sherdog and I are right...
this is definitel a case o murder.
Even our paper...
Just has this tiny little story on it.
Woman Hangs
off Apartment Roof
RUSTLE...
...But...

Case 9: ⚜ The Stolen Face, Part 4

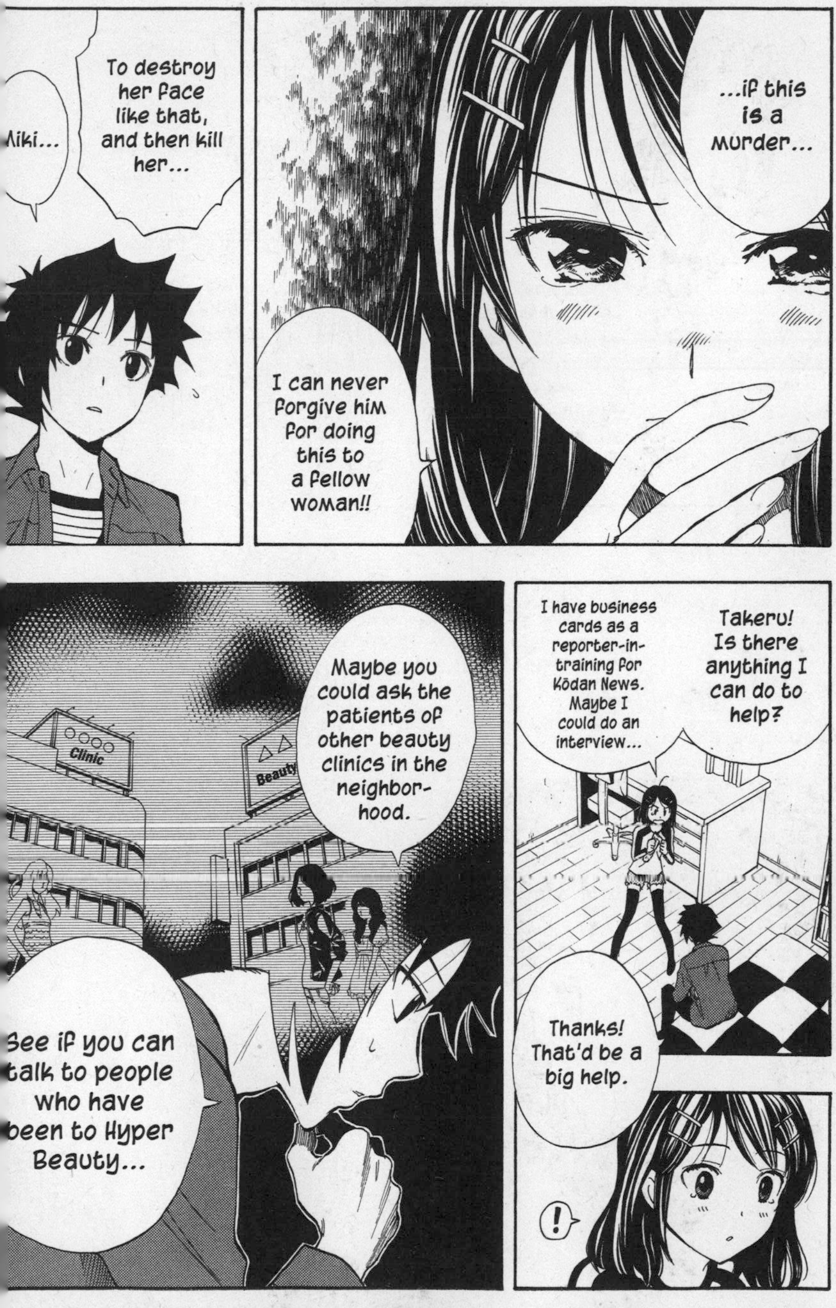
...if this is a murder...
I can never forgive him for doing this to a fellow woman!!
To destroy her face like that, and then kill her...
Miki...
Takeru! Is there anything I can do to help?
I have business cards as a reporter-in-training for Kōdan News. Maybe I could do an interview...
Thanks! That'd be a big help.
!
Maybe you could ask the patients of other beauty clinics in the neighbor-hood.
Clinic
Beauty
See if you can talk to people who have been to Hyper Beauty...

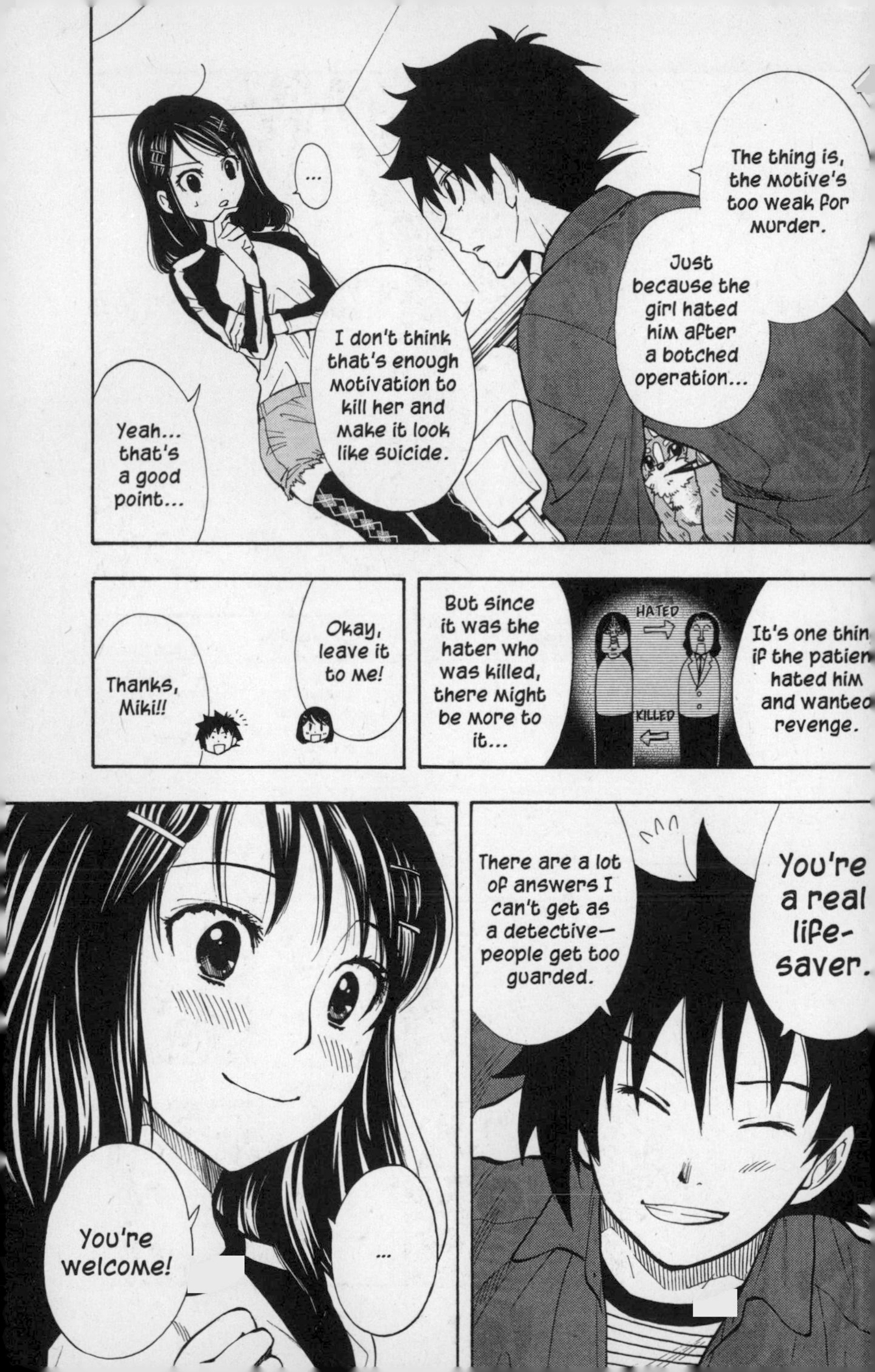
The thing is, the motive's too weak for murder.
Just because the girl hated him after a botched operation...
I don't think that's enough motivation to kill her and make it look like suicide.
...
Yeah... that's a good point...
It's one thin if the patien hated him and wante revenge.
HATED
KILLED
But since it was the hater who was killed, there might be more to it...
Okay, leave it to me!
Thanks, Miki!!
You're a real life-saver.
There are a lot of answers I can't get as a detective—people get too guarded.
...
You're welcome!

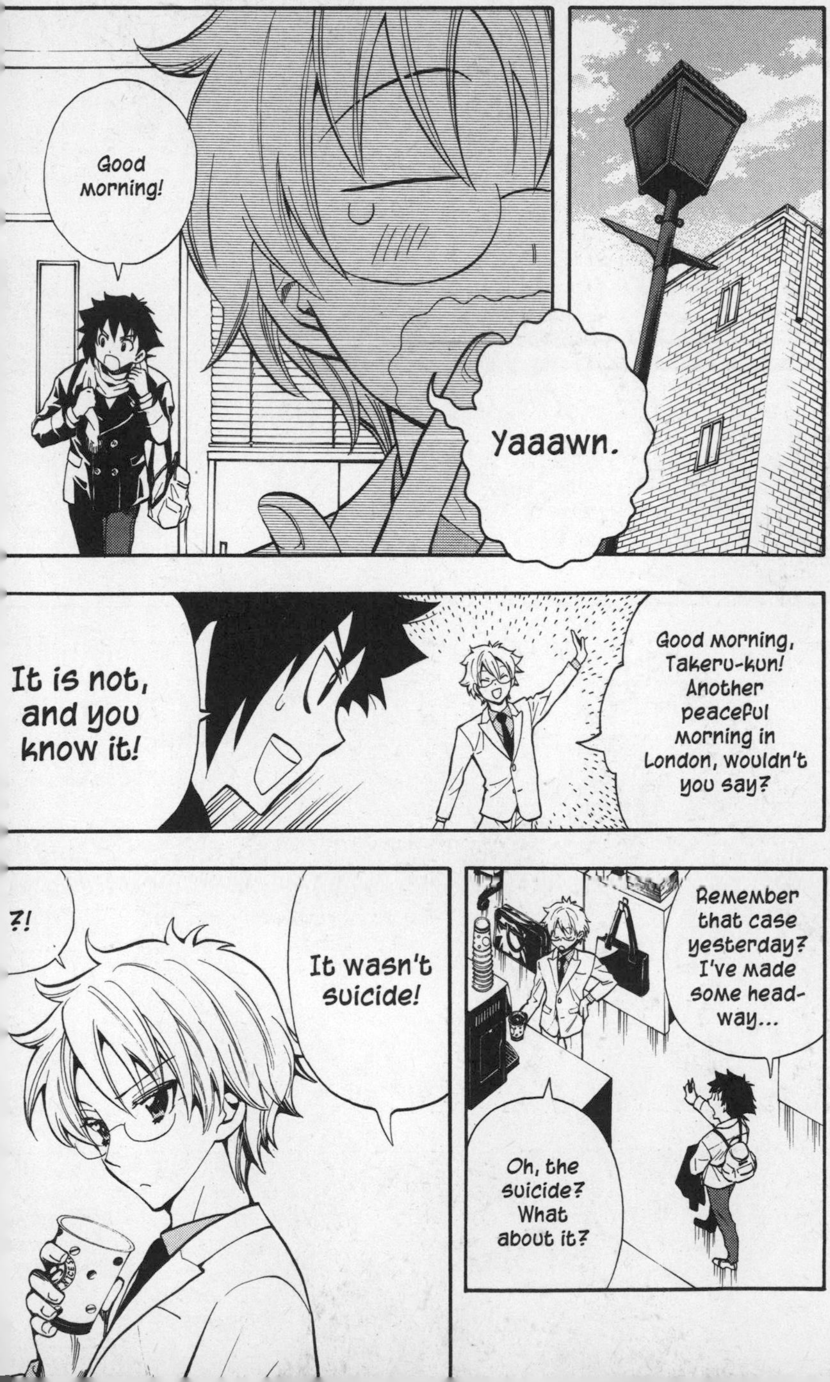
Yaaawn.
Good morning!
Good morning, Takeru-kun! Another peaceful morning in London, wouldn't you say?
It is not, and you know it!
Remember that case yesterday? I've made some head-way...
Oh, the suicide? What about it?
It wasn't suicide!
?!

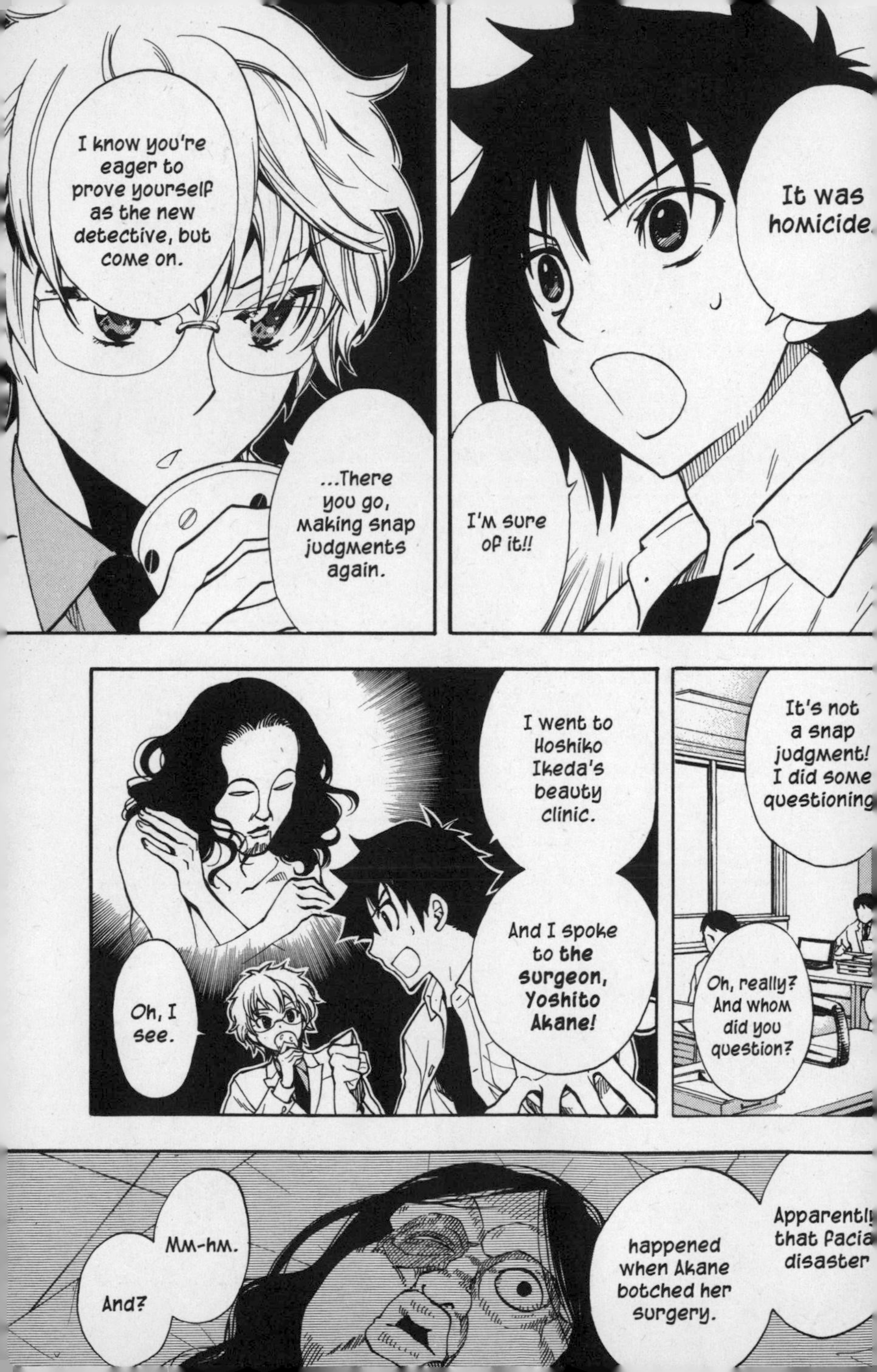

It was homicide.
I'm sure of it!!
I know you're eager to prove yourself as the new detective, but come on.
...There you go, making snap judgments again.
It's not a snap judgment! I did some questioning
Oh, really? And whom did you question?
I went to Hoshiko Ikeda's beauty clinic.
And I spoke to the surgeon, Yoshito Akane!
Oh, I see.
Apparently that facia disaster
happened when Akane botched her surgery.
Mm-hm.
And?

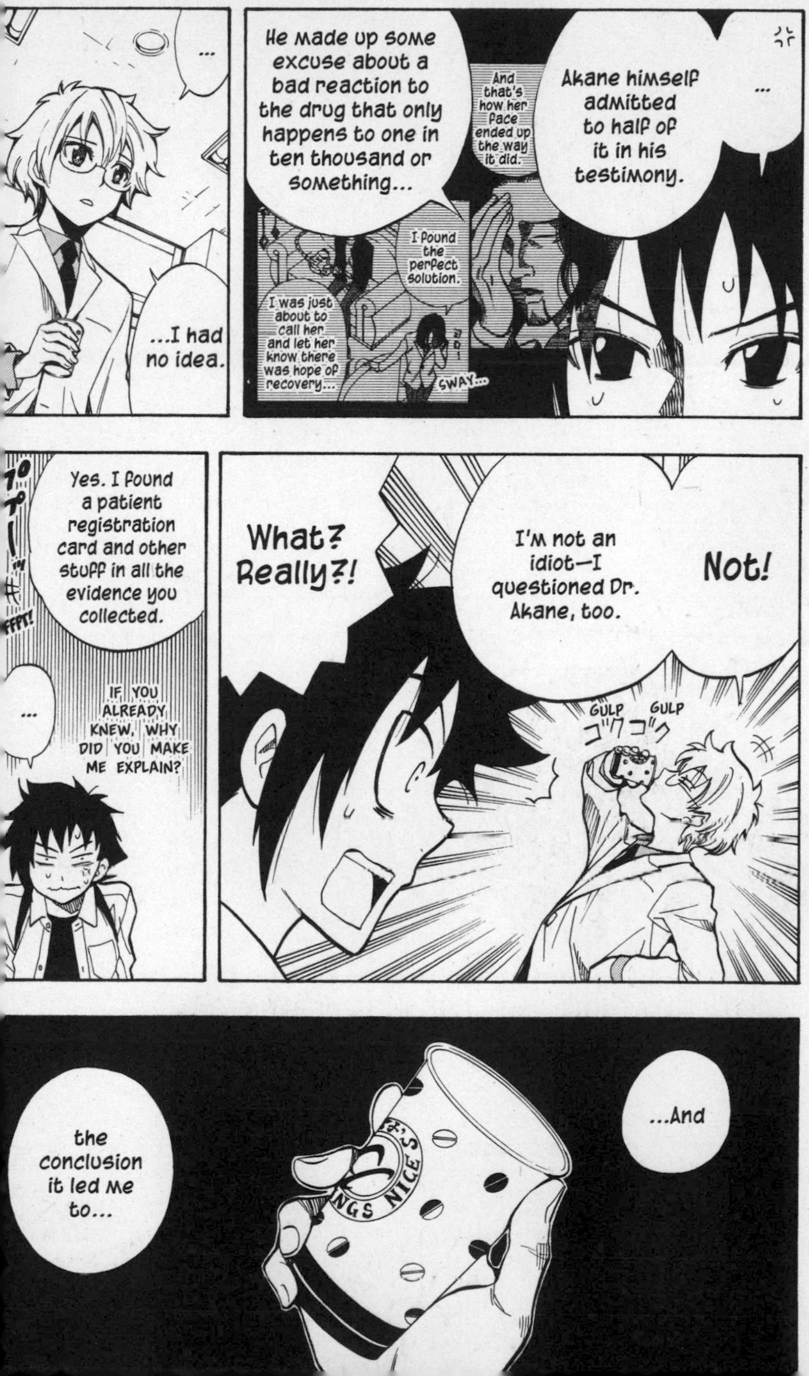
...
Akane himself admitted to half of it in his testimony.
And that's how her face ended up the way it did.
He made up some excuse about a bad reaction to the drug that only happens to one in ten thousand or something...
I found the perfect solution.
SWAY...
I was just about to call her and let her know there was hope of recovery...
...
...I had no idea.
Not!
I'm not an idiot—I questioned Dr. Akane, too.
What? Really?!
GULP GULP
Yes. I found a patient registration card and other stuff in all the evidence you collected.
IF YOU ALREADY KNEW, WHY DID YOU MAKE ME EXPLAIN?
...
...And
the conclusion it led me to...

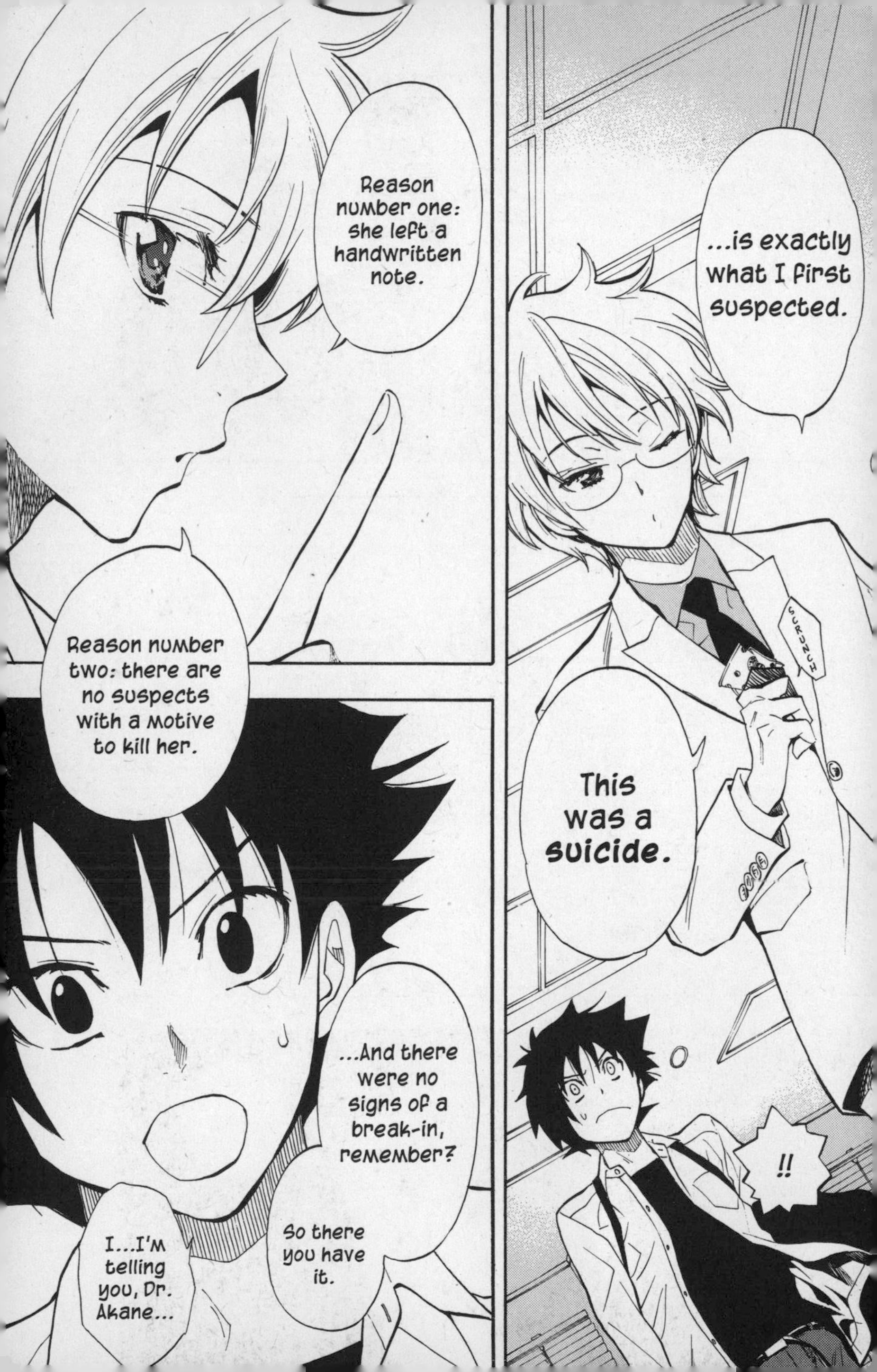
...is exactly what I first suspected.
SCRUNCH
This was a suicide.
!!
Reason number one: she left a handwritten note.
Reason number two: there are no suspects with a motive to kill her.
...And there were no signs of a break-in, remember?
So there you have it.
I...I'm telling you, Dr. Akane...

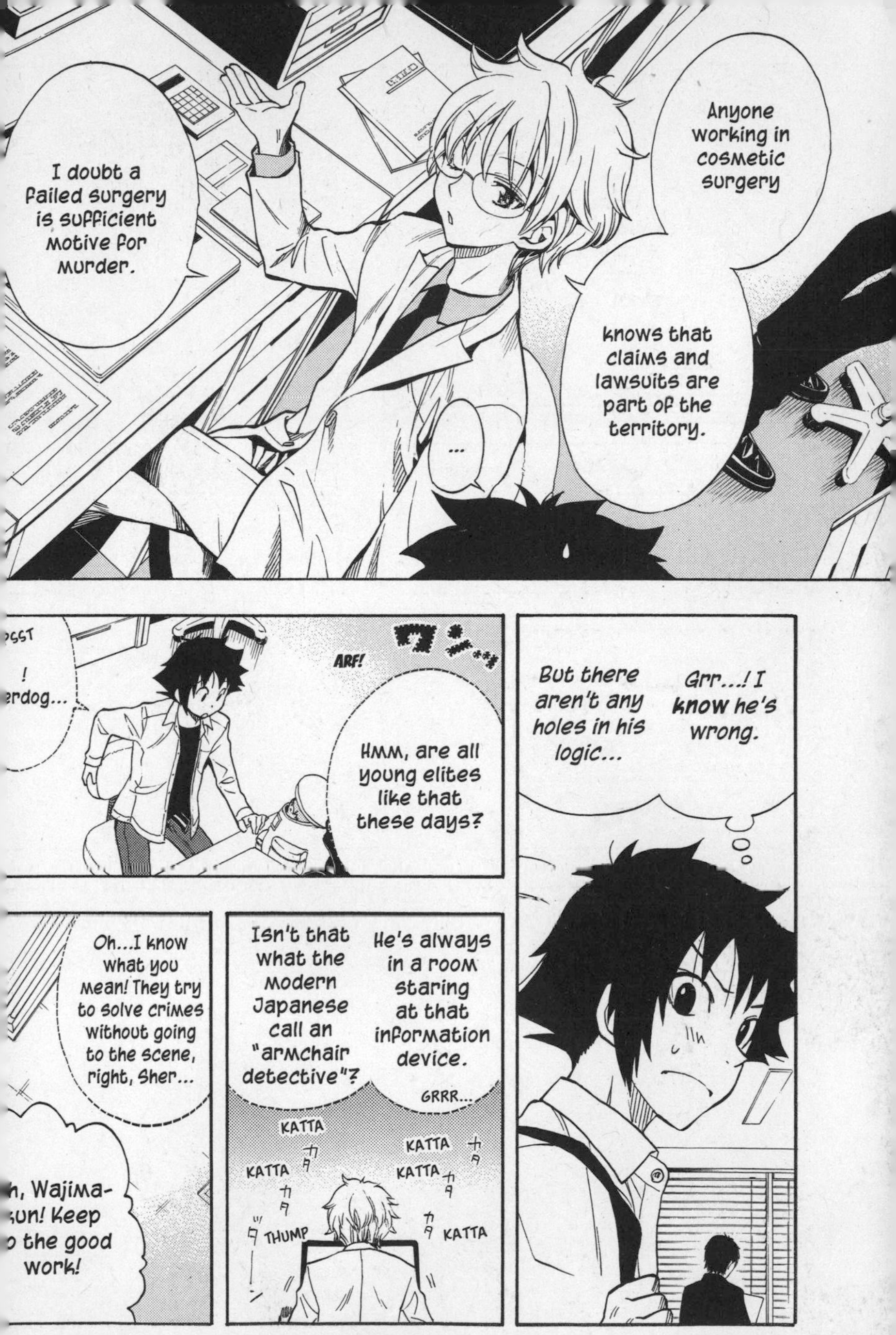
Anyone working in cosmetic surgery
knows that claims and lawsuits are part of the territory.
...
I doubt a failed surgery is sufficient motive for murder.
Grr...! I know he's wrong.
But there aren't any holes in his logic...
ARF!
Hmm, are all young elites like that these days?
PSST
!
erdog...
He's always in a room staring at that information device.
Isn't that what the modern Japanese call an "armchair detective"?
GRRR...
KATTA
KATTA
KATTA
KATTA
KATTA
THUMP
Oh...I know what you mean! They try to solve crimes without going to the scene, right, Sher...
h, Wajima-
un! Keep
o the good
work!

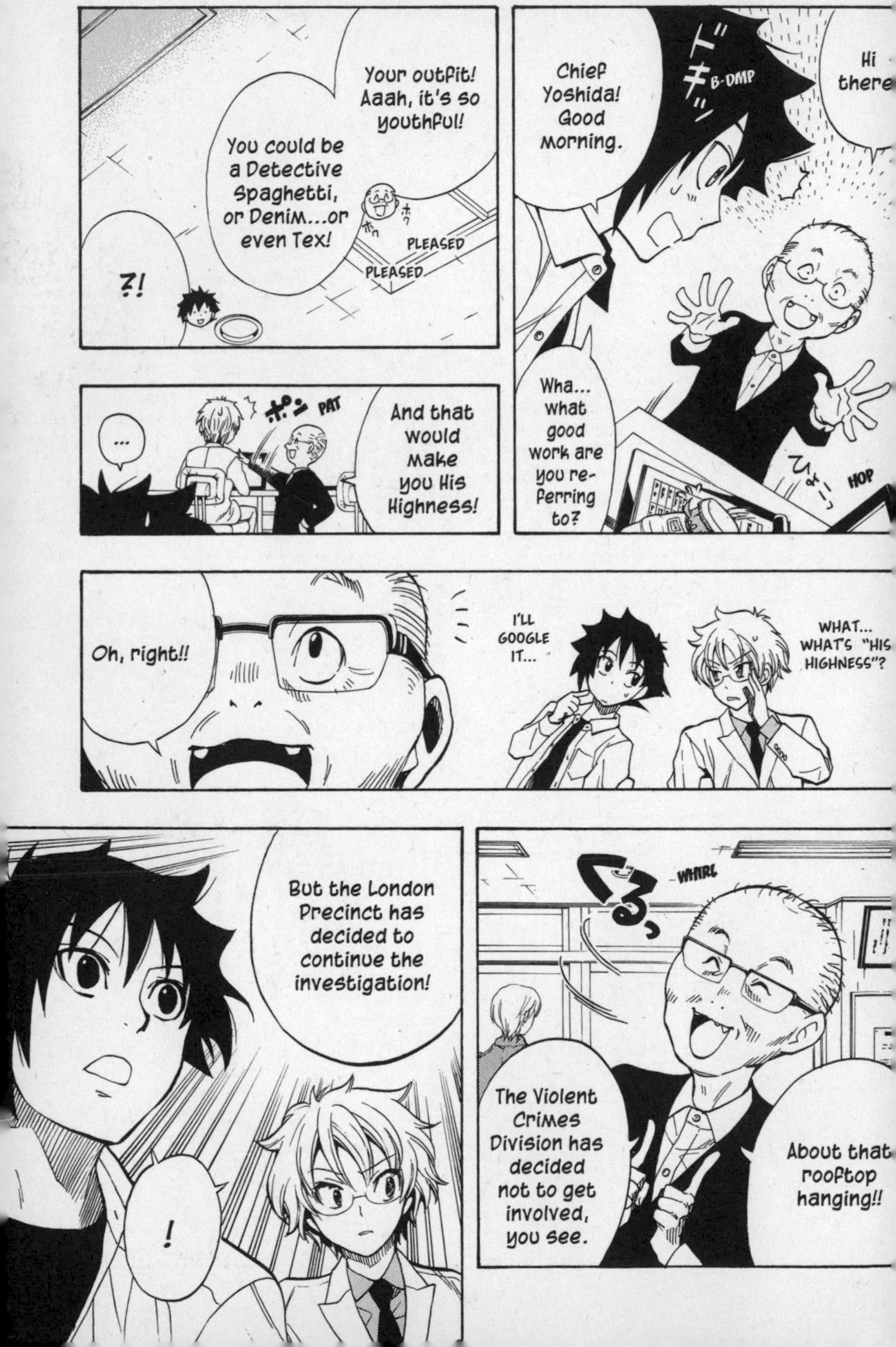

Hi there
B-DMP
Chief Yoshida! Good Morning.
HOP
Wha... what good work are you re-ferring to?
Your outfit! Aaah, it's so youthful!
You could be a Detective Spaghetti, or Denim...or even Tex!
PLEASED
PLEASED
?!
And that would make you His Highness!
PAT
...
WHAT... WHAT'S "HIS HIGHNESS"?
I'LL GOOGLE IT...
Oh, right!!
About that rooftop hanging!!
WHIRL
The Violent Crimes Division has decided not to get involved, you see.
But the London Precinct has decided to continue the investigation!
!

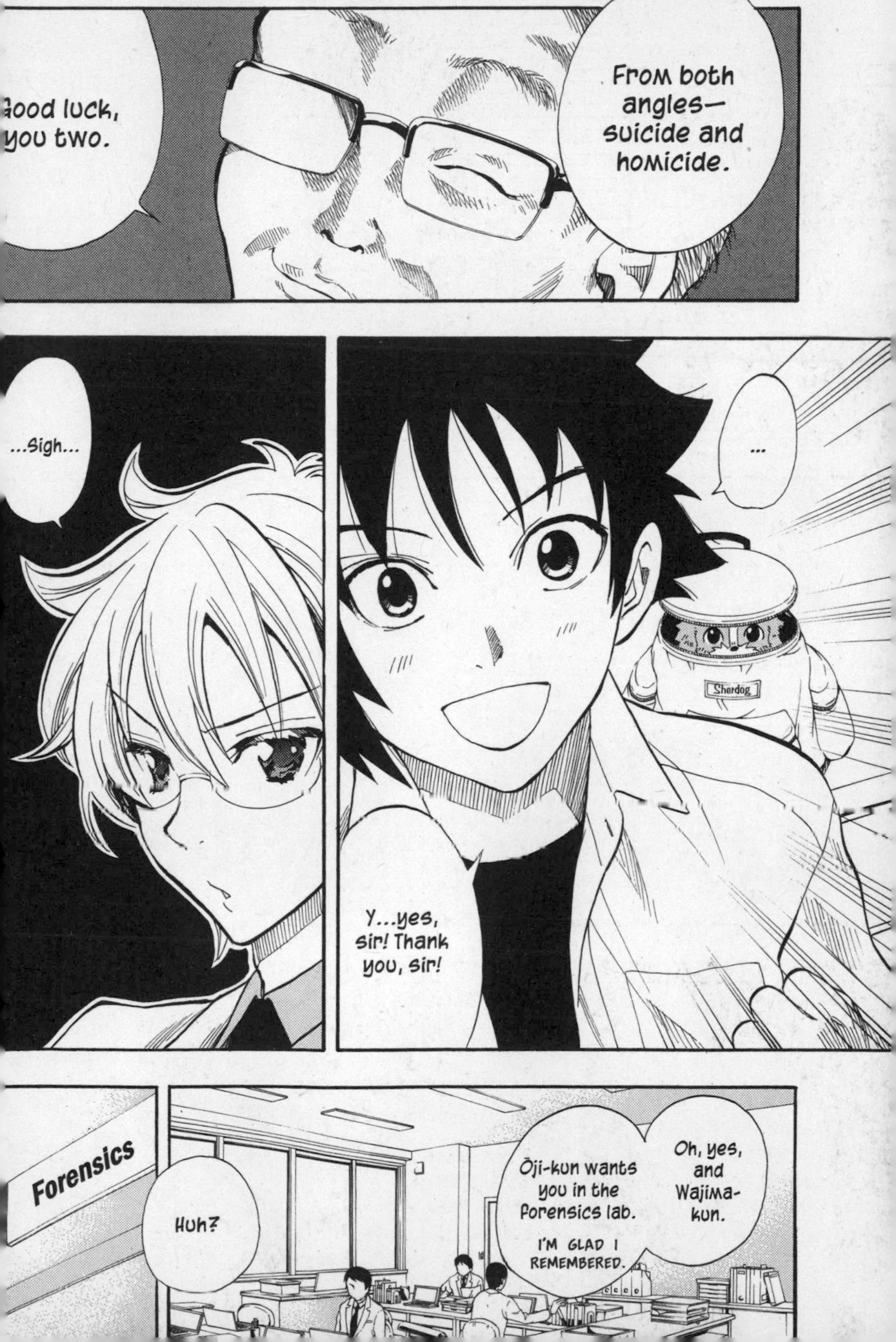
From both angles—suicide and homicide.
Good luck, you two.
...
Sherdog
Y...yes, sir! Thank you, sir!
...Sigh...
Oh, yes, and Wajima-kun.
Ōji-kun wants you in the forensics lab.
I'M GLAD I REMEMBERED.
Huh?
Forensics

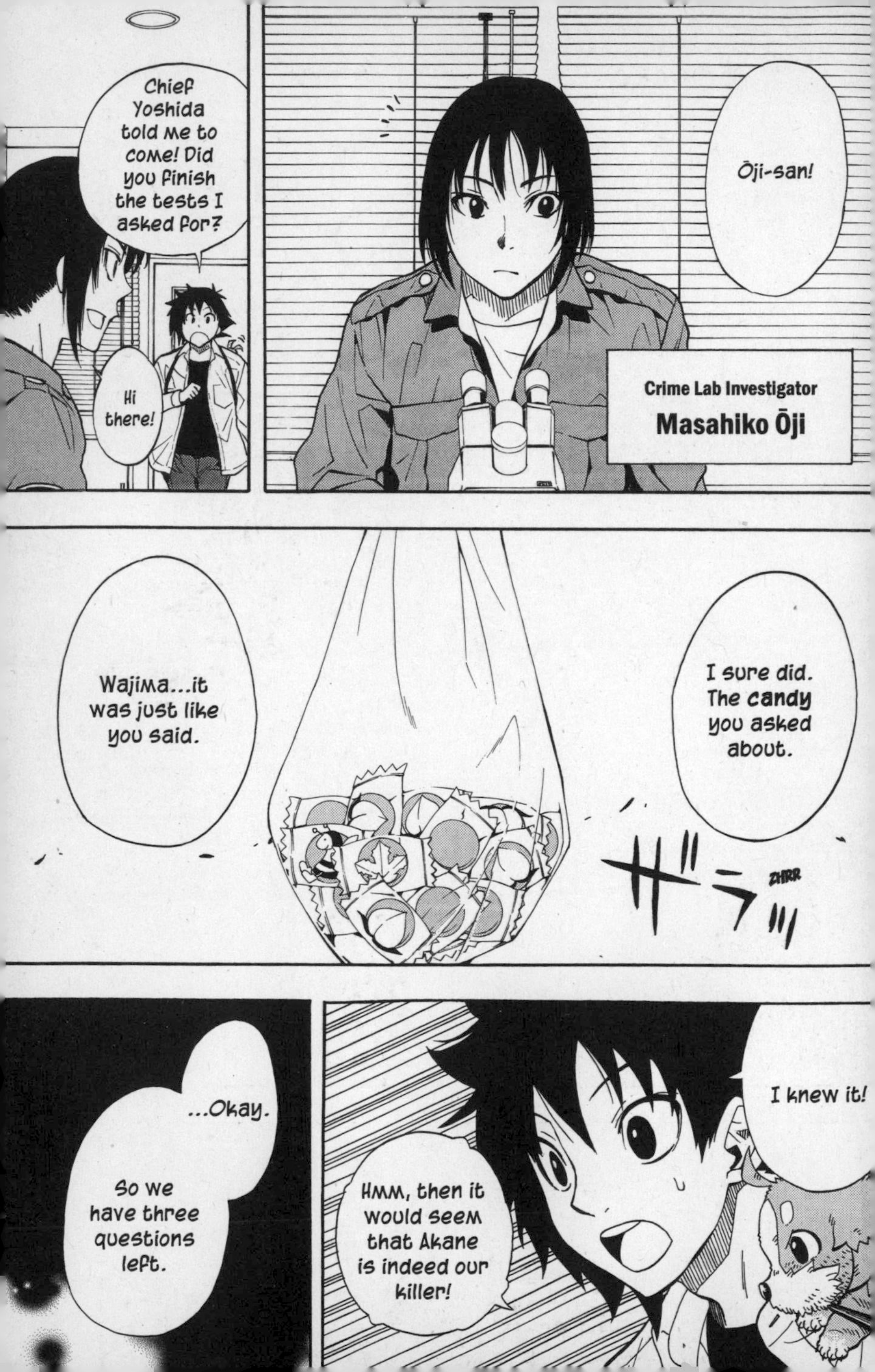
Ōji-san!
Crime Lab Investigator
Masahiko Ōji
Chief Yoshida told me to come! Did you finish the tests I asked for?
Hi there!
I sure did. The candy you asked about.
ZHRR
Wajima...it was just like you said.
I knew it!
HMM, then it would seem that Akane is indeed our killer!
...Okay.
So we have three questions left.

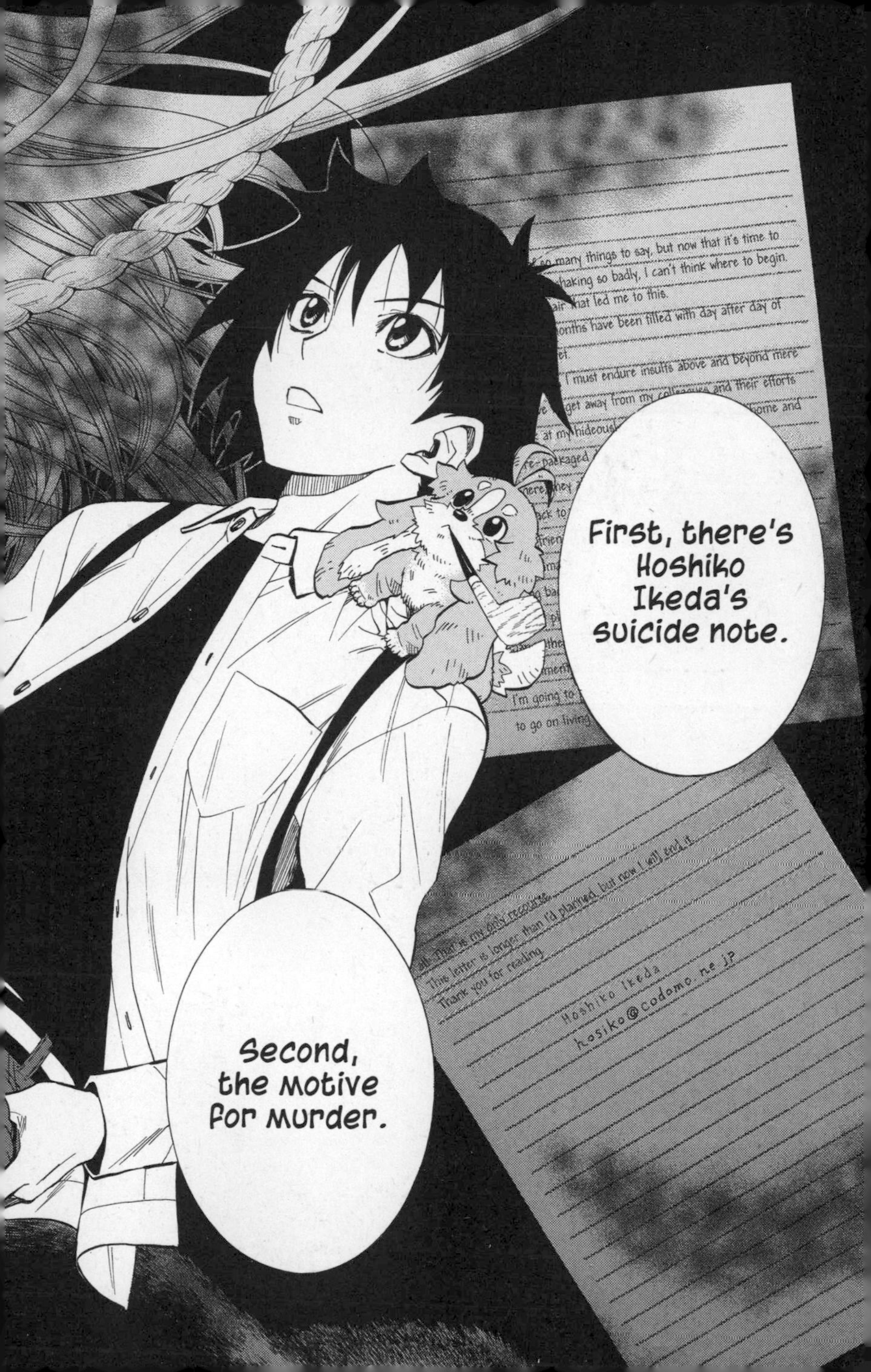
First, there's Hoshiko Ikeda's suicide note.
Second, the motive for murder.

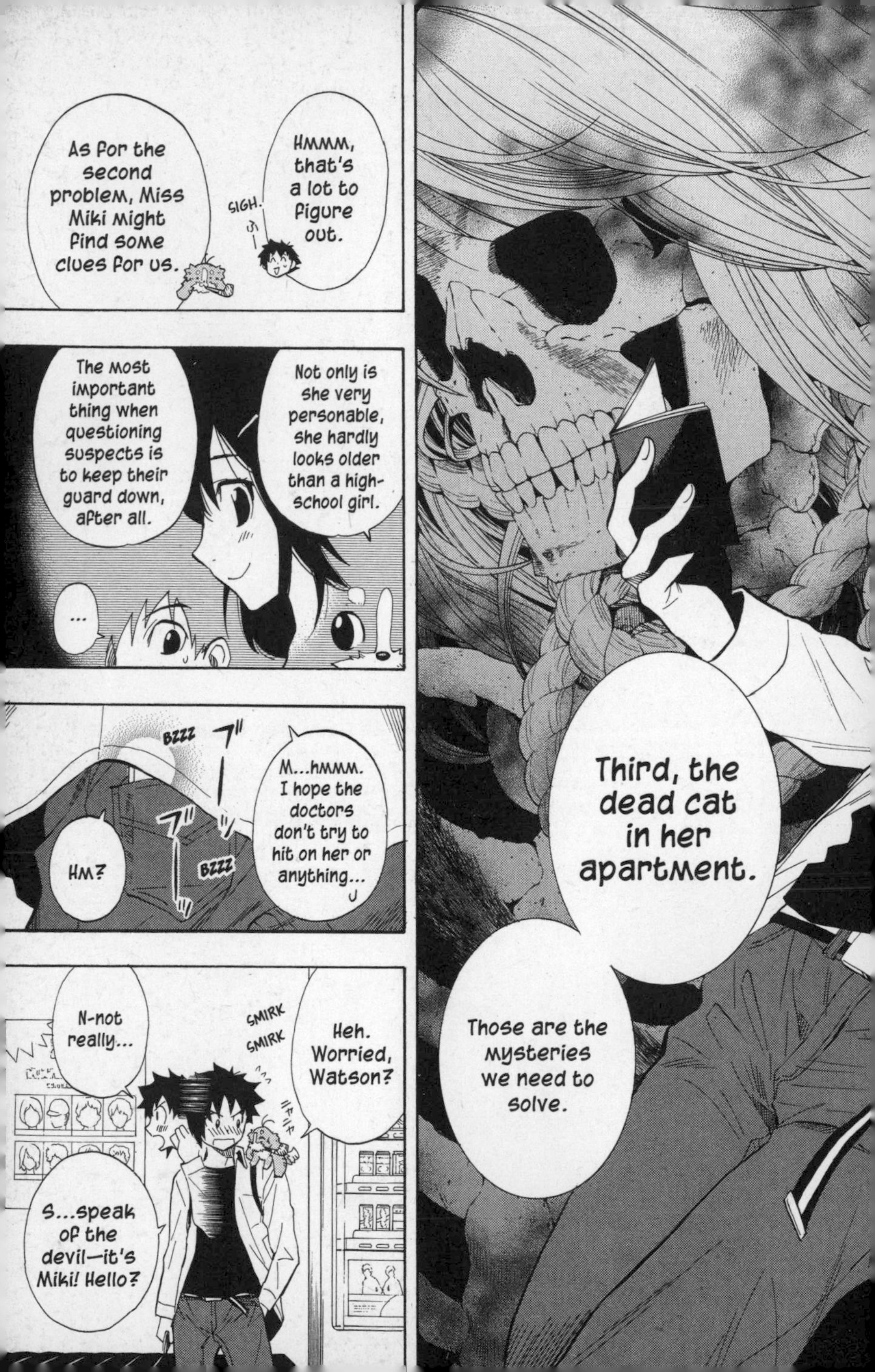
Third, the dead cat in her apartment.
Those are the mysteries we need to solve.
Hmmm, that's a lot to figure out.
SIGH.
As for the second problem, Miss Miki might find some clues for us.
Not only is she very personable, she hardly looks older than a high-school girl.
The most important thing when questioning suspects is to keep their guard down, after all.
...
BZZZ
M...hmmm. I hope the doctors don't try to hit on her or anything...
BZZZ
Hm?
Heh. Worried, Watson?
SMIRK SMIRK
N-not really...
S...speak of the devil—it's Miki! Hello?

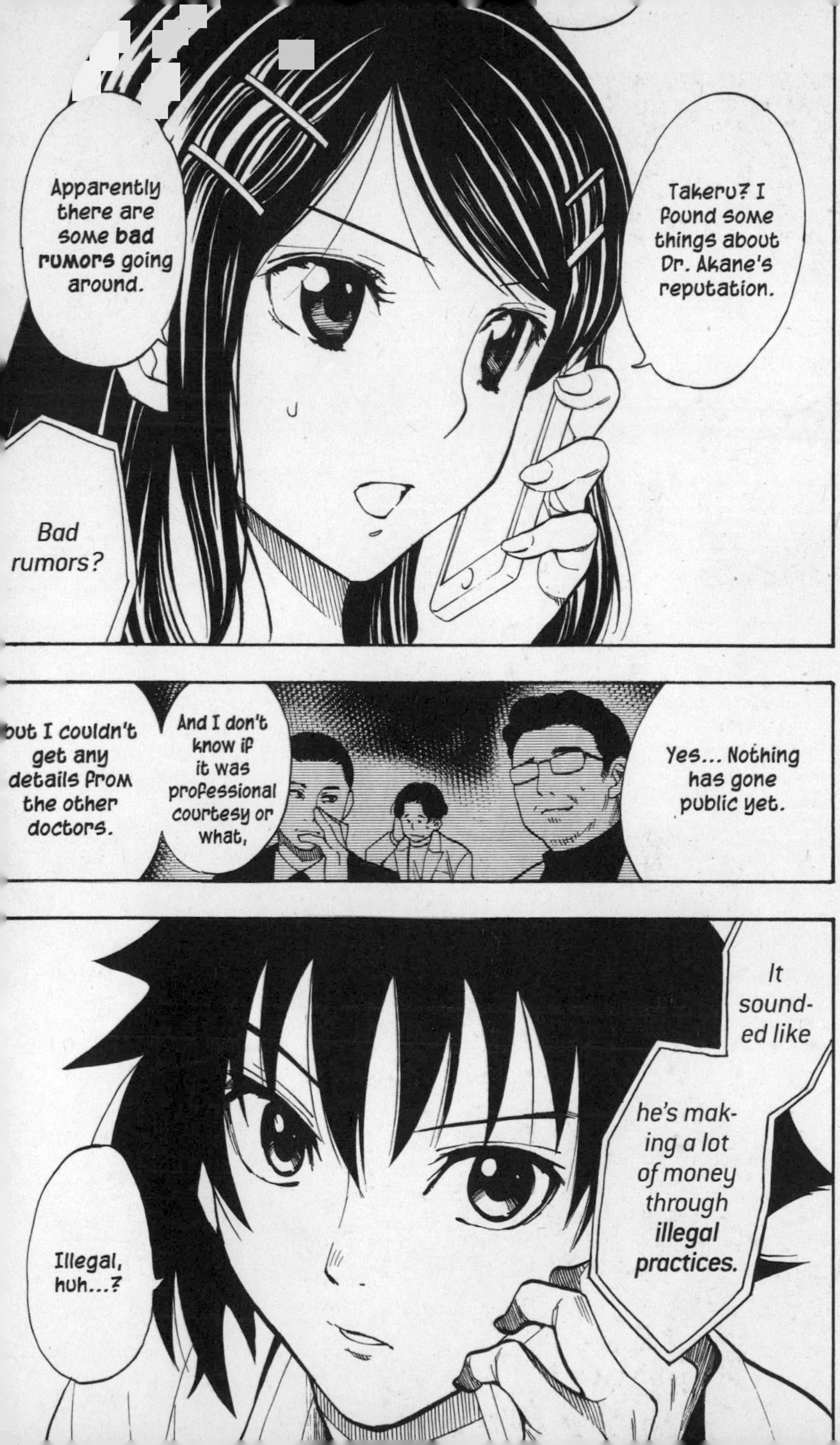
Takeru? I found some things about Dr. Akane's reputation.
Apparently there are some bad rumors going around.
Bad rumors?
Yes... Nothing has gone public yet.
And I don't know if it was professional courtesy or what,
but I couldn't get any details from the other doctors.
It sounded like
he's making a lot of money through illegal practices.
Illegal, huh...?

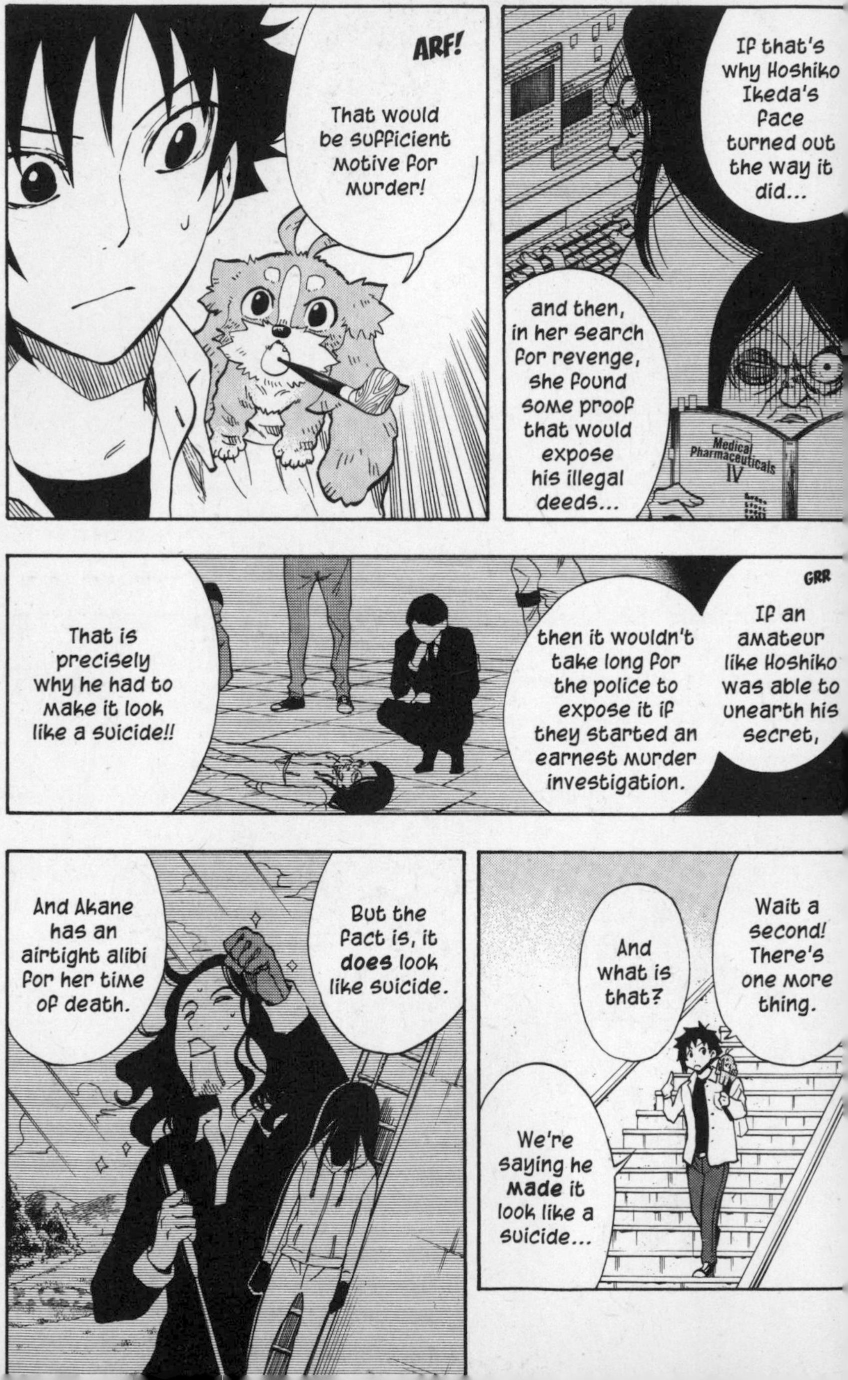
If that's why Hoshiko Ikeda's face turned out the way it did...
and then, in her search for revenge, she found some proof that would expose his illegal deeds...
Medical Pharmaceuticals IV
ARF!
That would be sufficient motive for murder!
GRR
If an amateur like Hoshiko was able to unearth his secret,
then it wouldn't take long for the police to expose it if they started an earnest murder investigation.
That is precisely why he had to make it look like a suicide!!
Wait a second! There's one more thing.
And what is that?
We're saying he **made** it look like a suicide...
But the fact is, it **does** look like suicide.
And Akane has an airtight alibi for her time of death.

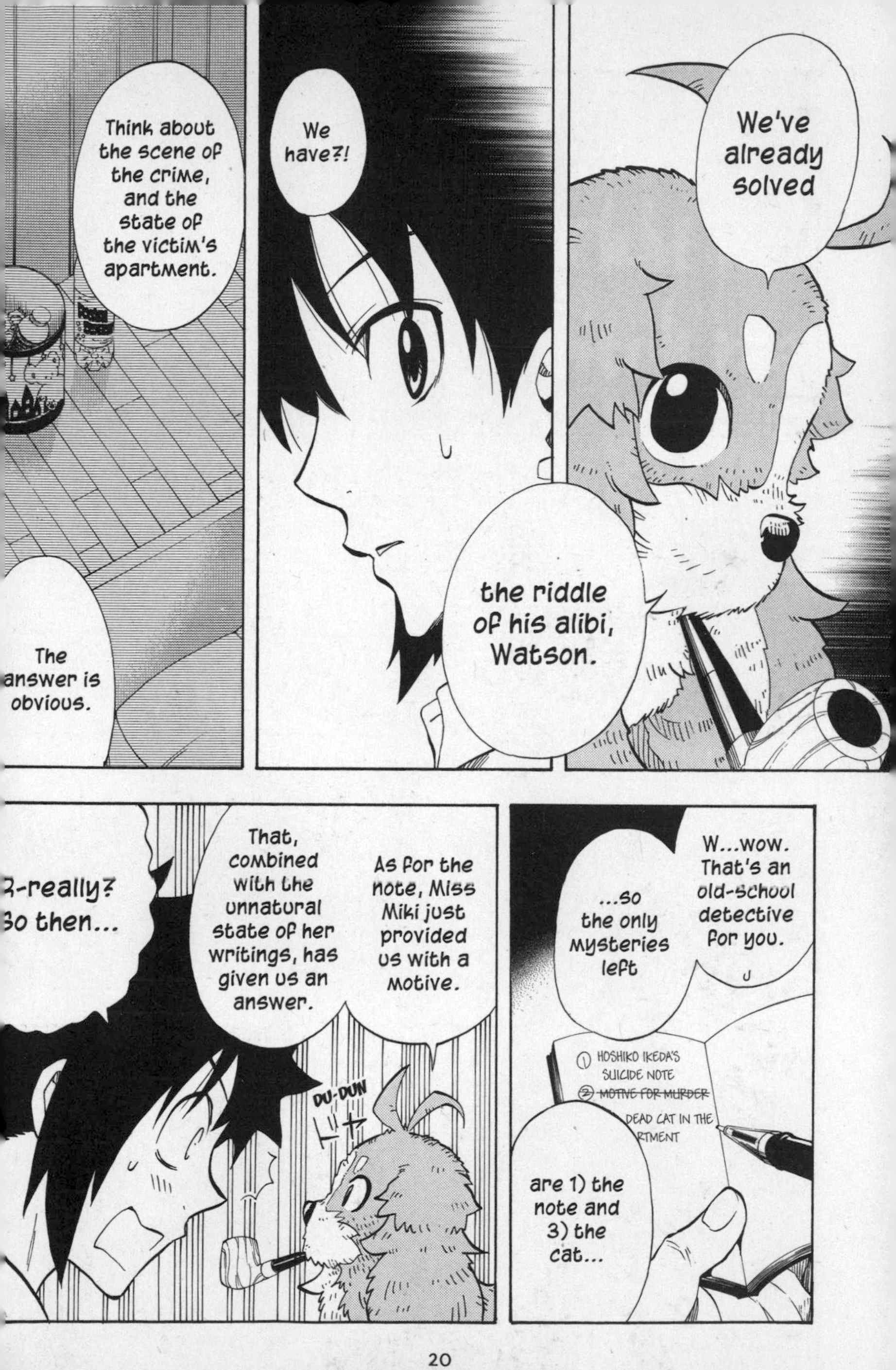
We've already solved
the riddle of his alibi, Watson.
We have?!
Think about the scene of the crime, and the state of the victim's apartment.
The answer is obvious.
W...wow. That's an old-school detective for you.
...so the only mysteries left
1 HOSHIKO IKEDA'S SUICIDE NOTE
2 ~~MOTIVE FOR MURDER~~
DEAD CAT IN THE
are 1) the note and 3) the cat...
As for the note, Miss Miki just provided us with a motive.
That, combined with the unnatural state of her writings, has given us an answer.
DU-DUN
R-really? So then...

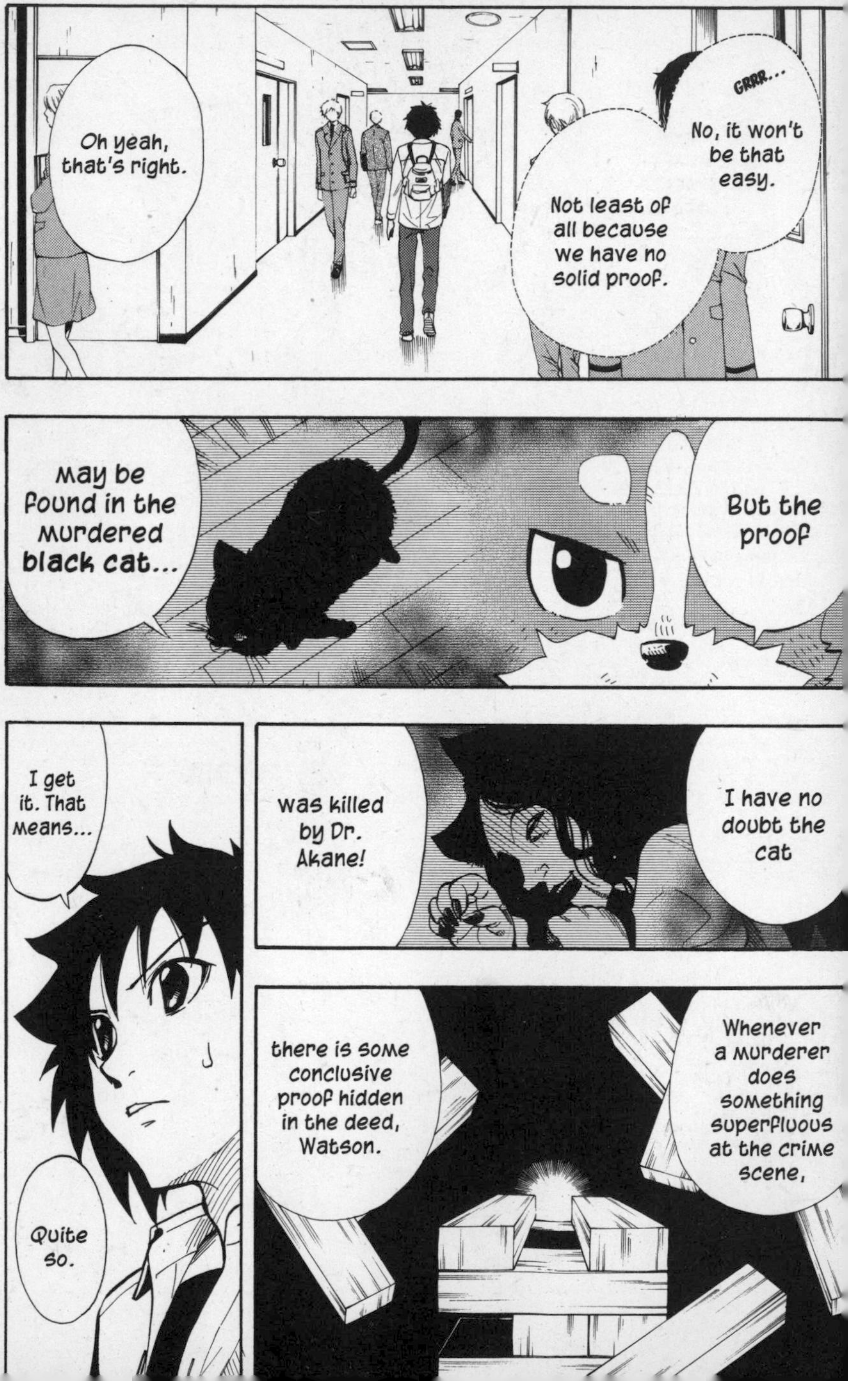
GRRR...
No, it won't be that easy.
Not least of all because we have no solid proof.
Oh yeah, that's right.
But the proof
May be found in the murdered black cat...
I have no doubt the cat
was killed by Dr. Akane!
Whenever a murderer does something superfluous at the crime scene,
there is some conclusive proof hidden in the deed, Watson.
I get it. That means...
Quite so.

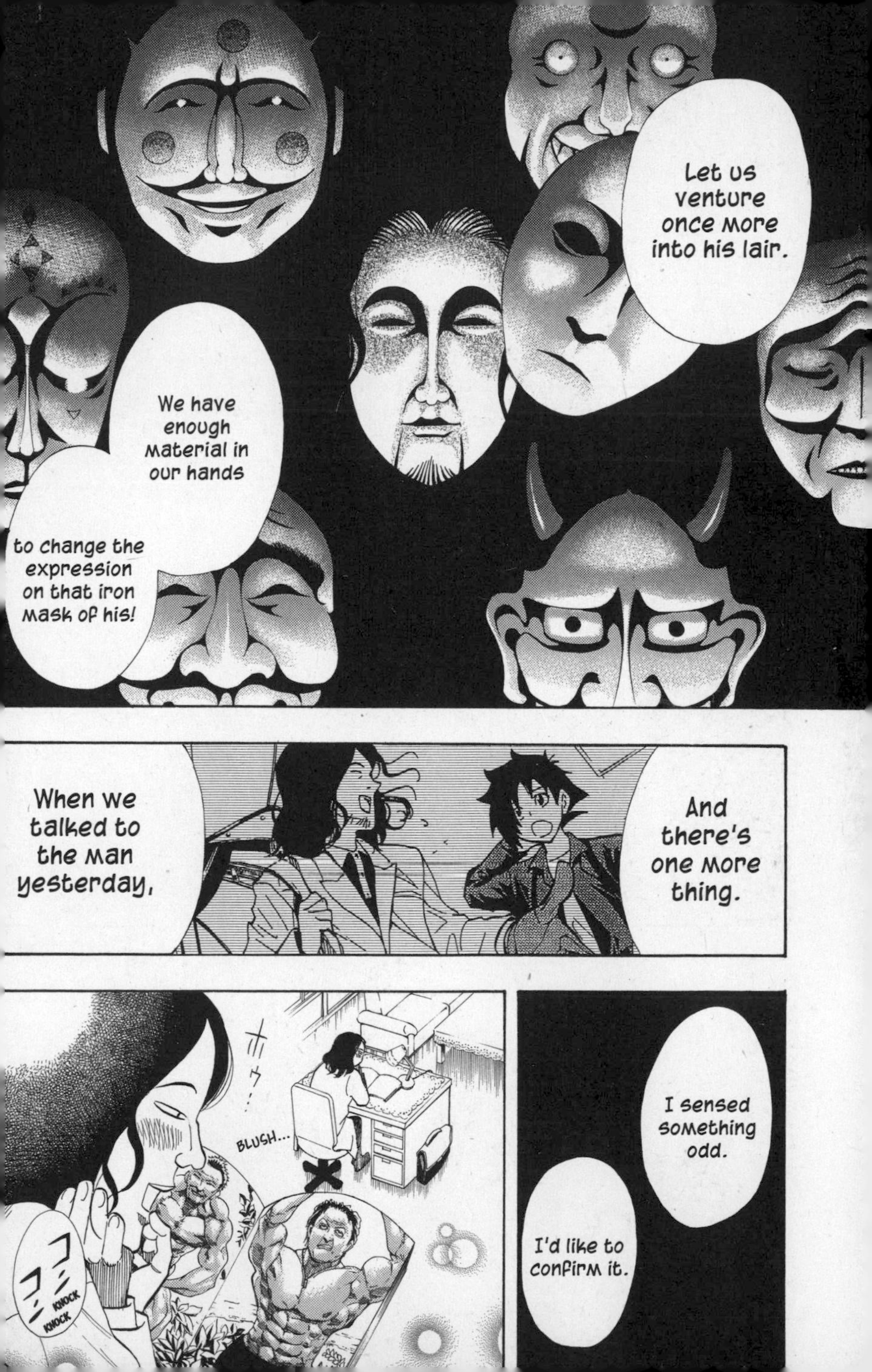
Let us venture once more into his lair.
We have enough material in our hands
to change the expression on that iron mask of his!
And there's one more thing.
When we talked to the man yesterday,
I sensed something odd.
I'd like to confirm it.
BLUSH...
KNOCK KNOCK

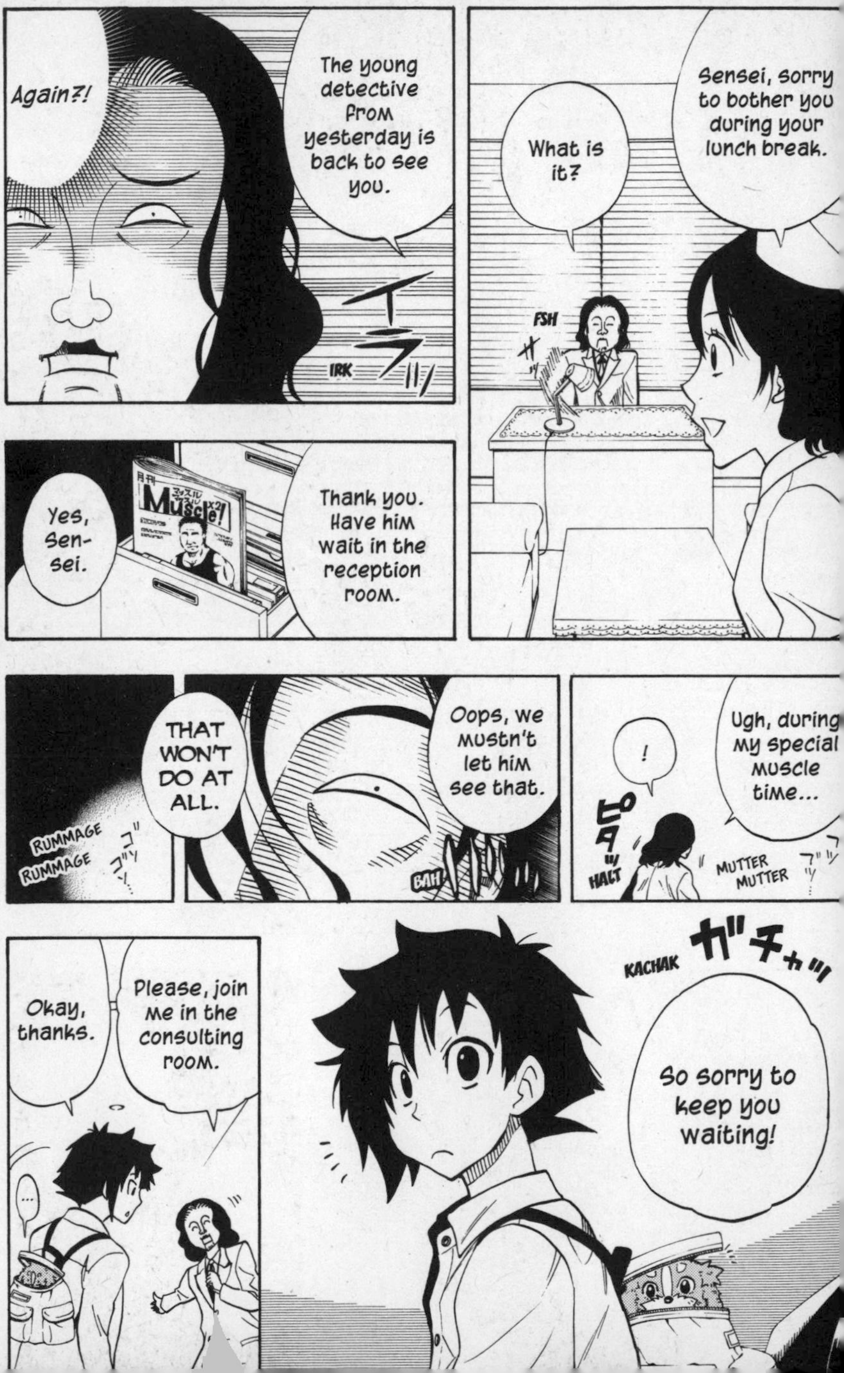
Sensei, sorry to bother you during your lunch break.
What is it?
FSH
The young detective from yesterday is back to see you.
Again?!
IRK
Thank you. Have him wait in the reception room.
Muscle
Yes, Sen-sei.
Ugh, during my special muscle time...
MUTTER MUTTER
!
HALT
Oops, we mustn't let him see that.
BAH
THAT WON'T DO AT ALL.
RUMMAGE RUMMAGE
KACHAK
So sorry to keep you waiting!
Please, join me in the consulting room.
Okay, thanks.
...

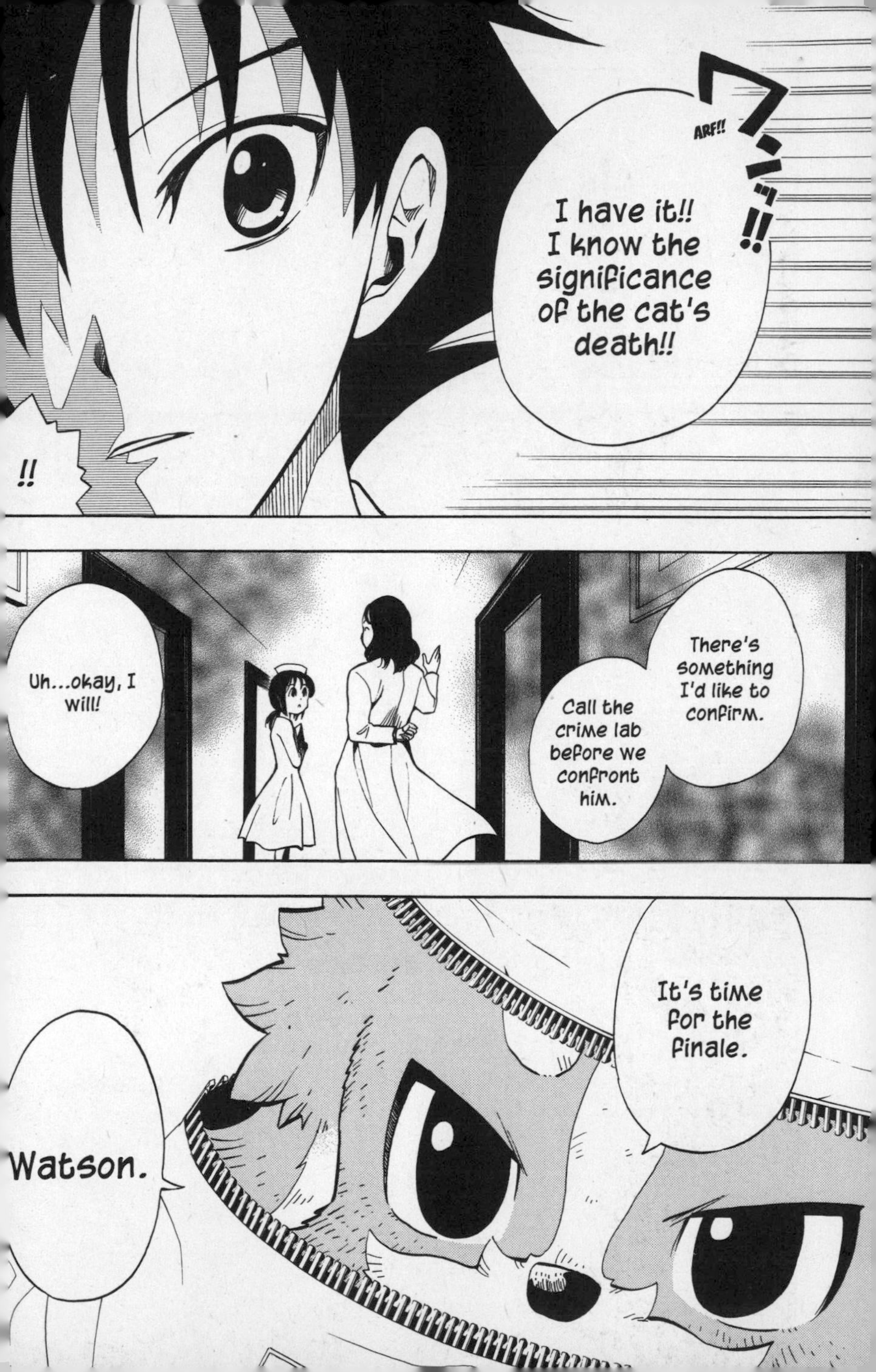
ARF!!
I have it!! I know the significance of the cat's death!!
!!
There's something I'd like to confirm.
Call the crime lab before we confront him.
Uh...okay, I will!
It's time for the finale.
Watson.

Case 9: ⚜ The Stolen Face, Part 5

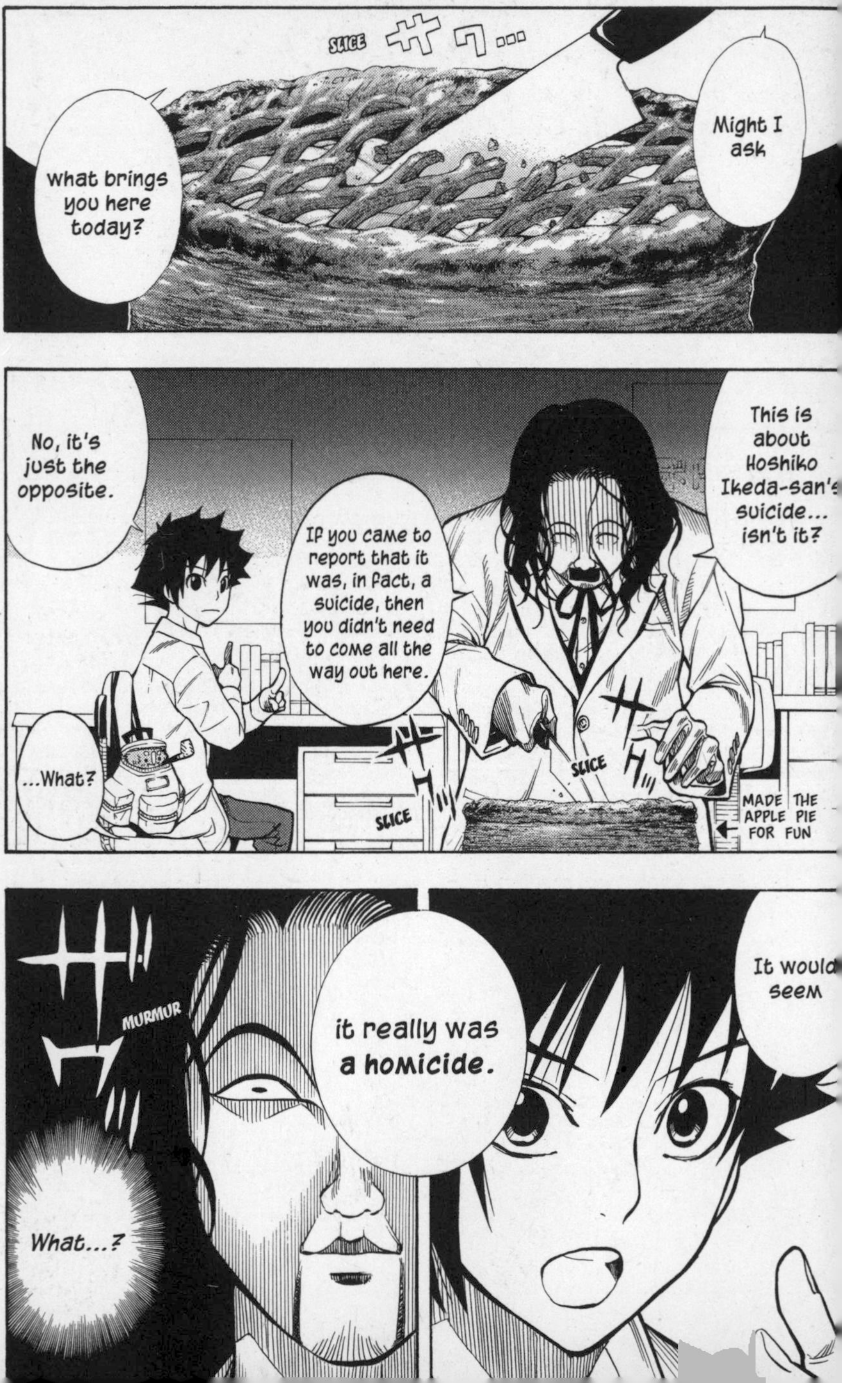
SLICE
Might I ask
what brings you here today?
This is about Hoshiko Ikeda-san's suicide... isn't it?
If you came to report that it was, in fact, a suicide, then you didn't need to come all the way out here.
SLICE
SLICE
MADE THE APPLE PIE FOR FUN
No, it's just the opposite.
...What?
It would seem
it really was a homicide.
MURMUR
What...?

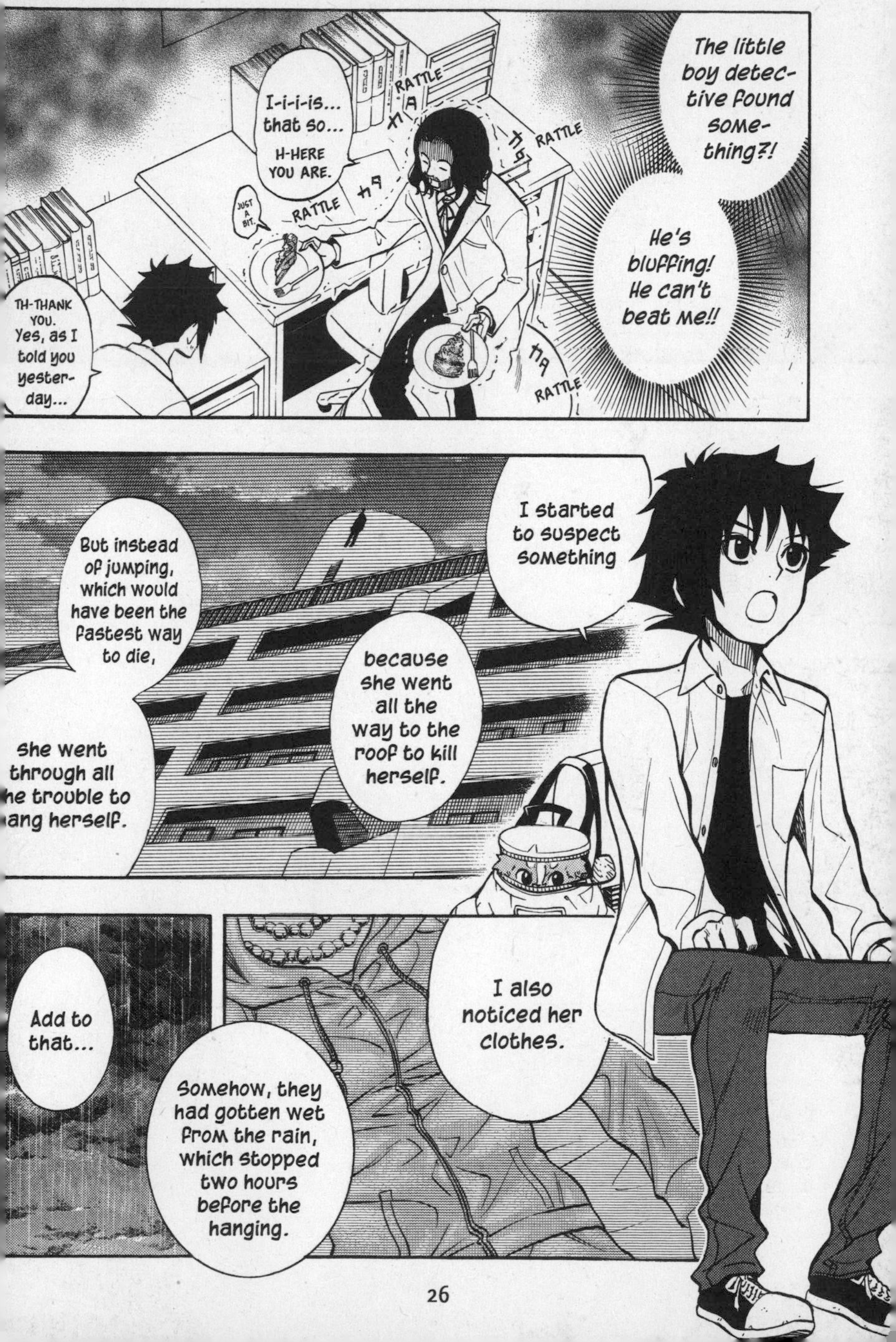

The little boy detective found something?!
He's bluffing! He can't beat me!!
RATTLE
RATTLE
I-i-i-is... that so...
H-HERE YOU ARE.
RATTLE
RATTLE
JUST A BIT.
TH-THANK YOU. Yes, as I told you yesterday...
I started to suspect something
because she went all the way to the roof to kill herself.
But instead of jumping, which would have been the fastest way to die,
she went through all he trouble to ang herself.
I also noticed her clothes.
Somehow, they had gotten wet from the rain, which stopped two hours before the hanging.
Add to that...

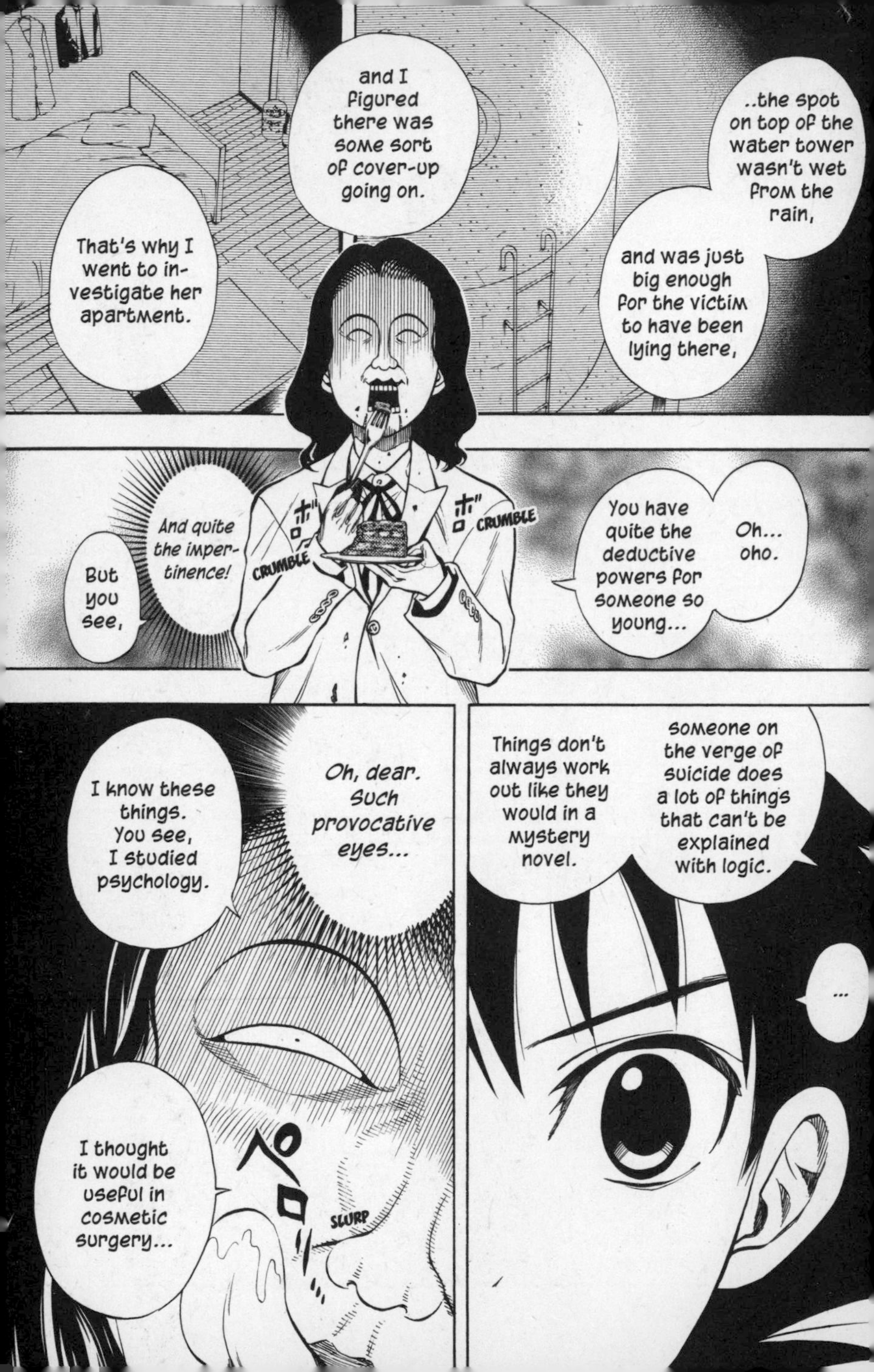
..the spot on top of the water tower wasn't wet from the rain,
and was just big enough for the victim to have been lying there,
and I figured there was some sort of cover-up going on.
That's why I went to investigate her apartment.
Oh... oho.
You have quite the deductive powers for someone so young...
CRUMBLE
CRUMBLE
And quite the impertinence!
But you see,
Someone on the verge of suicide does a lot of things that can't be explained with logic.
Things don't always work out like they would in a mystery novel.
...
Oh, dear. Such provocative eyes...
I know these things. You see, I studied psychology.
I thought it would be useful in cosmetic surgery...
SLURP

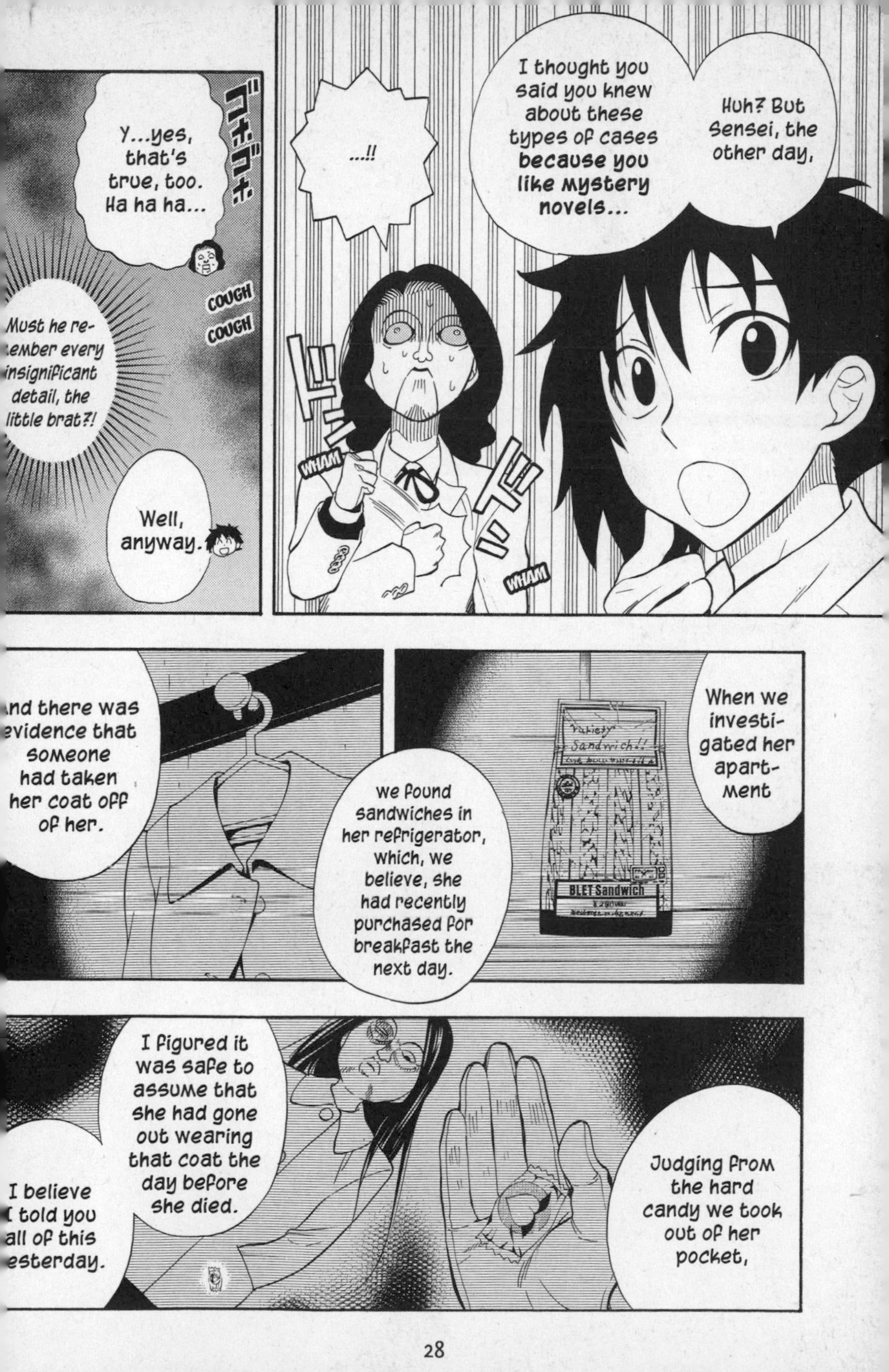
Huh? But Sensei, the other day,
I thought you said you knew about these types of cases because you like mystery novels...
...!!
WHAM
WHAM
Y...yes, that's true, too. Ha ha ha...
COUGH
COUGH
Must he remember every insignificant detail, the little brat?!
Well, anyway.
When we investigated her apartment
Variety Sandwich!!
BLET Sandwich
we found sandwiches in her refrigerator, which, we believe, she had recently purchased for breakfast the next day.
nd there was evidence that someone had taken her coat off of her.
Judging from the hard candy we took out of her pocket,
I figured it was safe to assume that she had gone out wearing that coat the day before she died.
I believe I told you all of this esterday.

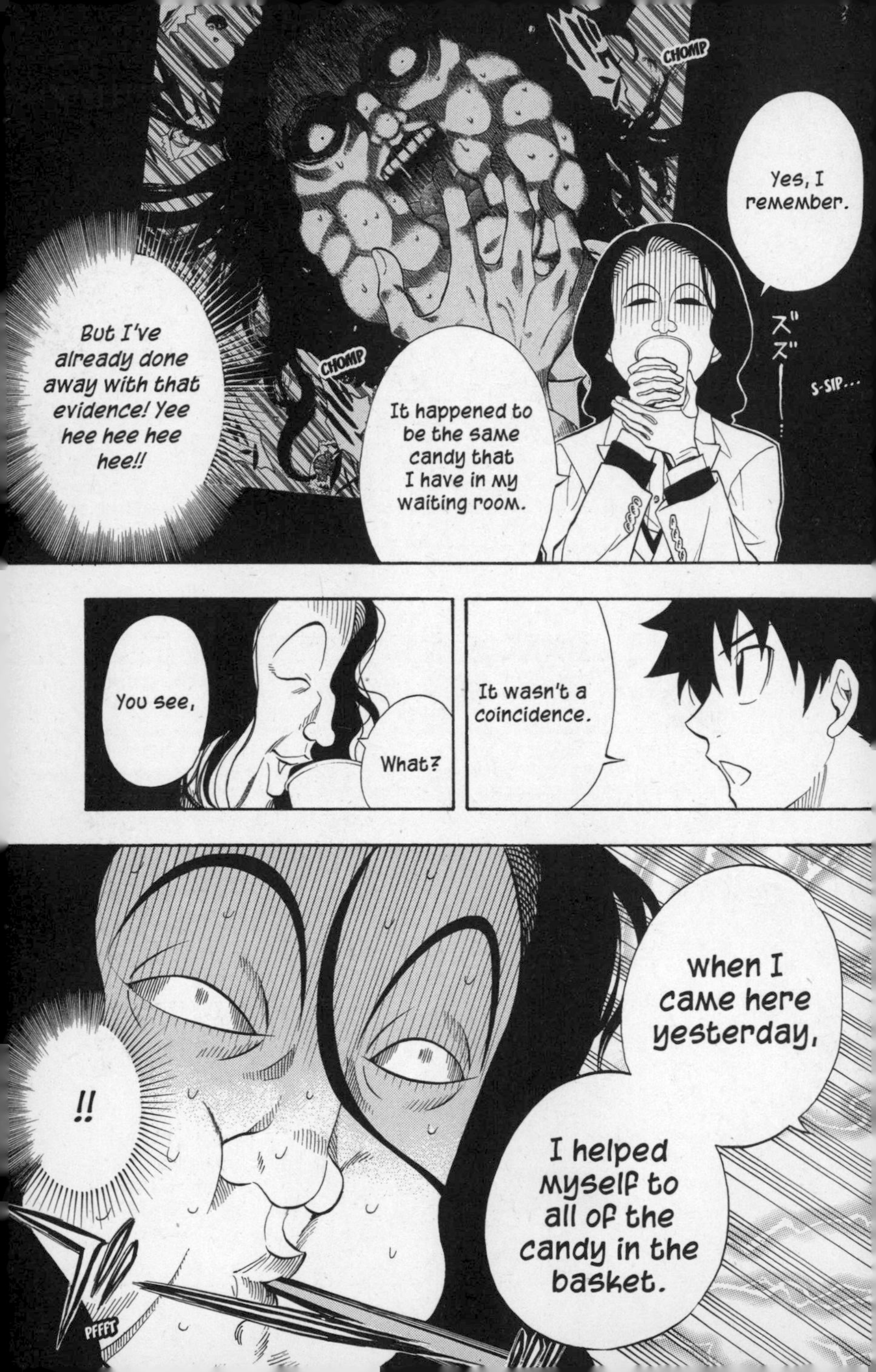
CHOMP
Yes, I remember.
ズズ
S-SIP...
It happened to be the same candy that I have in my waiting room.
CHOMP
But I've already done away with that evidence! Yee hee hee hee hee!!
It wasn't a coincidence.
What?
You see,
when I came here yesterday,
I helped myself to all of the candy in the basket.
!!
PFFFT

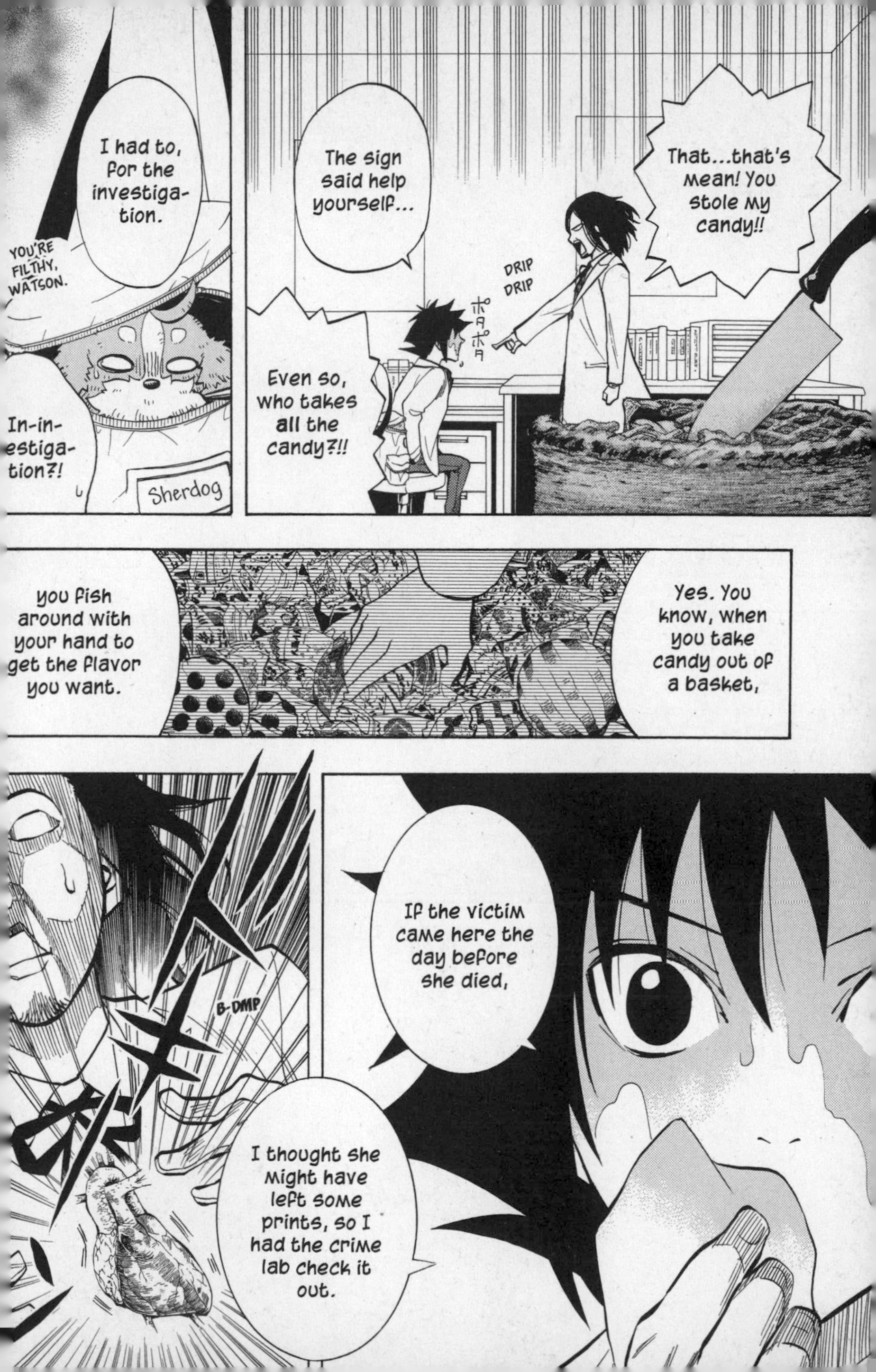

That...that's mean! You stole my candy!!
The sign said help yourself...
DRIP DRIP
ポタポタ
Even so, who takes all the candy?!!
I had to, for the investigation.
YOU'RE FILTHY, WATSON.
In-investigation?!
Sherdog
Yes. You know, when you take candy out of a basket,
you fish around with your hand to get the flavor you want.
If the victim came here the day before she died,
I thought she might have left some prints, so I had the crime lab check it out.
B-DMP

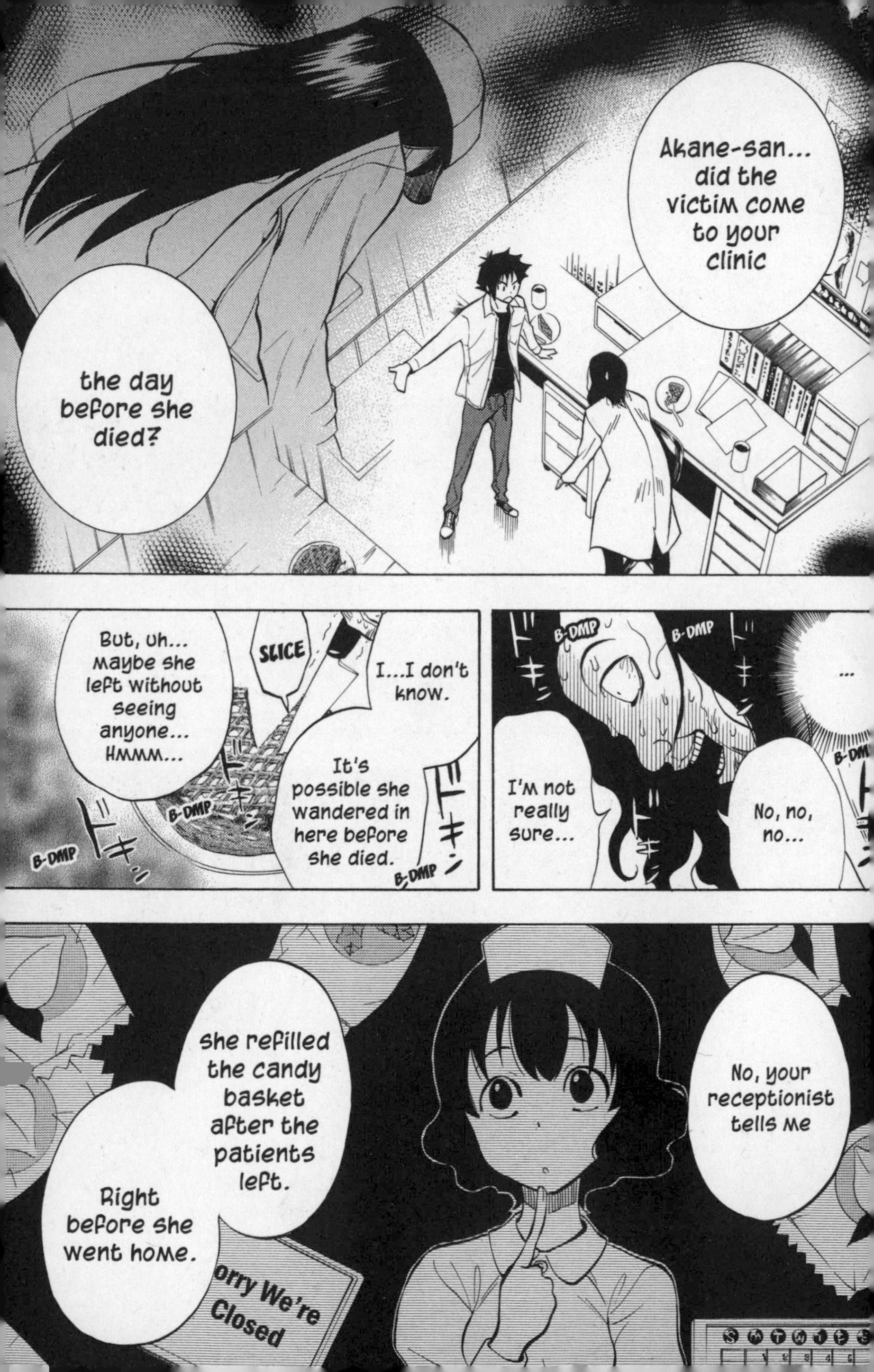
Akane-san... did the victim come to your clinic
the day before she died?
...
B-DMP
B-DMP
B-DMP
No, no, no...
I'm not really sure...
SLICE
I...I don't know.
It's possible she wandered in here before she died.
B-DMP
But, uh... maybe she left without seeing anyone... HMMM...
B-DMP
B-DMP
No, your receptionist tells me
she refilled the candy basket after the patients left.
Right before she went home.
orry We're Closed

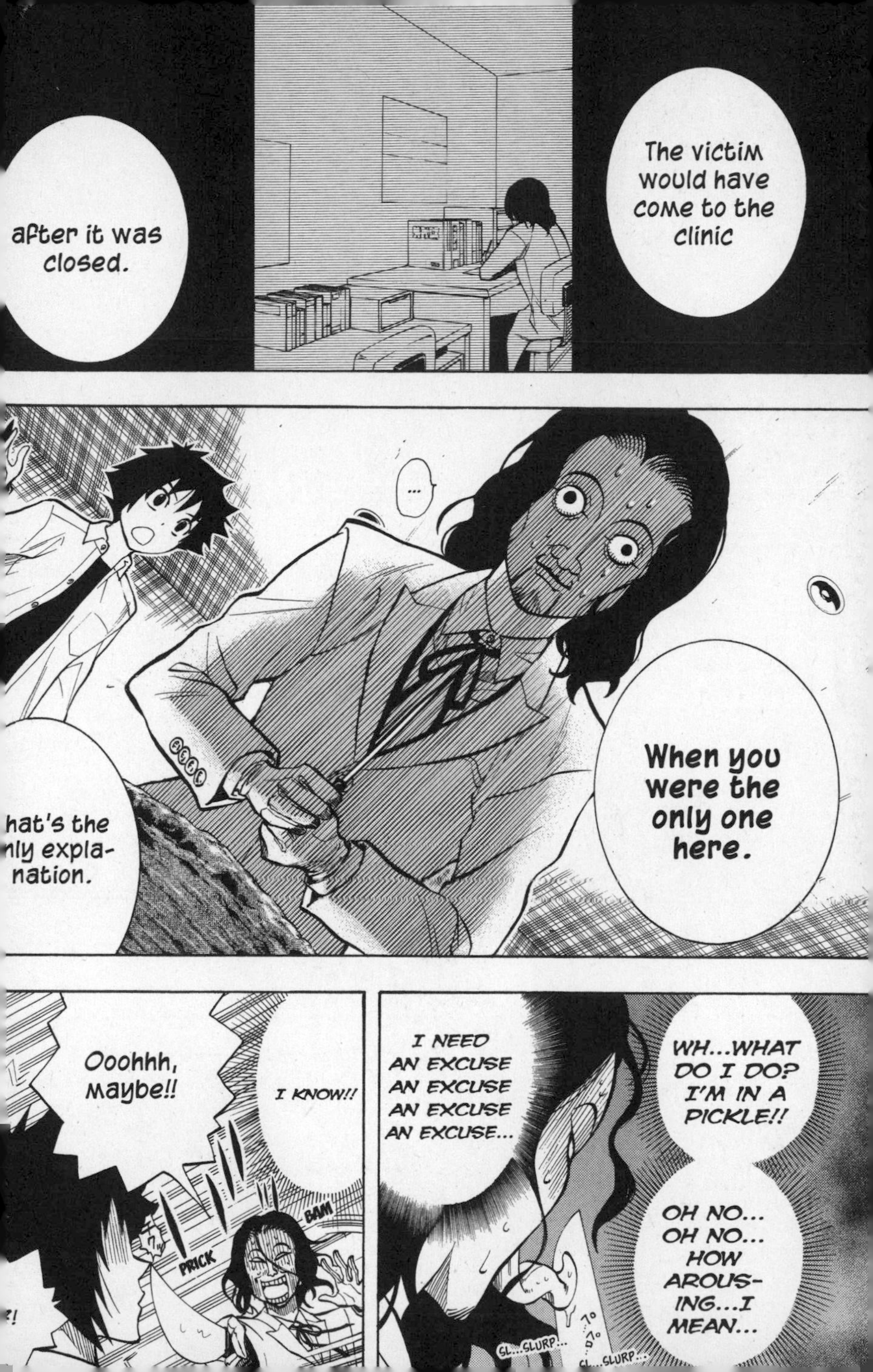
The victim would have come to the clinic
after it was closed.
...
When you were the only one here.
hat's the nly expla- nation.
WH...WHAT DO I DO? I'M IN A PICKLE!!
OH NO... OH NO... HOW AROUSING...I MEAN...
I NEED AN EXCUSE AN EXCUSE AN EXCUSE AN EXCUSE...
SL...SLURP...
SL...SLURP...
I KNOW!!
Ooohhh, Maybe!!
BAM
PRICK

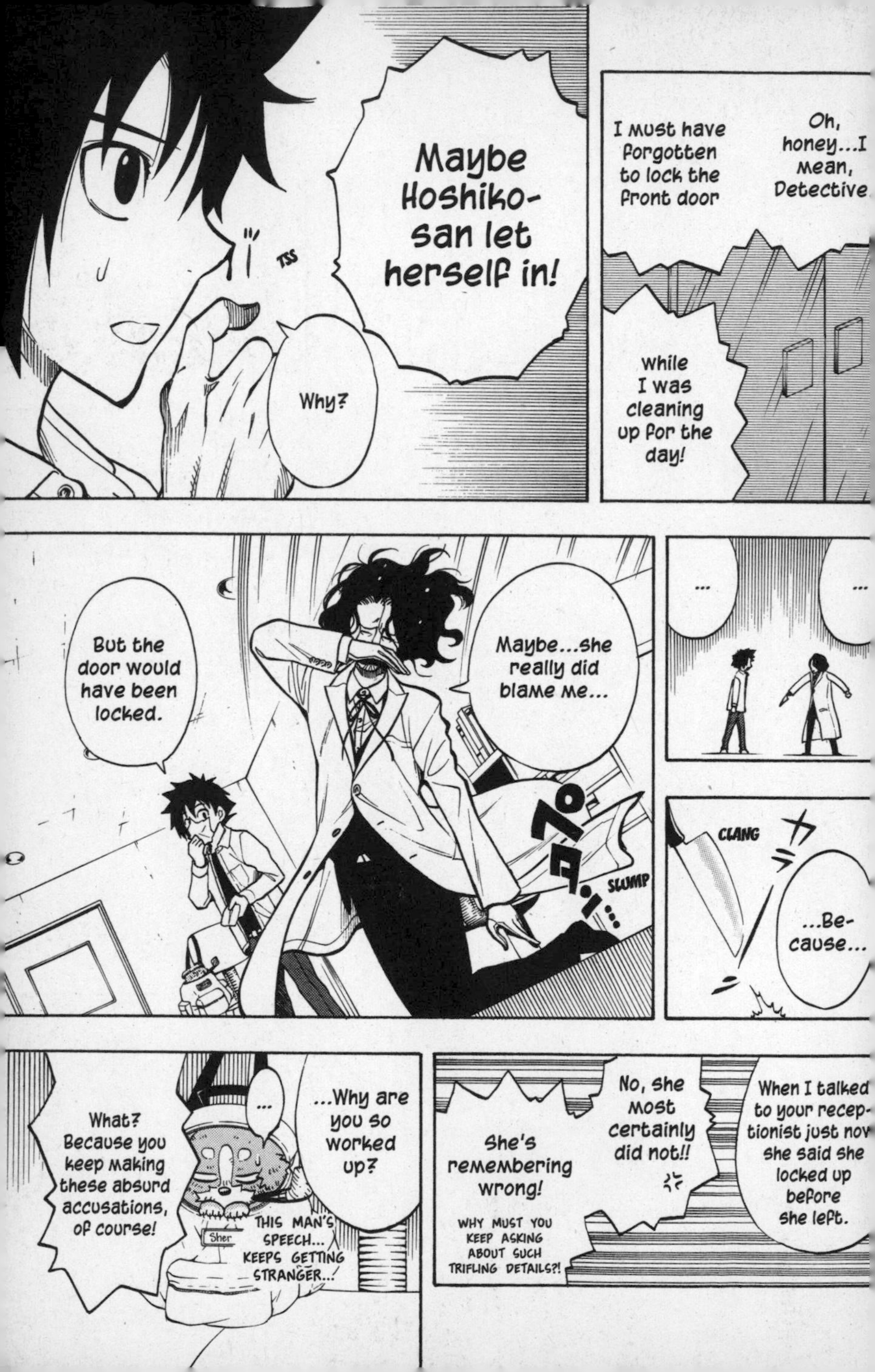
Oh, honey...I mean, Detective
I must have forgotten to lock the front door
while I was cleaning up for the day!
Maybe Hoshiko-san let herself in!
TSS
Why?
...
...
CLANG
...Be-cause...
Maybe...she really did blame me...
SLUMP
But the door would have been locked.
When I talked to your recep-tionist just now she said she locked up before she left.
No, she most certainly did not!!
She's remembering wrong!
WHY MUST YOU KEEP ASKING ABOUT SUCH TRIFLING DETAILS?!
...Why are you so worked up?
...
What? Because you keep making these absurd accusations, of course!
THIS MAN'S SPEECH... KEEPS GETTING STRANGER...
Sher

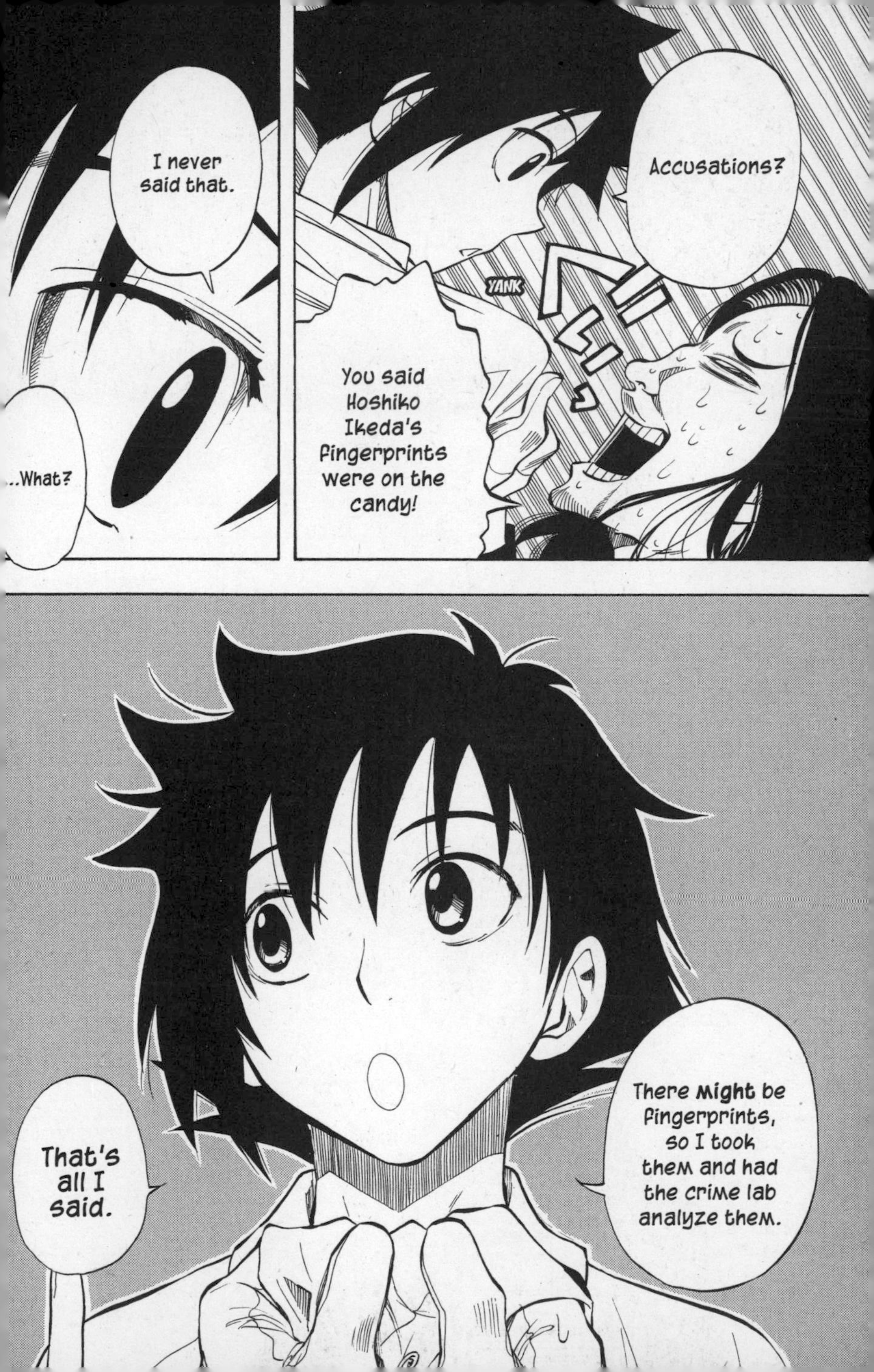
Accusations?
YANK
You said Hoshiko Ikeda's fingerprints were on the candy!
I never said that.
...What?
There might be fingerprints, so I took them and had the crime lab analyze them.
That's all I said.

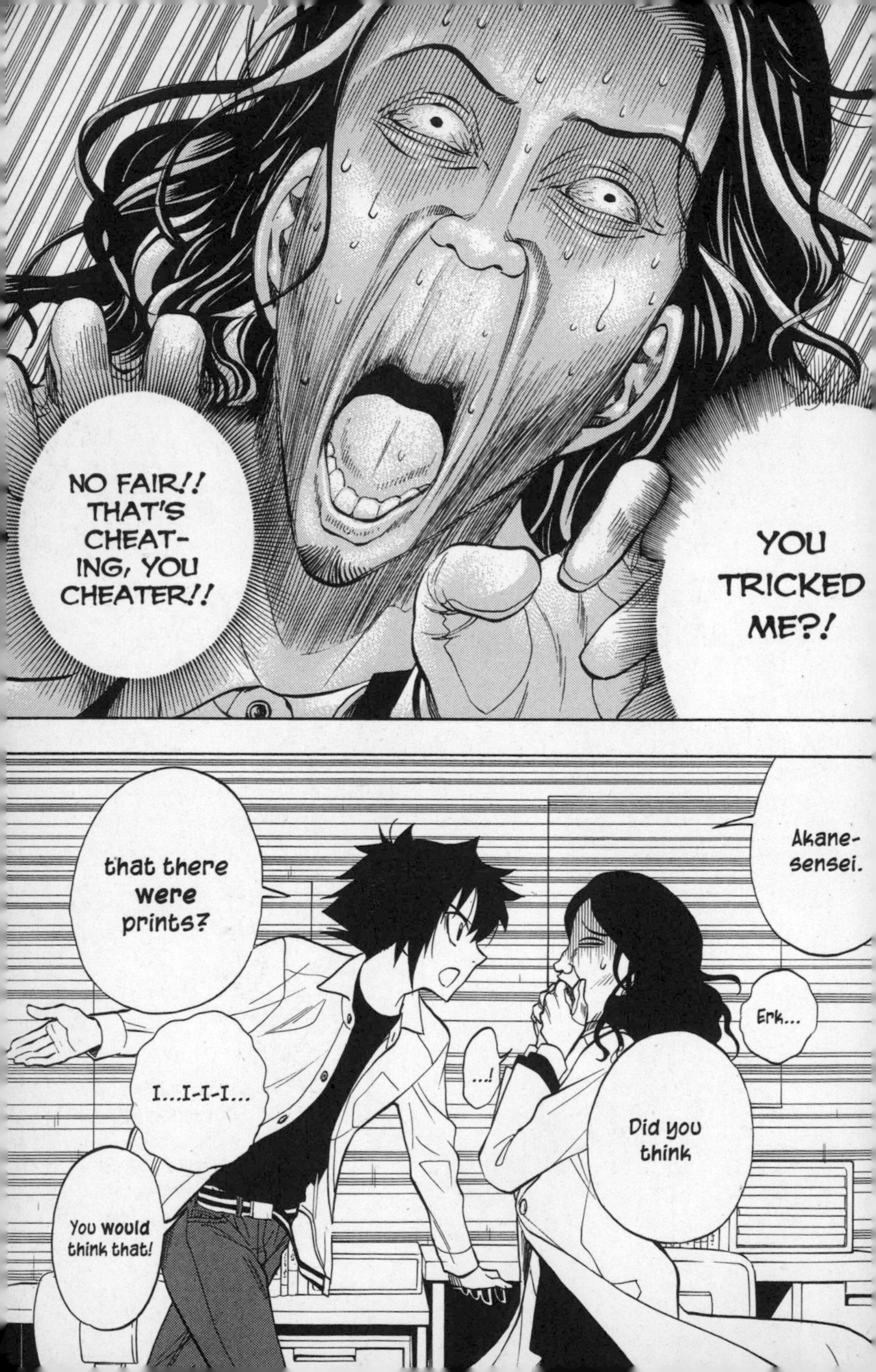
YOU TRICKED ME?!
NO FAIR!! THAT'S CHEAT-ING, YOU CHEATER!!
Akane-sensei.
Erk...
Did you think
...!
that there were prints?
I...I-I-I...
You would think that!

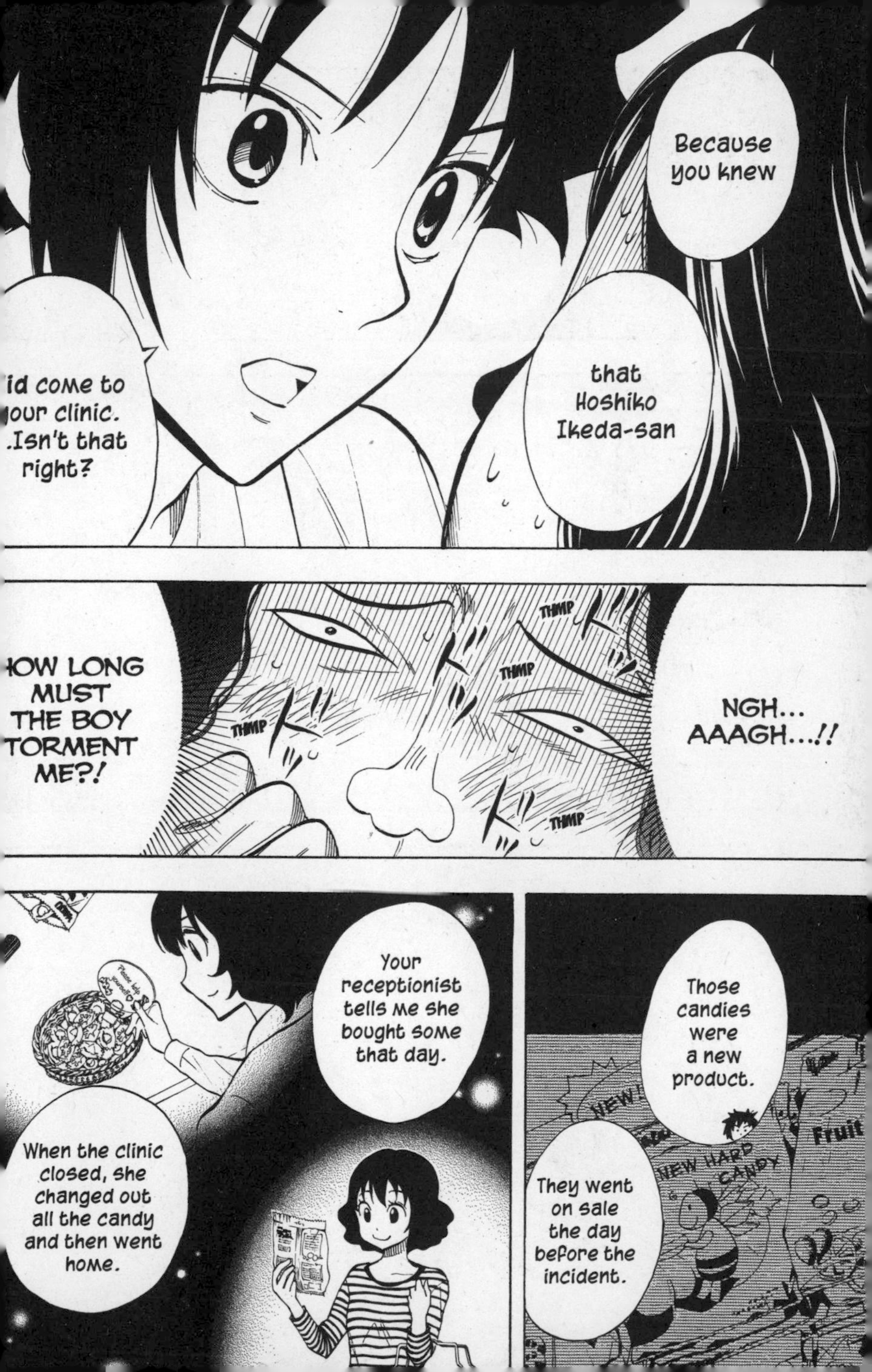
Because you knew
that Hoshiko Ikeda-san
id come to our clinic. .Isn't that right?
NGH... AAAGH...!!
THMP
THMP
THMP
THMP
OW LONG MUST THE BOY ORMENT ME?!
Those candies were a new product.
They went on sale the day before the incident.
NEW!
NEW HARD CANDY
Fruit
Your receptionist tells me she bought some that day.
When the clinic closed, she changed out all the candy and then went home.

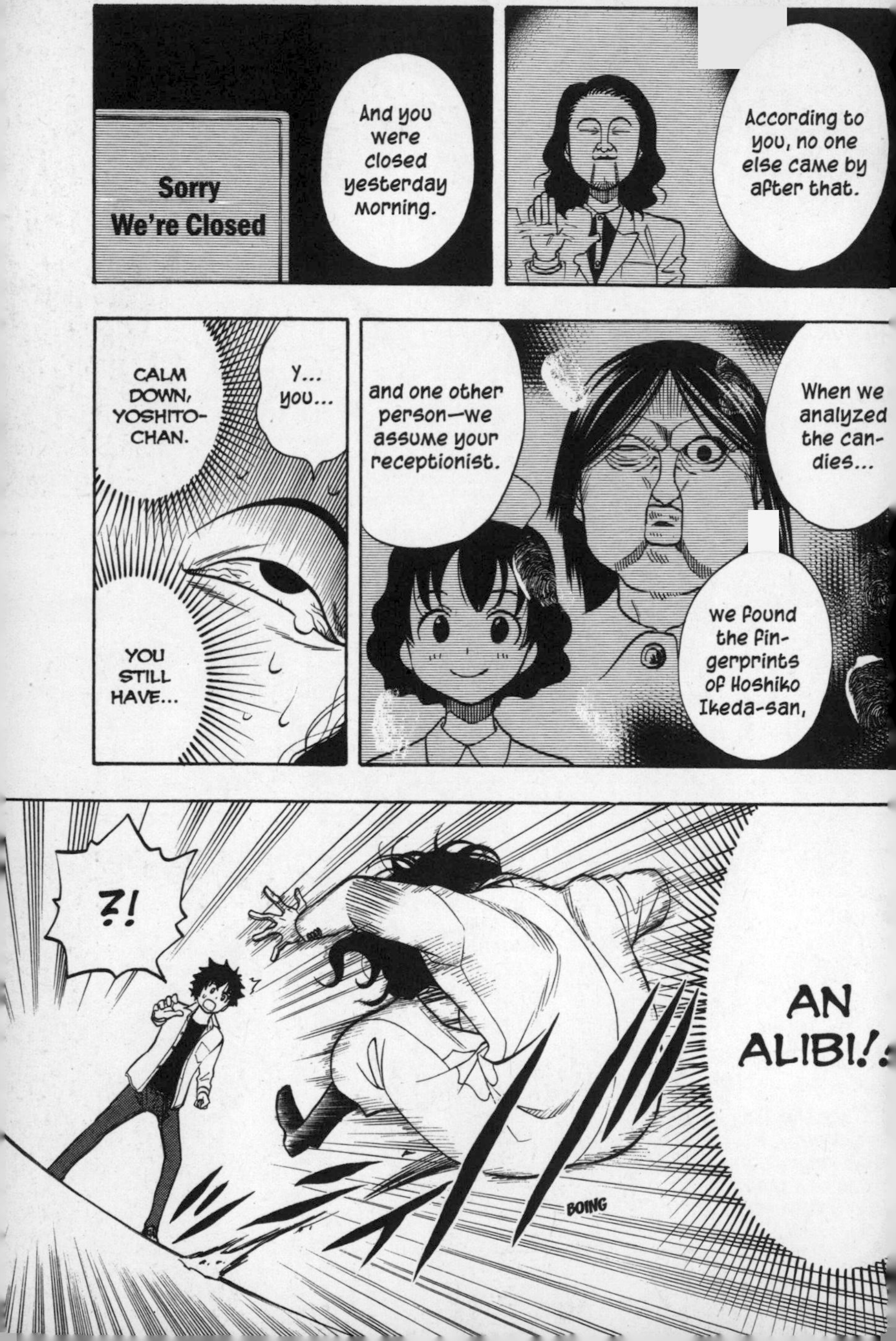
According to you, no one else came by after that.
And you were closed yesterday morning.
Sorry We're Closed
When we analyzed the candies...
we found the fingerprints of Hoshiko Ikeda-san,
and one other person—we assume your receptionist.
Y... you...
CALM DOWN, YOSHITO-CHAN.
YOU STILL HAVE...
AN ALIBI!!
?!
BOING

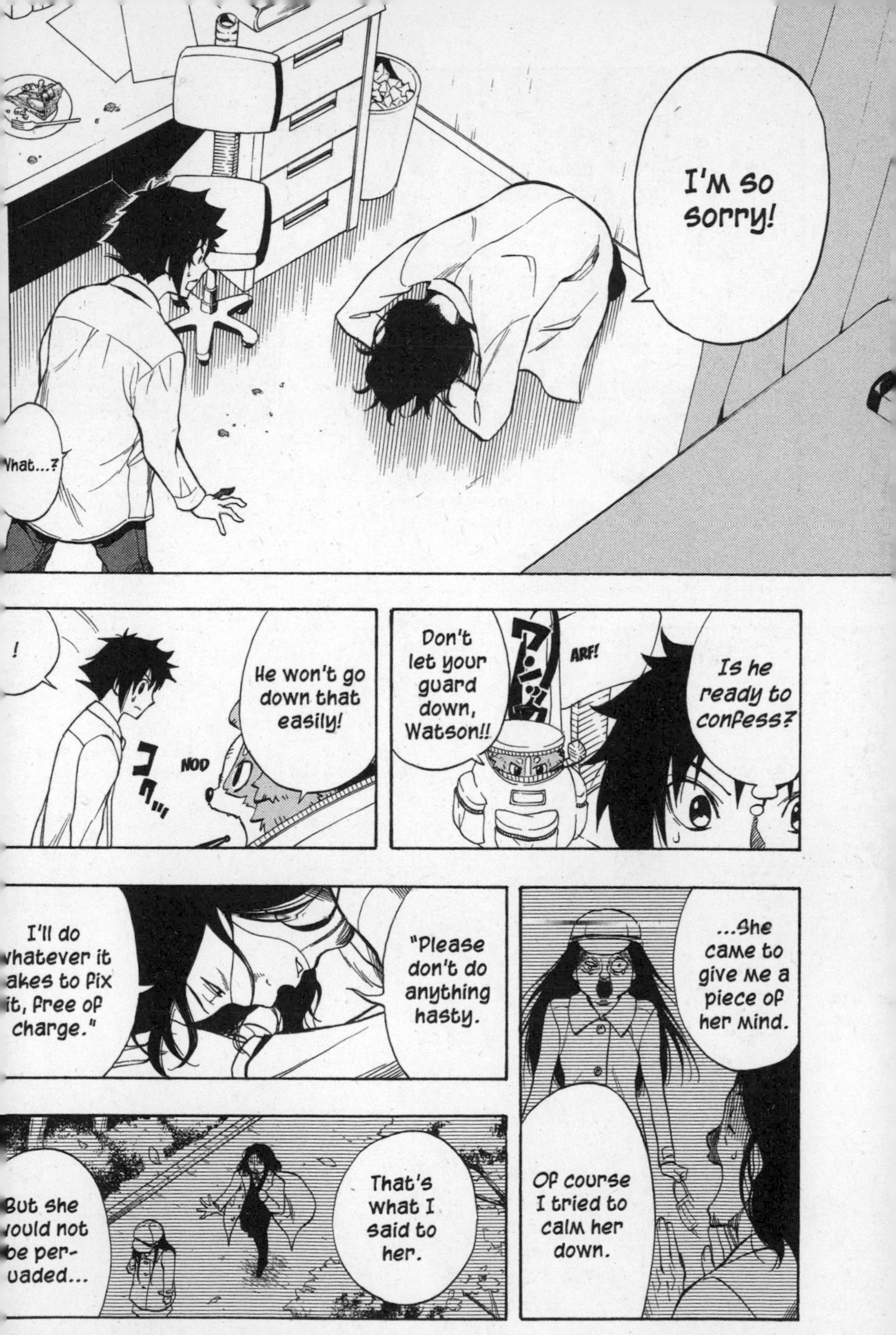
I'M SO sorry!
What...?
Is he ready to confess?
ARF!
Don't let your guard down, Watson!!
He won't go down that easily!
NOD
!
...She came to give me a piece of her mind.
Of course I tried to calm her down.
"Please don't do anything hasty.
I'll do whatever it takes to fix it, free of charge."
That's what I said to her.
But she would not be persuaded...

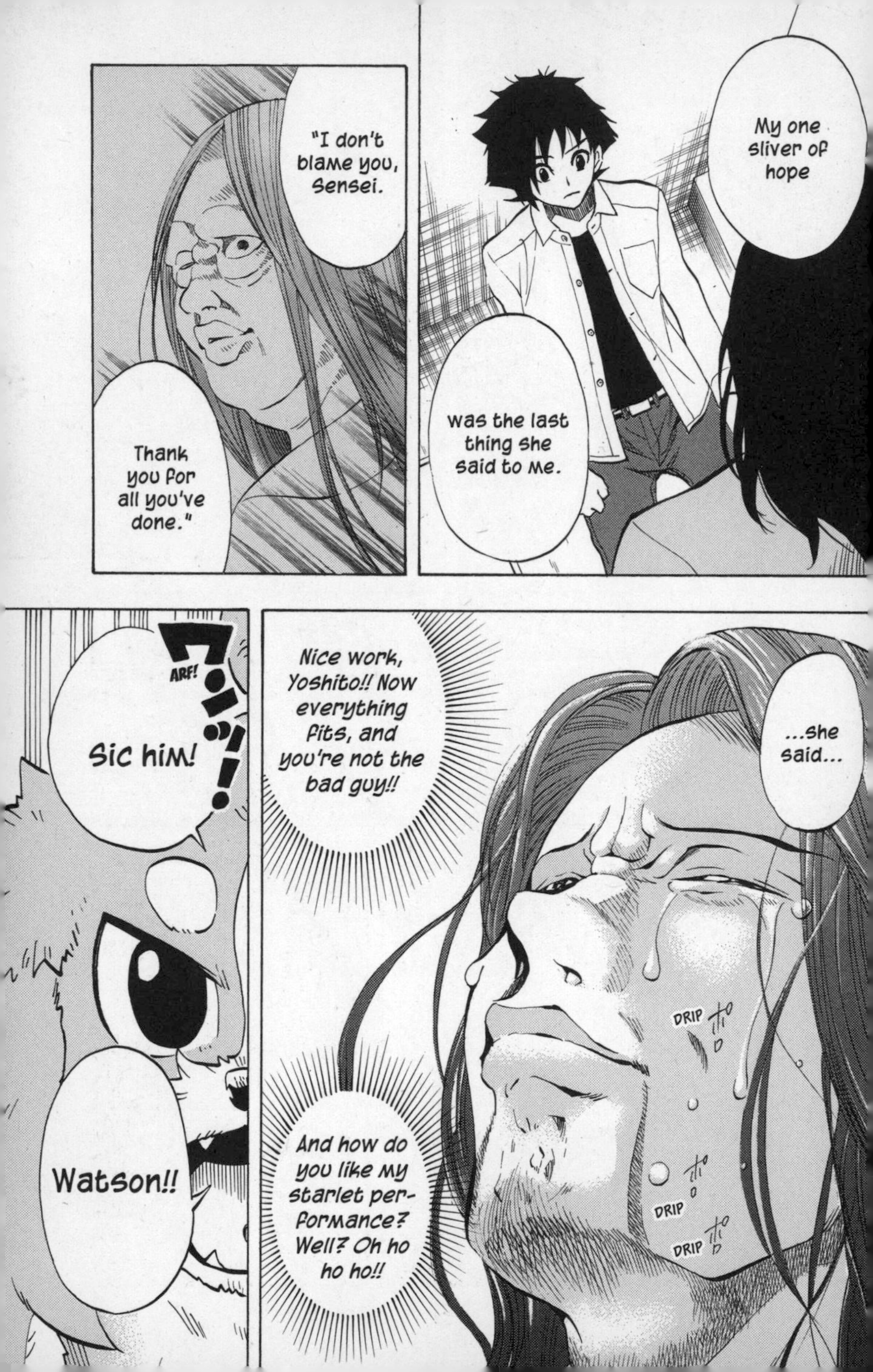
My one sliver of hope
was the last thing she said to me.
"I don't blame you, Sensei.
Thank you for all you've done."
...she said...
Nice work, Yoshito!! Now everything fits, and you're not the bad guy!!
DRIP
DRIP
DRIP
And how do you like my starlet per-formance? Well? Oh ho ho ho!!
ARF!
Sic him!
Watson!!

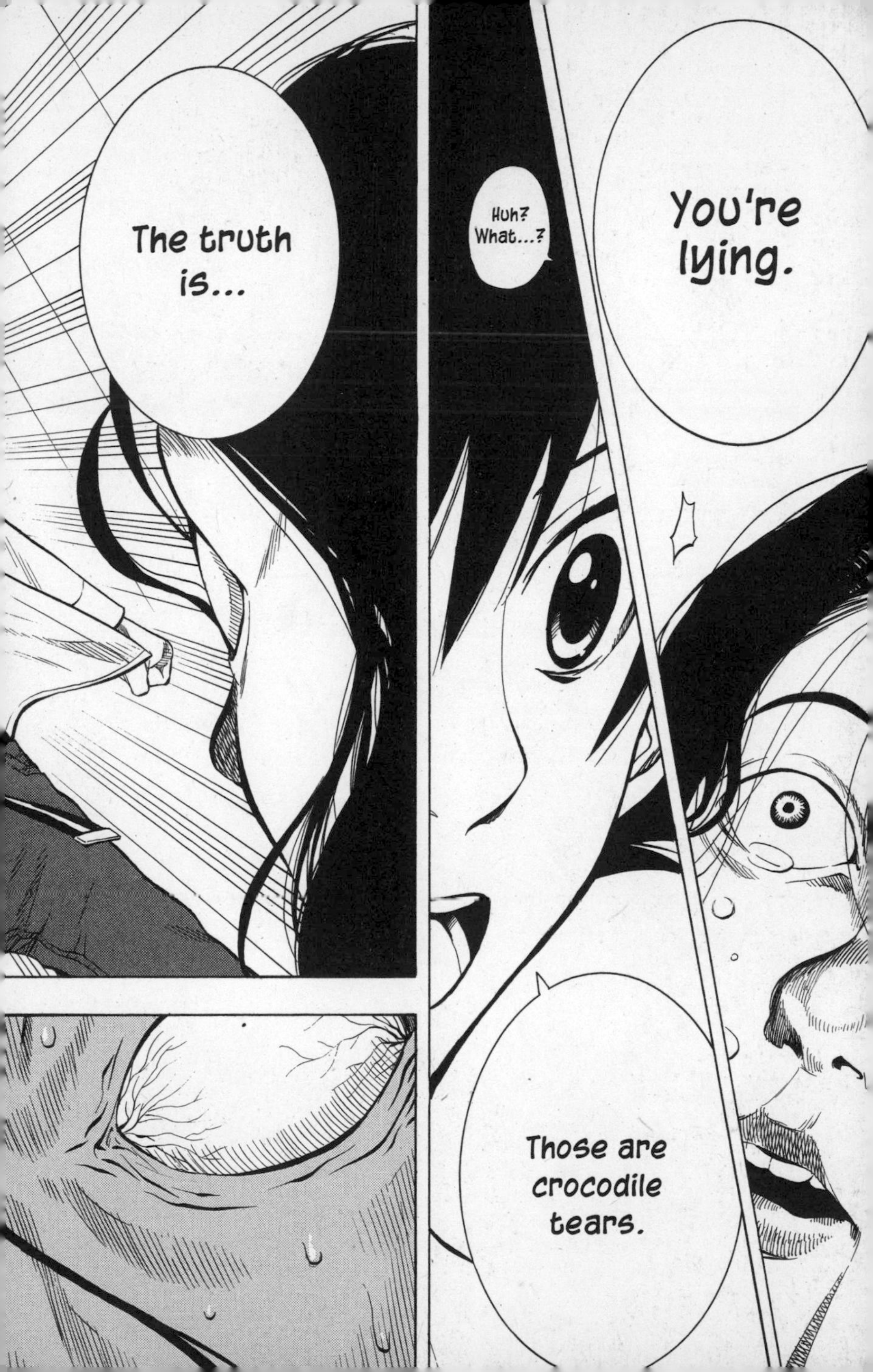
You're lying.
Huh? What...?
Those are crocodile tears.
The truth is...

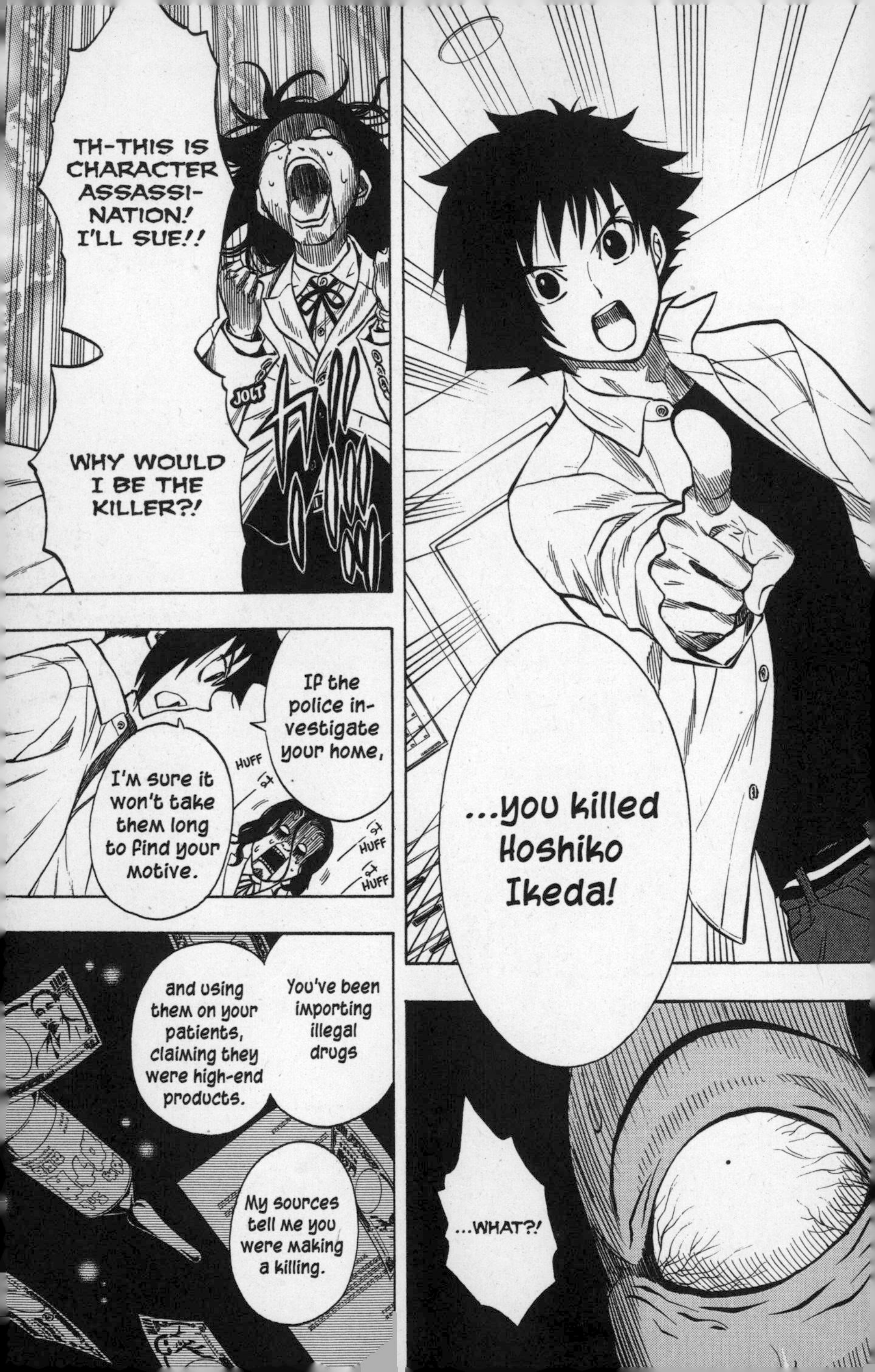
TH-THIS IS CHARACTER ASSASSI-NATION! I'LL SUE!!
JOLT
WHY WOULD I BE THE KILLER?!
If the police in-vestigate your home,
I'm sure it won't take them long to find your motive.
HUFF
HUFF
HUFF
You've been importing illegal drugs
and using them on your patients, claiming they were high-end products.
My sources tell me you were making a killing.
...you killed Hoshiko Ikeda!
...WHAT?!

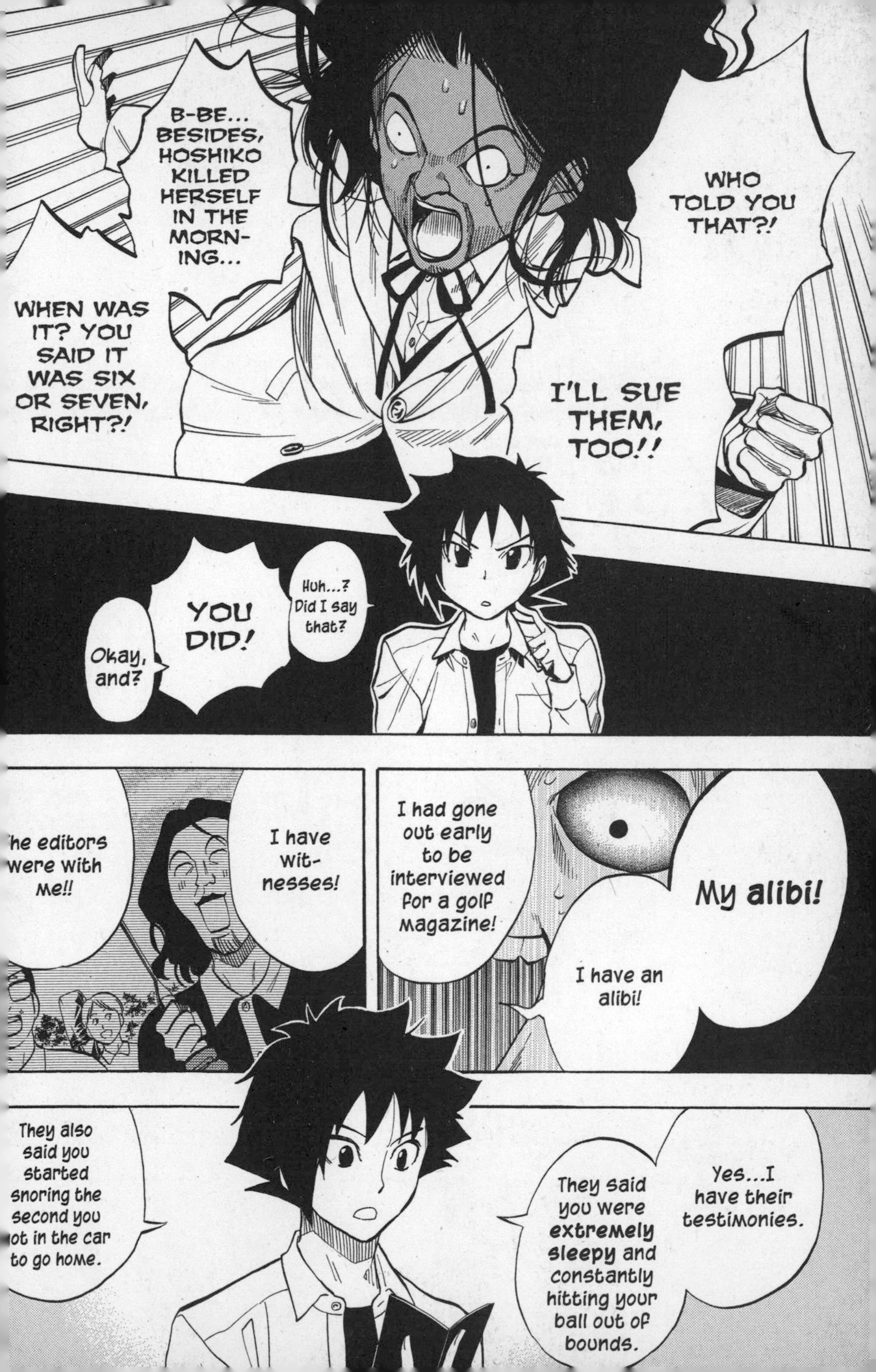
WHO TOLD YOU THAT?!
I'LL SUE THEM, TOO!!
B-BE... BESIDES, HOSHIKO KILLED HERSELF IN THE MORN-ING...
WHEN WAS IT? YOU SAID IT WAS SIX OR SEVEN, RIGHT?!
Huh...? Did I say that?
YOU DID!
Okay, and?
My alibi!
I have an alibi!
I had gone out early to be interviewed for a golf magazine!
I have wit-nesses!
he editors were with me!!
Yes...I have their testimonies.
They said you were extremely sleepy and constantly hitting your ball out of bounds.
They also said you started snoring the second you ot in the car to go home.

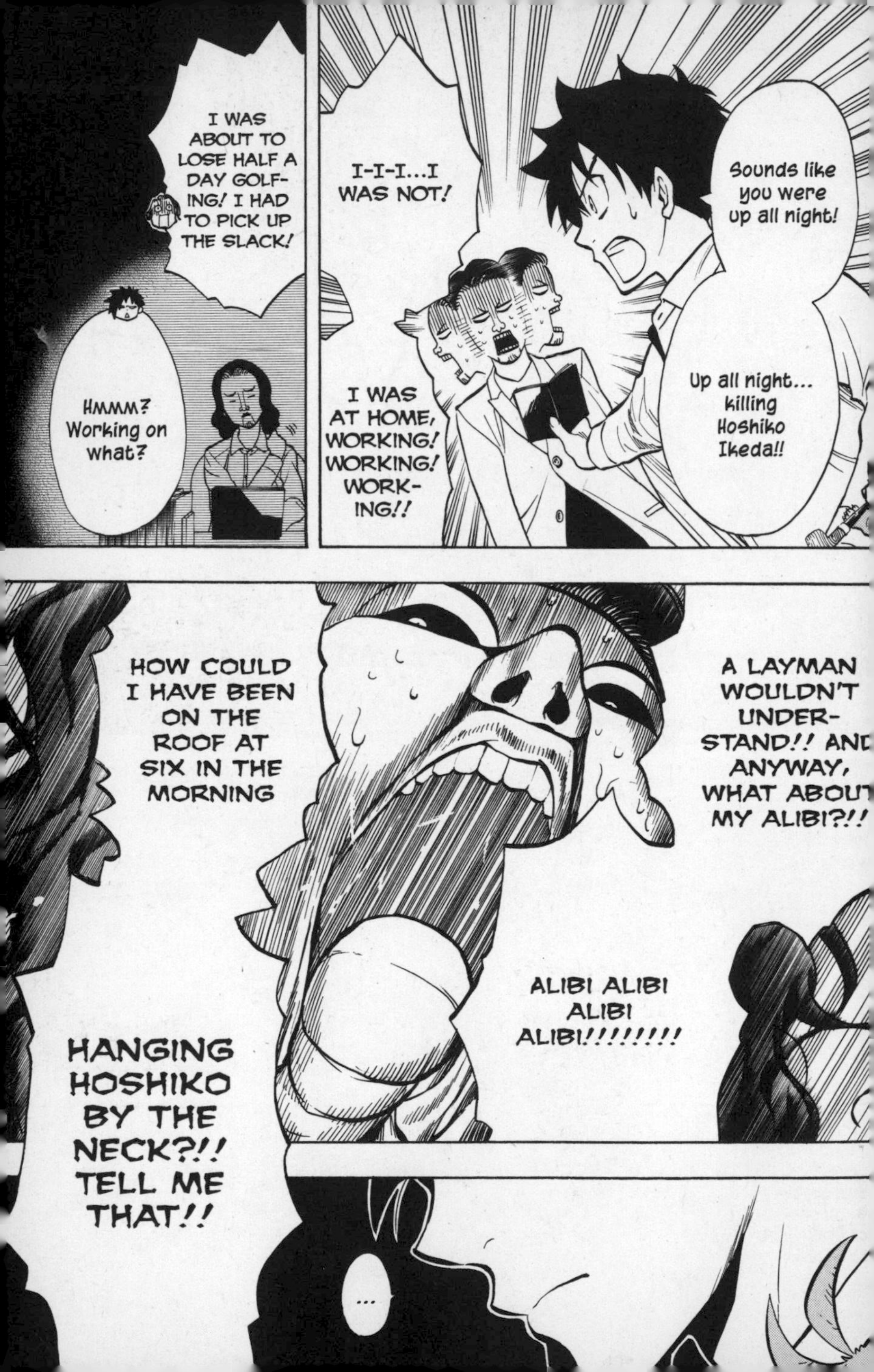
Sounds like you were up all night!
I-I-I...I WAS NOT!
Up all night... killing Hoshiko Ikeda!!
I WAS AT HOME, WORKING! WORKING! WORKING!!
I WAS ABOUT TO LOSE HALF A DAY GOLFING! I HAD TO PICK UP THE SLACK!
HMMM? Working on what?
A LAYMAN WOULDN'T UNDERSTAND!! AND ANYWAY, WHAT ABOUT MY ALIBI?!!
HOW COULD I HAVE BEEN ON THE ROOF AT SIX IN THE MORNING
ALIBI ALIBI ALIBI ALIBI!!!!!!!!!
HANGING HOSHIKO BY THE NECK?!! TELL ME THAT!!
...

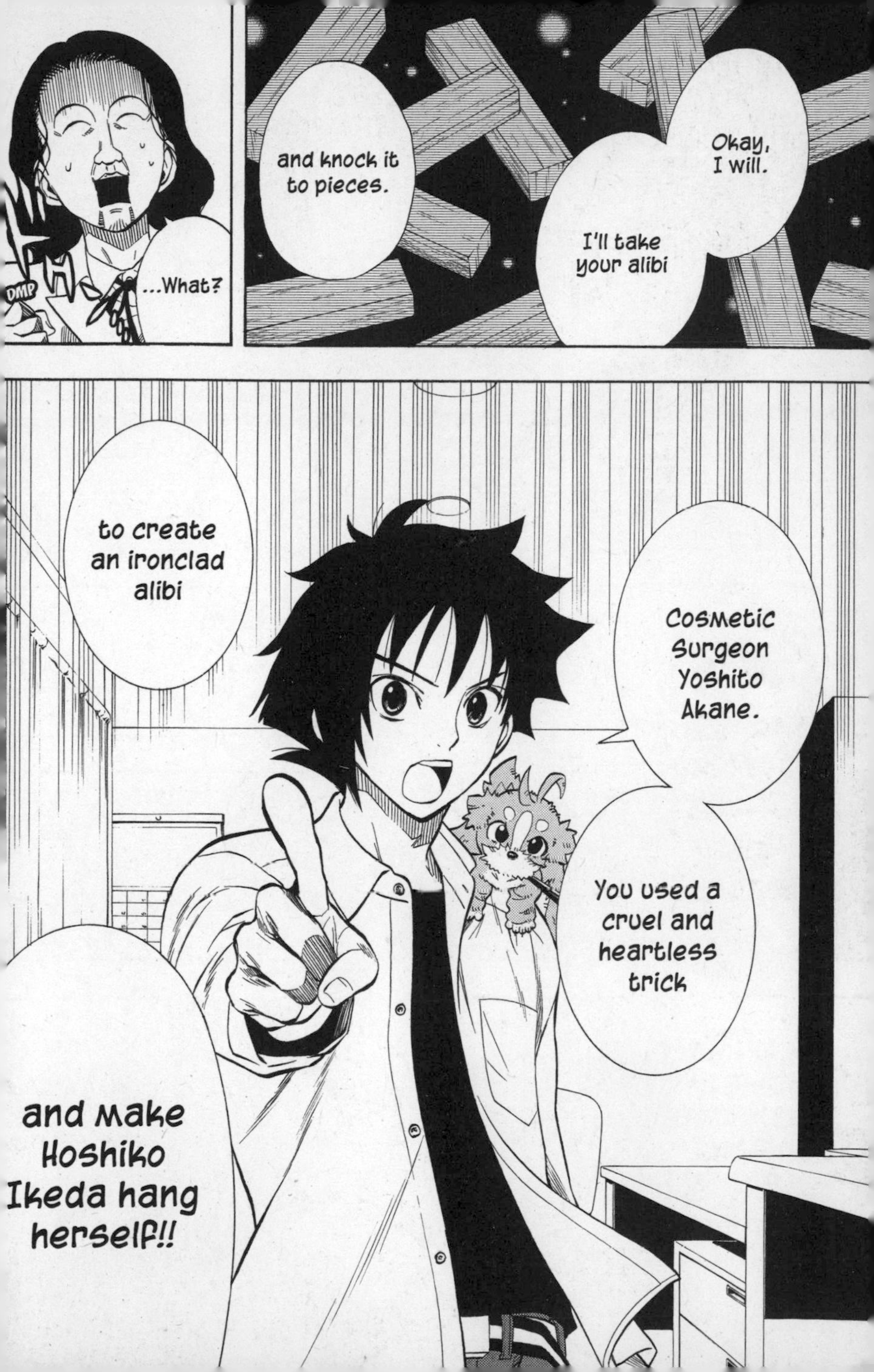
Okay, I will.
I'll take your alibi
and knock it to pieces.
DMP
...What?
Cosmetic Surgeon Yoshito Akane.
You used a cruel and heartless trick
to create an ironclad alibi
and make Hoshiko Ikeda hang herself!!

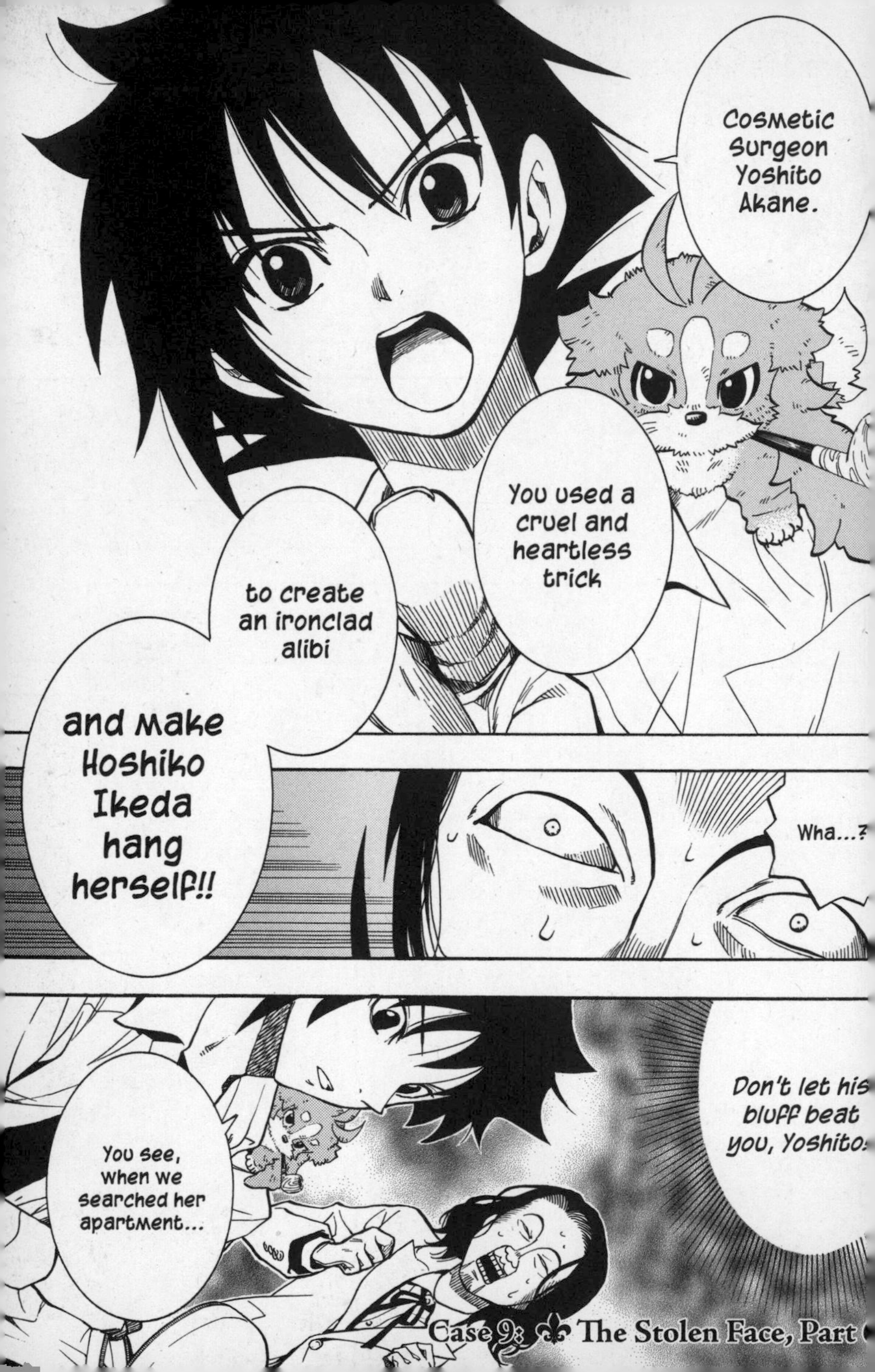
Cosmetic Surgeon Yoshito Akane.
You used a cruel and heartless trick
to create an ironclad alibi
and make Hoshiko Ikeda hang herself!!
Wha...?
Don't let his bluff beat you, Yoshito
You see, when we searched her apartment...
Case 9: The Stolen Face, Part

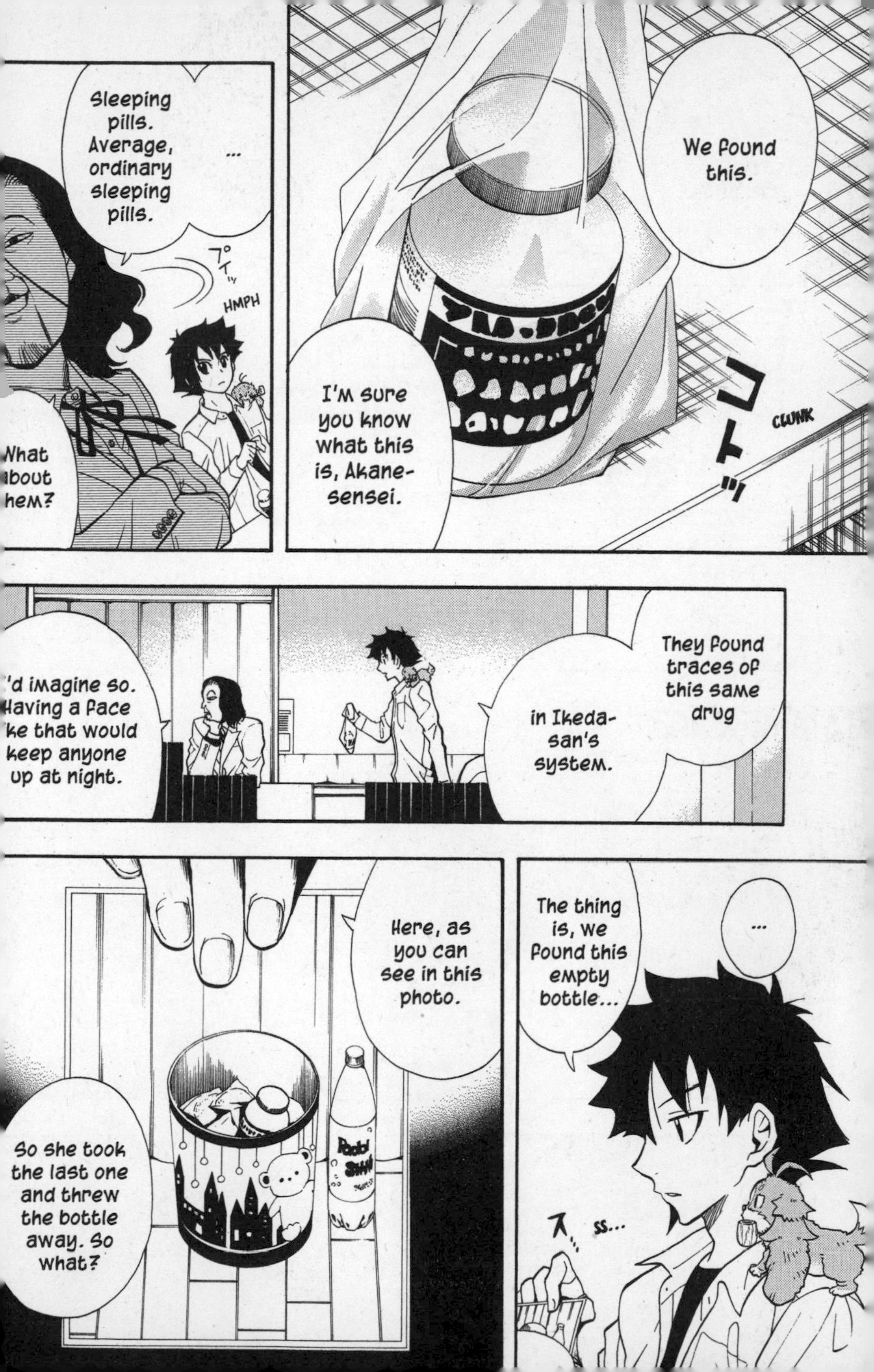

We found this.
CLUNK
I'm sure you know what this is, Akane-sensei.
Sleeping pills. Average, ordinary sleeping pills.
...
HMPH
What about hem?
They found traces of this same drug
in Ikeda-san's system.
'd imagine so. Having a face ke that would keep anyone up at night.
...
The thing is, we found this empty bottle...
SS...
Here, as you can see in this photo.
So she took the last one and threw the bottle away. So what?

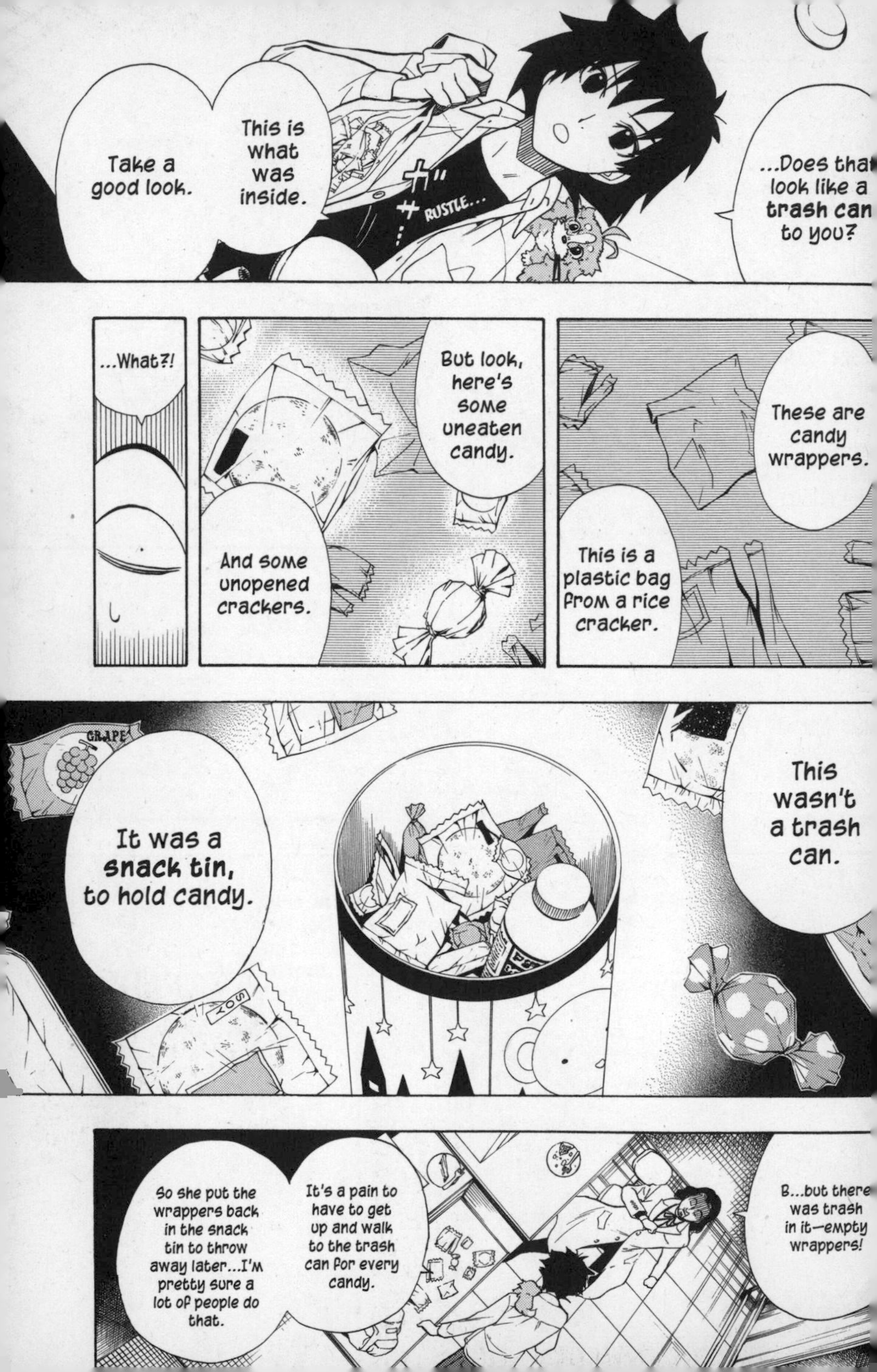
...Does tha look like a trash can to you?
This is what was inside.
RUSTLE...
Take a good look.
These are candy wrappers.
This is a plastic bag from a rice cracker.
But look, here's some uneaten candy.
And some unopened crackers.
...What?!
This wasn't a trash can.
GRAPE
It was a snack tin, to hold candy.
SOY
B...but there was trash in it—empty wrappers!
It's a pain to have to get up and walk to the trash can for every candy.
So she put the wrappers back in the snack tin to throw away later...I'm pretty sure a lot of people do that.

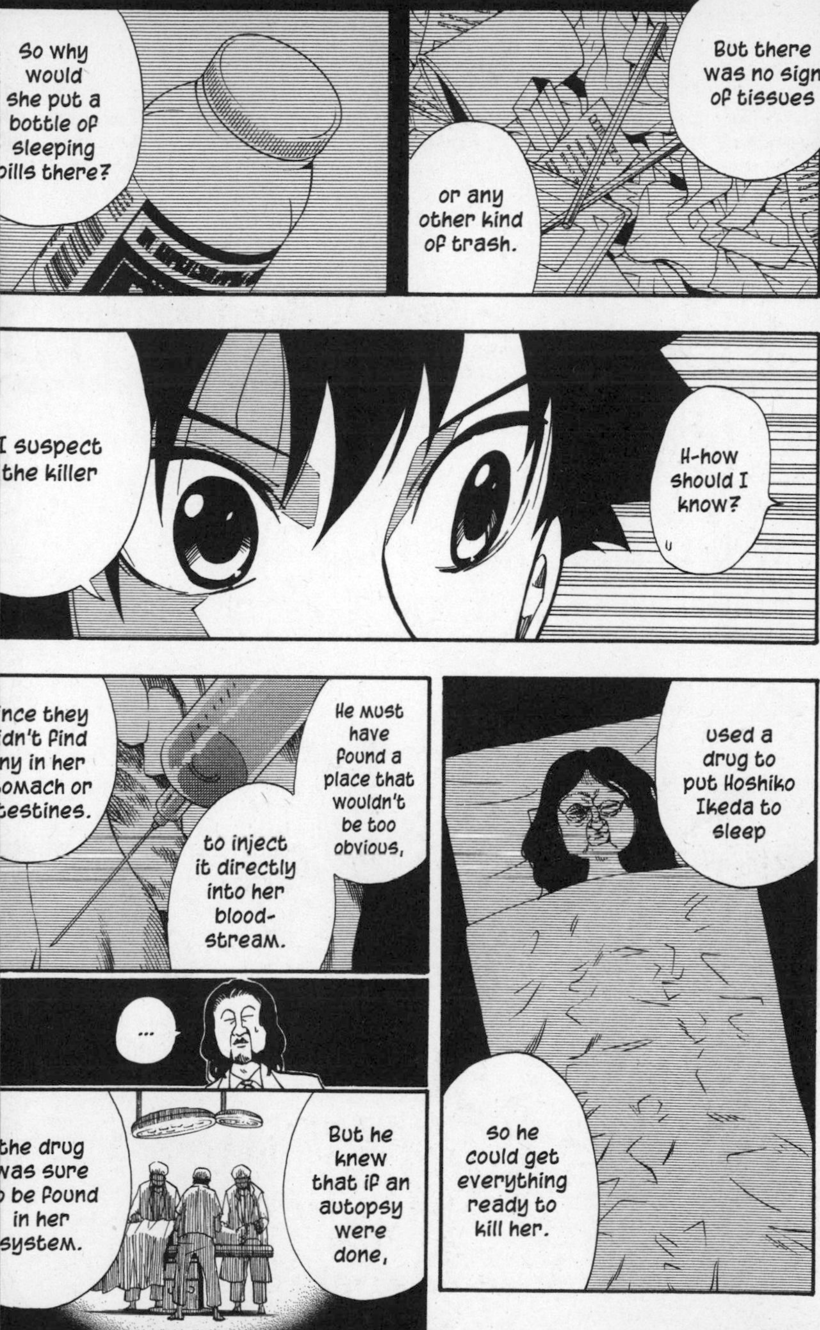

But there was no sign of tissues
or any other kind of trash.
So why would she put a bottle of sleeping pills there?
H-how should I know?
I suspect the killer
used a drug to put Hoshiko Ikeda to sleep
so he could get everything ready to kill her.
He must have found a place that wouldn't be too obvious,
to inject it directly into her blood-stream.
ince they idn't find ny in her omach or testines.
...
But he knew that if an autopsy were done,
the drug was sure o be found in her system.

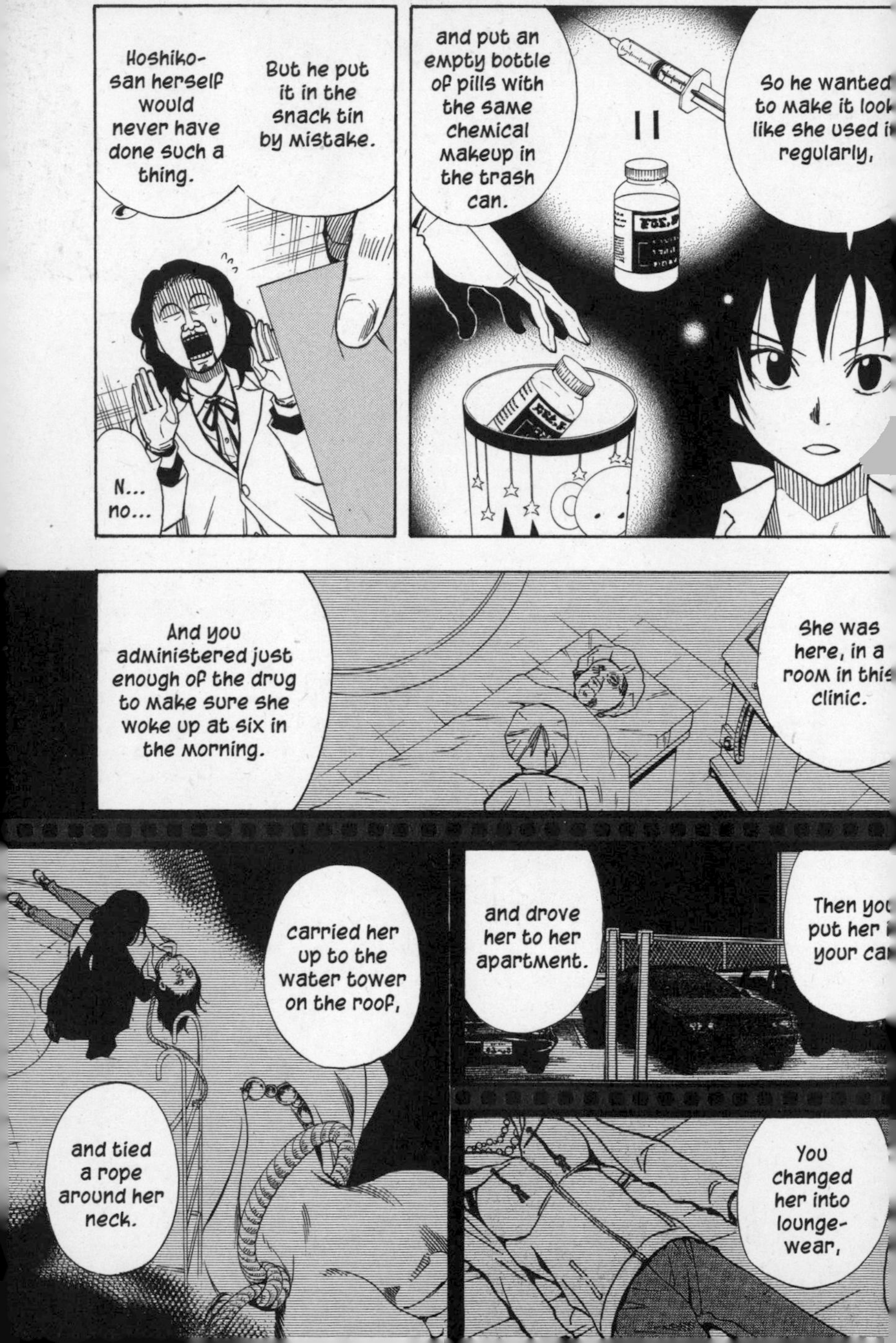

So he wanted to make it look like she used i regularly,
and put an empty bottle of pills with the same chemical makeup in the trash can.
But he put it in the snack tin by mistake.
Hoshiko-san herself would never have done such a thing.
N... no...
She was here, in a room in this clinic.
And you administered just enough of the drug to make sure she woke up at six in the morning.
Then you put her i your ca
and drove her to her apartment.
You changed her into lounge-wear,
carried her up to the water tower on the roof,
and tied a rope around her neck.

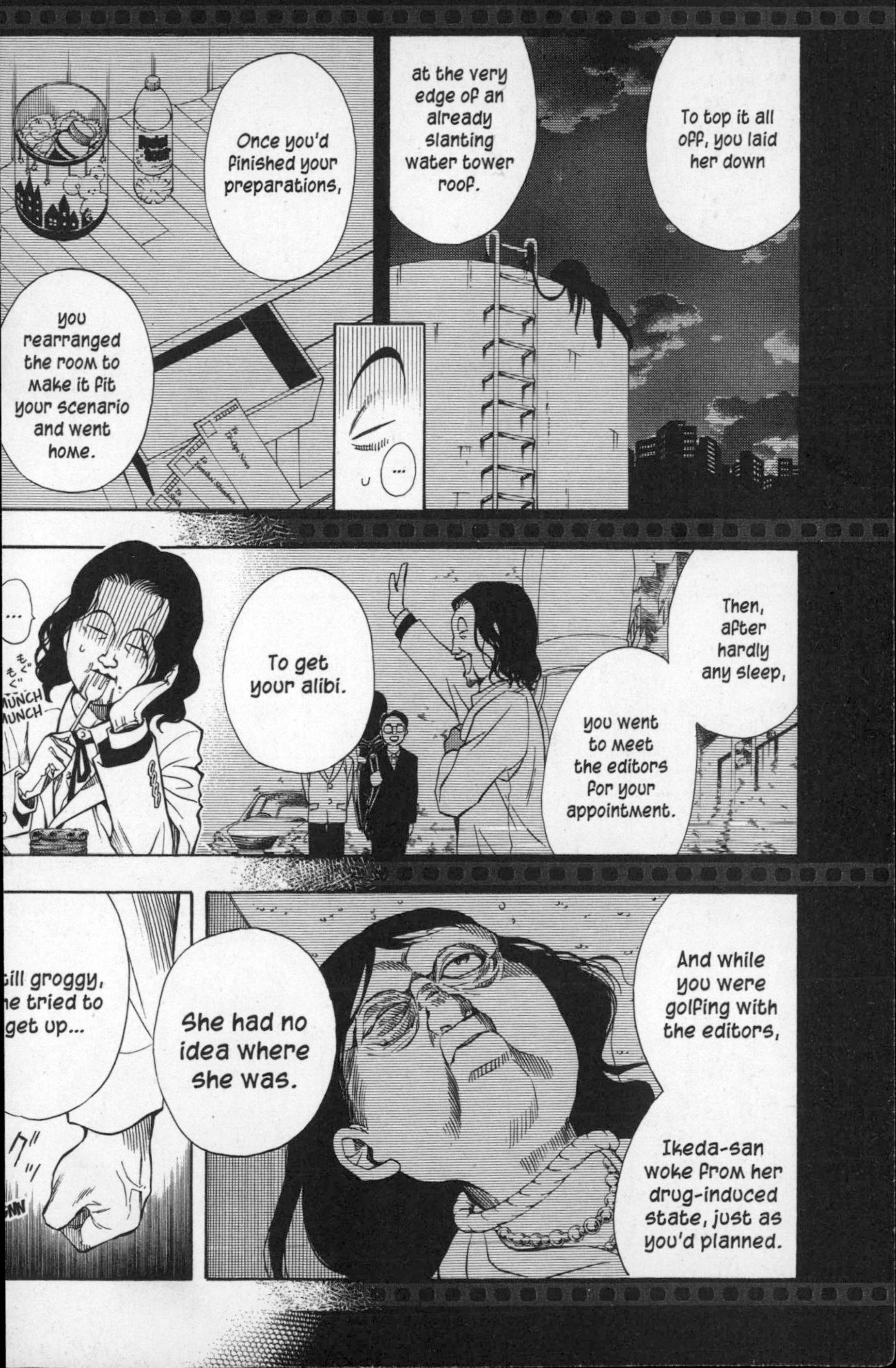
To top it all off, you laid her down
at the very edge of an already slanting water tower roof.
...
Once you'd finished your preparations,
you rearranged the room to make it fit your scenario and went home.
Then, after hardly any sleep,
you went to meet the editors for your appointment.
To get your alibi.
...
MUNCH MUNCH
And while you were golfing with the editors,
Ikeda-san woke from her drug-induced state, just as you'd planned.
She had no idea where she was.
till groggy, e tried to get up...

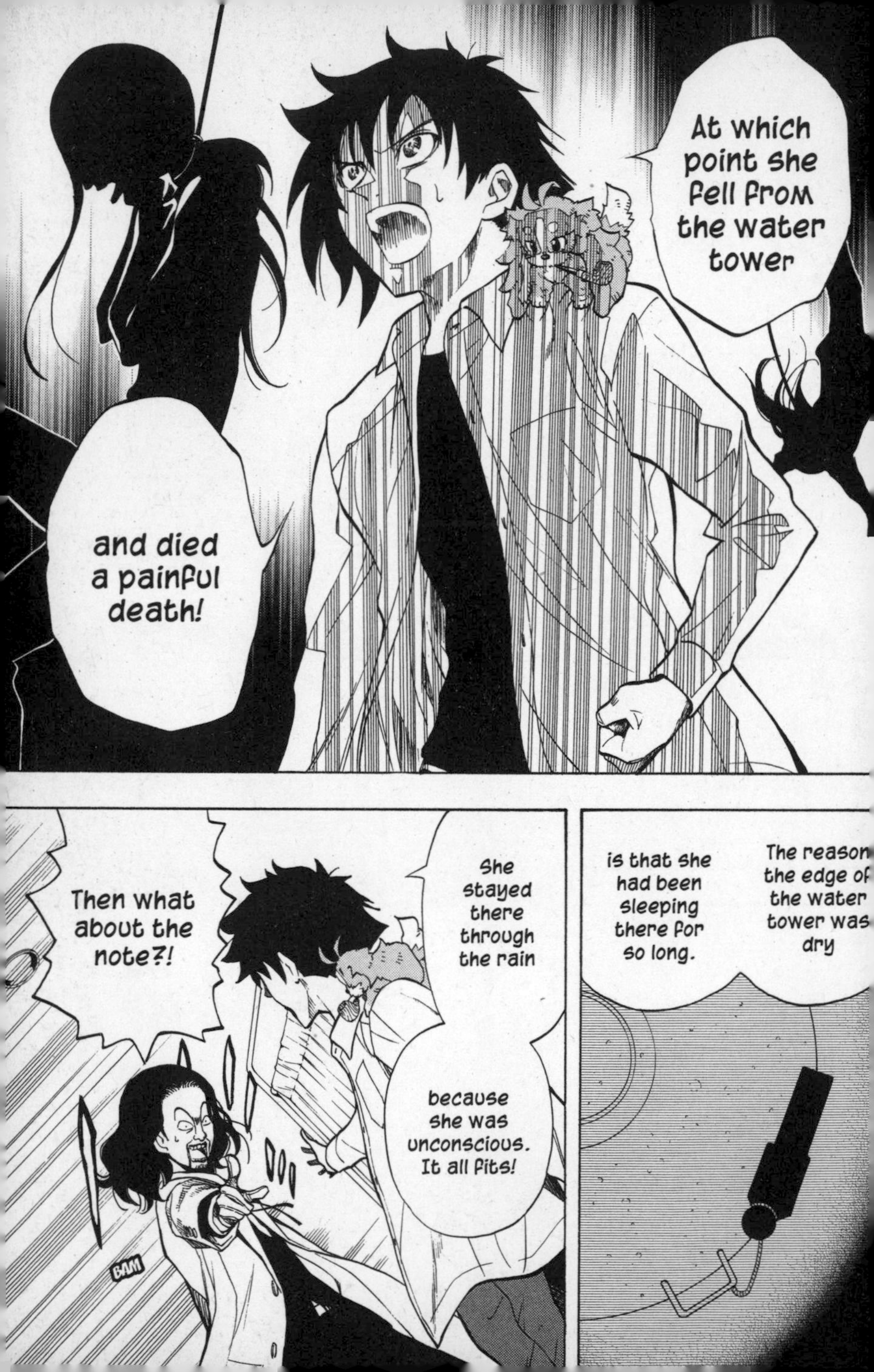
At which point she fell from the water tower
and died a painful death!
The reason the edge of the water tower was dry
is that she had been sleeping there for so long.
She stayed there through the rain
because she was unconscious. It all fits!
Then what about the note?!
BAM

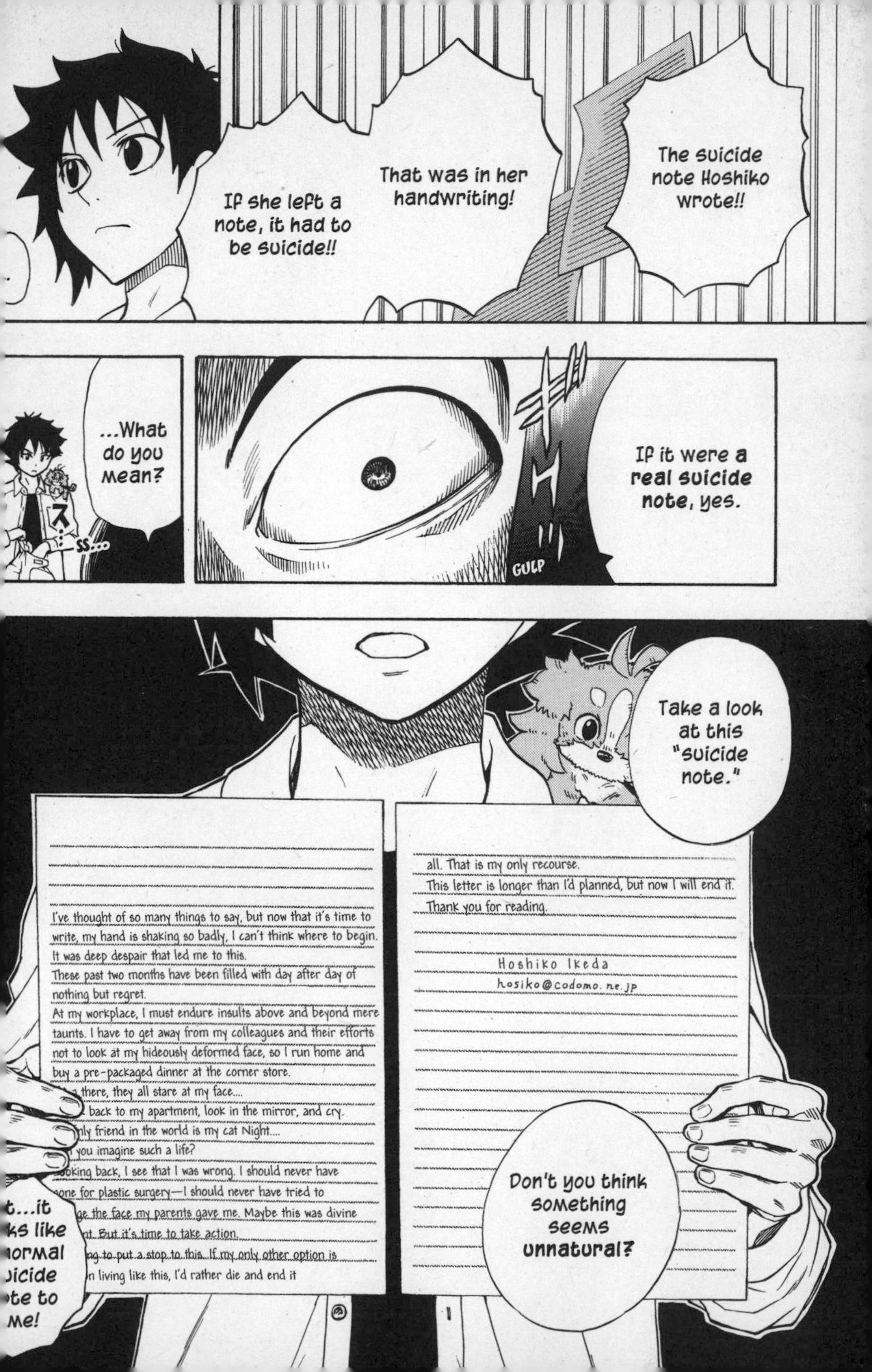
The suicide note Hoshiko wrote!!
That was in her handwriting!
If she left a note, it had to be suicide!!
If it were a real suicide note, yes.
GULP
...What do you mean?
SS...
Take a look at this "suicide note."
I've thought of so many things to say, but now that it's time to write, my hand is shaking so badly, I can't think where to begin.
It was deep despair that led me to this.
These past two months have been filled with day after day of nothing but regret.
At my workplace, I must endure insults above and beyond mere taunts. I have to get away from my colleagues and their efforts not to look at my hideously deformed face, so I run home and buy a pre-packaged dinner at the corner store.
there, they all stare at my face....
back to my apartment, look in the mirror, and cry.
nly friend in the world is my cat Night....
you imagine such a life?
ooking back, I see that I was wrong. I should never have
one for plastic surgery—I should never have tried to
ge the face my parents gave me. Maybe this was divine
nt. But it's time to take action.
ng to put a stop to this. If my only other option is
n living like this, I'd rather die and end it
all. That is my only recourse.
This letter is longer than I'd planned, but now I will end it.
Thank you for reading.
Hoshiko Ikeda
hosiko@codomo.ne.jp
Don't you think something seems unnatural?
t...it ks like normal uicide te to me!

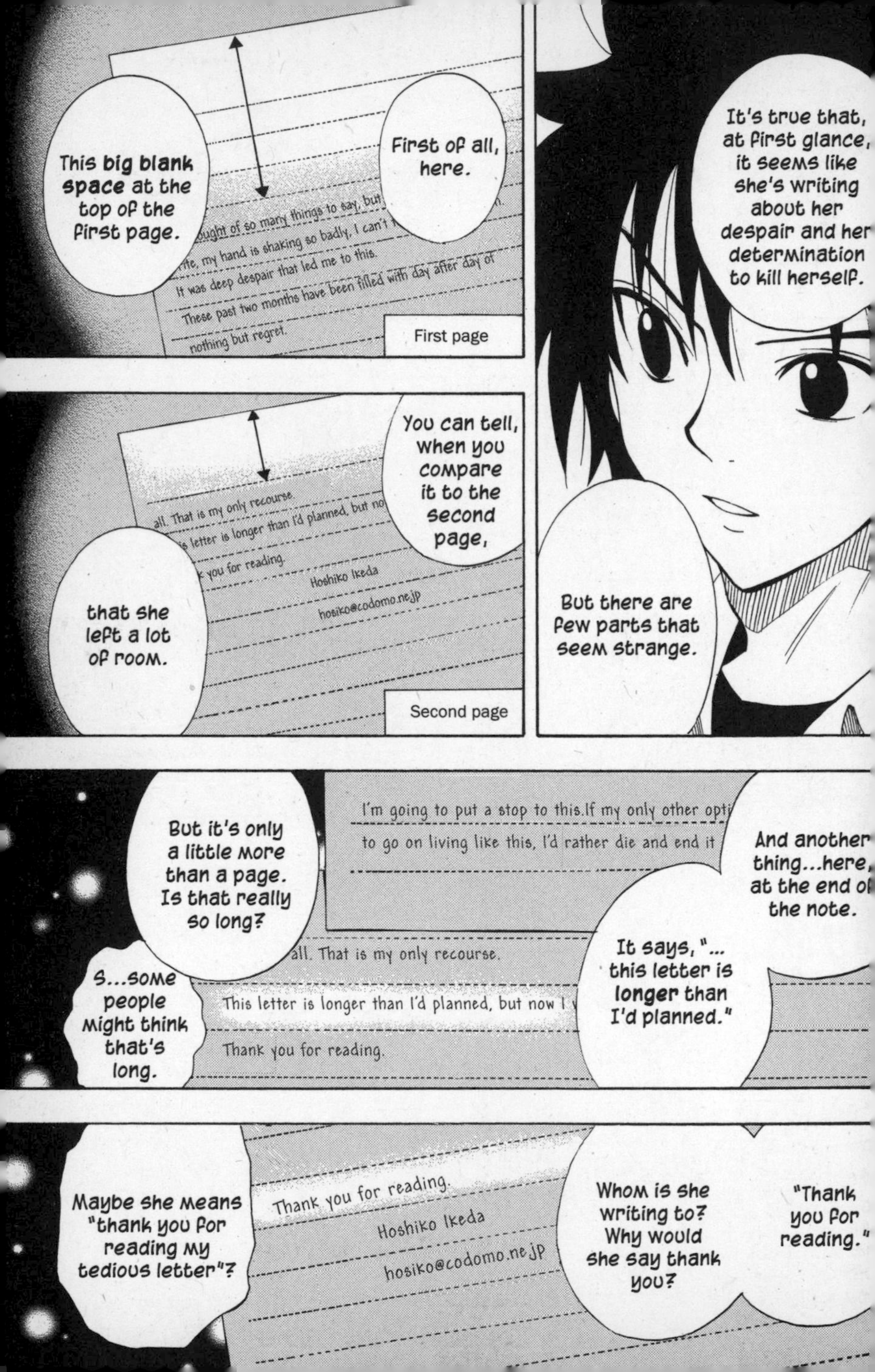

It's true that, at first glance, it seems like she's writing about her despair and her determination to kill herself.
But there are few parts that seem strange.
First of all, here.
This big blank space at the top of the first page.
It was deep despair that led me to this.
These past two months have been filled with day after day of nothing but regret.
First page
You can tell, when you compare it to the second page,
that she left a lot of room.
all. That is my only recourse.
Hoshiko Ikeda
hosiko@codomo.ne.jp
Second page
And another thing...here, at the end of the note.
It says, "...this letter is longer than I'd planned."
But it's only a little more than a page. Is that really so long?
S...some people might think that's long.
all. That is my only recourse.
Thank you for reading.
"Thank you for reading."
Whom is she writing to? Why would she say thank you?
Maybe she means "thank you for reading my tedious letter"?
Thank you for reading.
Hoshiko Ikeda
hosiko@codomo.ne.jp

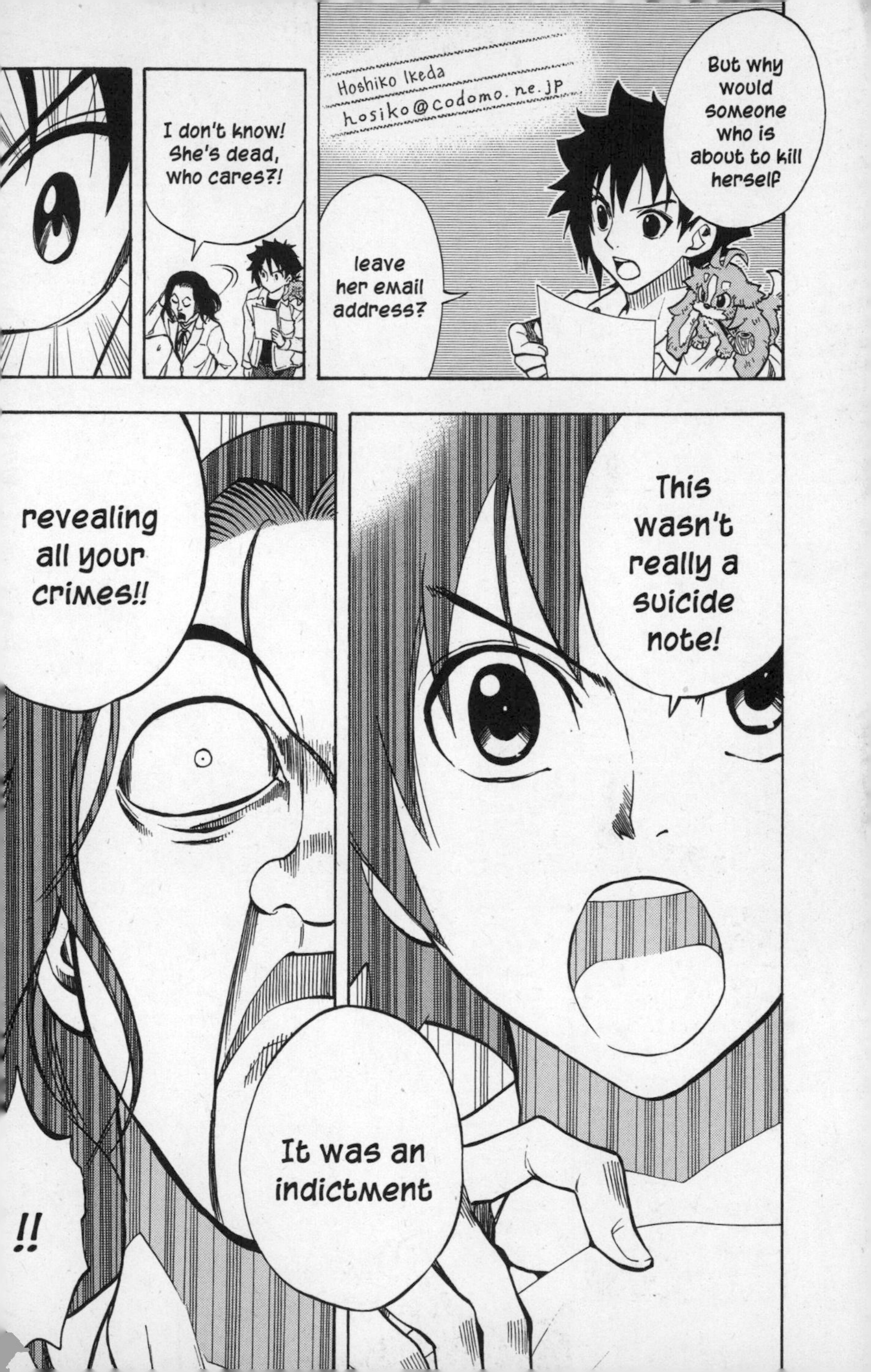
Hoshiko Ikeda
hosiko@codomo.ne.jp
But why would someone who is about to kill herself
leave her email address?
I don't know! She's dead, who cares?!
This wasn't really a suicide note!
It was an indictment
revealing all your crimes!!
!!

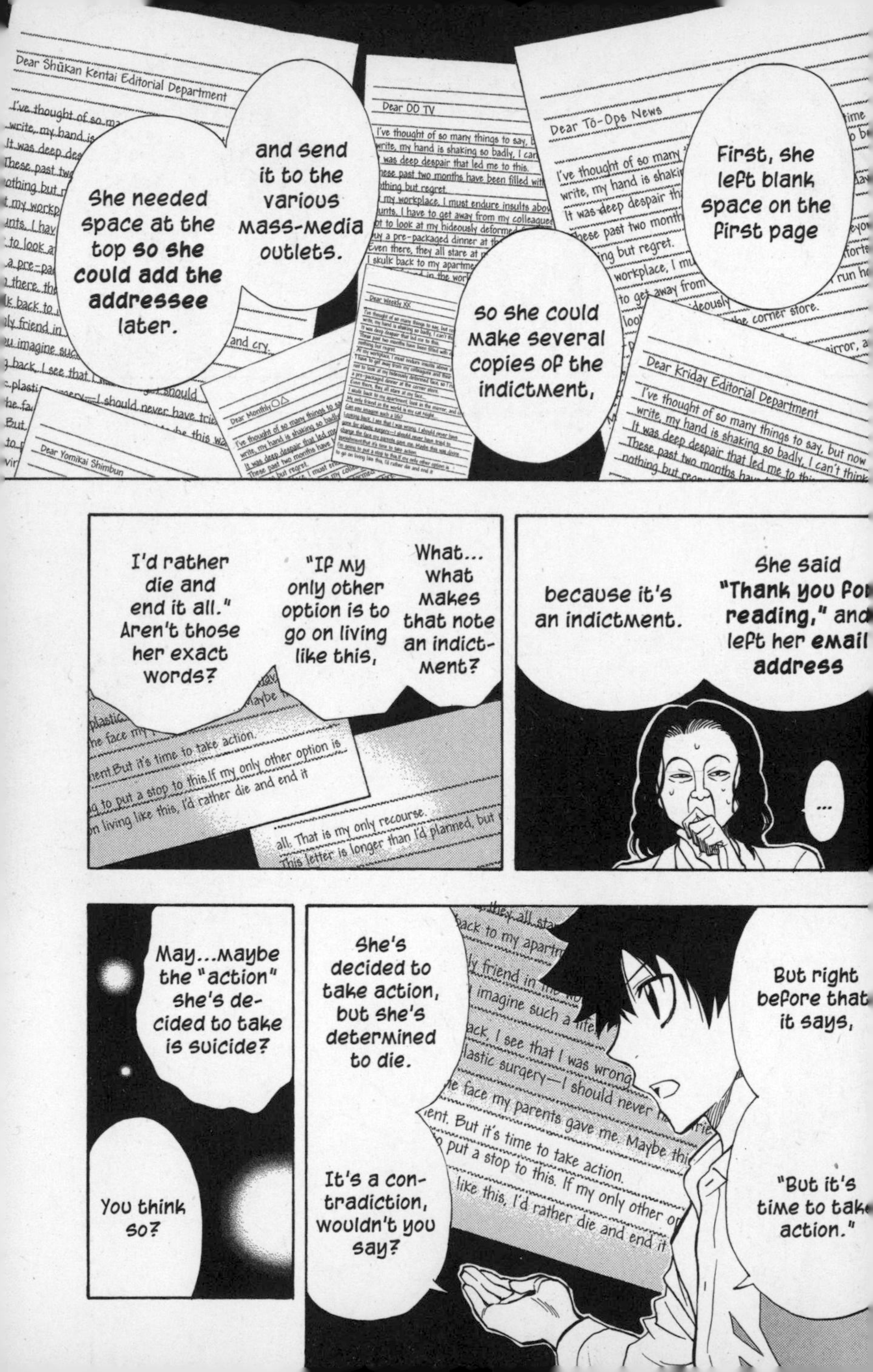
Dear Shūkan Kentai Editorial Department
Dear OO TV
Dear Tō-Ops News
Dear Kriday Editorial Department
Dear Monthly○△
Dear Yomikai Shimbun
I've thought of so many things to say, but now
write, my hand is shaking so badly, I can't think
It was deep despair that led me to this.
These past two months have been filled with
nothing but regret.
First, she left blank space on the first page
so she could make several copies of the indictment,
and send it to the various mass-media outlets.
She needed space at the top so she could add the addressee later.
She said "Thank you for reading," and left her email address
because it's an indictment.
...
What... what makes that note an indict-ment?
"If my only other option is to go on living like this,
I'd rather die and end it all." Aren't those her exact words?
ment.But it's time to take action.
to put a stop to this.If my only other option is
on living like this, I'd rather die and end it
all. That is my only recourse.
This letter is longer than I'd planned, but
But right before that it says,
"But it's time to take action."
She's decided to take action, but she's determined to die.
It's a con-tradiction, wouldn't you say?
plastic surgery—I should never have
he face my parents gave me. Maybe this
ent. But it's time to take action.
put a stop to this. If my only other o
like this, I'd rather die and end it
May...maybe the "action" she's de-cided to take is suicide?
You think so?

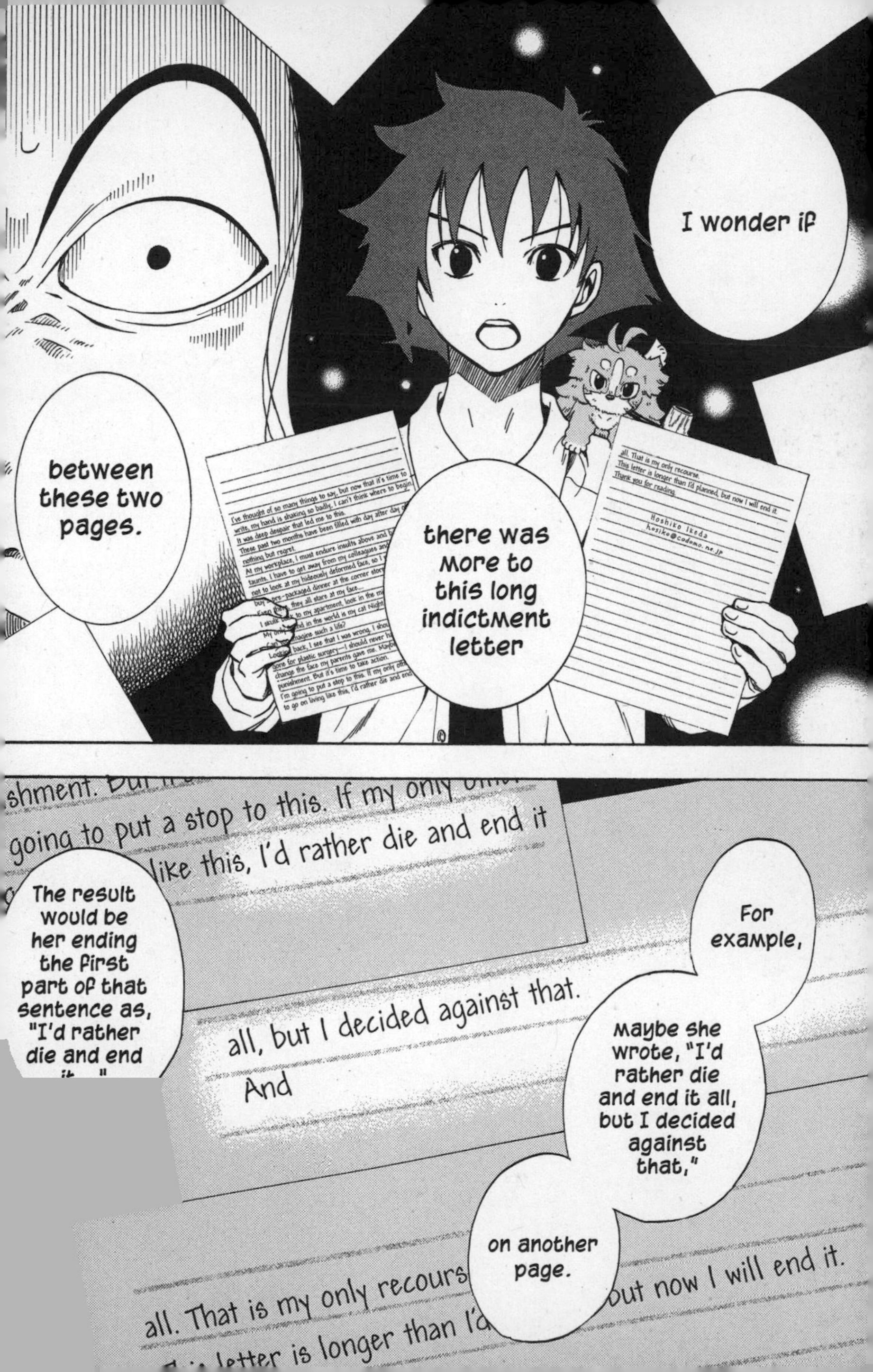
I wonder if
there was more to this long indictment letter
between these two pages.
I've thought of so many things to say, but now that it's time to write, my hand is shaking so badly, I can't think where to begin.
It was deep despair that led me to this.
These past two months have been filled with day after day of nothing but regret.
all. That is my only recourse.
This letter is longer than I'd planned, but now I will end it.
Thank you for reading.
Hoshiko Ikeda
hosiko@codomo.ne.jp
For example,
Maybe she wrote, "I'd rather die and end it all, but I decided against that,"
on another page.
going to put a stop to this. If my only
like this, I'd rather die and end it
all, but I decided against that.
And
all. That is my only recours
but now I will end it.
letter is longer than I'
The result would be her ending the first part of that sentence as, "I'd rather die and end

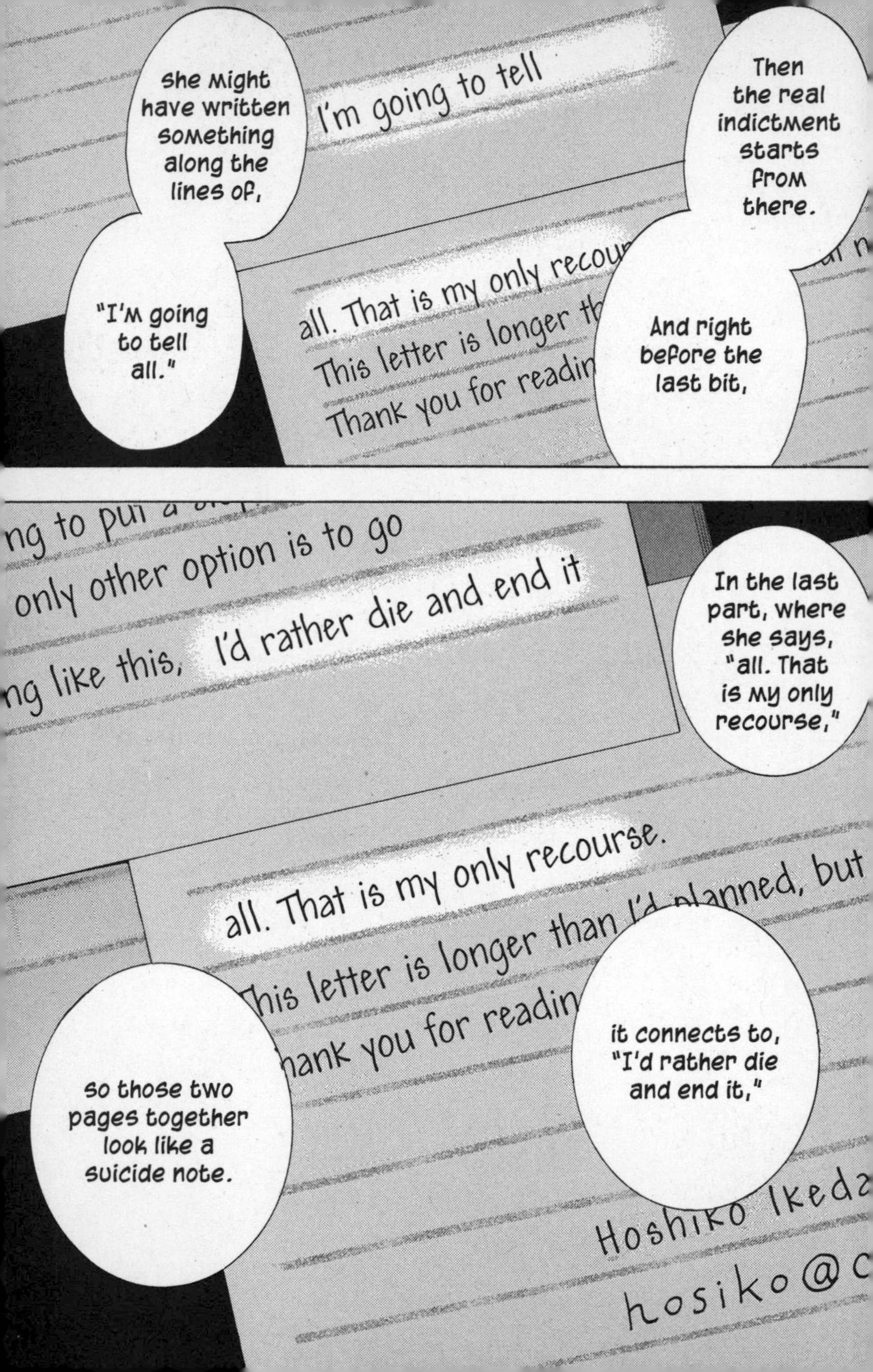

she might have written something along the lines of,

I'm going to tell

Then the real indictment starts from there.

"I'M going to tell all."

all. That is my only recour...

This letter is longer th...

Thank you for readin...

And right before the last bit,

...ng to put a st...

only other option is to go

...ng like this, I'd rather die and end it

In the last part, where she says, "all. That is my only recourse,"

all. That is my only recourse.

This letter is longer than I'd planned, but

...hank you for readin...

so those two pages together look like a suicide note.

it connects to, "I'd rather die and end it,"

Hoshiko Ikeda

hosiko@c...

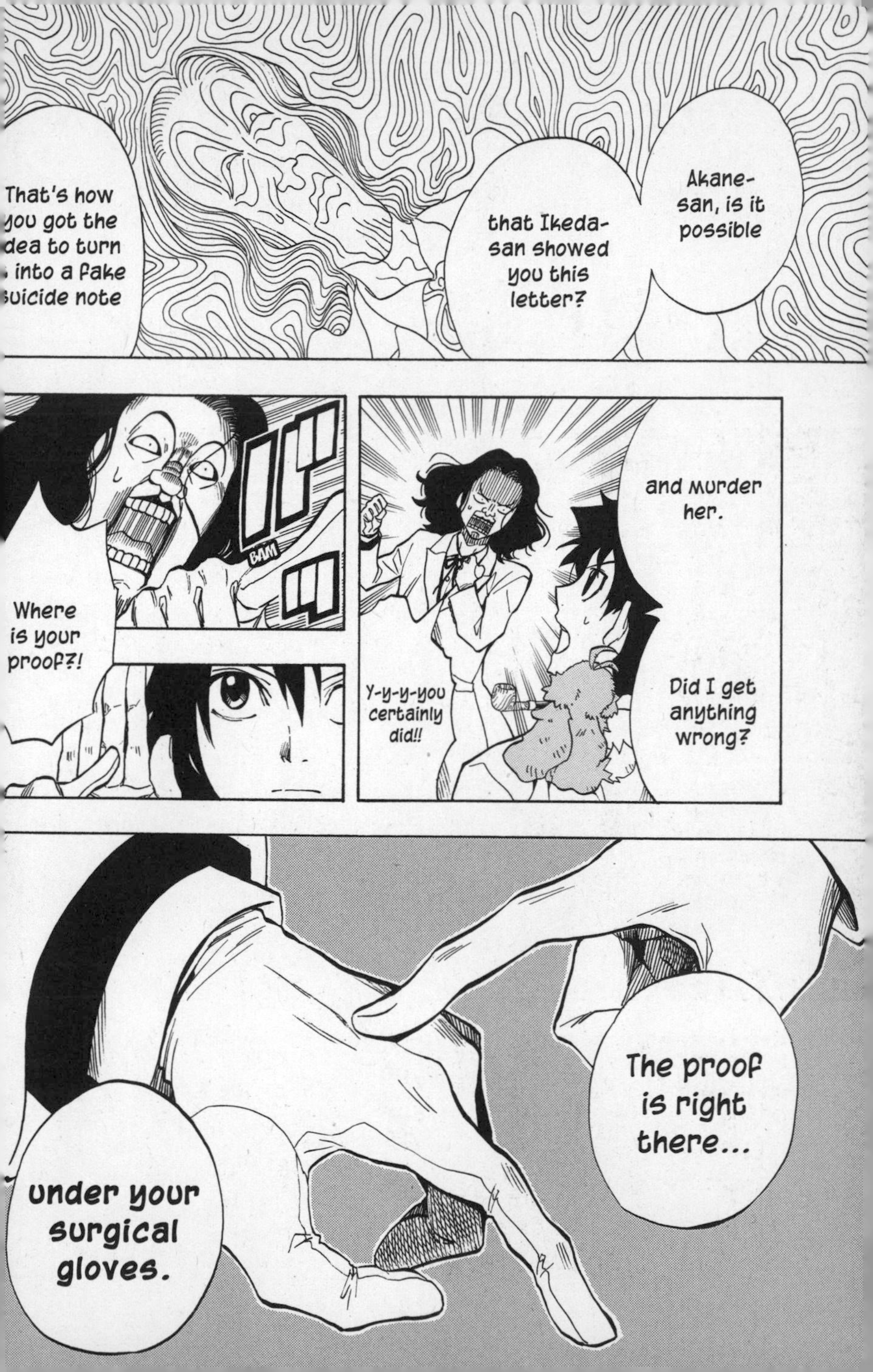
Akane-san, is it possible
that Ikeda-san showed you this letter?
That's how you got the dea to turn into a fake uicide note
and murder her.
Did I get anything wrong?
Y-y-y-you certainly did!!
BAM
Where is your proof?!
The proof is right there...
under your surgical gloves.

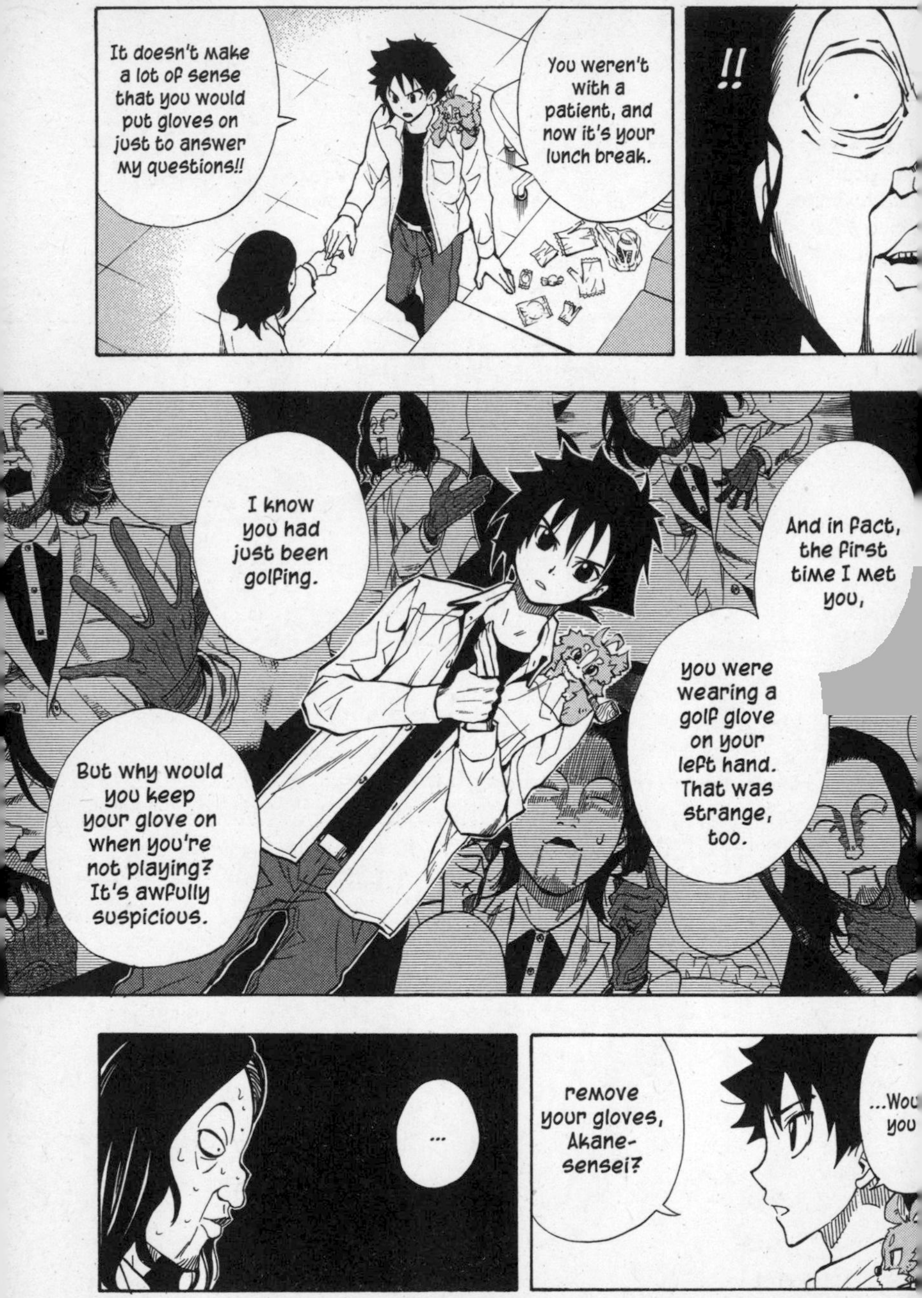
!!
You weren't with a patient, and now it's your lunch break.
It doesn't make a lot of sense that you would put gloves on just to answer my questions!!
And in fact, the first time I met you,
you were wearing a golf glove on your left hand. That was strange, too.
I know you had just been golfing.
But why would you keep your glove on when you're not playing? It's awfully suspicious.
...Wou you
remove your gloves, Akane-sensei?
...

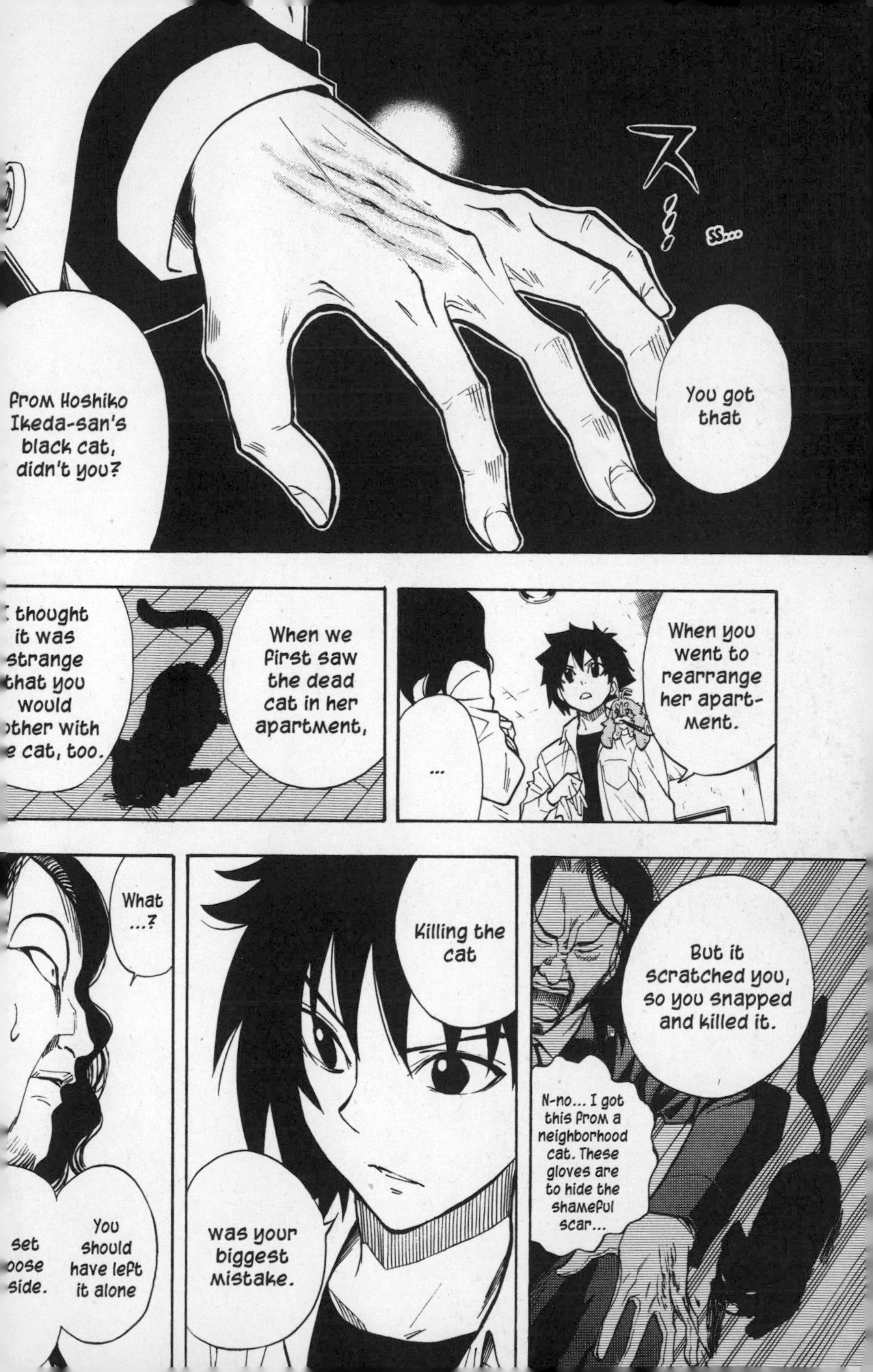
ス
SS...
You got that
from Hoshiko Ikeda-san's black cat, didn't you?
When you went to rearrange her apartment.
...
When we first saw the dead cat in her apartment,
thought it was strange that you would other with e cat, too.
But it scratched you, so you snapped and killed it.
N-no... I got this from a neighborhood cat. These gloves are to hide the shameful scar...
Killing the cat
was your biggest mistake.
What ...?
You should have left it alone
set oose side.

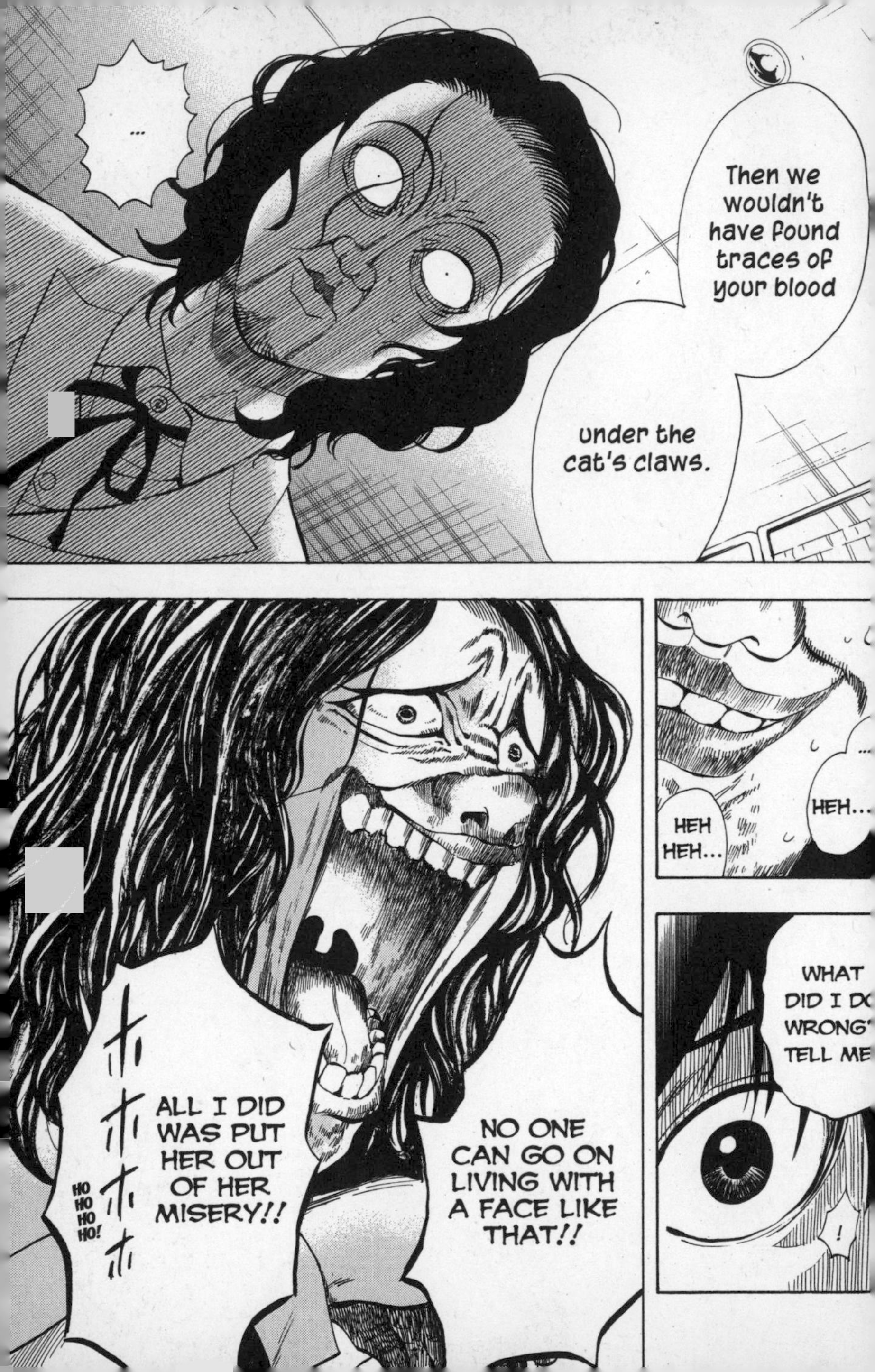
Then we wouldn't have found traces of your blood
under the cat's claws.
...
...
HEH...
HEH HEH...
WHAT DID I DO WRONG? TELL ME
!
NO ONE CAN GO ON LIVING WITH A FACE LIKE THAT!!
ALL I DID WAS PUT HER OUT OF HER MISERY!!
HO HO HO HO!

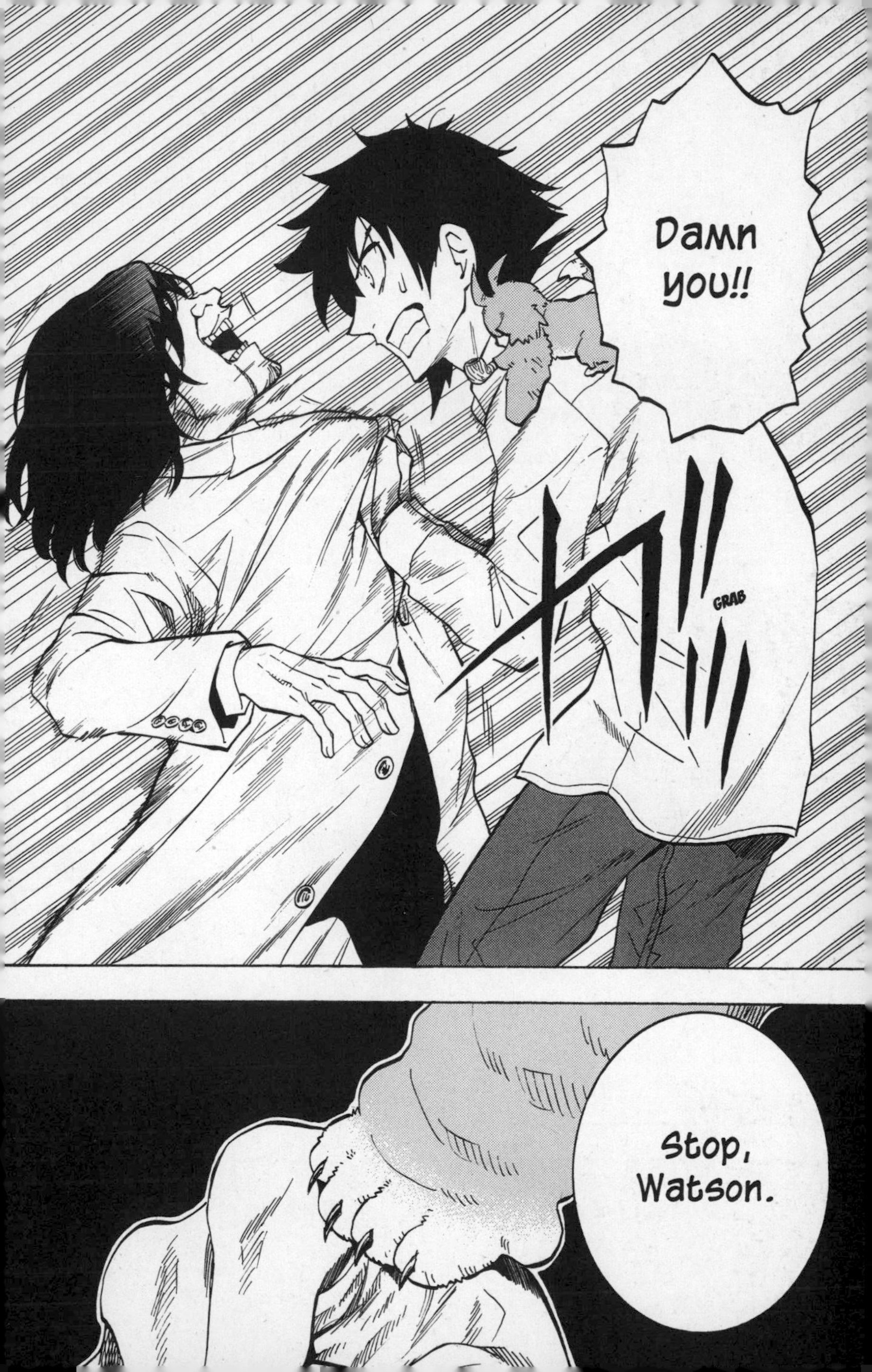
Damn you!!
GRAB
Stop, Watson.

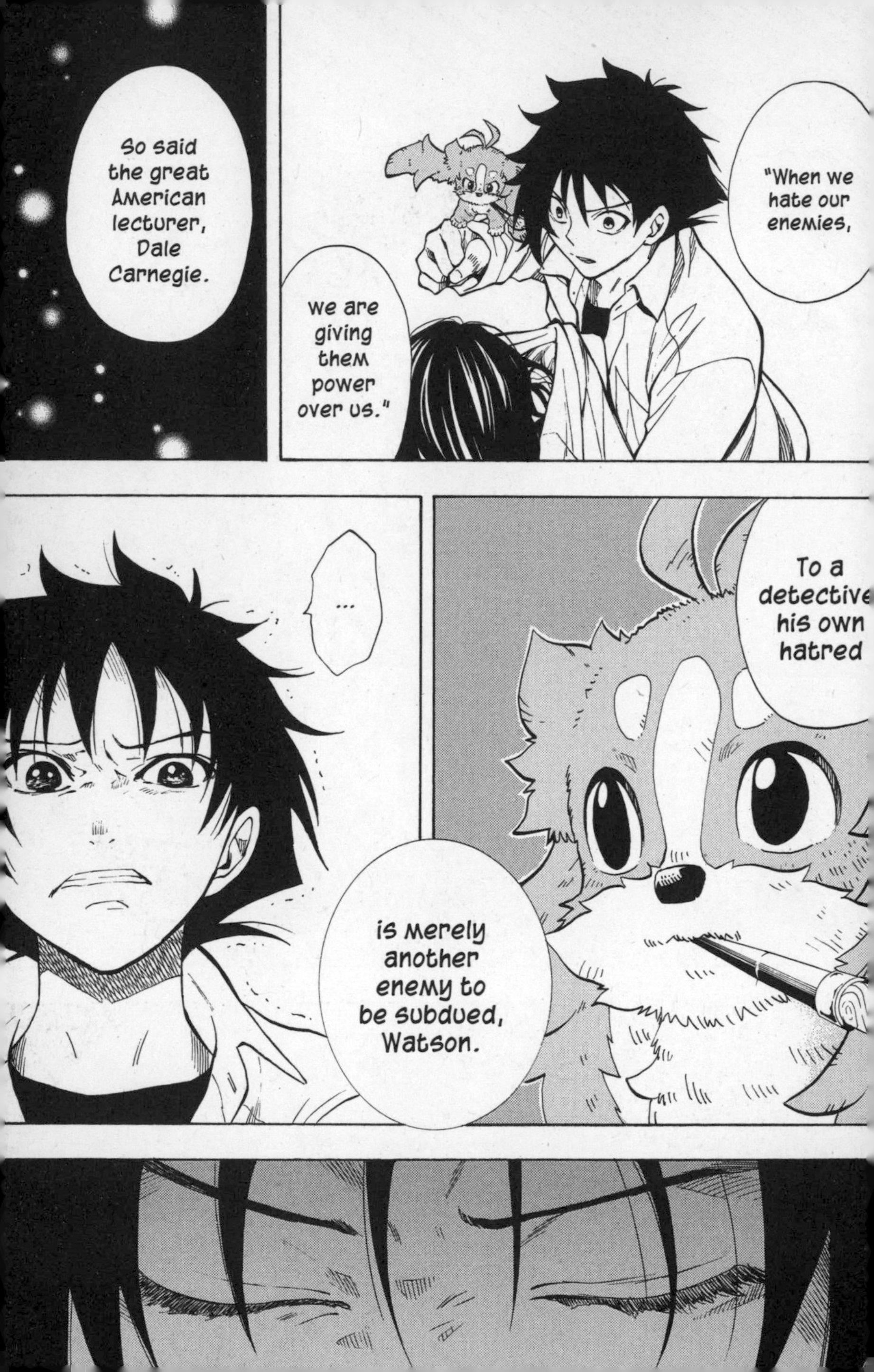
"When we hate our enemies,
we are giving them power over us."
So said the great American lecturer, Dale Carnegie.
To a detective his own hatred
is merely another enemy to be subdued, Watson.
...

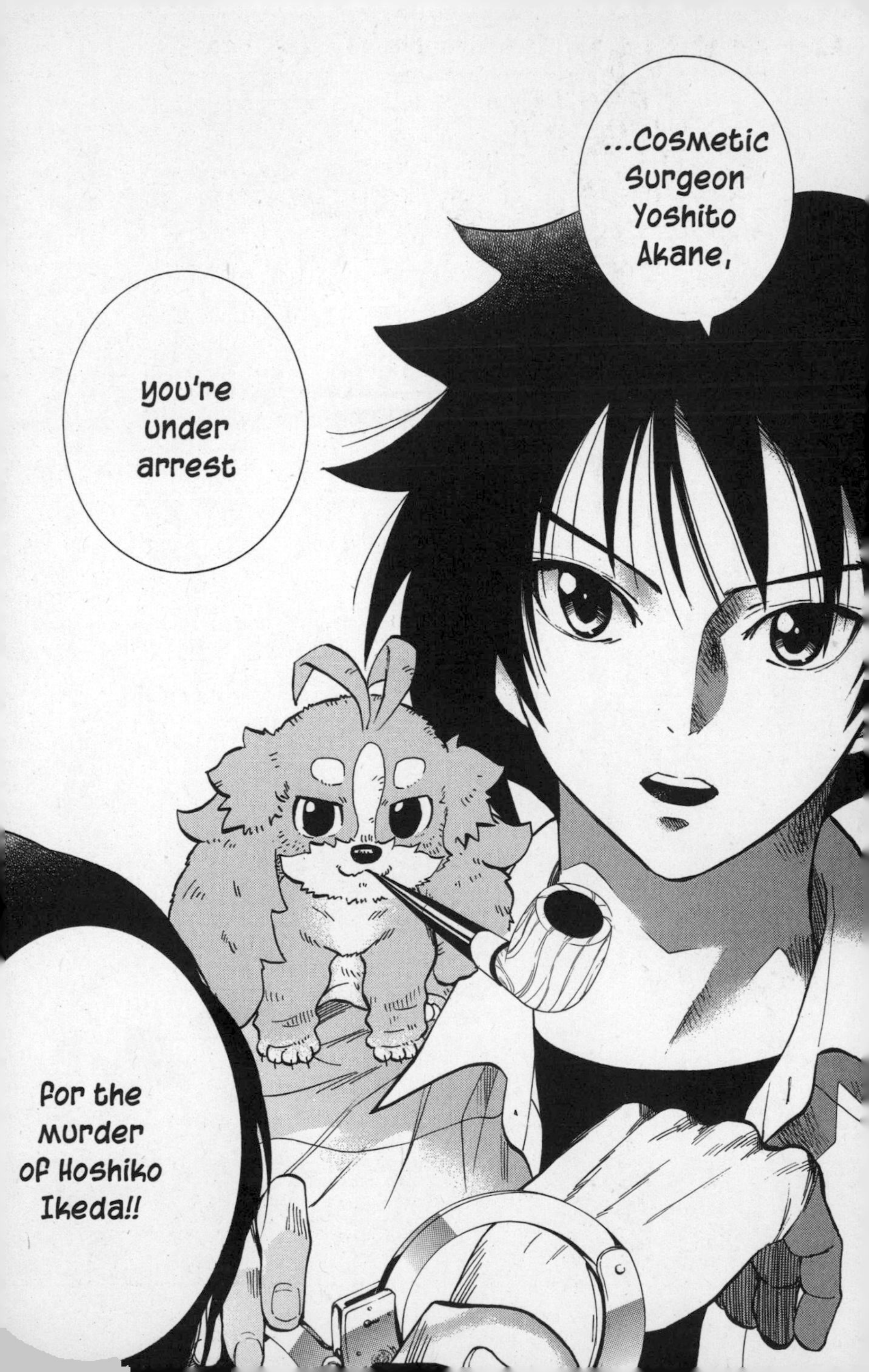
...Cosmetic Surgeon Yoshito Akane,
you're under arrest
for the murder of Hoshiko Ikeda!!

Case 10: ⚜ A Certain Policewoman's Crime, Part 1

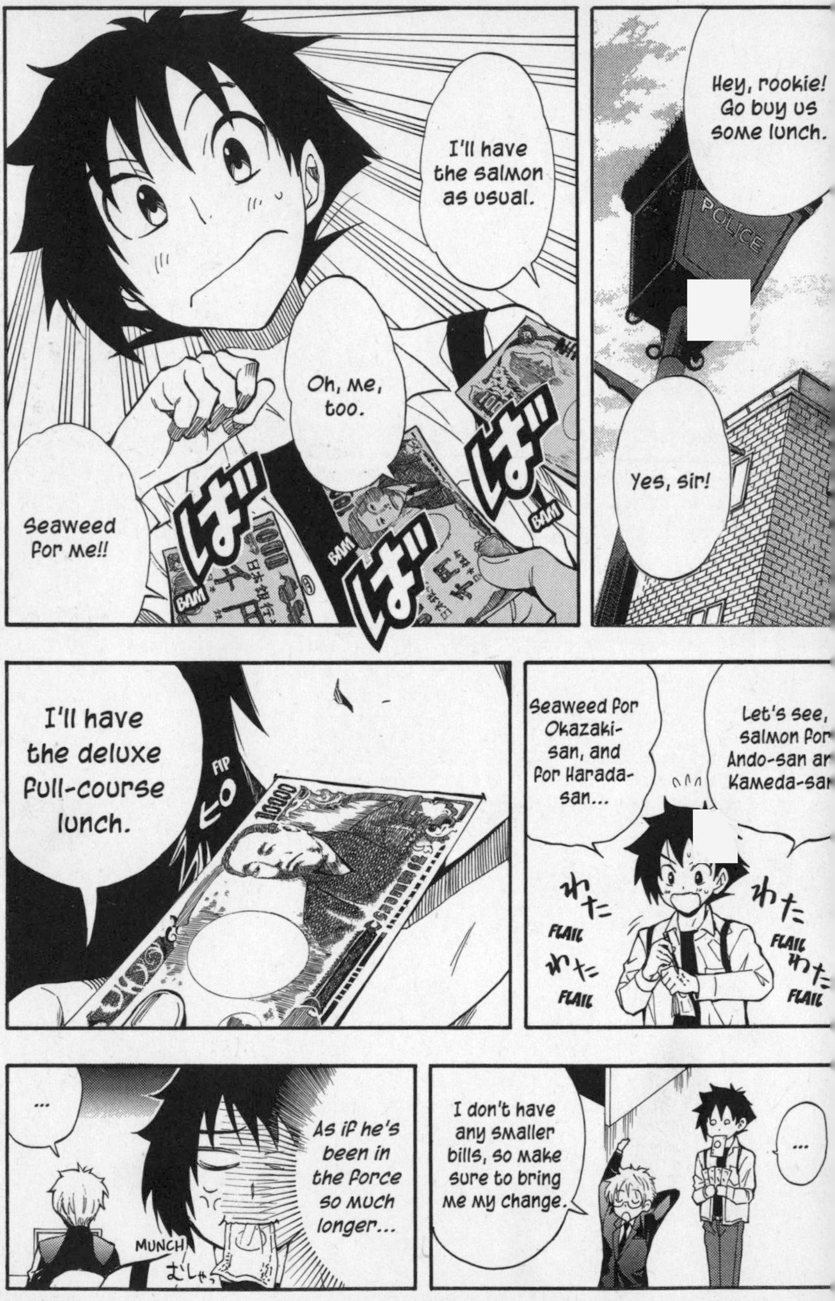
POLICE
Hey, rookie! Go buy us some lunch.
Yes, sir!
I'll have the salmon as usual.
Oh, me, too.
Seaweed for me!!
BAM
BAM
BAM
Let's see, salmon for Ando-san ar Kameda-sar
Seaweed for Okazaki-san, and for Harada-san...
FLAIL
FLAIL
FLAIL
FLAIL
FIP
I'll have the deluxe full-course lunch.
...
I don't have any smaller bills, so make sure to bring me my change.
As if he's been in the force so much longer...
...
MUNCH

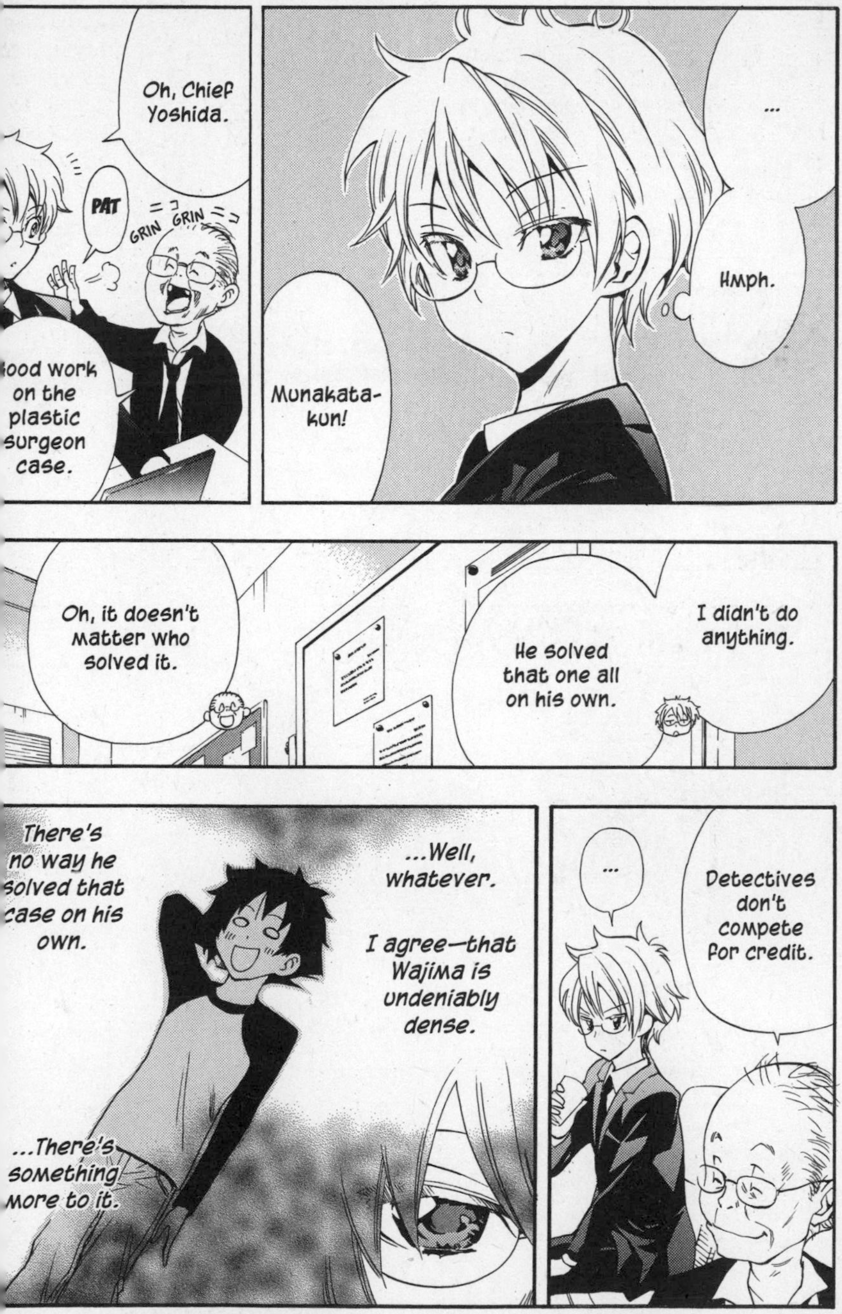
...
Hmph.
Munakata-kun!
Oh, Chief Yoshida.
PAT
GRIN GRIN
Good work on the plastic surgeon case.
I didn't do anything.
He solved that one all on his own.
Oh, it doesn't matter who solved it.
Detectives don't compete for credit.
...
...Well, whatever.
I agree—that Wajima is undeniably dense.
There's no way he solved that case on his own.
...There's something more to it.

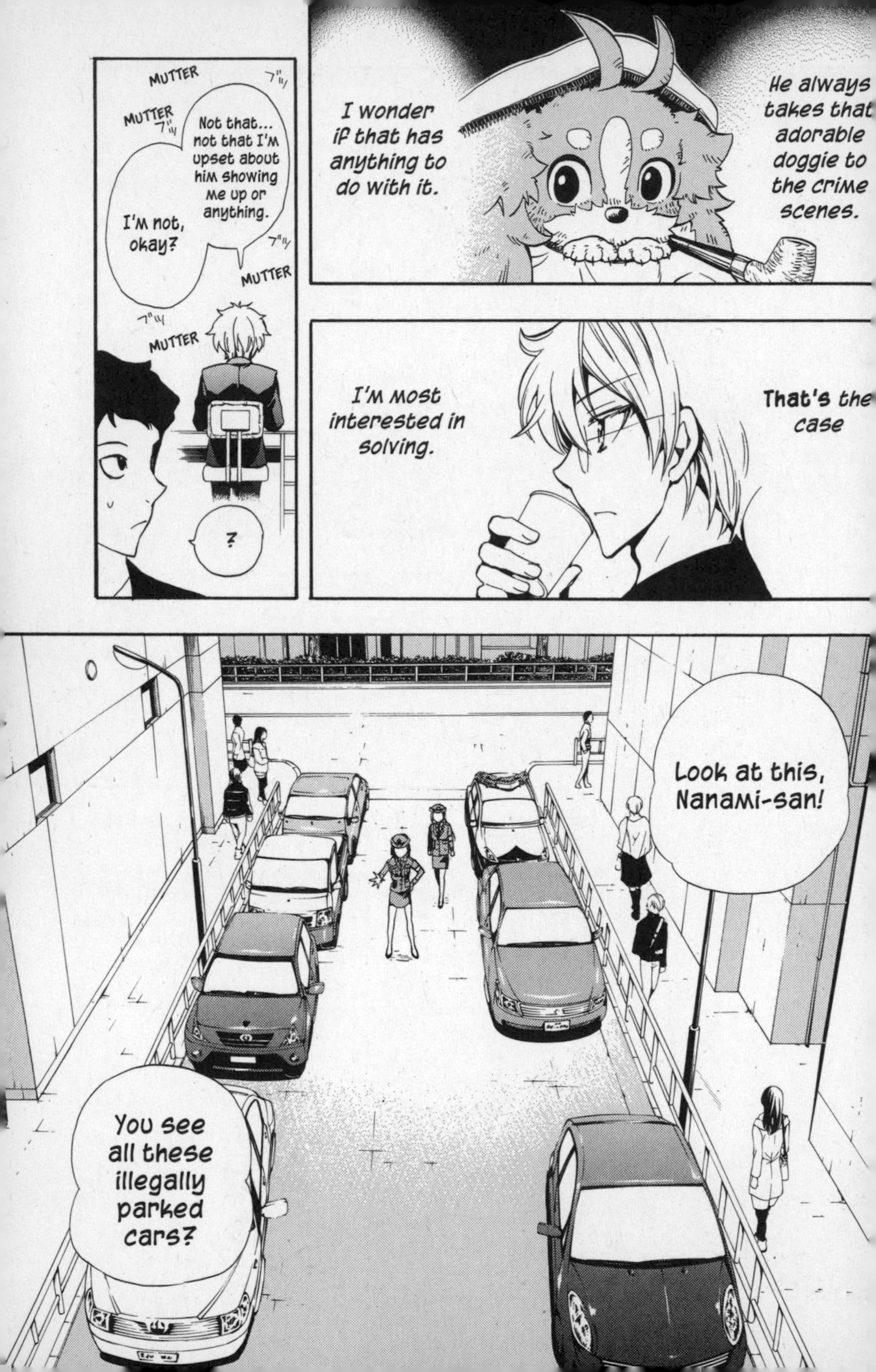
He always takes that adorable doggie to the crime scenes.
I wonder if that has anything to do with it.
That's the case
I'm most interested in solving.
MUTTER
MUTTER
Not that... not that I'm upset about him showing me up or anything.
I'm not, okay?
MUTTER
MUTTER
?
Look at this, Nanami-san!
You see all these illegally parked cars?

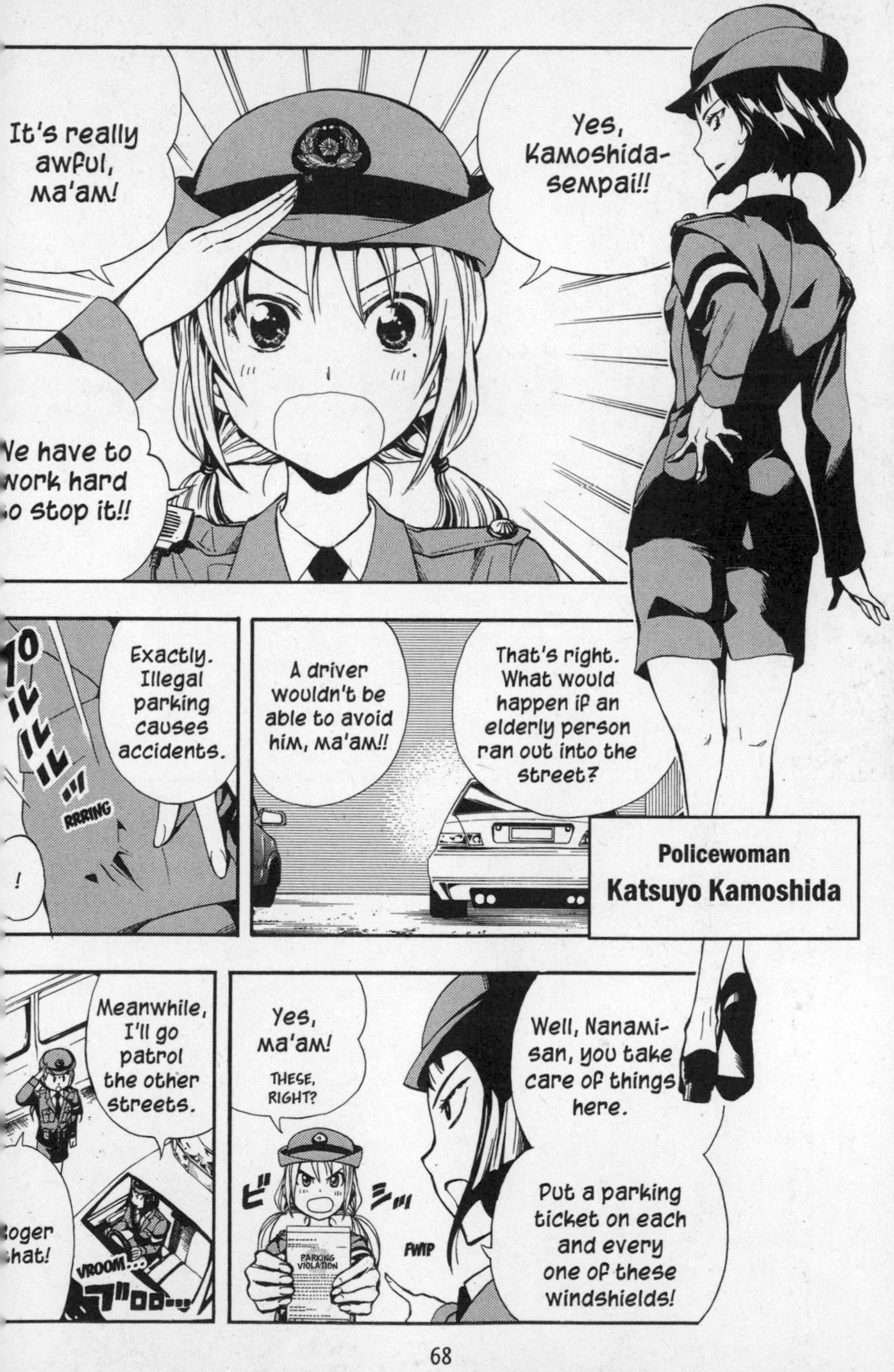
Yes, Kamoshida-sempai!!
It's really awful, ma'am!
Ve have to vork hard o stop it!!
That's right. What would happen if an elderly person ran out into the street?
A driver wouldn't be able to avoid him, ma'am!!
Policewoman Katsuyo Kamoshida
Exactly. Illegal parking causes accidents.
RRRING
!
Well, Nanami-san, you take care of things here.
Put a parking ticket on each and every one of these windshields!
Yes, ma'am!
THESE, RIGHT?
FWIP
PARKING VIOLATION
Meanwhile, I'll go patrol the other streets.
oger hat!
VROOM...

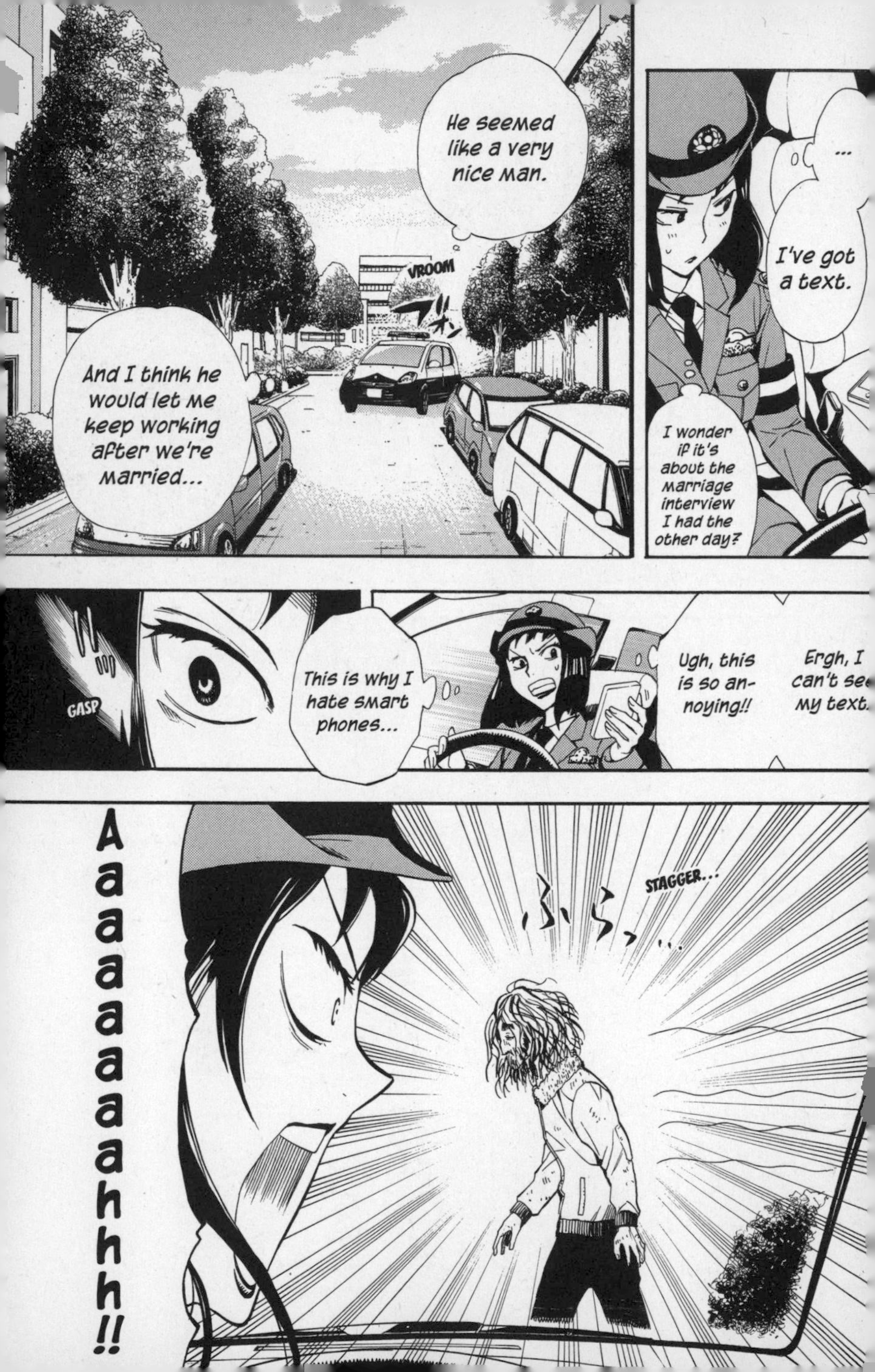
...
I've got a text.
I wonder if it's about the marriage interview I had the other day?
He seemed like a very nice man.
VROOM
And I think he would let me keep working after we're married...
Ergh, I can't see my text.
Ugh, this is so annoying!!
This is why I hate smart phones...
GASP
STAGGER...
Aaaaaaaaaahhh!!

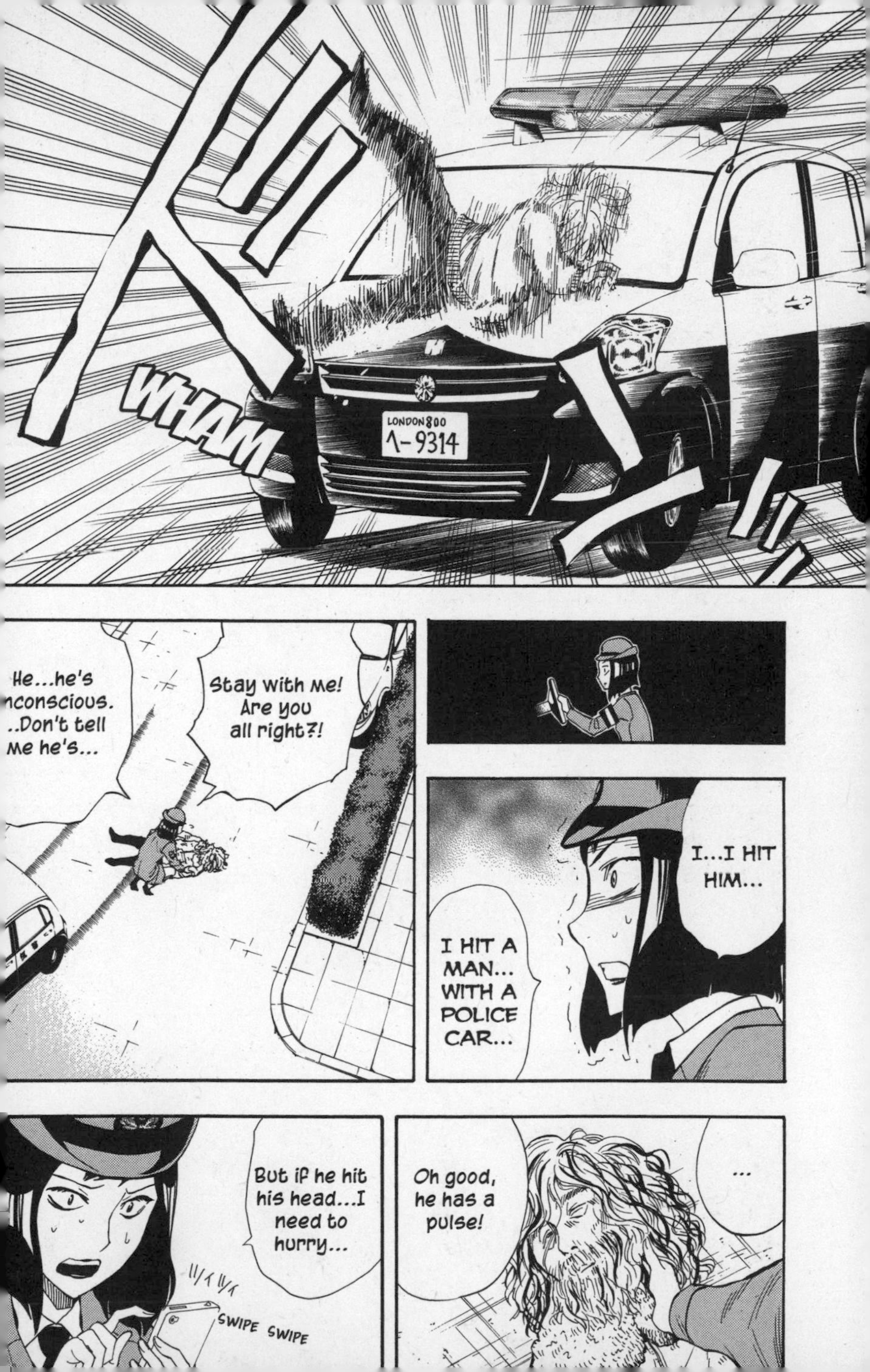

WHAM
LONDON800
ヘ-9314
I...I HIT HIM...
I HIT A MAN... WITH A POLICE CAR...
Stay with me! Are you all right?!
He...he's nconscious. ..Don't tell me he's...
...
Oh good, he has a pulse!
But if he hit his head...I need to hurry...
SWIPE SWIPE

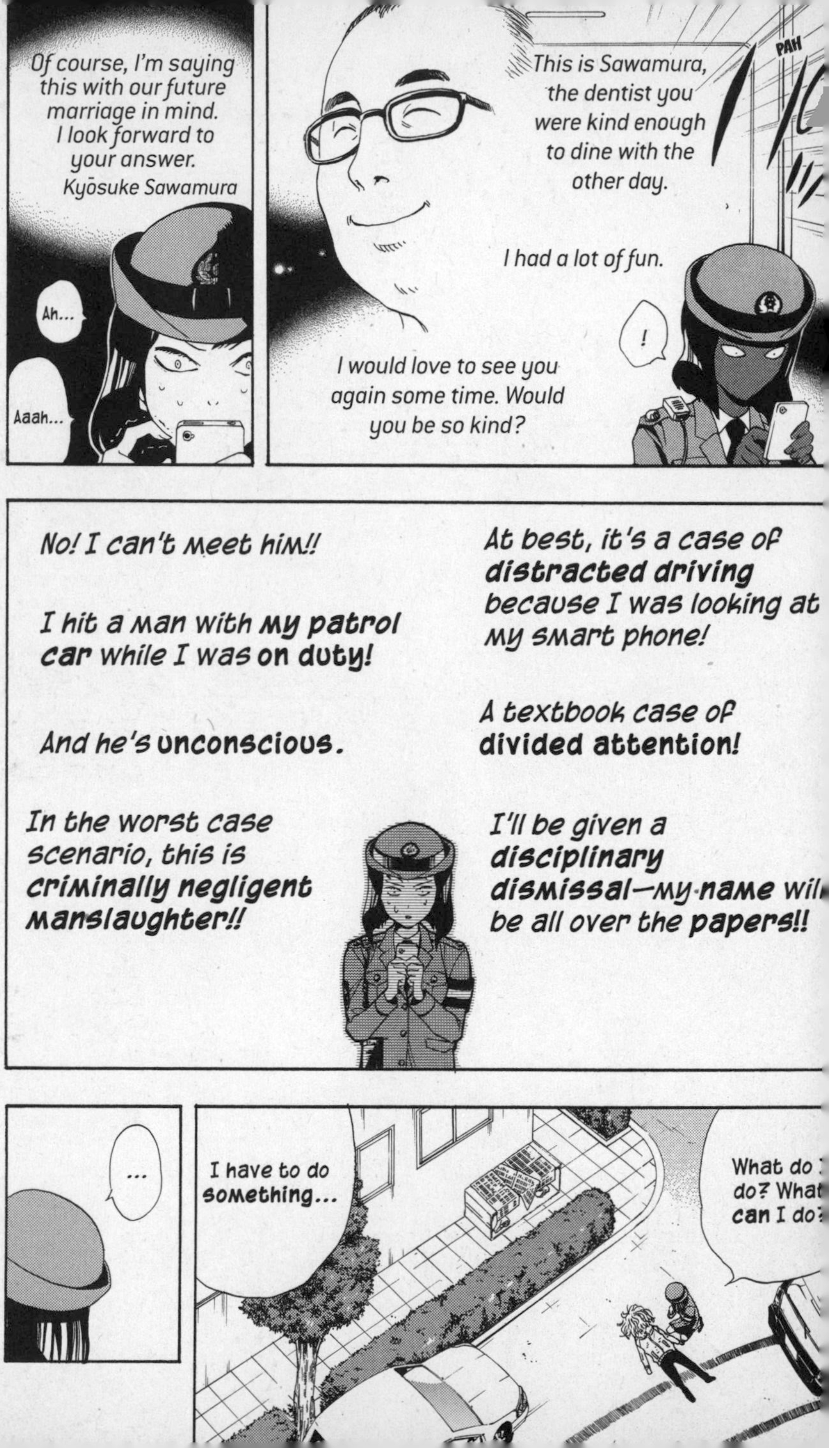
PAH
This is Sawamura, the dentist you were kind enough to dine with the other day.
I had a lot of fun.
!
I would love to see you again some time. Would you be so kind?
Of course, I'm saying this with our future marriage in mind. I look forward to your answer. Kyōsuke Sawamura
Ah...
Aaah...
No! I can't meet him!!
I hit a man with my patrol car while I was on duty!
And he's unconscious.
In the worst case scenario, this is criminally negligent manslaughter!!
At best, it's a case of distracted driving because I was looking at my smart phone!
A textbook case of divided attention!
I'll be given a disciplinary dismissal—my name wil
be all over the papers!!
What do
do? Wha
can I do
I have to do something...
...

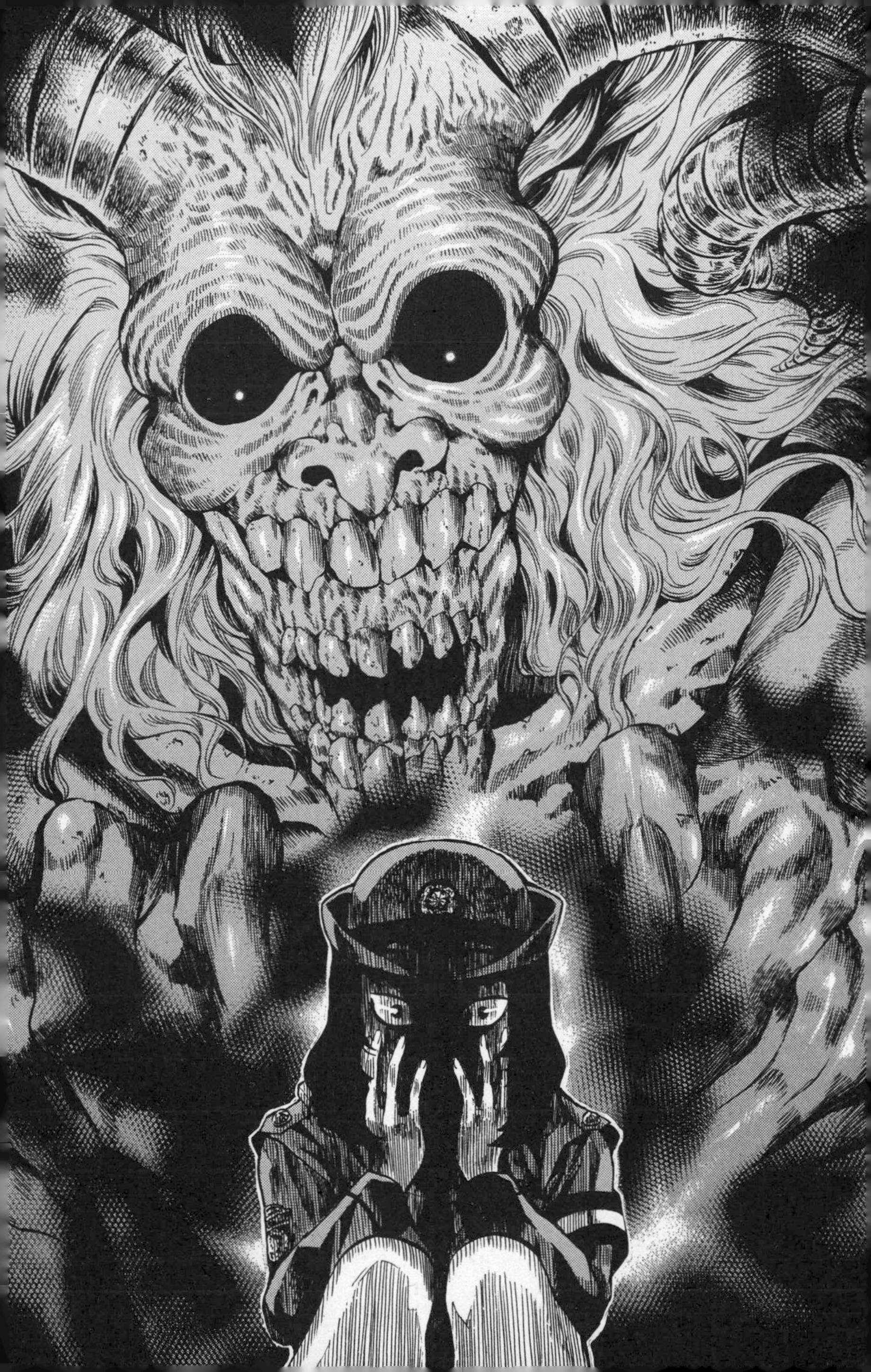

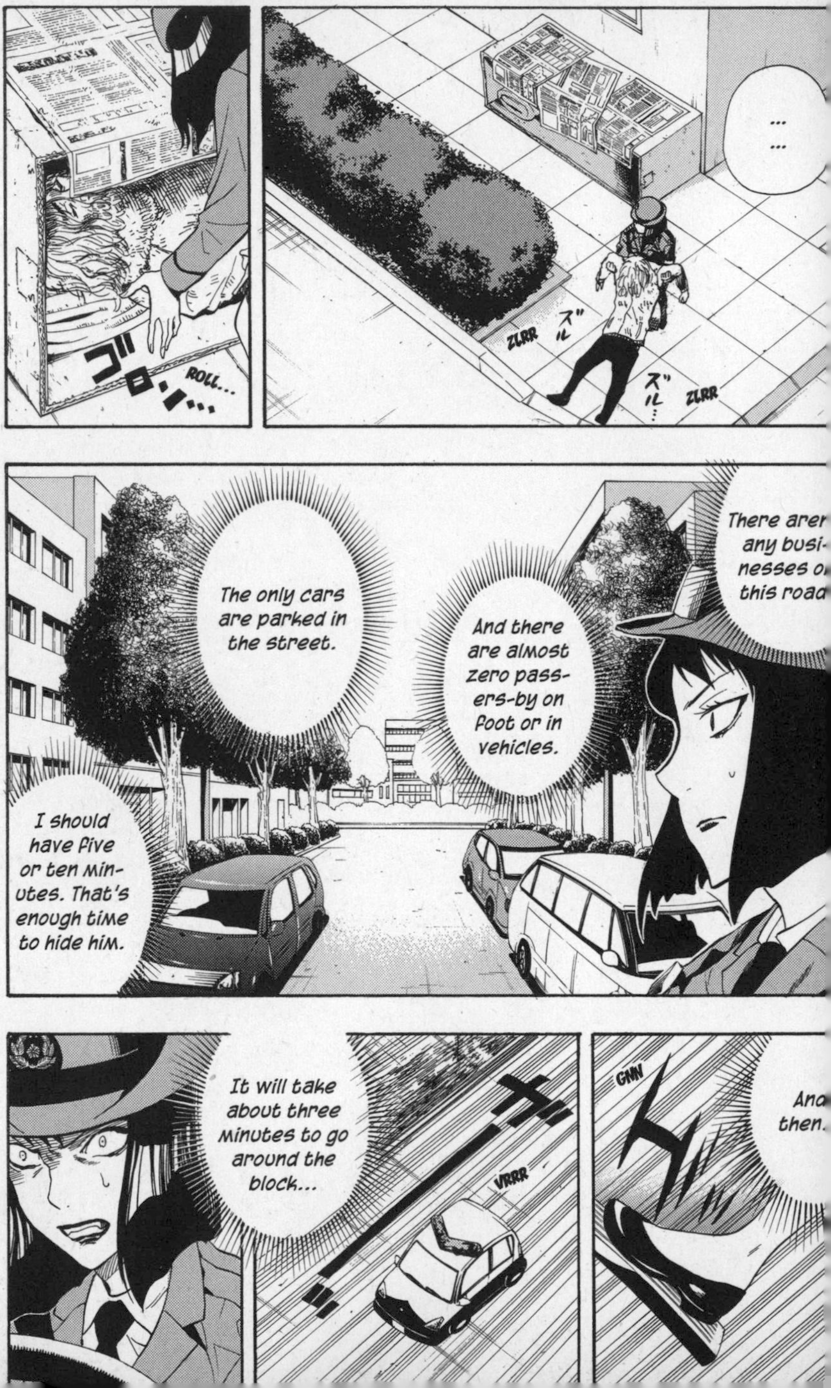

... ...
ズル ZLRR
ズル... ZLRR
ゴロン... ROLL...
There are any busi- nesses o this roa
And there are almost zero passers-by on foot or in vehicles.
The only cars are parked in the street.
I should have five or ten minutes. That's enough time to hide him.
And then.
GNN
It will take about three minutes to go around the block...
VRRR

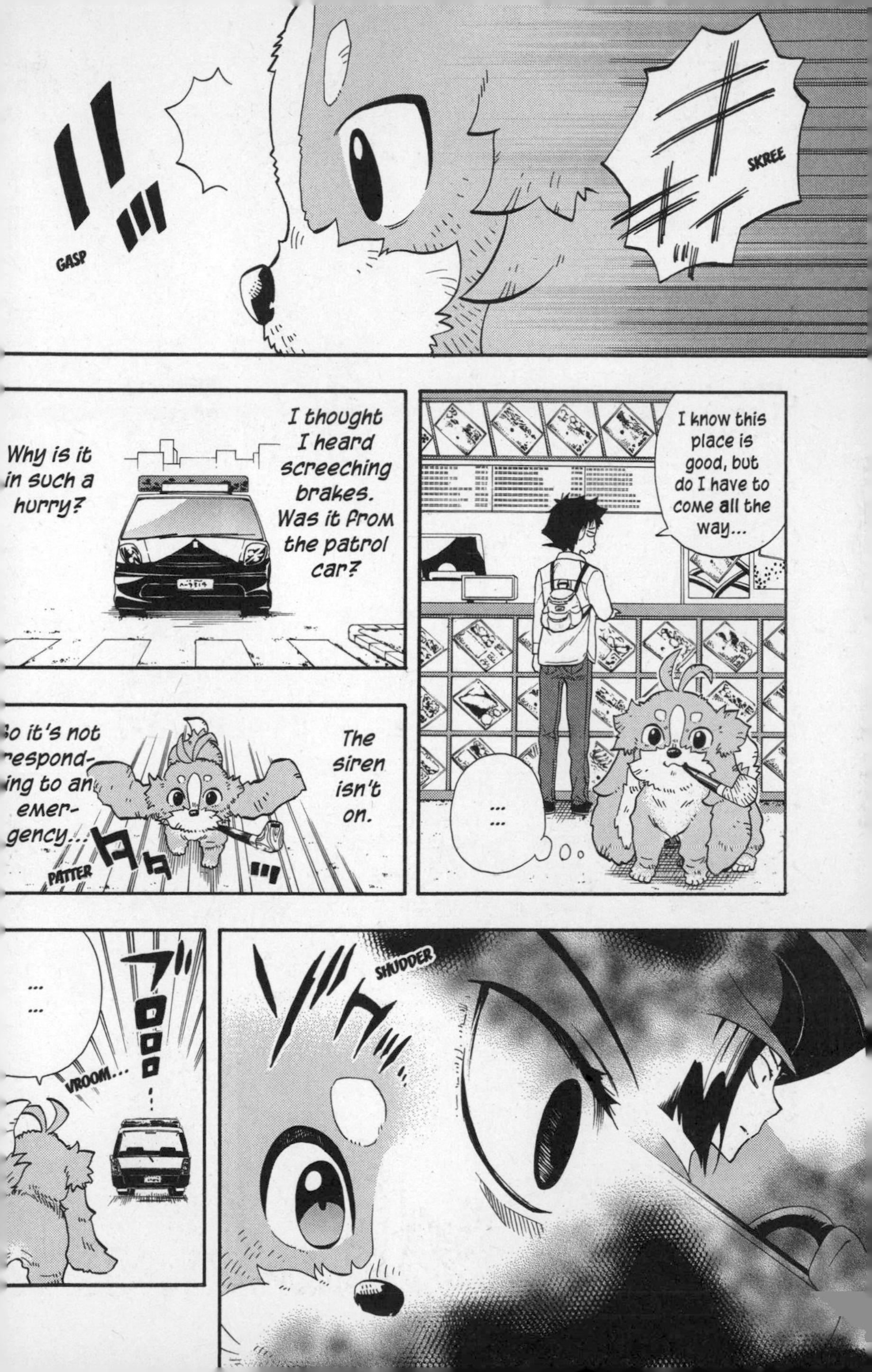
SKREE
GASP
I know this place is good, but do I have to come all the way...
... ...
I thought I heard screeching brakes. Was it from the patrol car?
Why is it in such a hurry?
The siren isn't on.
So it's not responding to an emergency...
PATTER
SHUDDER
... ...
VROOM...

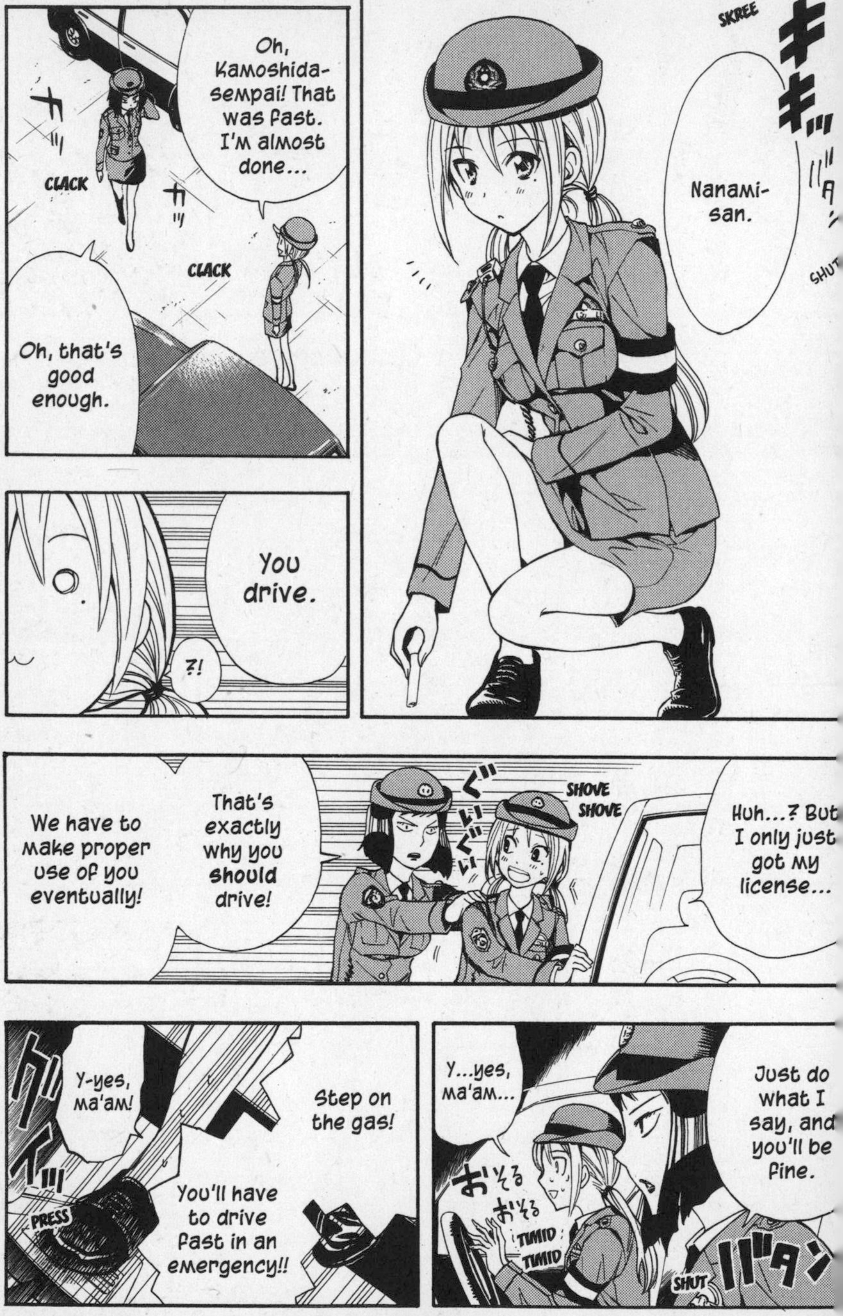
SKREE
キキッ
Nanami-san.
SHUT
Oh, Kamoshida-sempai! That was fast. I'm almost done...
CLACK
CLACK
Oh, that's good enough.
You drive.
?!
Huh...? But I only just got my license...
SHOVE SHOVE
That's exactly why you should drive!
We have to make proper use of you eventually!
Just do what I say, and you'll be fine.
Y...yes, ma'am...
おそるおそる
TIMID TIMID
SHUT
バタン
Step on the gas!
Y-yes, ma'am!
You'll have to drive fast in an emergency!!
PRESS

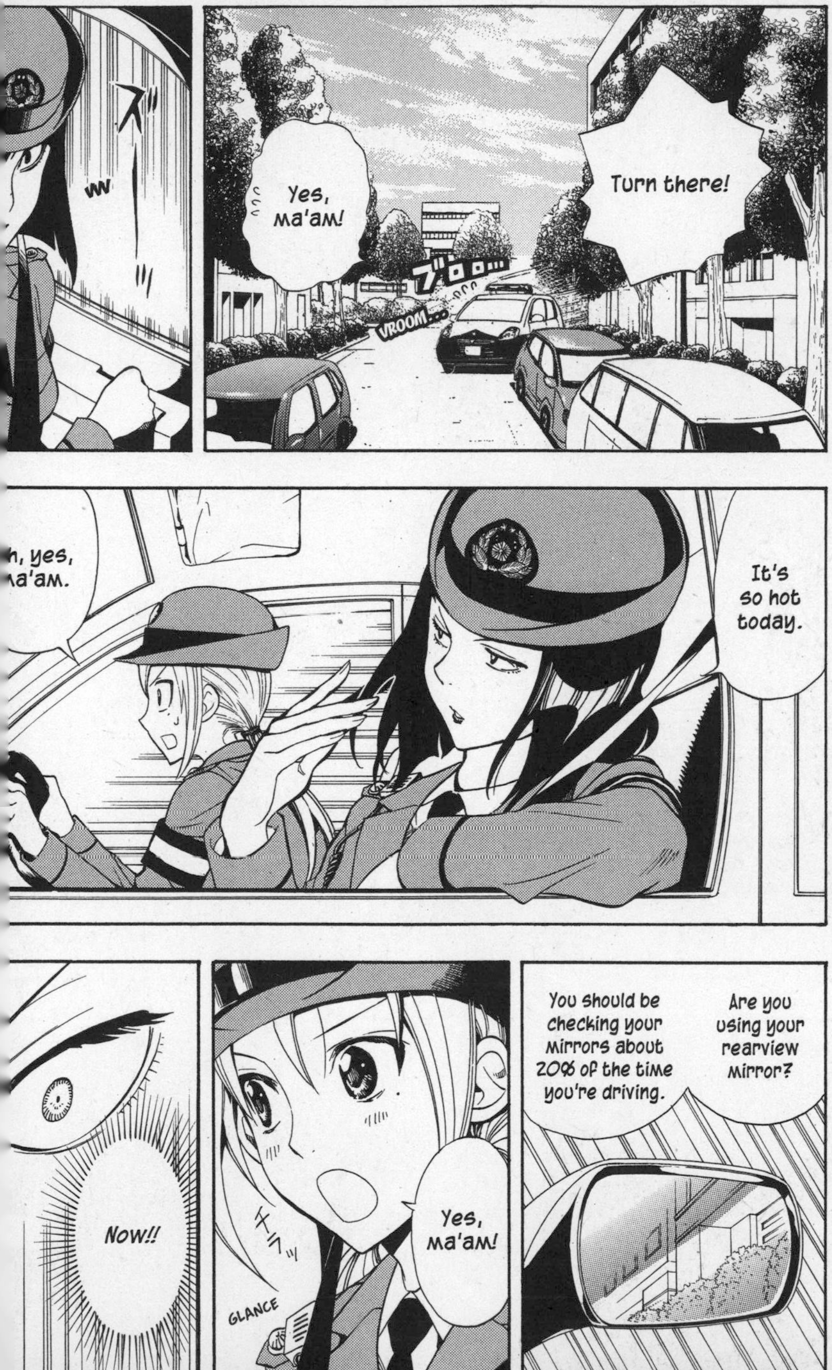
Turn there!
Yes, ma'am!
VROOM...
It's so hot today.
h, yes, a'am.
Are you using your rearview mirror?
You should be checking your mirrors about 20% of the time you're driving.
Yes, ma'am!
GLANCE
Now!!

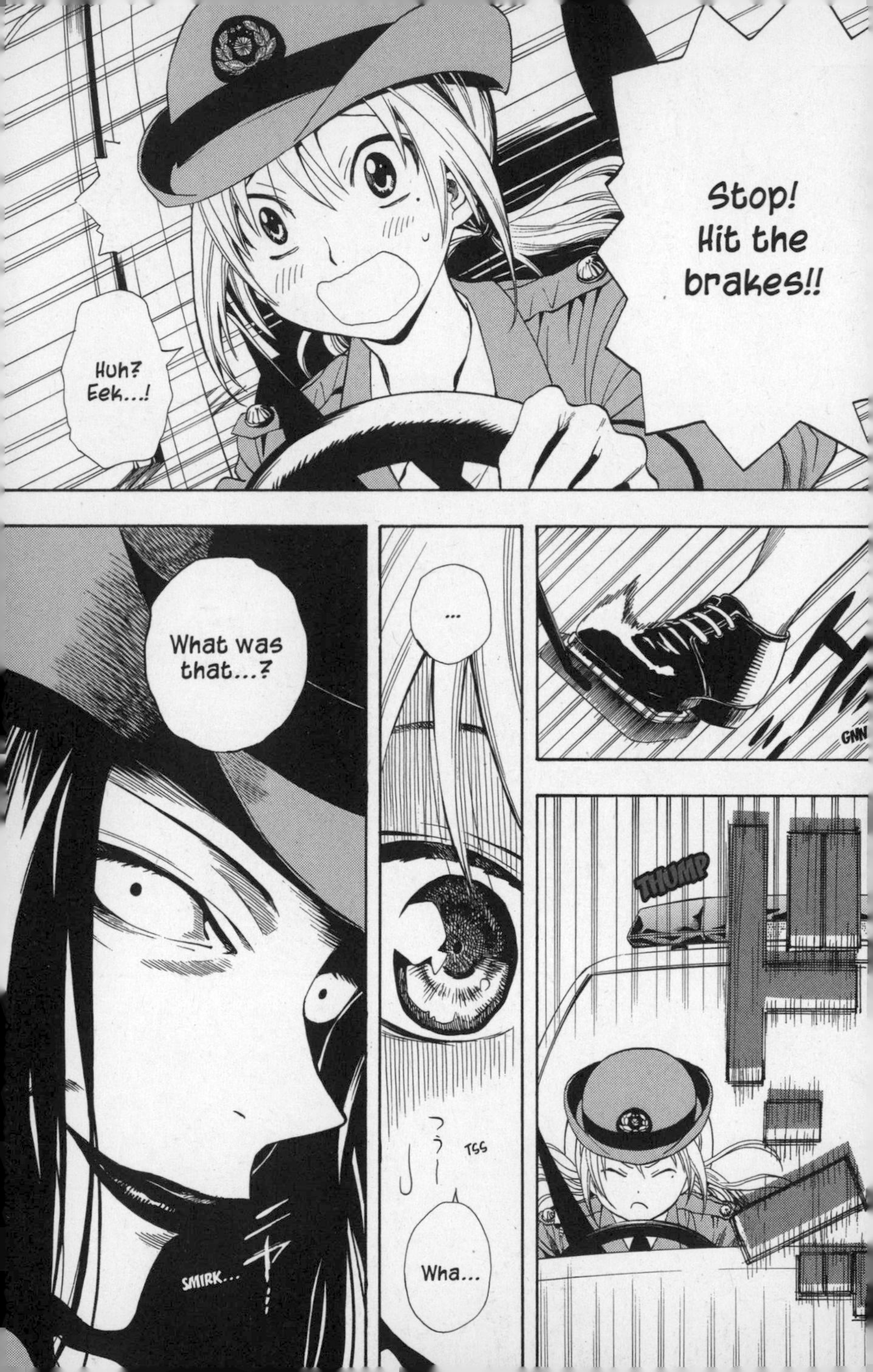
Stop! Hit the brakes!!
Huh? Eek...!
GNN
THUMP
...
TSS
Wha...
What was that...?
SMIRK...

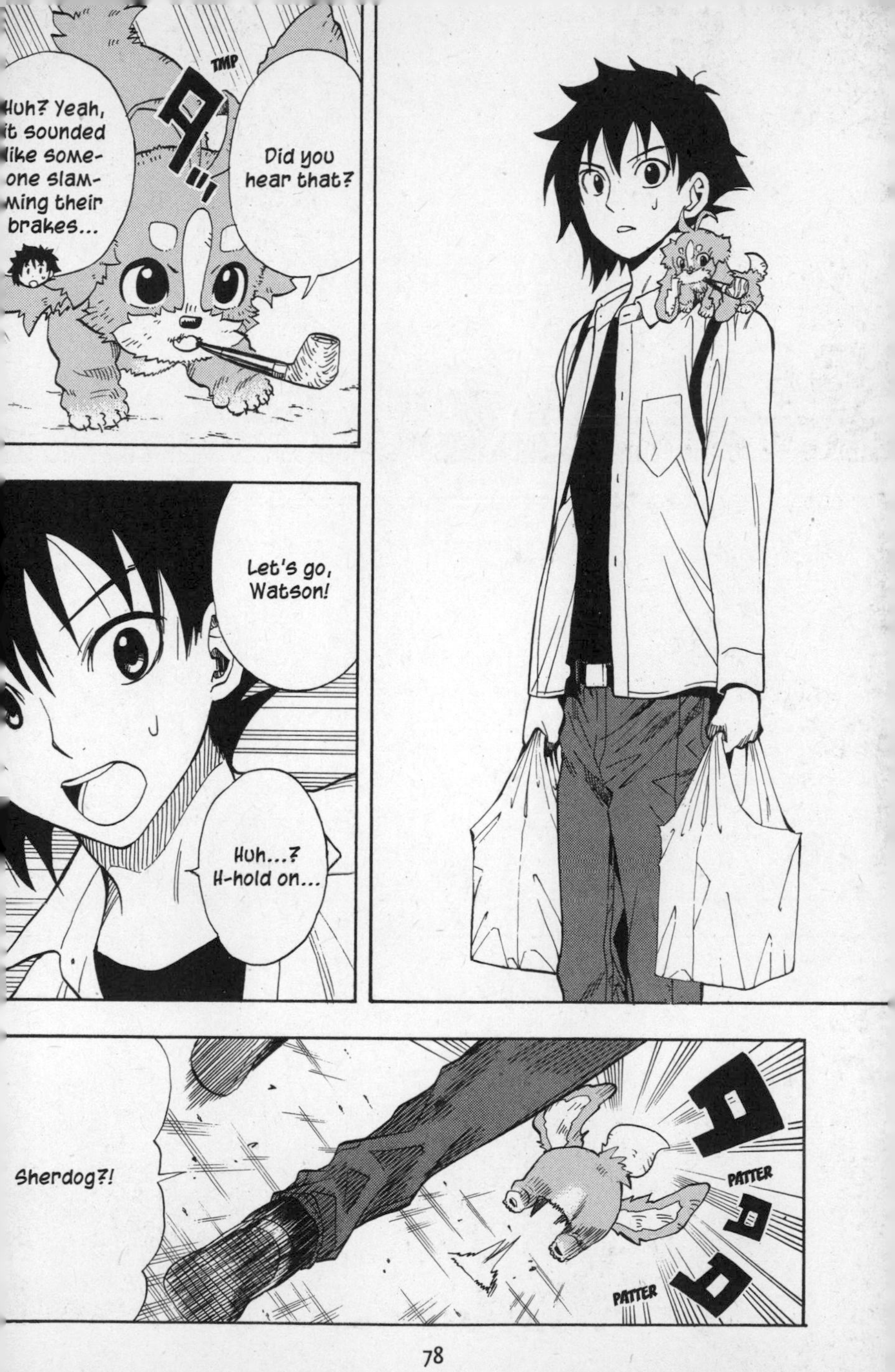
TMP
Did you hear that?
Huh? Yeah, it sounded like someone slamming their brakes...
Let's go, Watson!
Huh...? H-hold on...
PATTER
PATTER
Sherdog?!

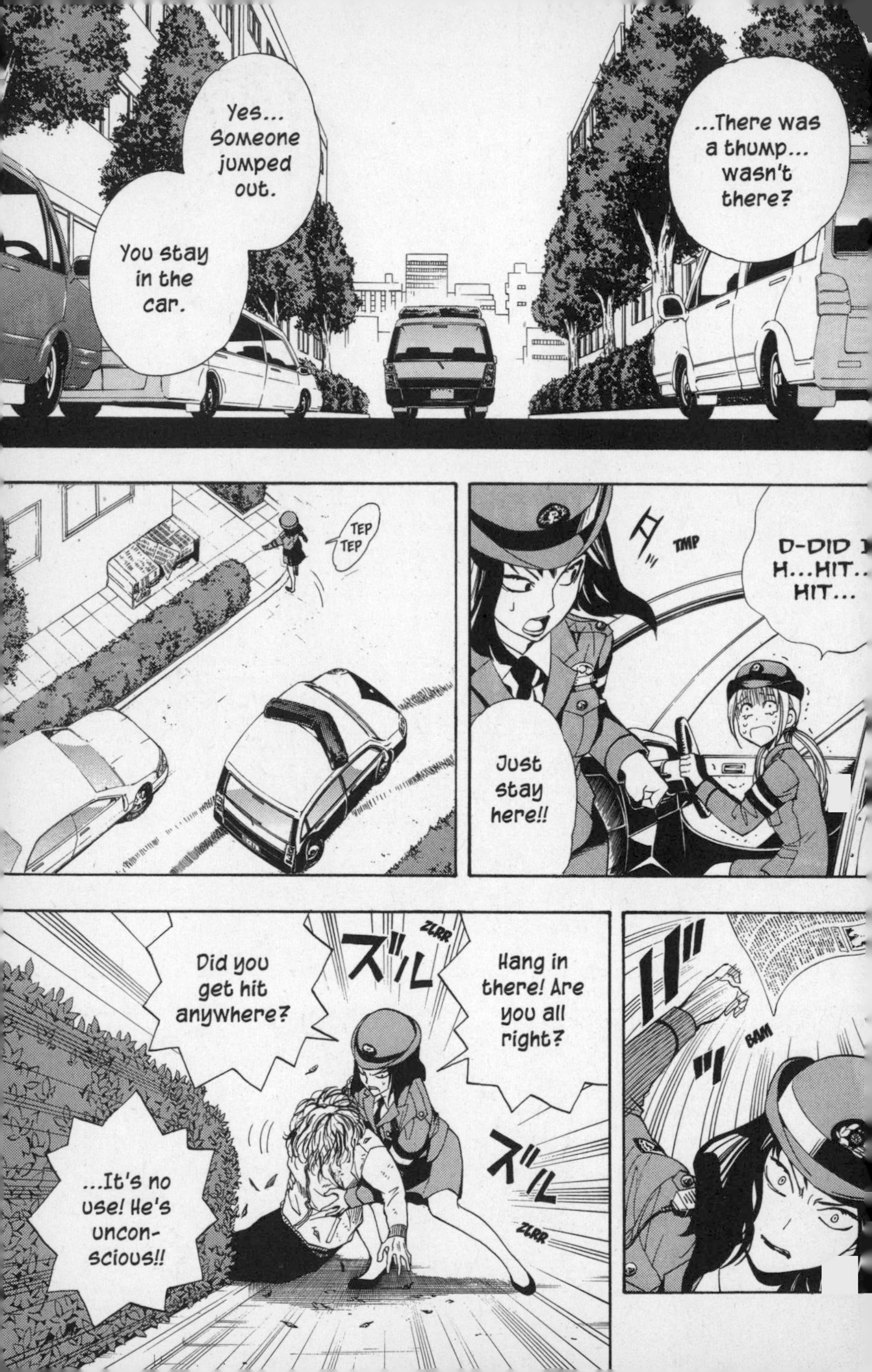
...There was a thump... wasn't there?
Yes... Someone jumped out.
You stay in the car.
TMP
D-DID I H...HIT... HIT...
Just stay here!!
TEP TEP
BAM
Hang in there! Are you all right?
ズル
ZLRR
Did you get hit anywhere?
ズル
ZLRR
...It's no use! He's uncon-scious!!

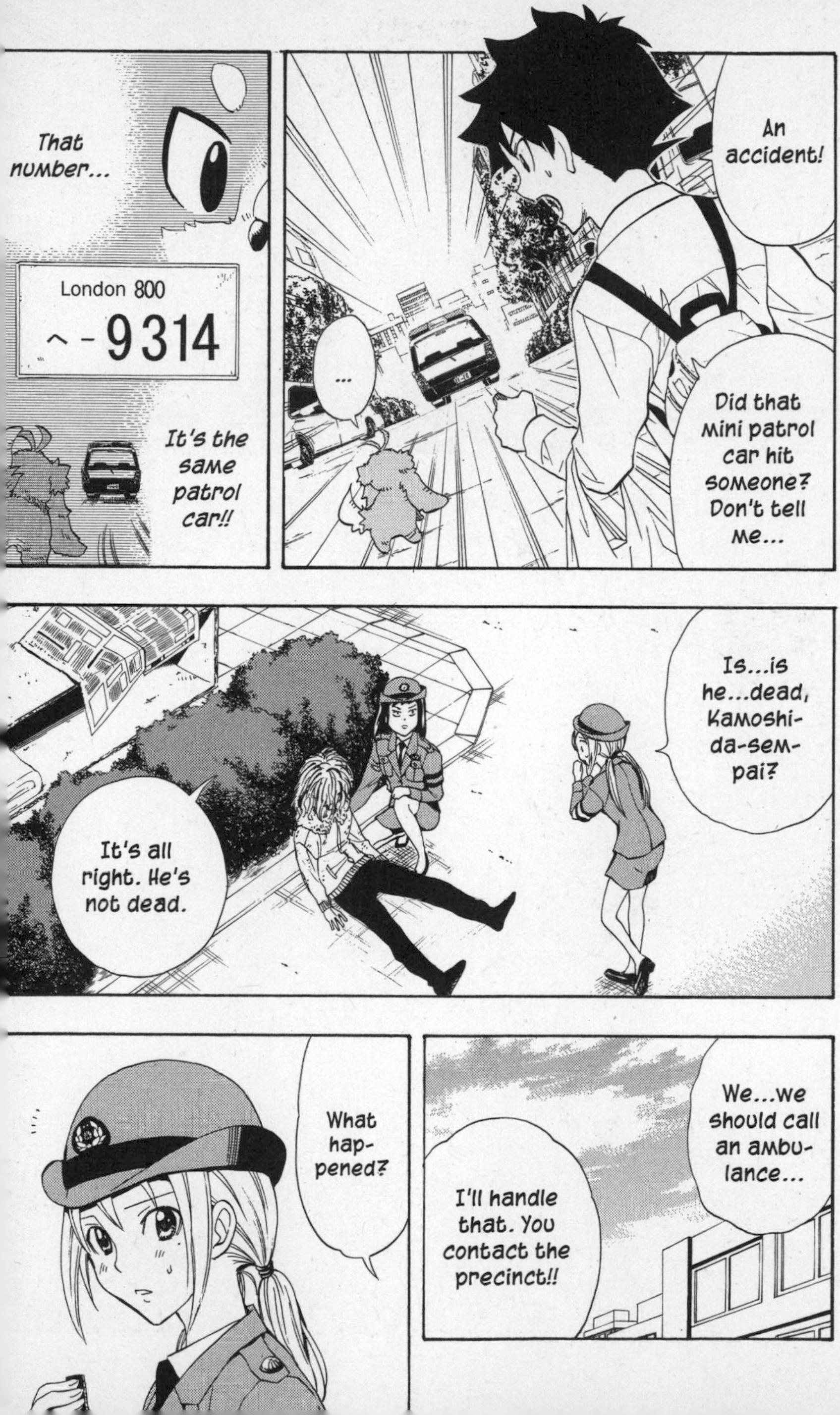

An accident!
Did that mini patrol car hit someone? Don't tell me...
...
That number...
London 800
へ-9314
It's the same patrol car!!
Is...is he...dead, Kamoshida-sempai?
It's all right. He's not dead.
We...we should call an ambulance...
I'll handle that. You contact the precinct!!
What happened?

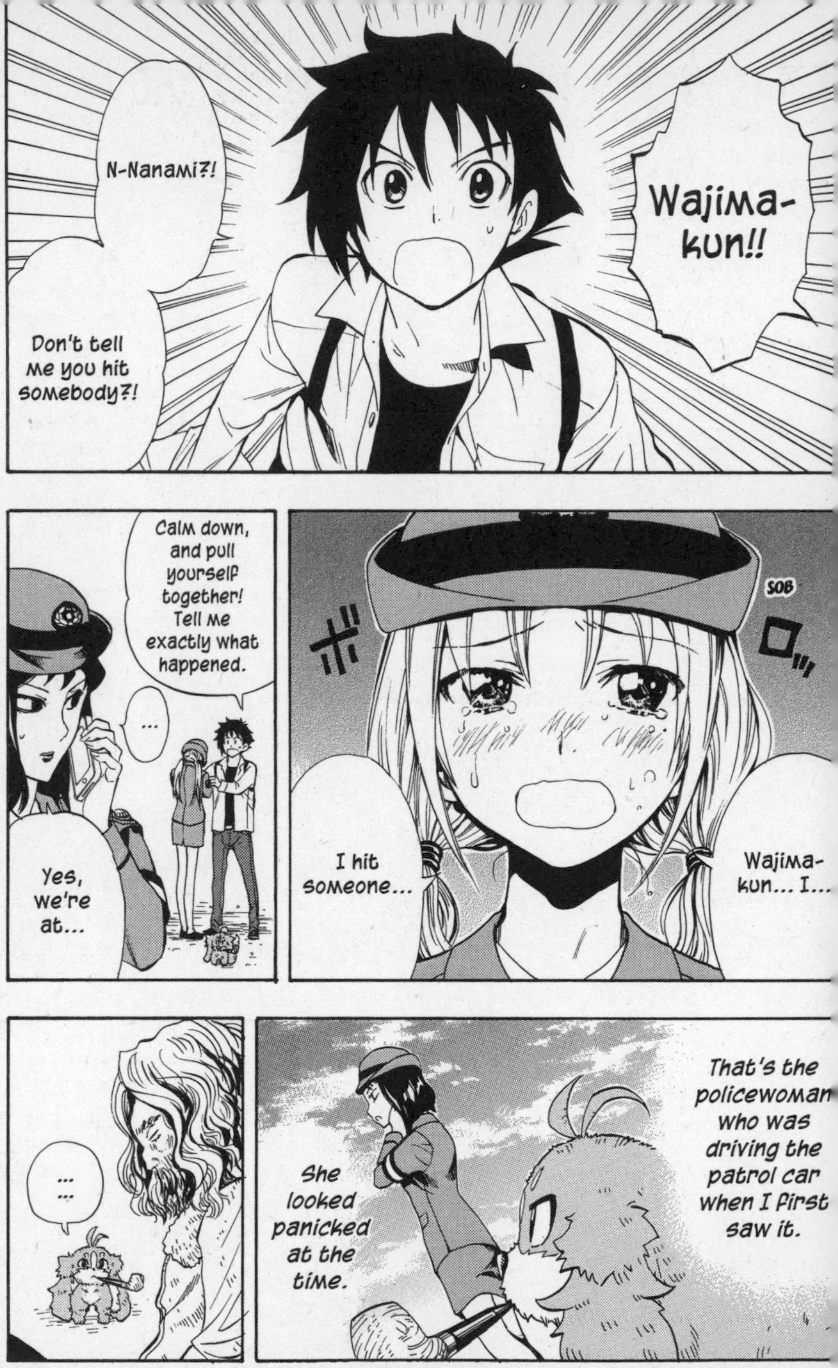
Wajima-kun!!
N-Nanami?!
Don't tell me you hit somebody?!
SOB
Wajima-kun... I...
I hit someone...
Calm down, and pull yourself together! Tell me exactly what happened.
...
Yes, we're at...
That's the policewoman who was driving the patrol car when I first saw it.
She looked panicked at the time.
... ...

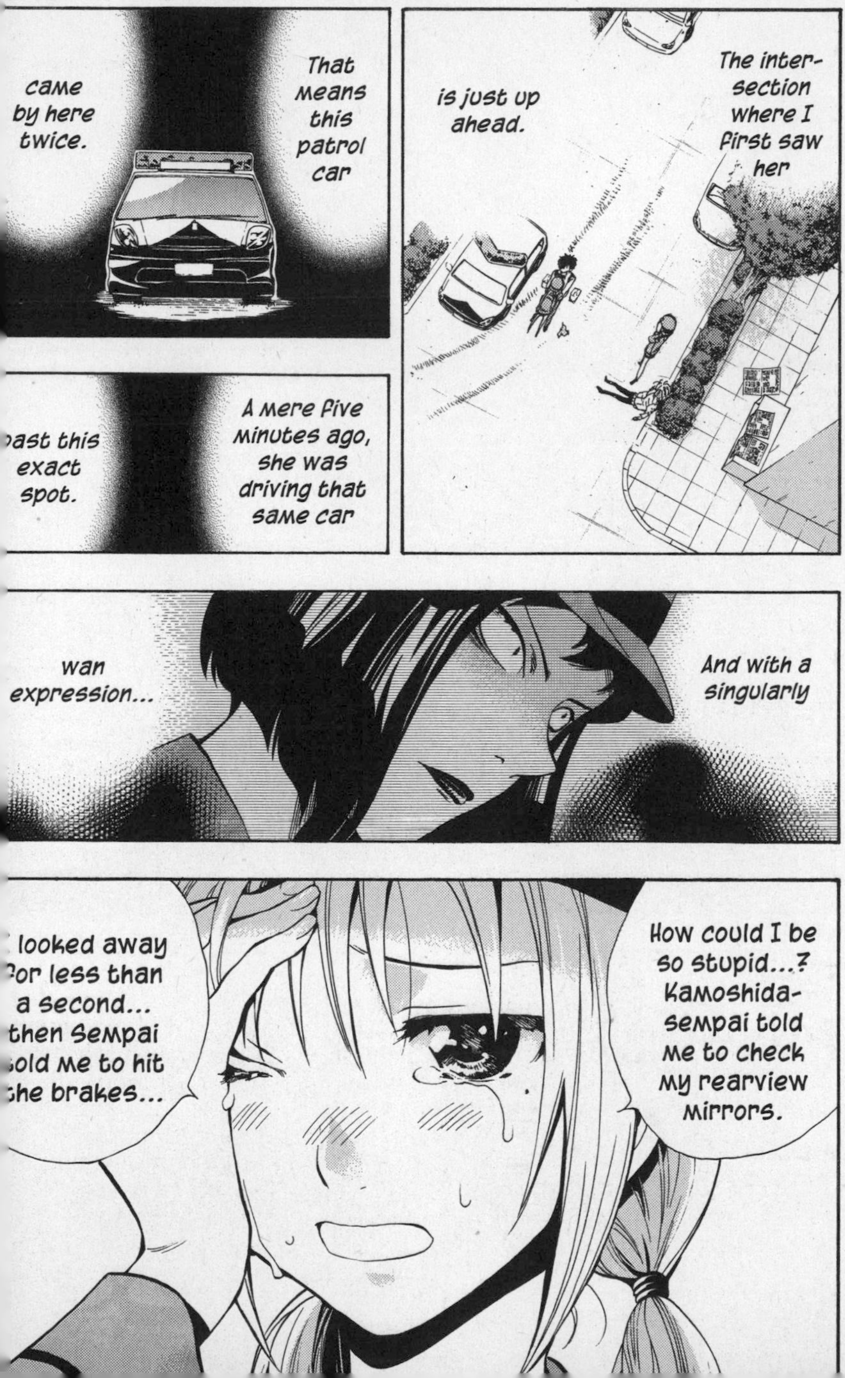
The inter-section where I first saw her
is just up ahead.
That means this patrol car
came by here twice.
A mere five minutes ago, she was driving that same car
past this exact spot.
And with a singularly
wan expression...
How could I be so stupid...? Kamoshida-sempai told me to check my rearview mirrors.
I looked away for less than a second... then Sempai told me to hit the brakes...

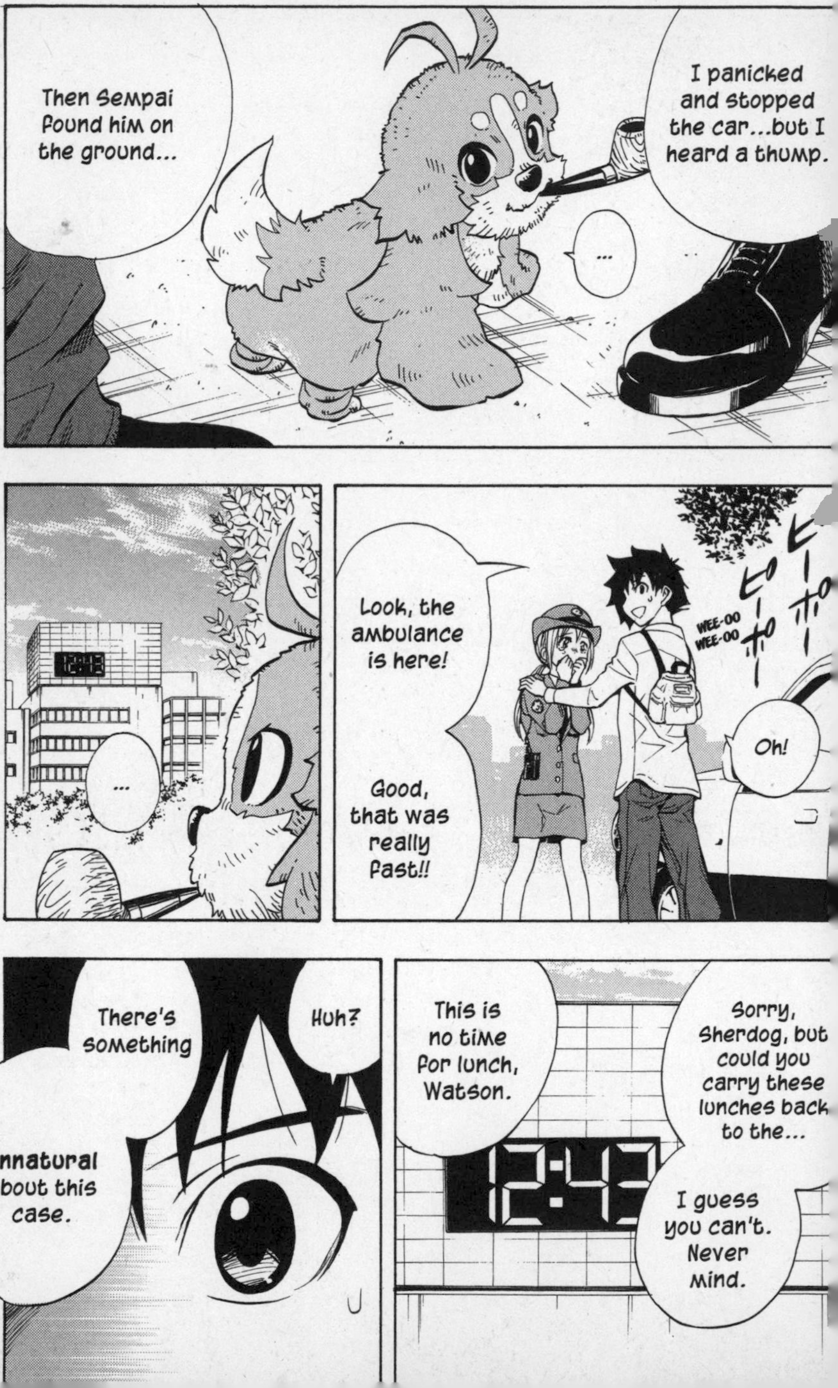
I panicked and stopped the car...but I heard a thump.
...
Then Sempai found him on the ground...
WEE-OO WEE-OO
Look, the ambulance is here!
Oh!
Good, that was really fast!!
...
Sorry, Sherdog, but could you carry these lunches back to the...
This is no time for lunch, Watson.
I guess you can't. Never mind.
Huh?
There's something
unnatural about this case.

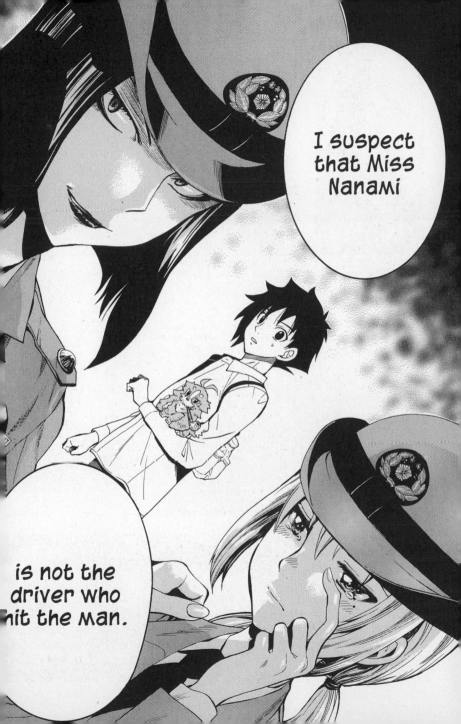

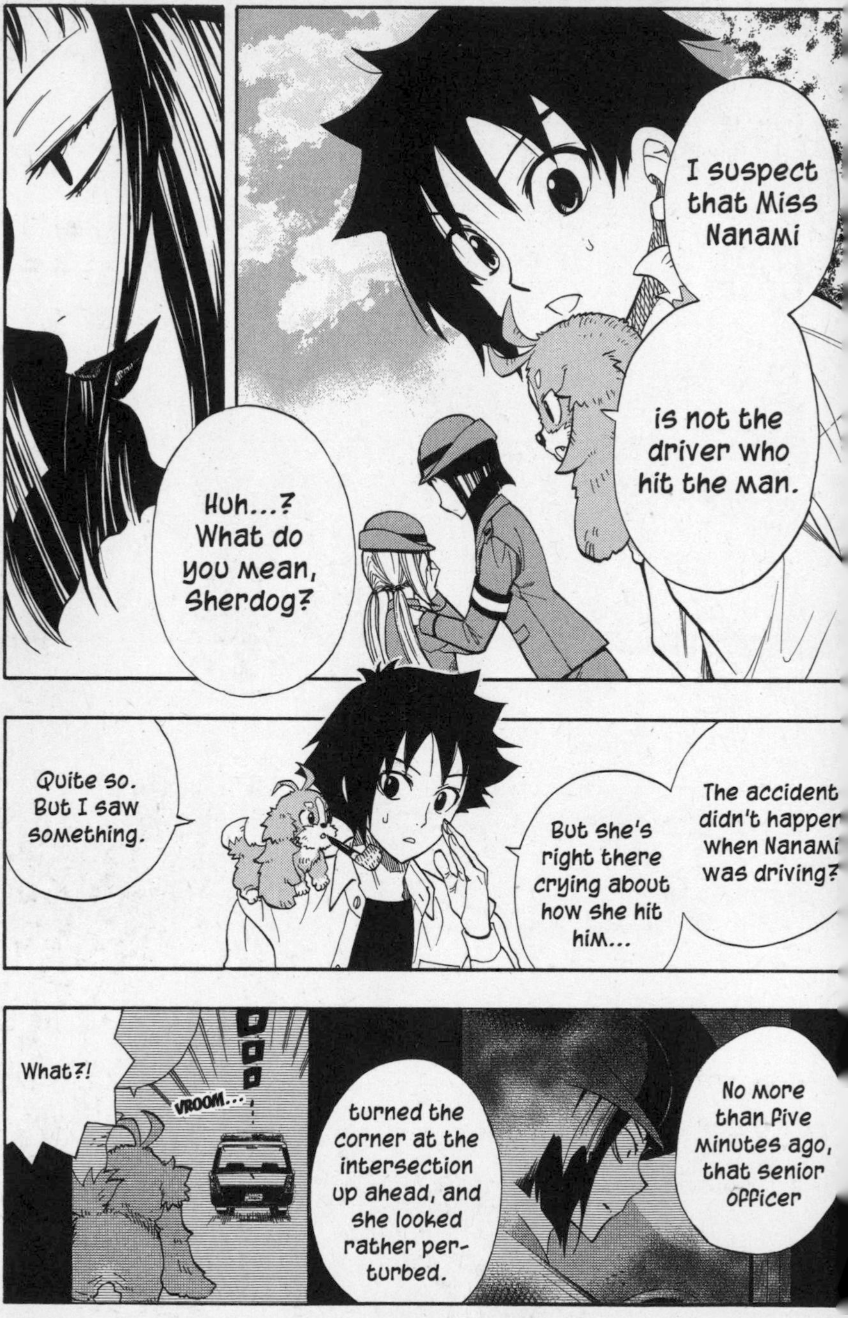
I suspect that Miss Nanami
is not the driver who hit the man.
Huh...? What do you mean, Sherdog?
The accident didn't happen when Nanami was driving?
But she's right there crying about how she hit him...
Quite so. But I saw something.
No more than five minutes ago, that senior officer
turned the corner at the intersection up ahead, and she looked rather per-turbed.
VROOM...
What?!

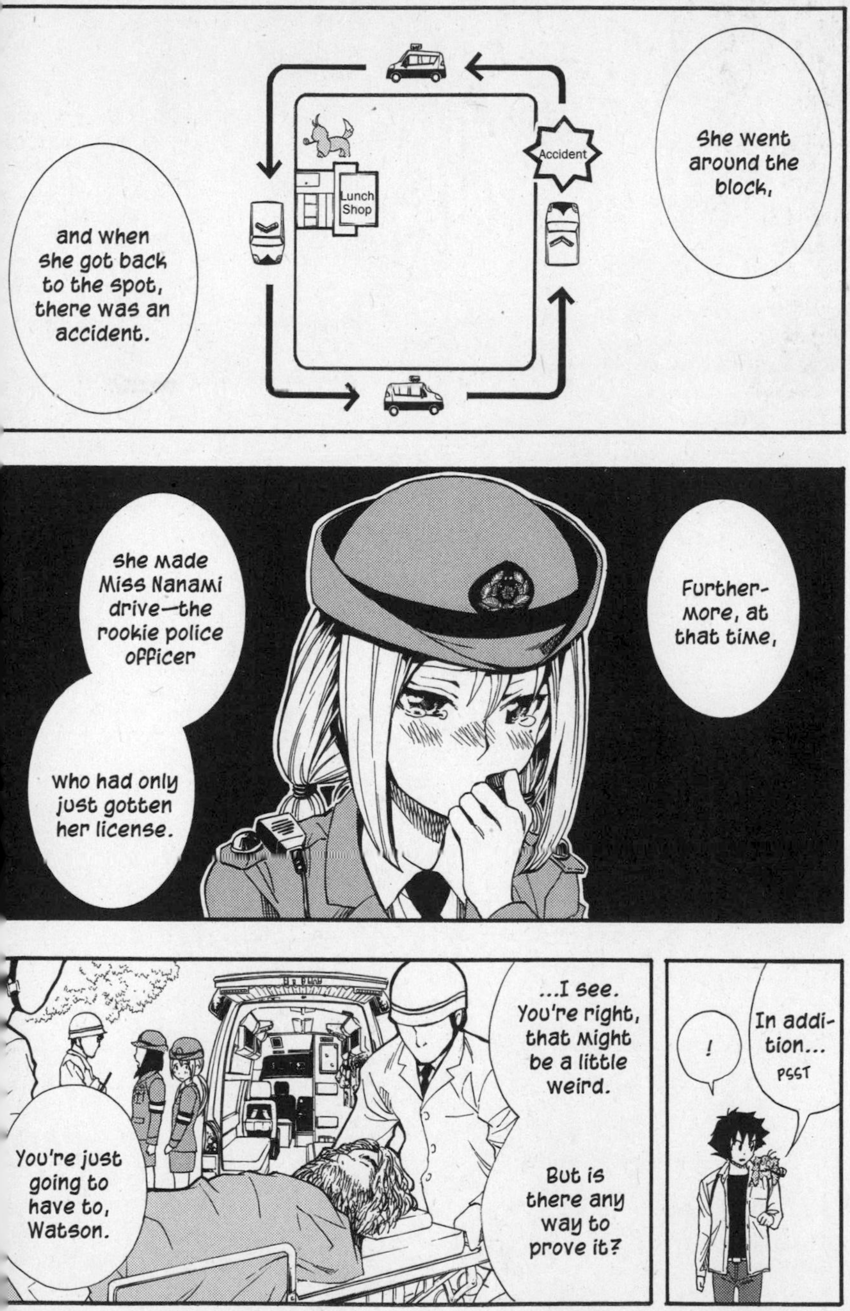
She went around the block,
Accident
Lunch Shop
and when she got back to the spot, there was an accident.
Further-more, at that time,
She made Miss Nanami drive—the rookie police officer
who had only just gotten her license.
In addi-tion...
PSST
!
...I see. You're right, that might be a little weird.
But is there any way to prove it?
You're just going to have to, Watson.

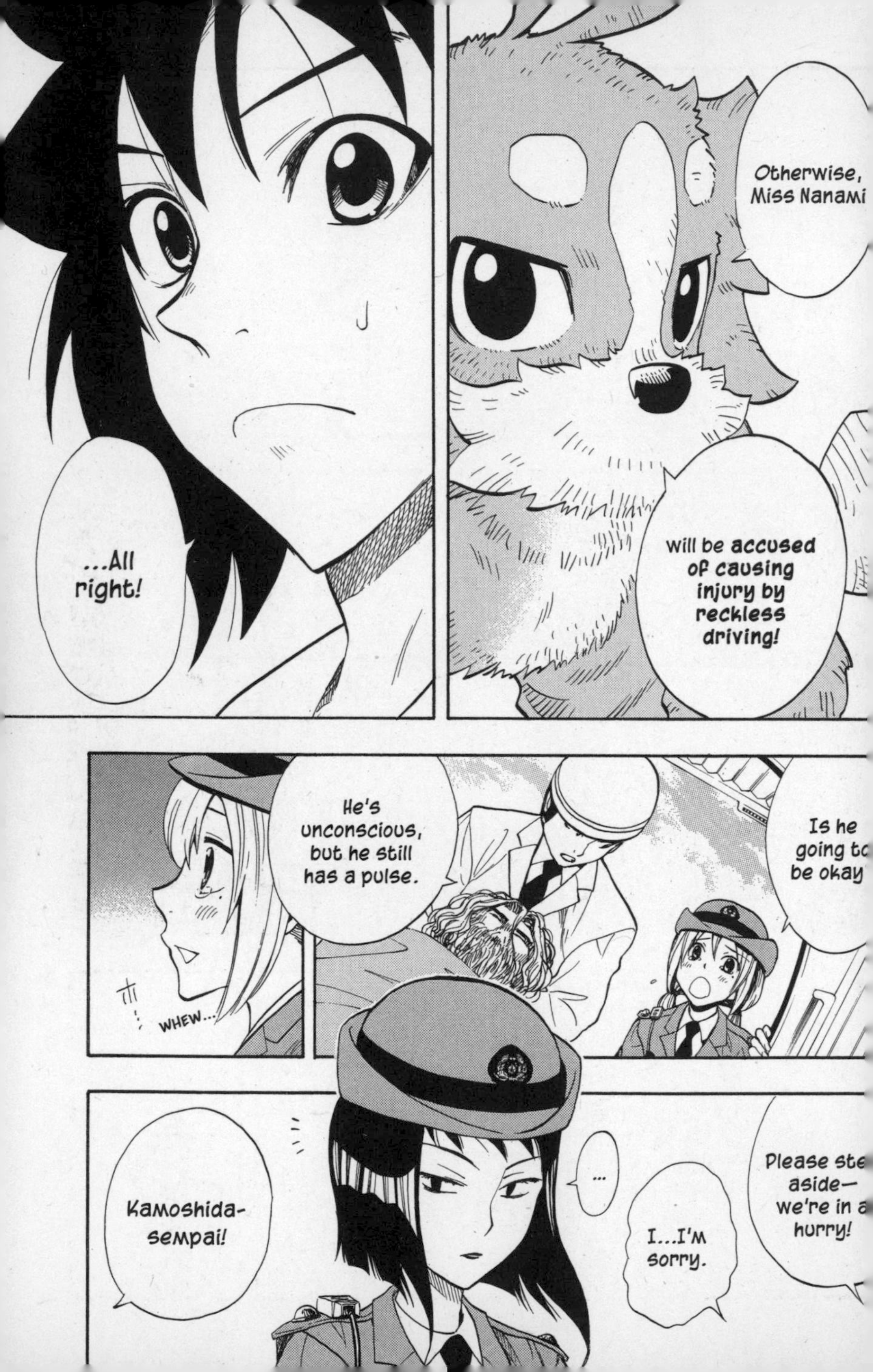
Otherwise, Miss Nanami
will be accused of causing injury by reckless driving!
...All right!
Is he going to be okay
He's unconscious, but he still has a pulse.
WHEW...
Please ste aside— we're in a hurry!
...
I...I'M sorry.
Kamoshida-sempai!

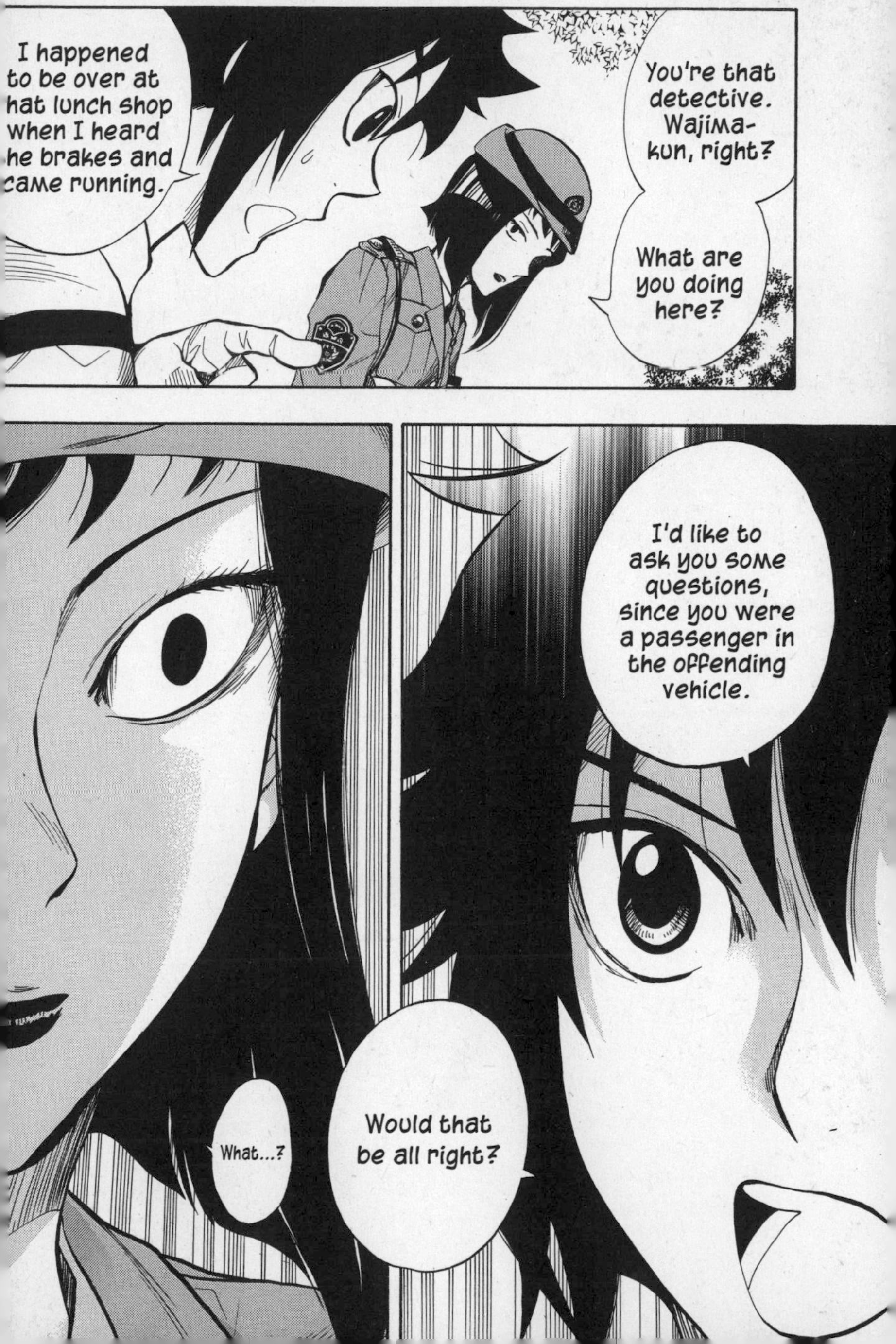
You're that detective. Wajima-kun, right?
What are you doing here?
I happened to be over at hat lunch shop when I heard he brakes and came running.
I'd like to ask you some questions, since you were a passenger in the offending vehicle.
Would that be all right?
What...?

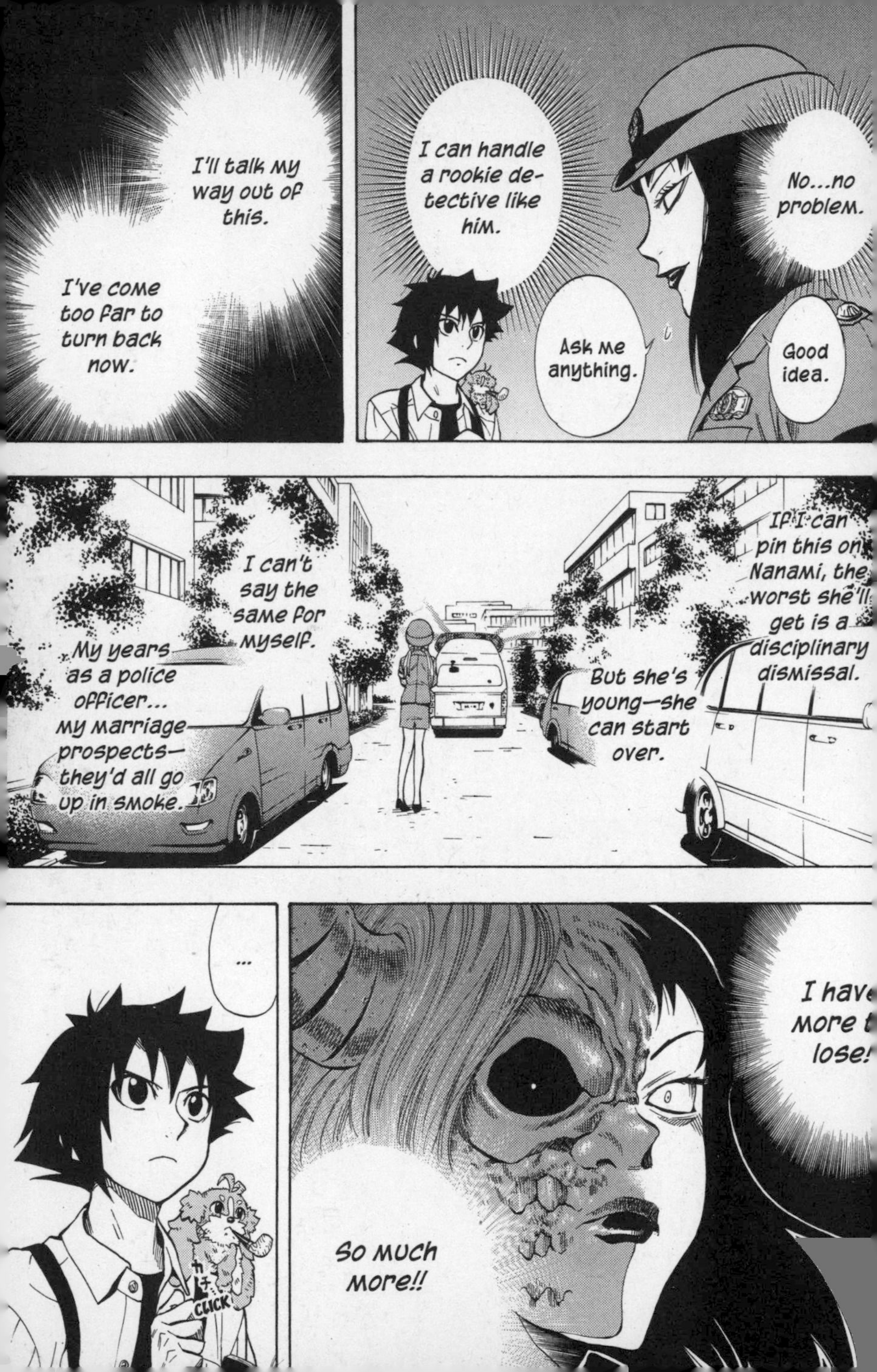
No...no problem.
I can handle a rookie detective like him.
Good idea.
Ask me anything.
I'll talk my way out of this.
I've come too far to turn back now.
If I can pin this on Nanami, the worst she'll get is a disciplinary dismissal.
But she's young—she can start over.
I can't say the same for myself.
My years as a police officer... my marriage prospects—they'd all go up in smoke.
I have more t lose!
So much more!!
...
カチ
CLICK

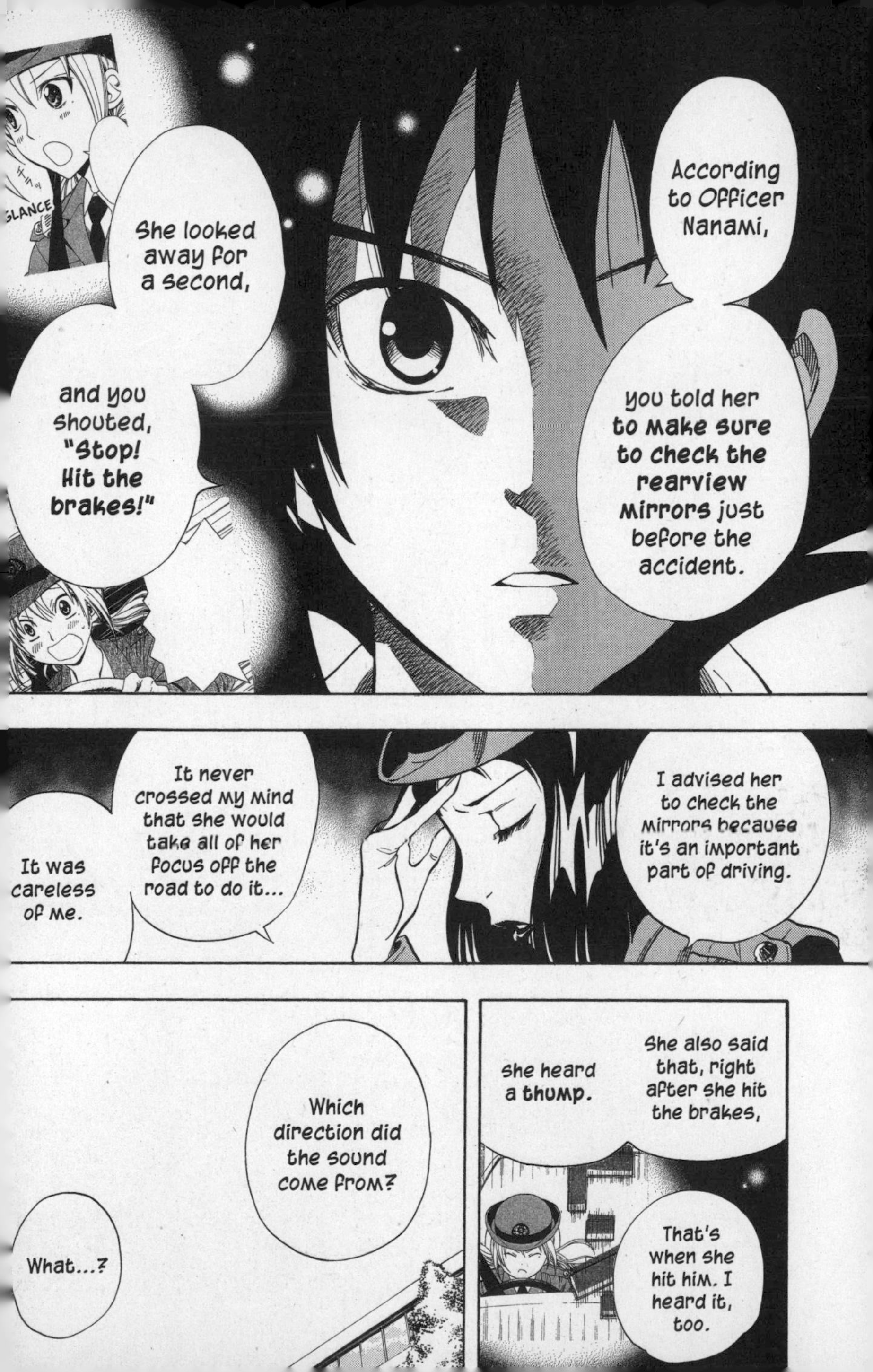
According to Officer Nanami,
you told her to make sure to check the rearview mirrors just before the accident.
She looked away for a second,
GLANCE
and you shouted, "Stop! Hit the brakes!"
I advised her to check the mirrors because it's an important part of driving.
It never crossed my mind that she would take all of her focus off the road to do it...
It was careless of me.
She also said that, right after she hit the brakes,
she heard a thump.
That's when she hit him. I heard it, too.
Which direction did the sound come from?
What...?

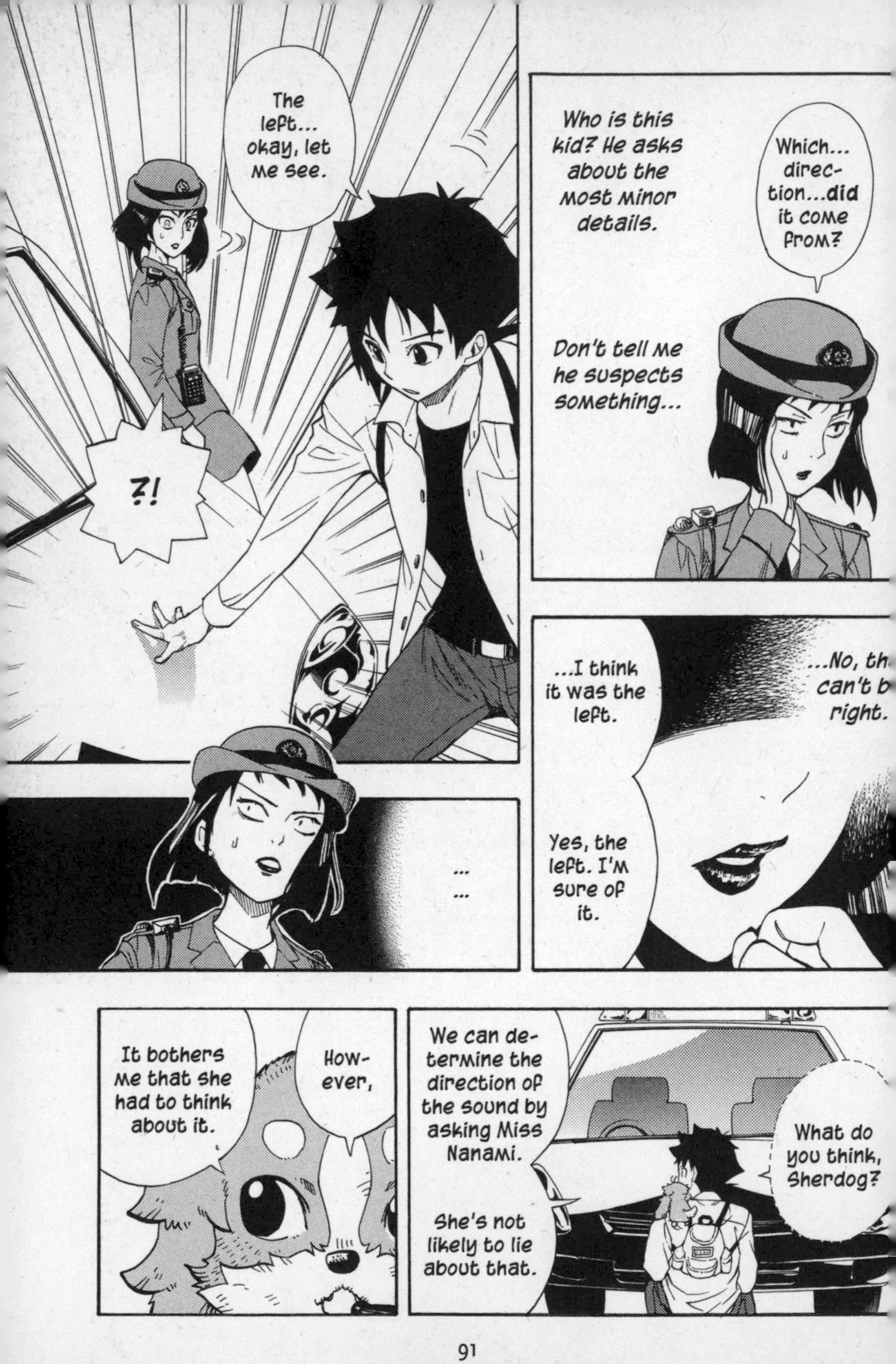
Which... direction...did it come from?
Who is this kid? He asks about the most minor details.
Don't tell me he suspects something...
The left... okay, let me see.
?!
...No, th can't b right.
...I think it was the left.
Yes, the left. I'm sure of it.
......
What do you think, Sherdog?
We can determine the direction of the sound by asking Miss Nanami.
She's not likely to lie about that.
How-ever,
It bothers me that she had to think about it.

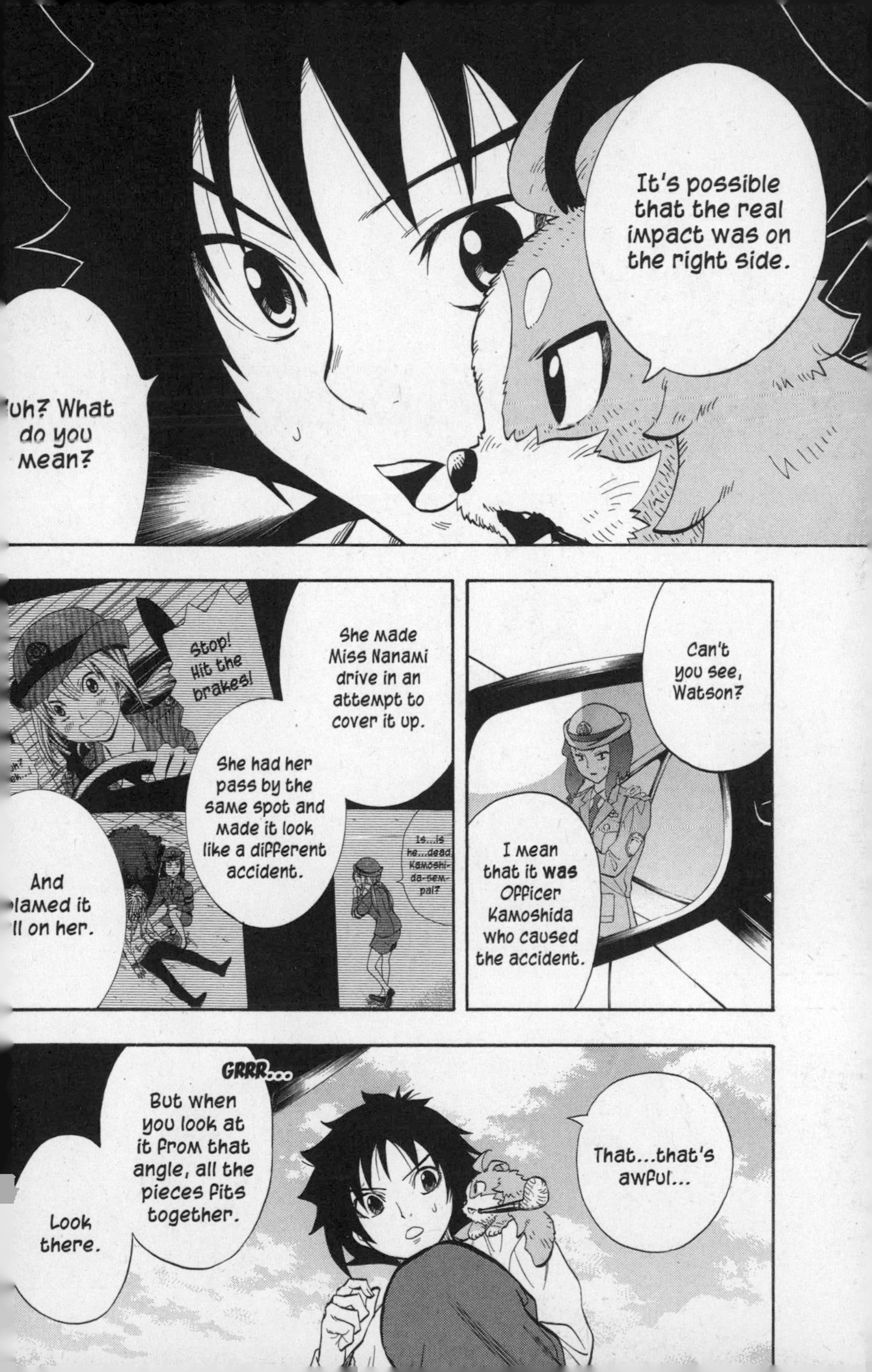
It's possible that the real impact was on the right side.
uh? What do you mean?
Can't you see, Watson?
I mean that it was Officer Kamoshida who caused the accident.
She made Miss Nanami drive in an attempt to cover it up.
Stop! Hit the brakes!
She had her pass by the same spot and made it look like a different accident.
Is...is he...dead, Kamoshida-sempai?
And lamed it ll on her.
That...that's awful...
GRRR...
But when you look at it from that angle, all the pieces fits together.
Look there.

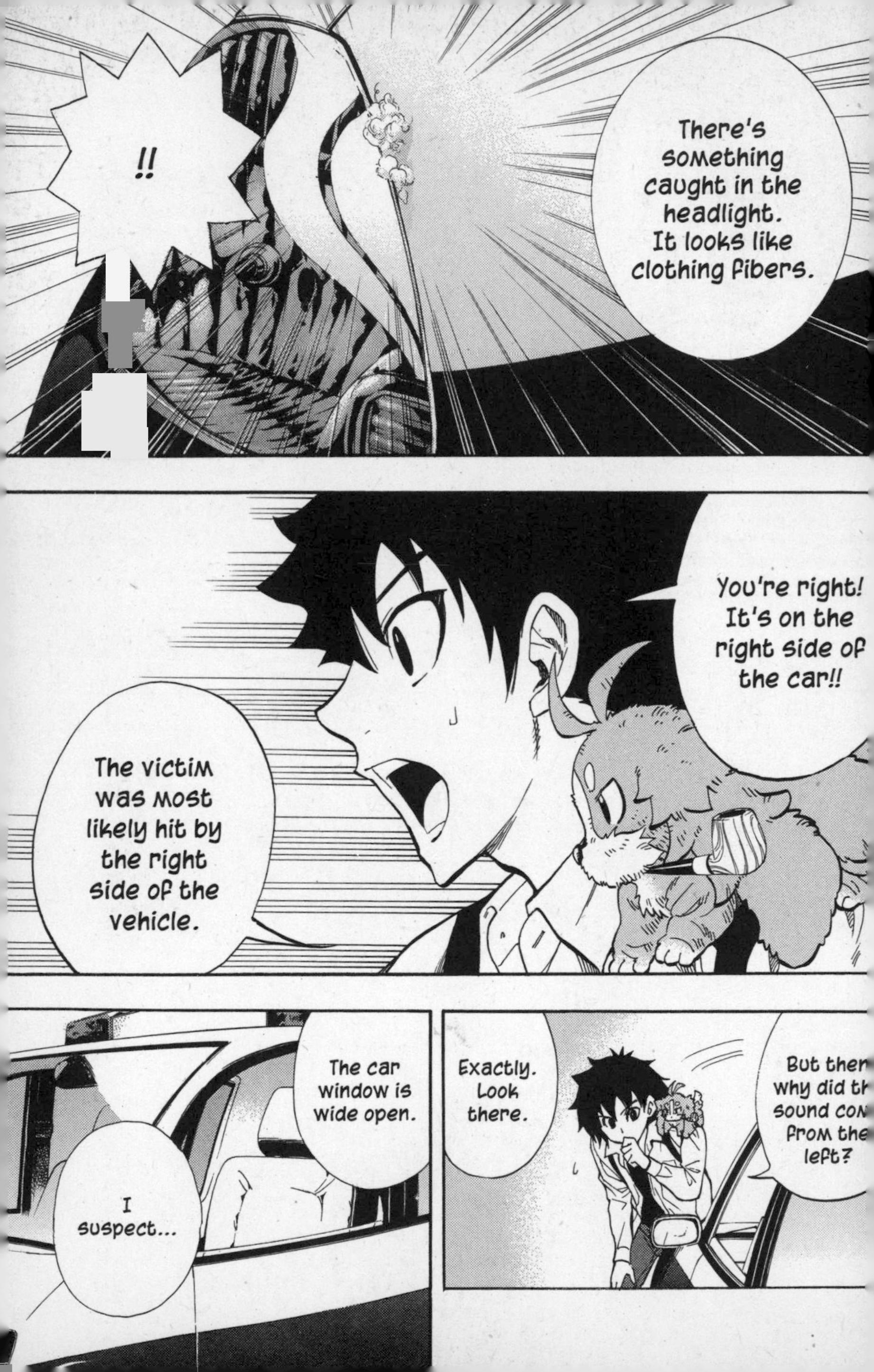
There's something caught in the headlight. It looks like clothing fibers.
!!
You're right! It's on the right side of the car!!
The victim was most likely hit by the right side of the vehicle.
But then why did th sound com from the left?
Exactly. Look there.
The car window is wide open.
I suspect...

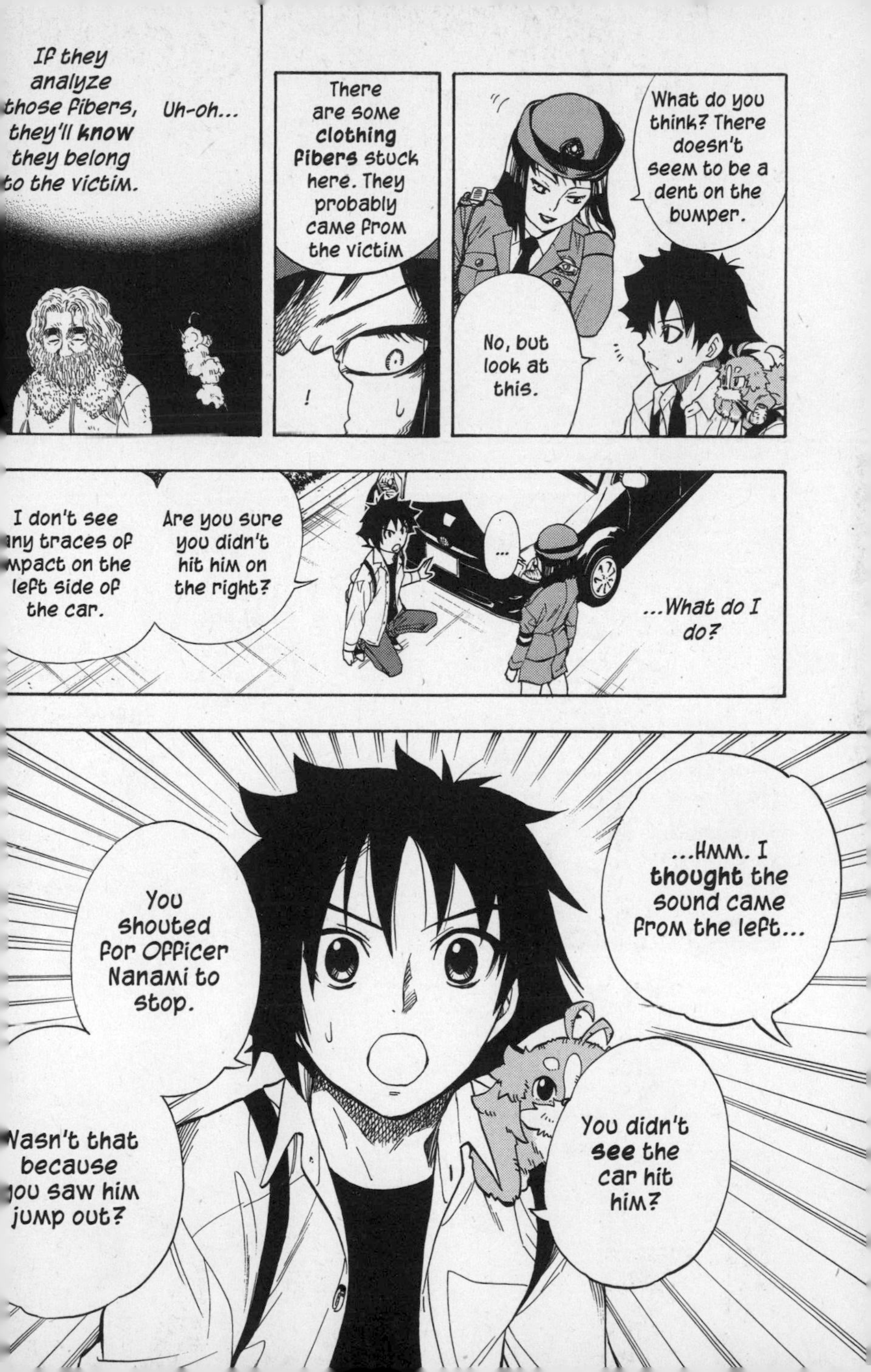
What do you think? There doesn't seem to be a dent on the bumper.
No, but look at this.
There are some **clothing fibers** stuck here. They probably came from the victim
!
Uh-oh...
If they analyze those fibers, they'll **know** they belong to the victim.
...What do I do?
...
Are you sure you didn't hit him on the right?
I don't see ny traces of mpact on the left side of the car.
...HMM. I **thought** the sound came from the left...
You shouted for Officer Nanami to stop.
You didn't **see** the car hit him?
Nasn't that because jou saw him jump out?

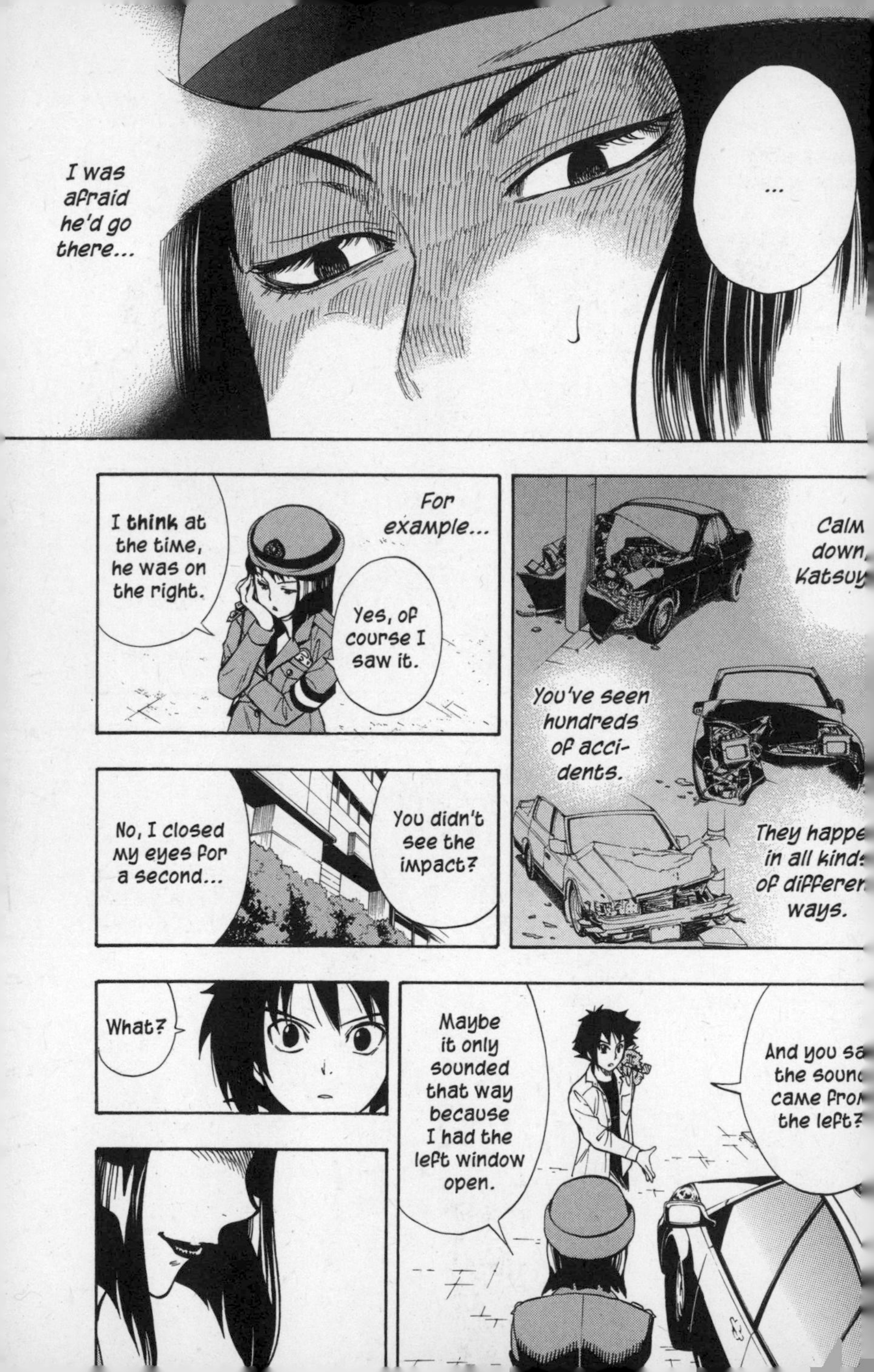
...
I was afraid he'd go there...
Calm down, Katsuy
You've seen hundreds of acci-dents.
They happe in all kinds of differen ways.
For example...
Yes, of course I saw it.
I think at the time, he was on the right.
You didn't see the impact?
No, I closed my eyes for a second...
And you sa the sounc came fron the left?
Maybe it only sounded that way because I had the left window open.
What?

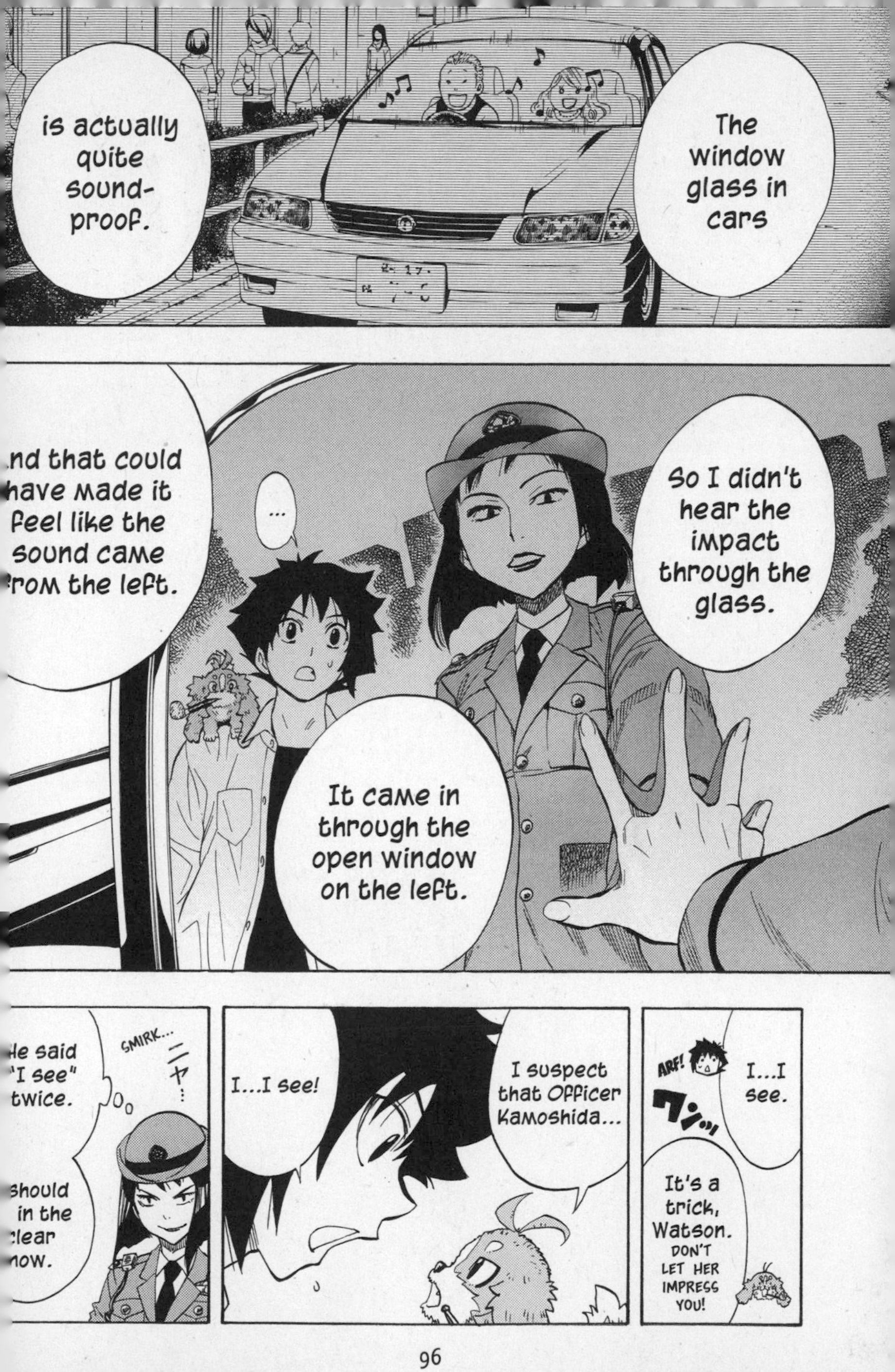
The window glass in cars
is actually quite sound-proof.
So I didn't hear the impact through the glass.
It came in through the open window on the left.
...
nd that could have made it feel like the sound came from the left.
I...I see.
ARF!
ワン
It's a trick, Watson. DON'T LET HER IMPRESS YOU!
I suspect that Officer Kamoshida...
I...I see!
SMIRK...
ニヤ…
He said "I see" twice.
should in the clear now.

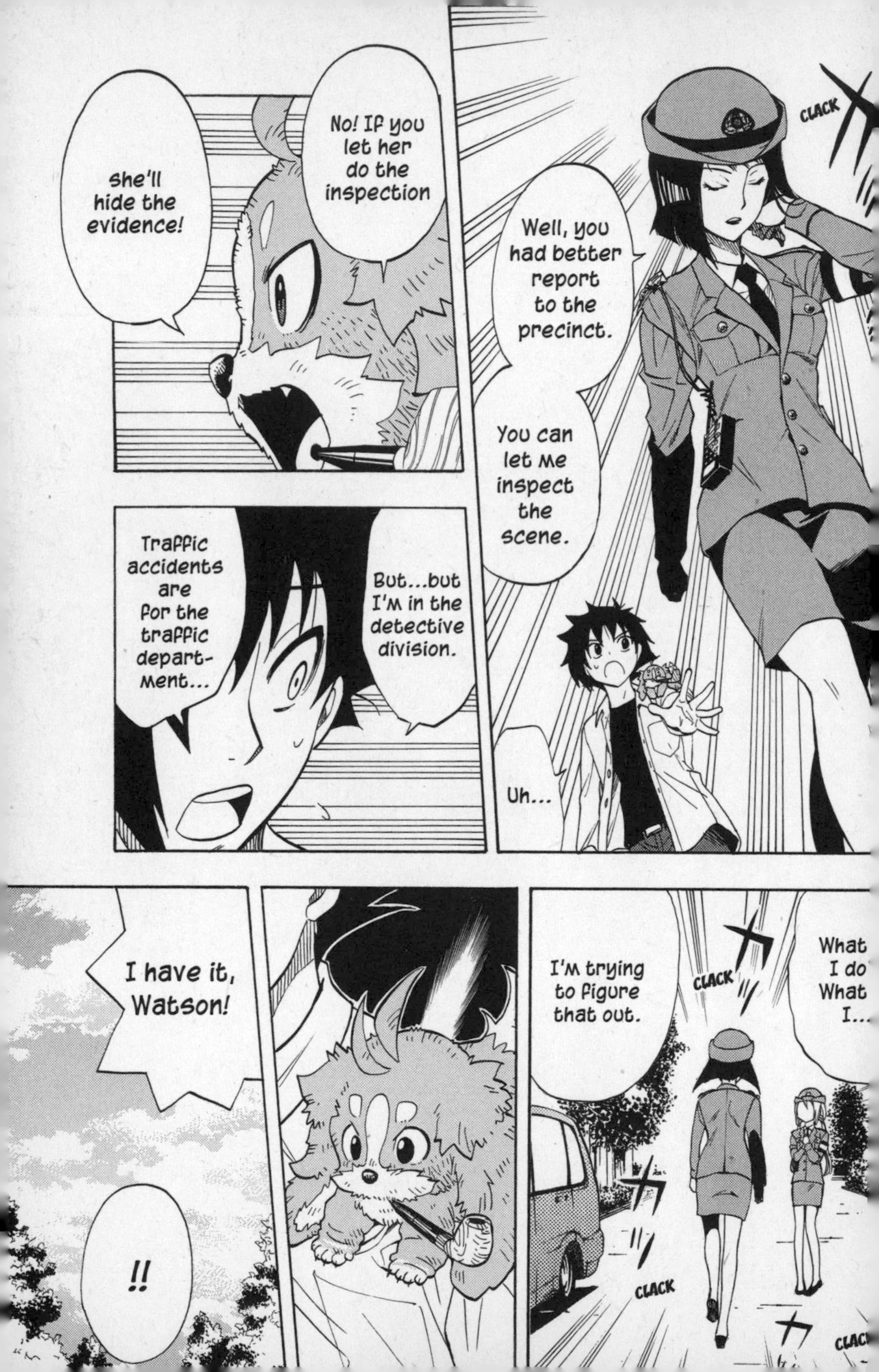
CLACK
Well, you had better report to the precinct.
You can let me inspect the scene.
Uh...
No! If you let her do the inspection
She'll hide the evidence!
But...but I'm in the detective division.
Traffic accidents are for the traffic department...
What I do What I...
CLACK
I'm trying to figure that out.
CLACK
CLAC
I have it, Watson!
!!

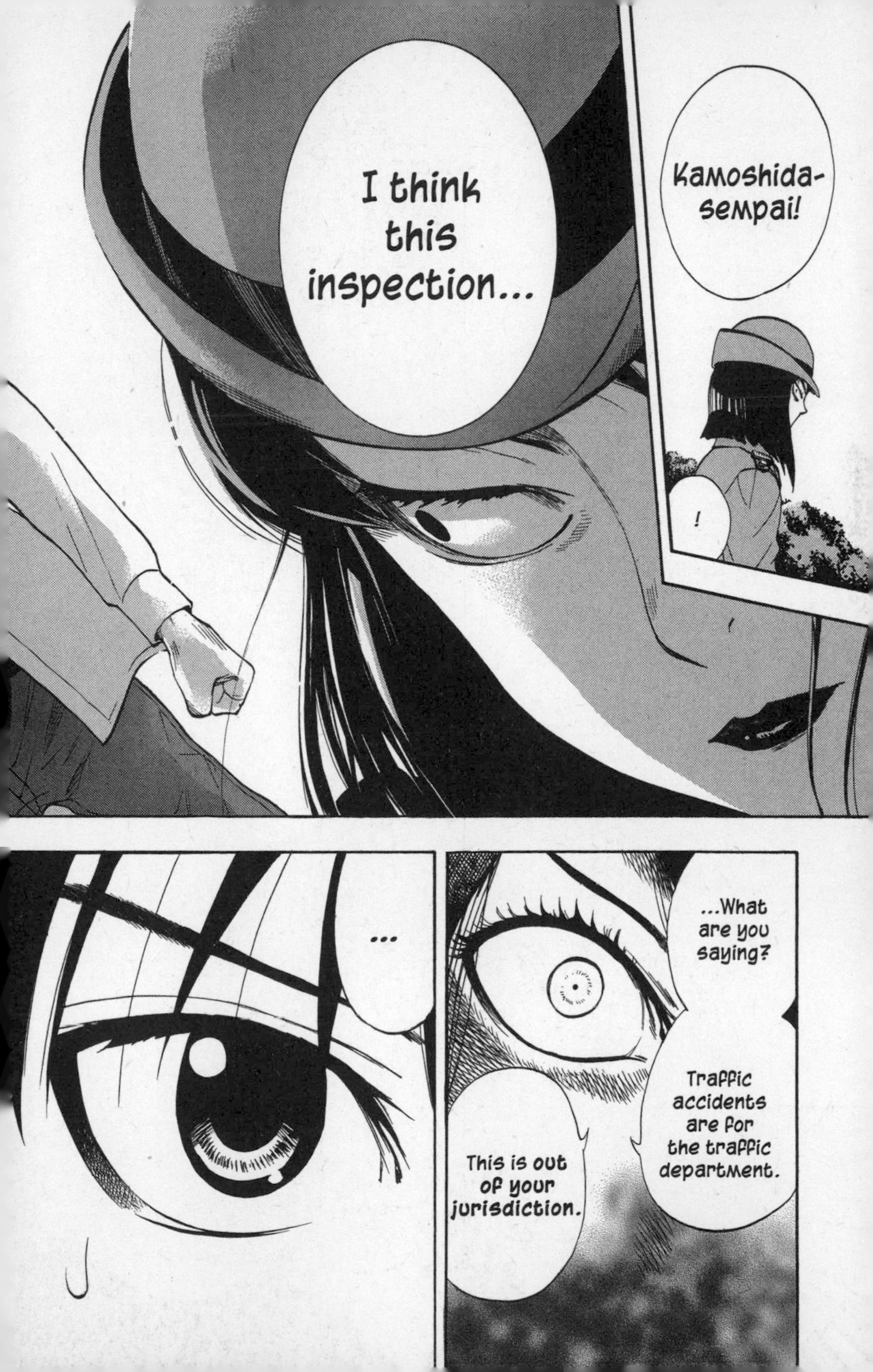
Kamoshida-sempai!
!
I think this inspection...
...What are you saying?
Traffic accidents are for the traffic department.
This is out of your jurisdiction.
...

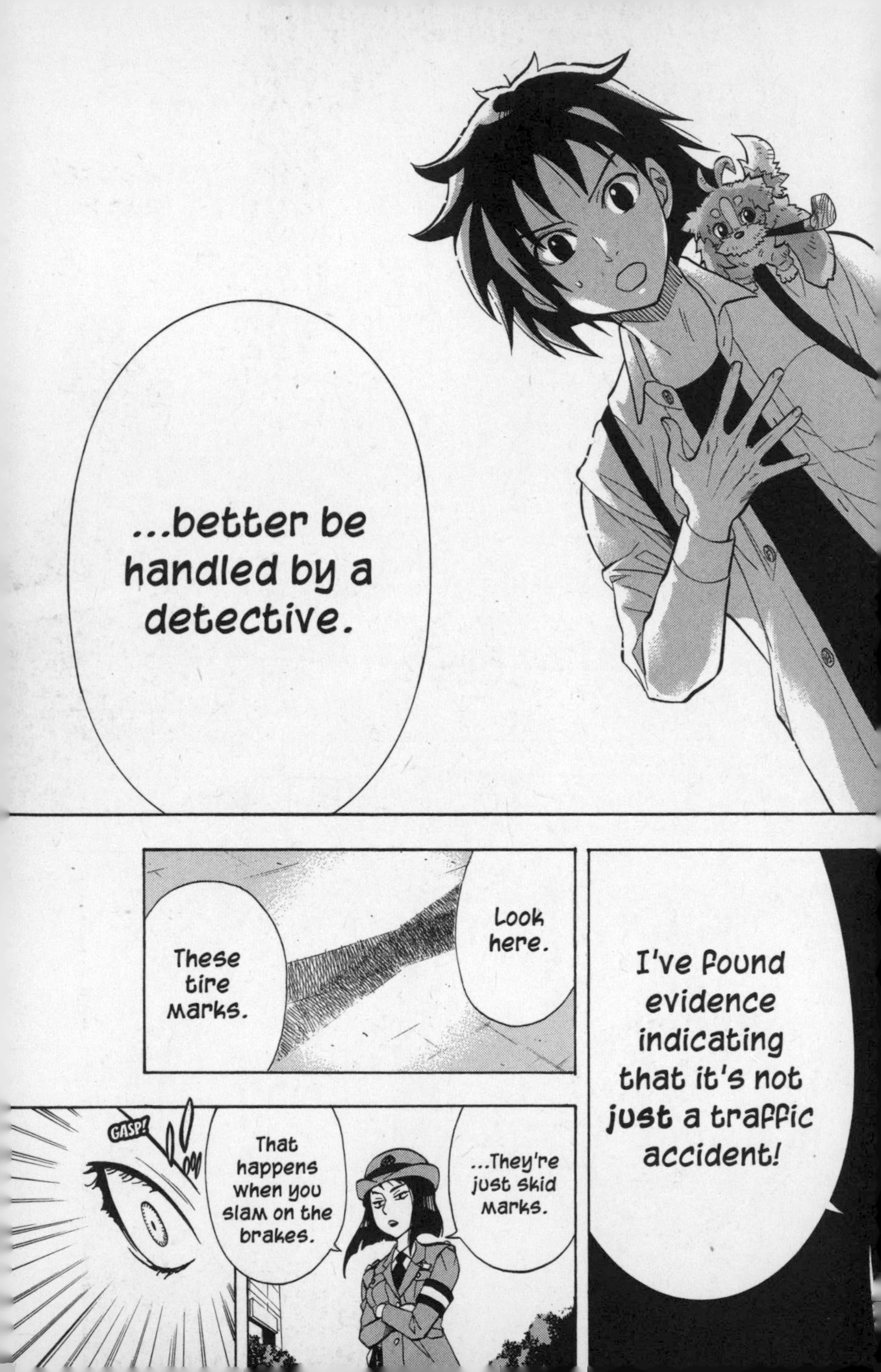
...better be handled by a detective.
I've found evidence indicating that it's not just a traffic accident!
Look here.
These tire marks.
...They're just skid marks.
That happens when you slam on the brakes.
GASP!

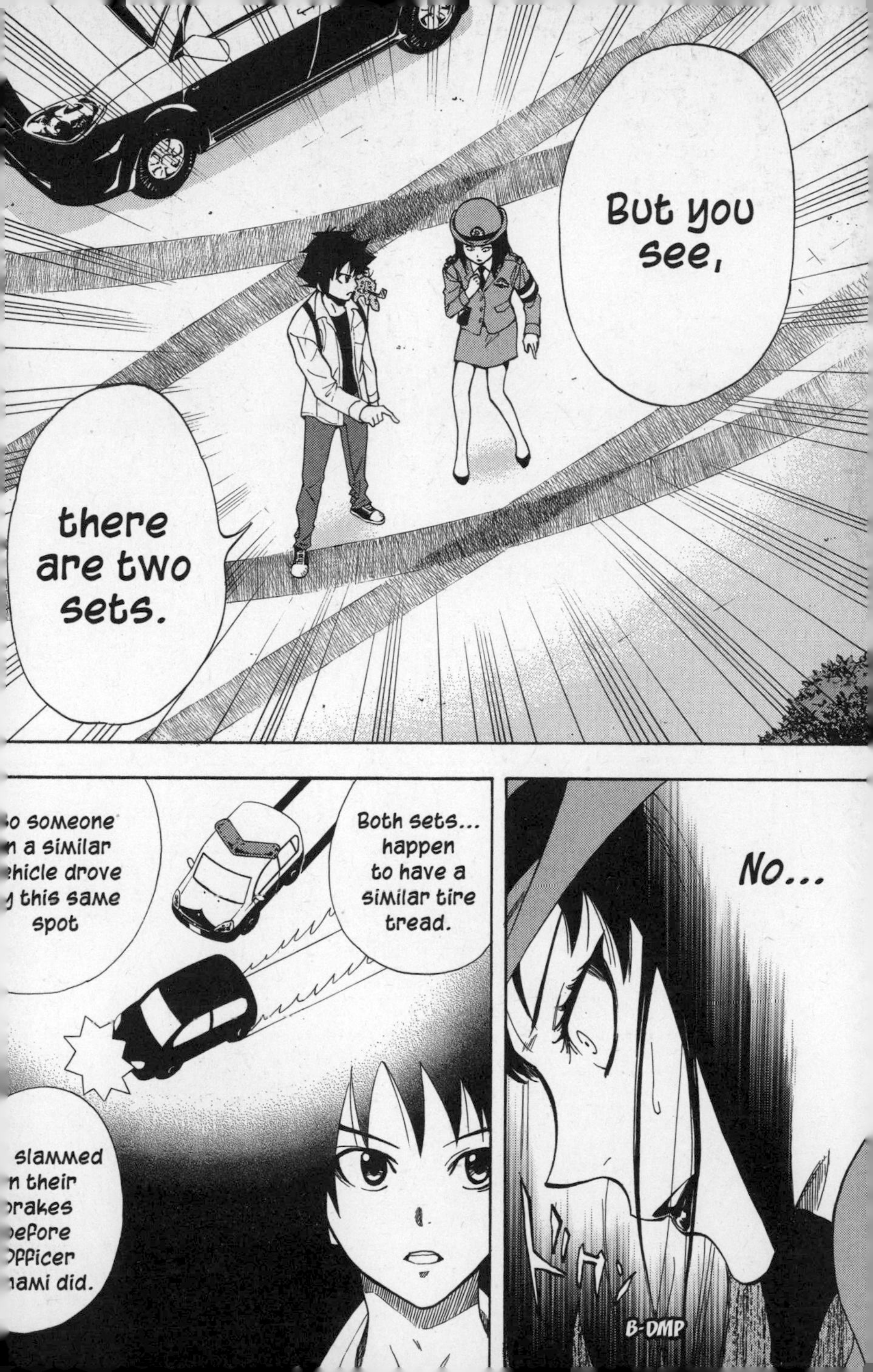
But you see,
there are two sets.
No...
B-DMP
Both sets... happen to have a similar tire tread.
o someone n a similar ehicle drove this same spot
slammed n their rakes efore Officer ami did.

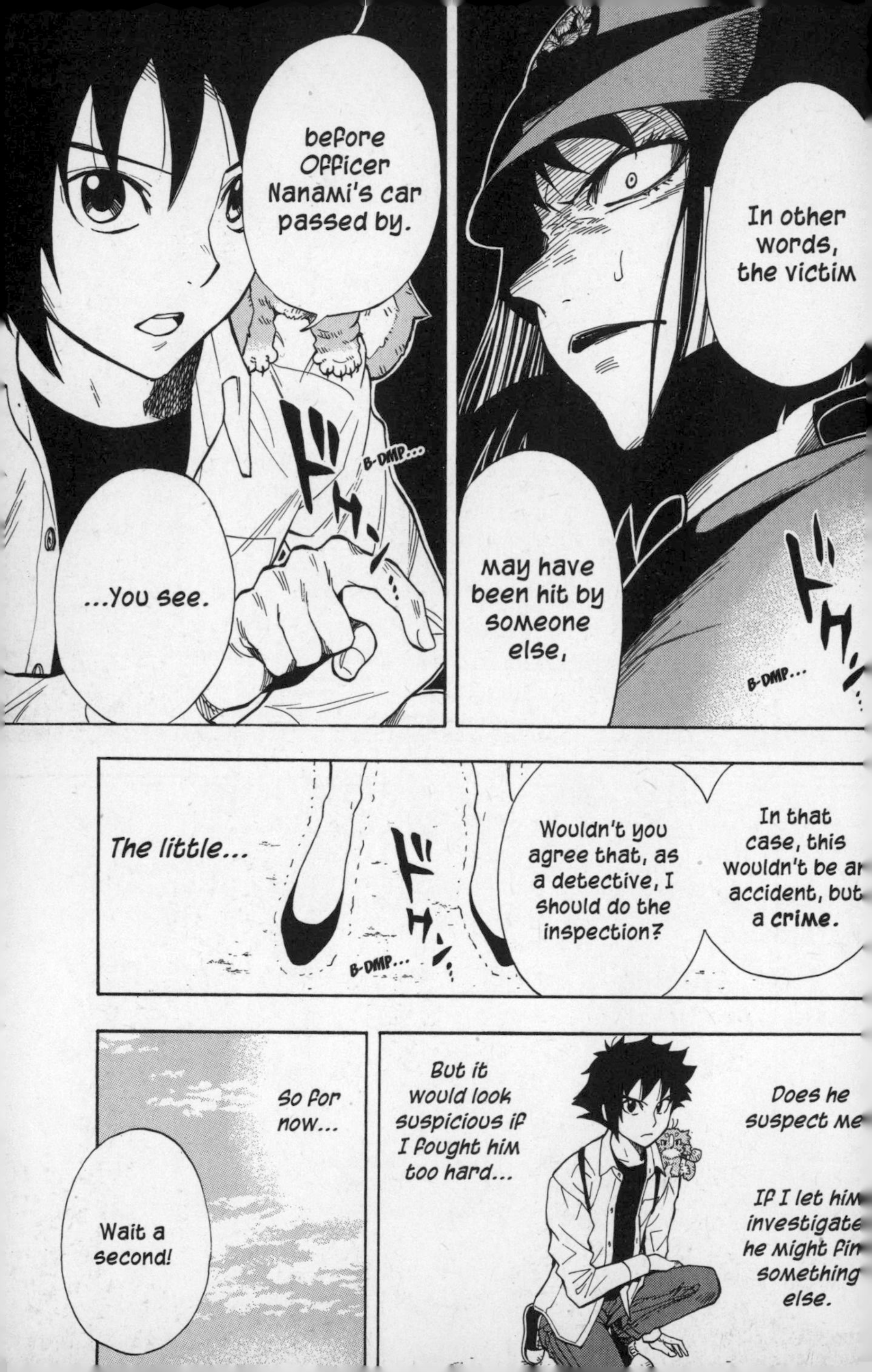
In other words, the victim
may have been hit by someone else,
B-DMP...
before Officer Nanami's car passed by.
B-DMP...
...You see.
In that case, this wouldn't be ar accident, but a crime.
Wouldn't you agree that, as a detective, I should do the inspection?
B-DMP...
The little...
Does he suspect me
If I let him investigate he might fin something else.
But it would look suspicious if I fought him too hard...
So for now...
Wait a second!

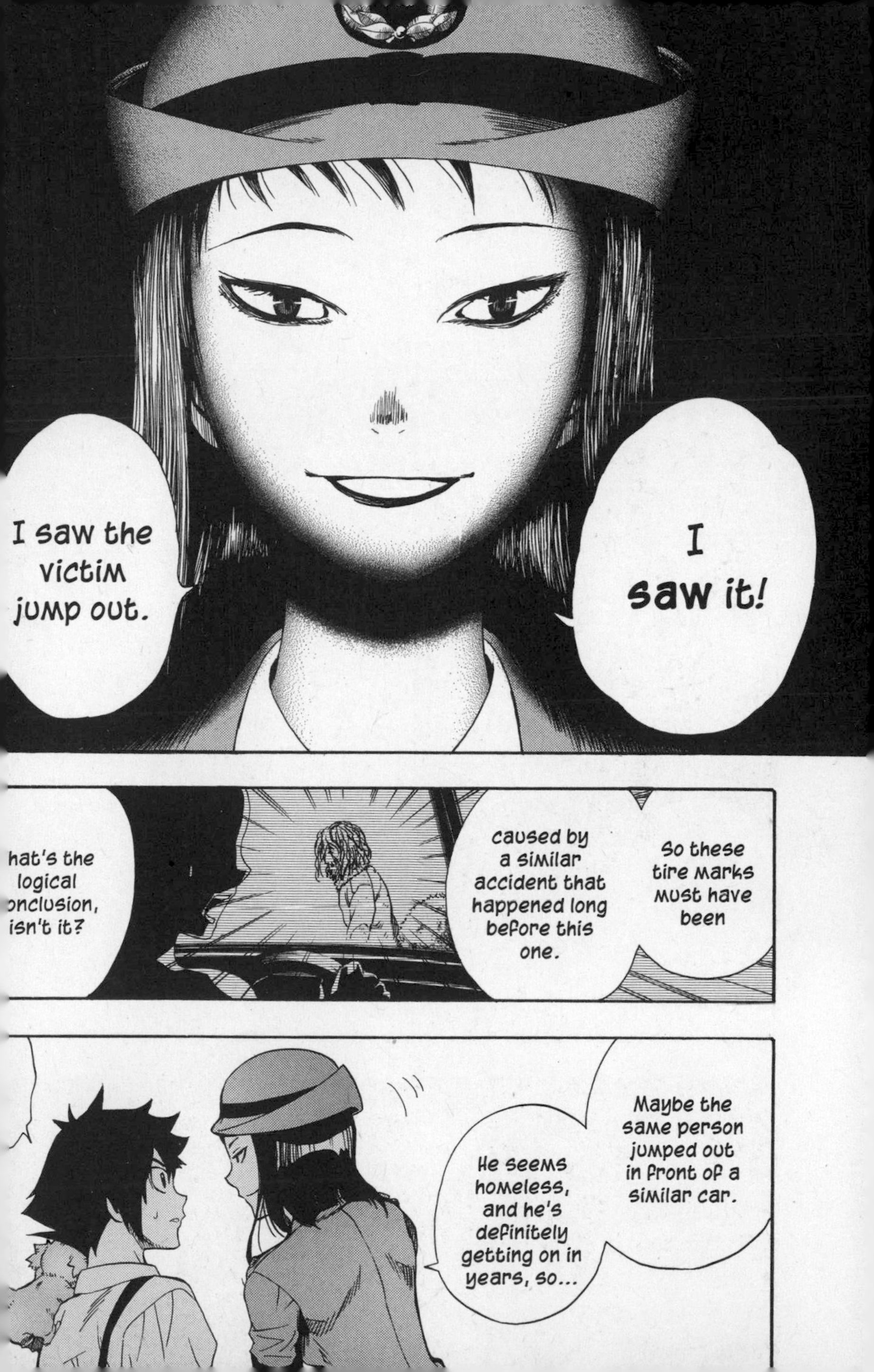

I saw it!
I saw the victim jump out.
So these tire marks must have been
caused by a similar accident that happened long before this one.
hat's the logical onclusion, isn't it?
Maybe the same person jumped out in front of a similar car.
He seems homeless, and he's definitely getting on in years, so...

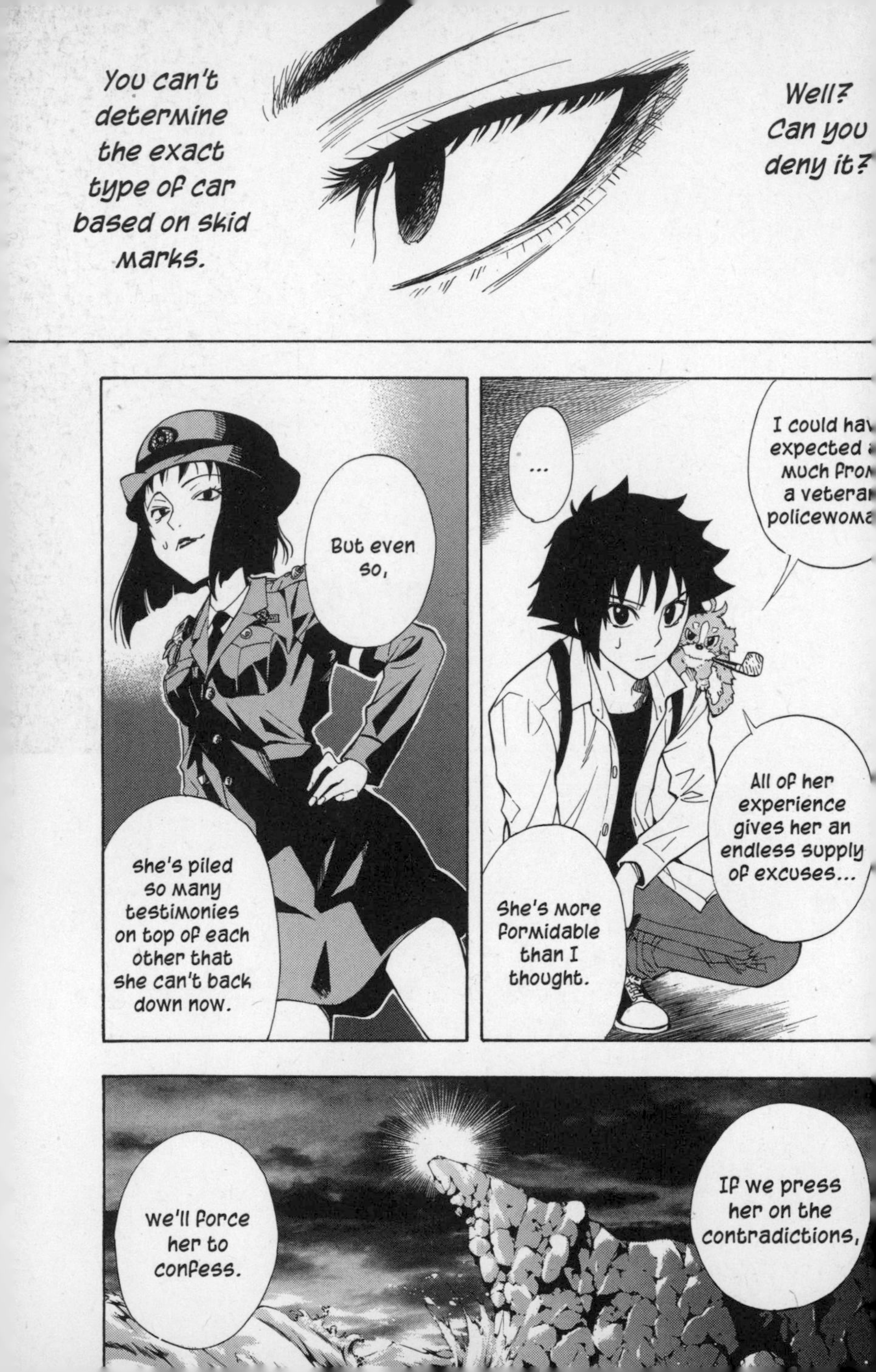
Well? Can you deny it?
You can't determine the exact type of car based on skid marks.
I could hav expected much from a vetera policewoma
...
All of her experience gives her an endless supply of excuses...
She's more formidable than I thought.
But even so,
she's piled so many testimonies on top of each other that she can't back down now.
If we press her on the contradictions,
we'll force her to confess.

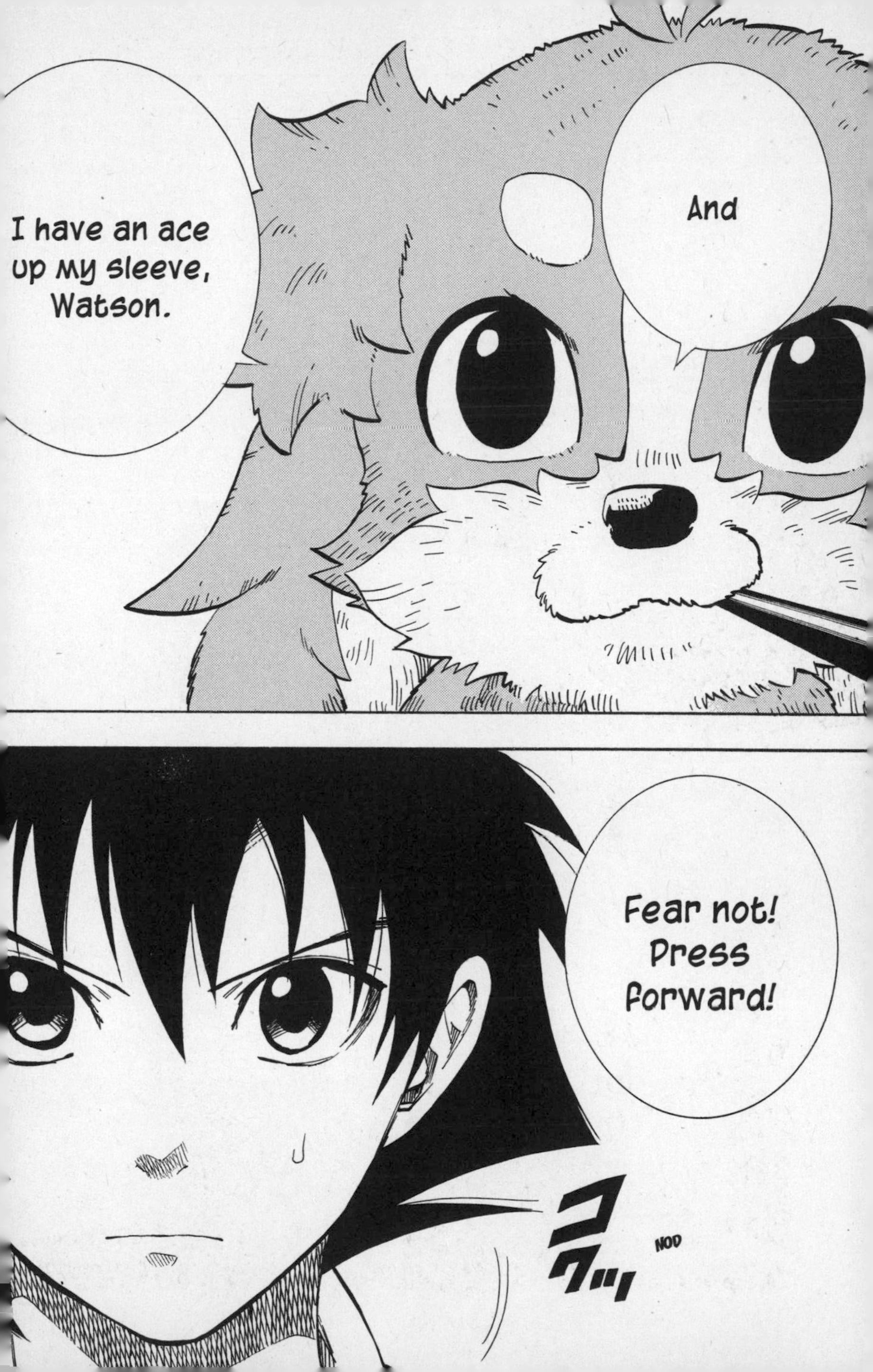
And
I have an ace up my sleeve, Watson.
Fear not! Press forward!
NOD

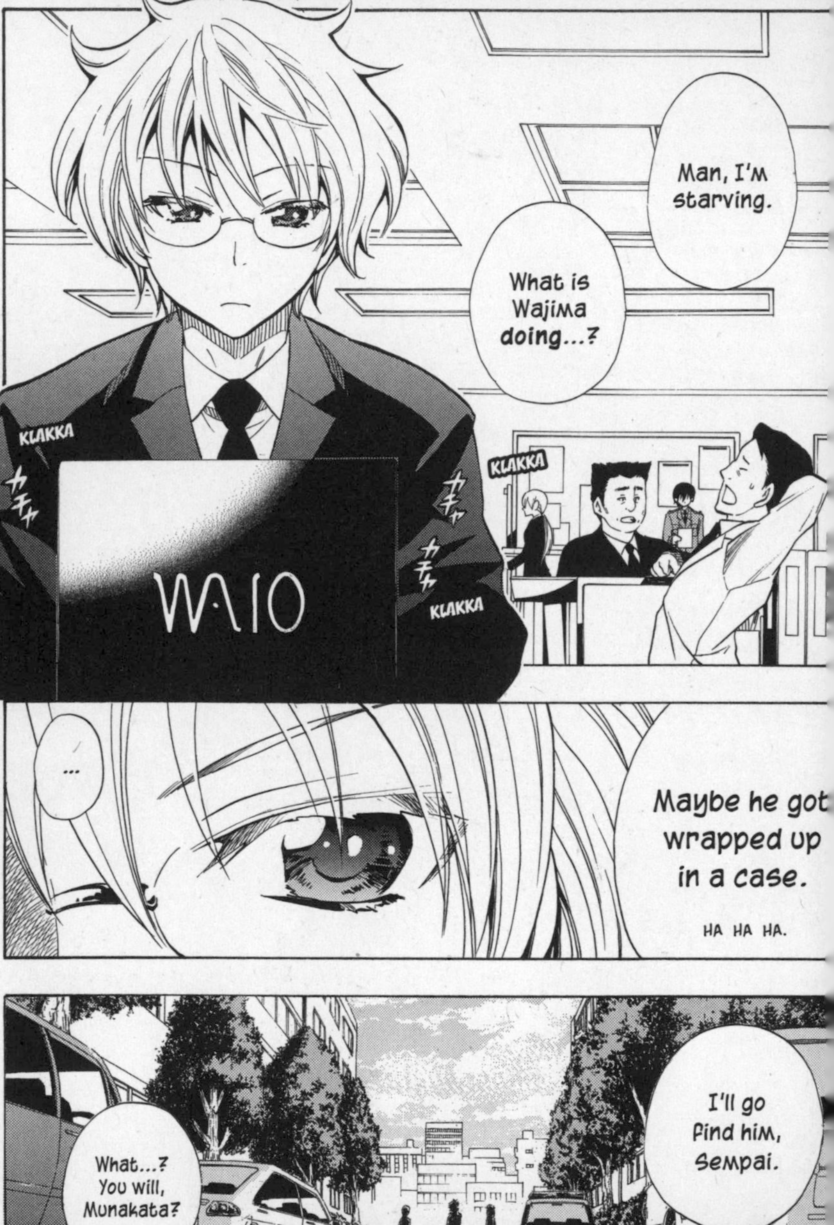
Man, I'm starving.
What is Wajima doing...?
KLAKKA
KLAKKA
カチャ
カチャ
カチャ
KLAKKA
Maybe he got wrapped up in a case.
HA HA HA.
...
I'll go find him, Sempai.
What...? You will, Munakata?
REALLY? ♪

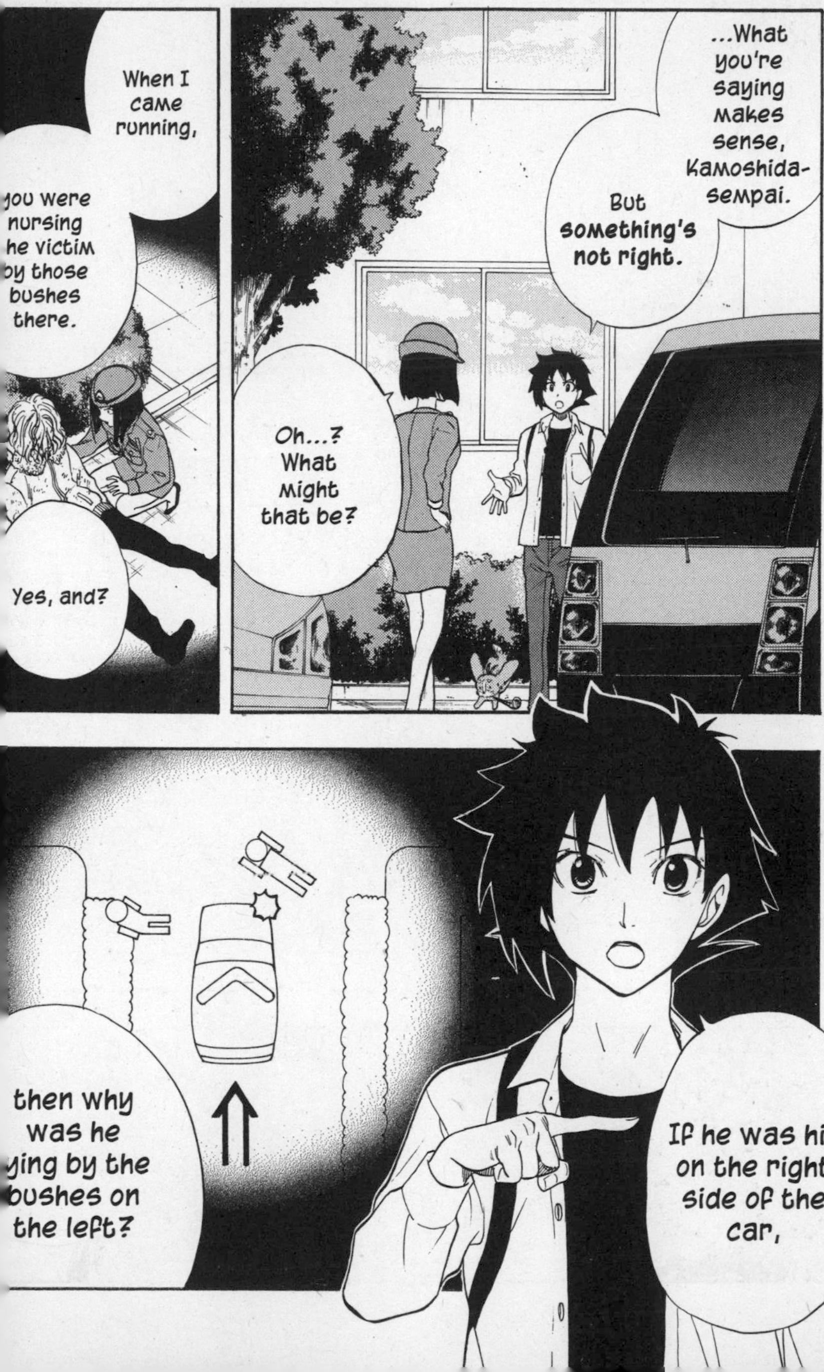
...What you're saying makes sense, Kamoshida-sempai.
But something's not right.
Oh...? What might that be?
When I came running,
you were nursing he victim by those bushes there.
Yes, and?
If he was hit on the right side of the car,
then why was he ying by the bushes on the left?

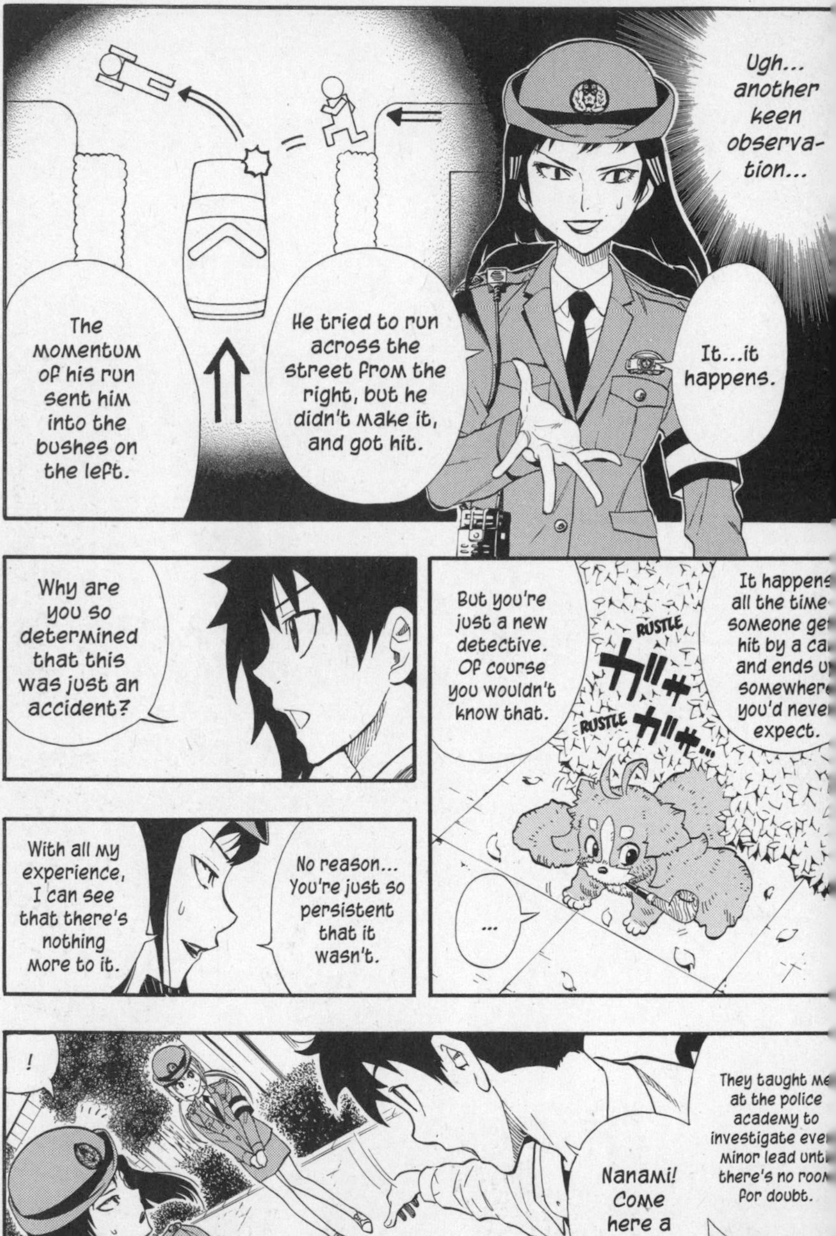
Ugh... another keen observation...
It...it happens.
He tried to run across the street from the right, but he didn't make it, and got hit.
The momentum of his run sent him into the bushes on the left.
It happens all the time someone ge hit by a ca and ends u somewhere you'd neve expect.
But you're just a new detective. Of course you wouldn't know that.
RUSTLE
ガサ
RUSTLE
ガサ...
...
Why are you so determined that this was just an accident?
No reason... You're just so persistent that it wasn't.
With all my experience, I can see that there's nothing more to it.
They taught me at the police academy to investigate eve minor lead unti there's no roo for doubt.
Nanami! Come here a sec.
!

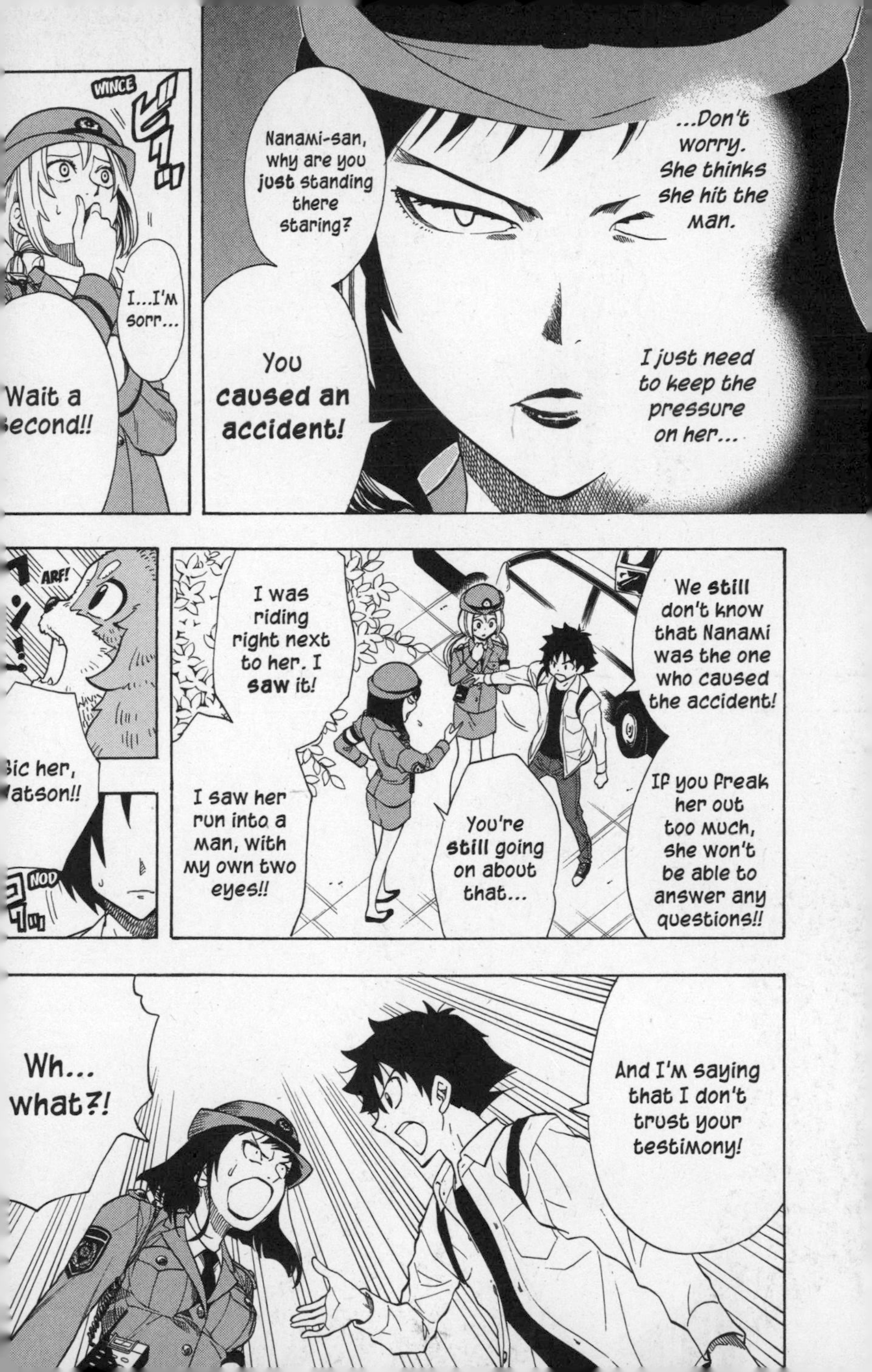
...Don't worry. She thinks she hit the man.
Nanami-san, why are you just standing there staring?
I just need to keep the pressure on her...
You caused an accident!
WINCE
I...I'm sorr...
Wait a second!!
We still don't know that Nanami was the one who caused the accident!
I was riding right next to her. I saw it!
If you freak her out too much, she won't be able to answer any questions!!
You're still going on about that...
I saw her run into a man, with my own two eyes!!
ARF!
Sic her, Watson!!
NOD
And I'm saying that I don't trust your testimony!
Wh... what?!

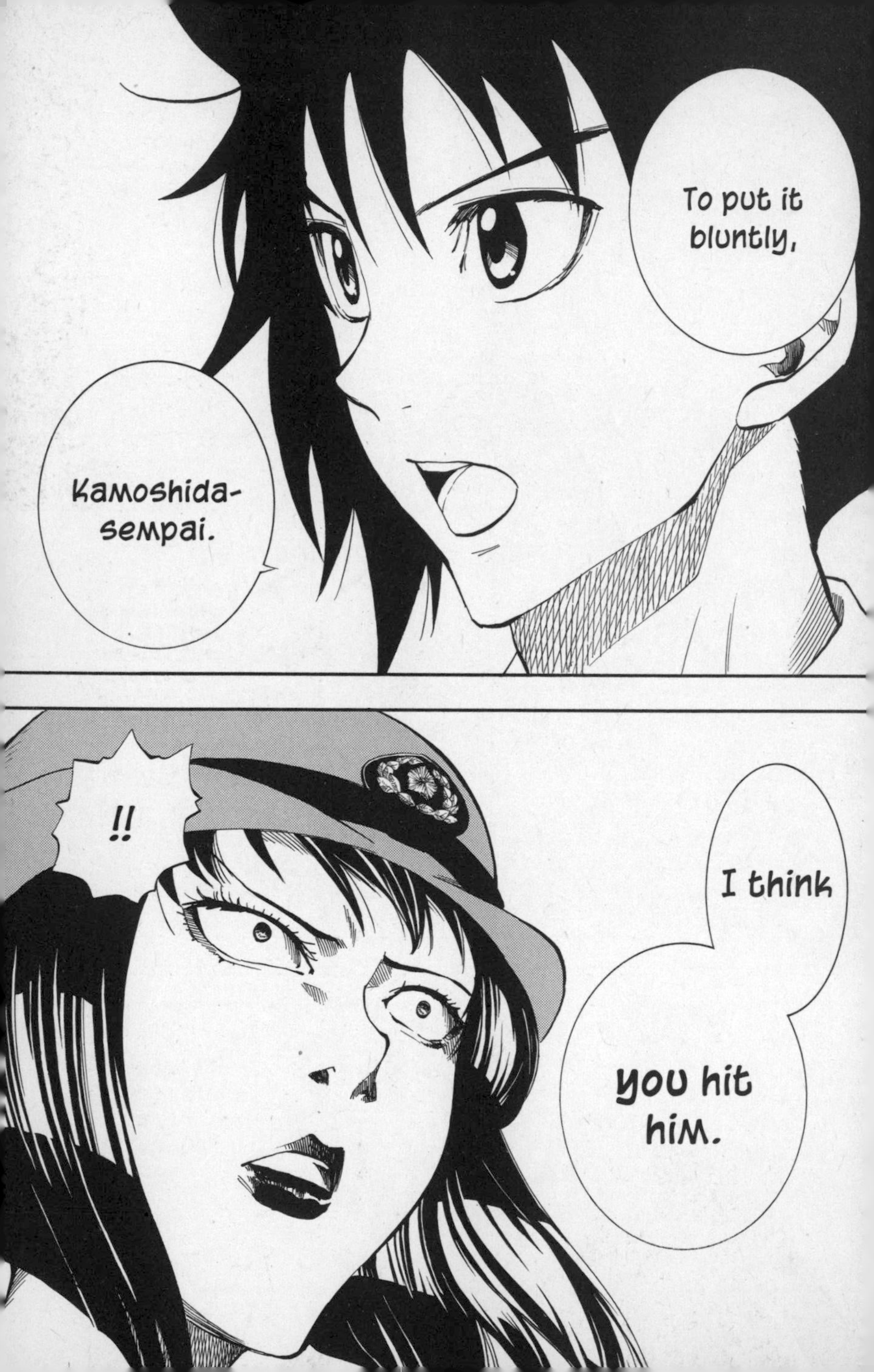
To put it bluntly,
Kamoshida-sempai.
!!
I think
you hit him.

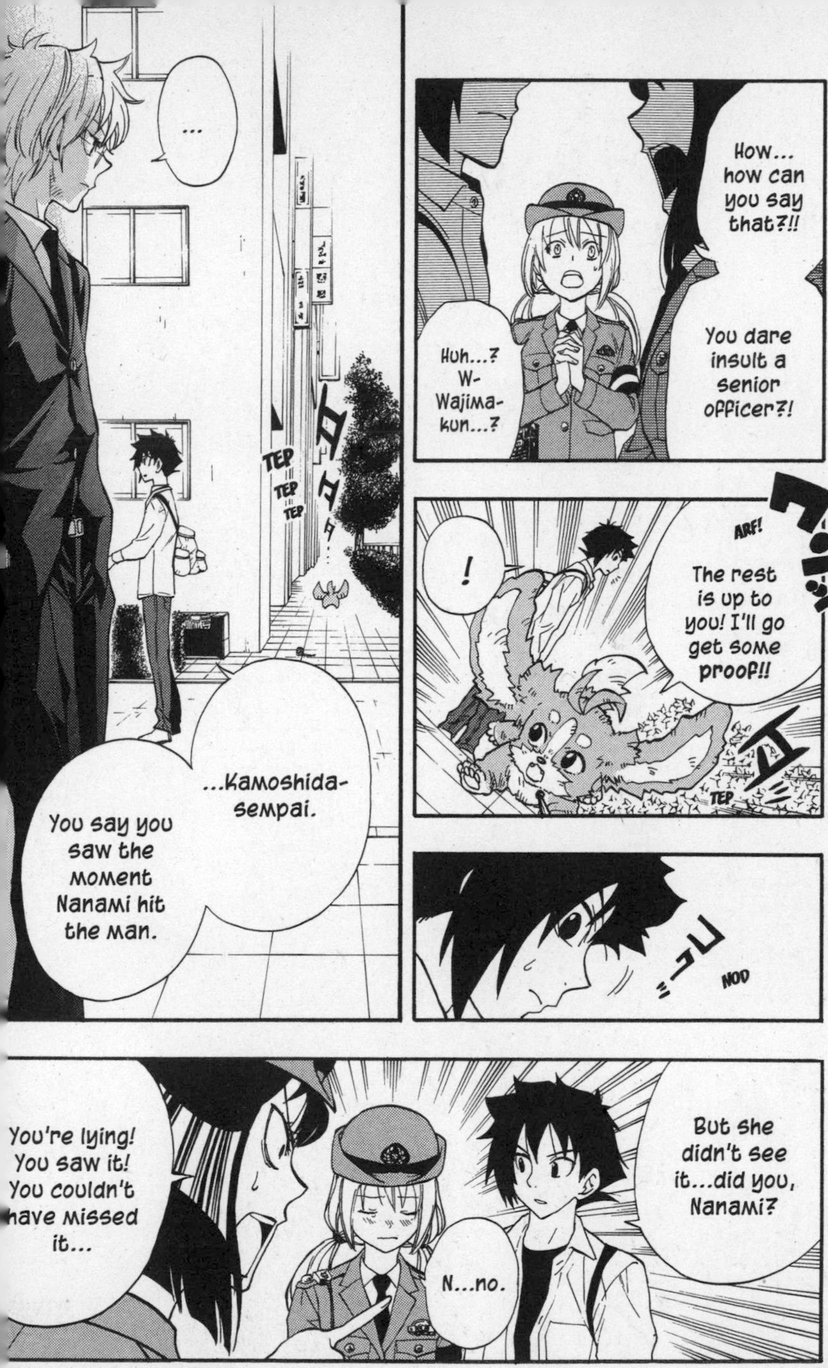
How... how can you say that?!!
You dare insult a senior officer?!
Huh...? W-Wajima-kun...?
ARF!
The rest is up to you! I'll go get some proof!!
!
TEP
NOD
...
TEP
TEP
TEP
...Kamoshida-sempai.
You say you saw the moment Nanami hit the man.
But she didn't see it...did you, Nanami?
N...no.
You're lying! You saw it! You couldn't have missed it...

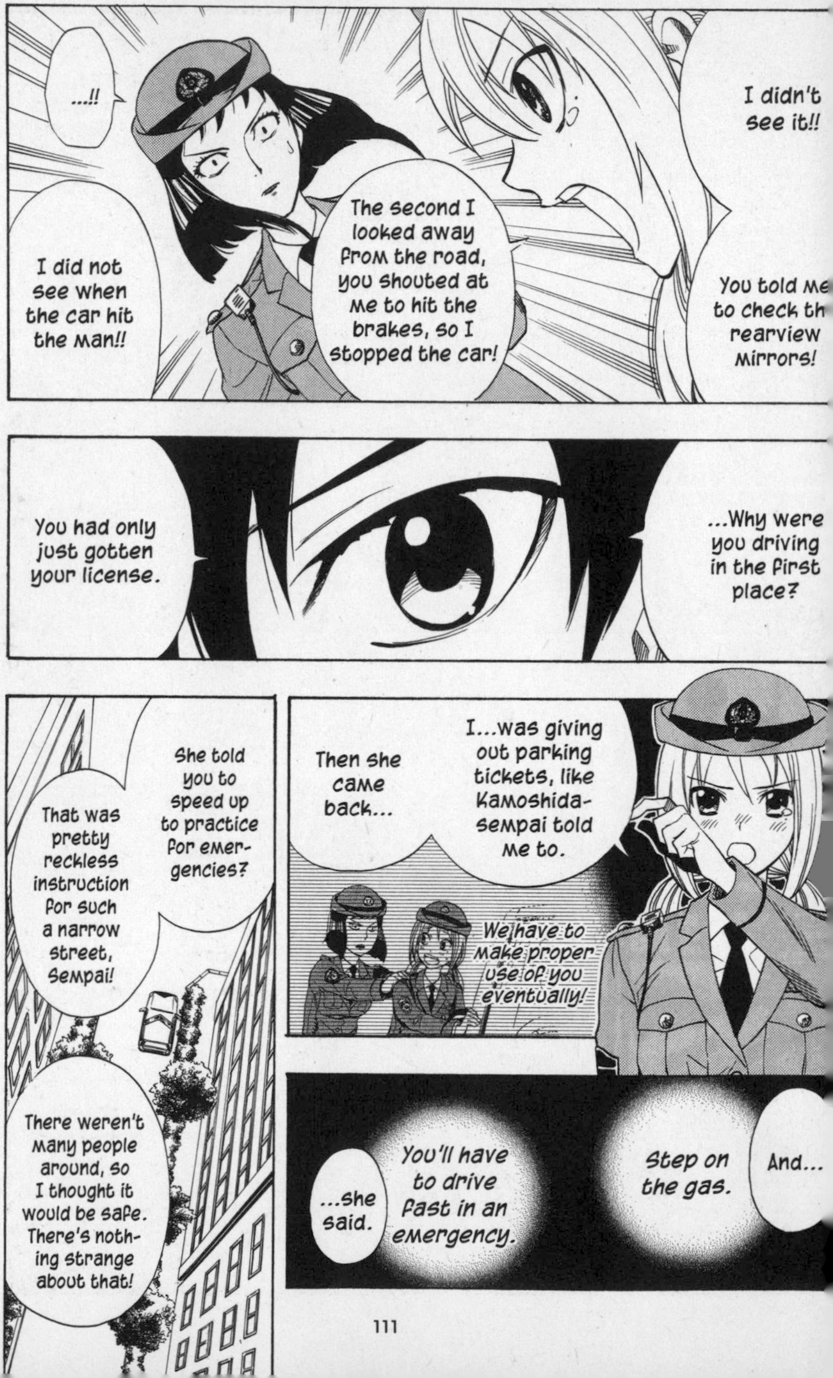
I didn't see it!!
You told me to check th rearview mirrors!
The second I looked away from the road, you shouted at me to hit the brakes, so I stopped the car!
...!!
I did not see when the car hit the man!!
...Why were you driving in the first place?
You had only just gotten your license.
I...was giving out parking tickets, like Kamoshida-sempai told me to.
Then she came back...
We have to make proper use of you eventually!
And...
Step on the gas.
You'll have to drive fast in an emergency.
...she said.
She told you to speed up to practice for emer-gencies?
That was pretty reckless instruction for such a narrow street, Sempai!
There weren't many people around, so I thought it would be safe. There's noth-ing strange about that!

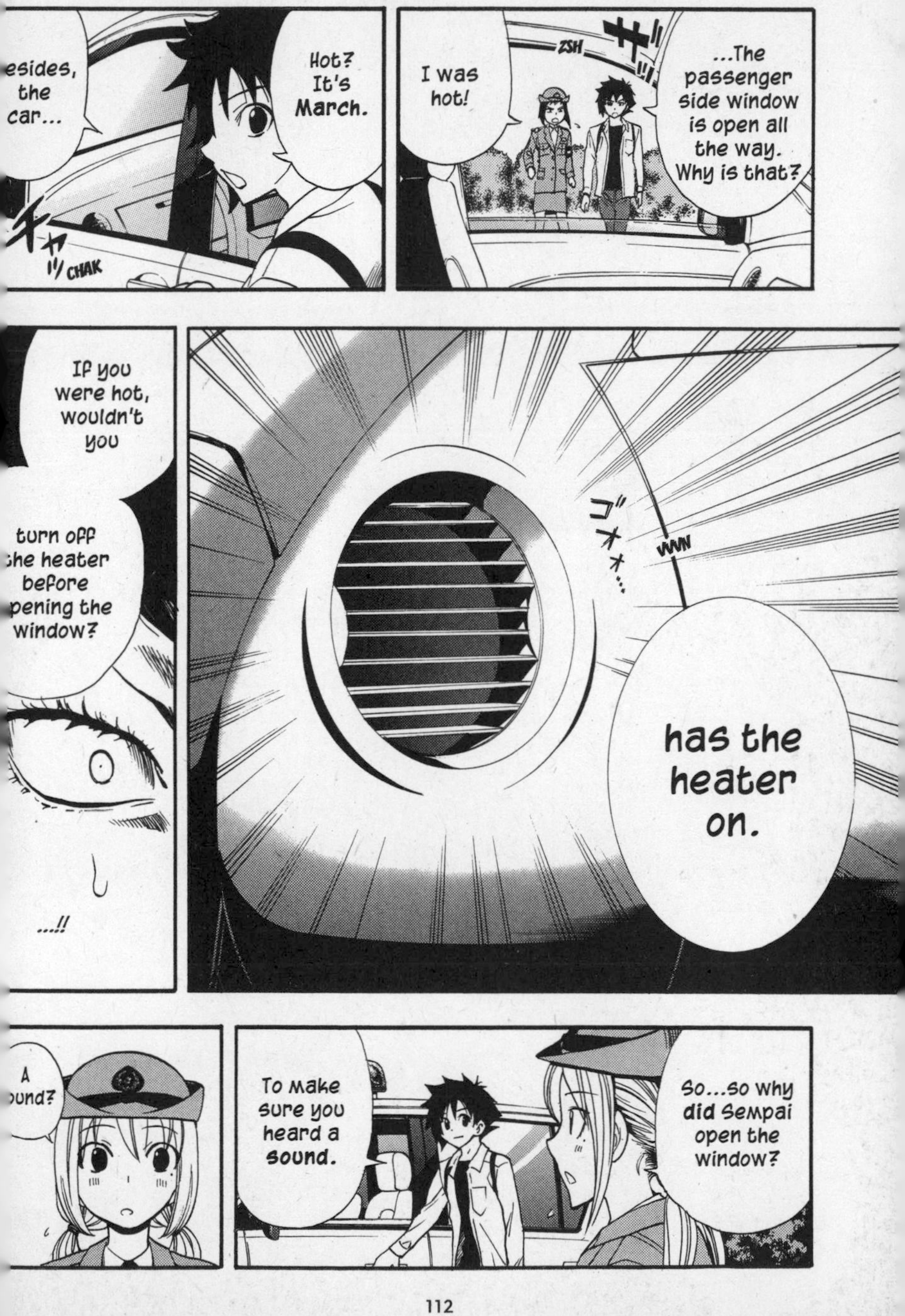
...The passenger side window is open all the way. Why is that?
ZSH
I was hot!
Hot? It's March.
esides, the car...
CHAK
WVVN
has the heater on.
If you were hot, wouldn't you
turn off the heater before pening the window?
...!!
So...so why did Sempai open the window?
To make sure you heard a sound.
A ound?

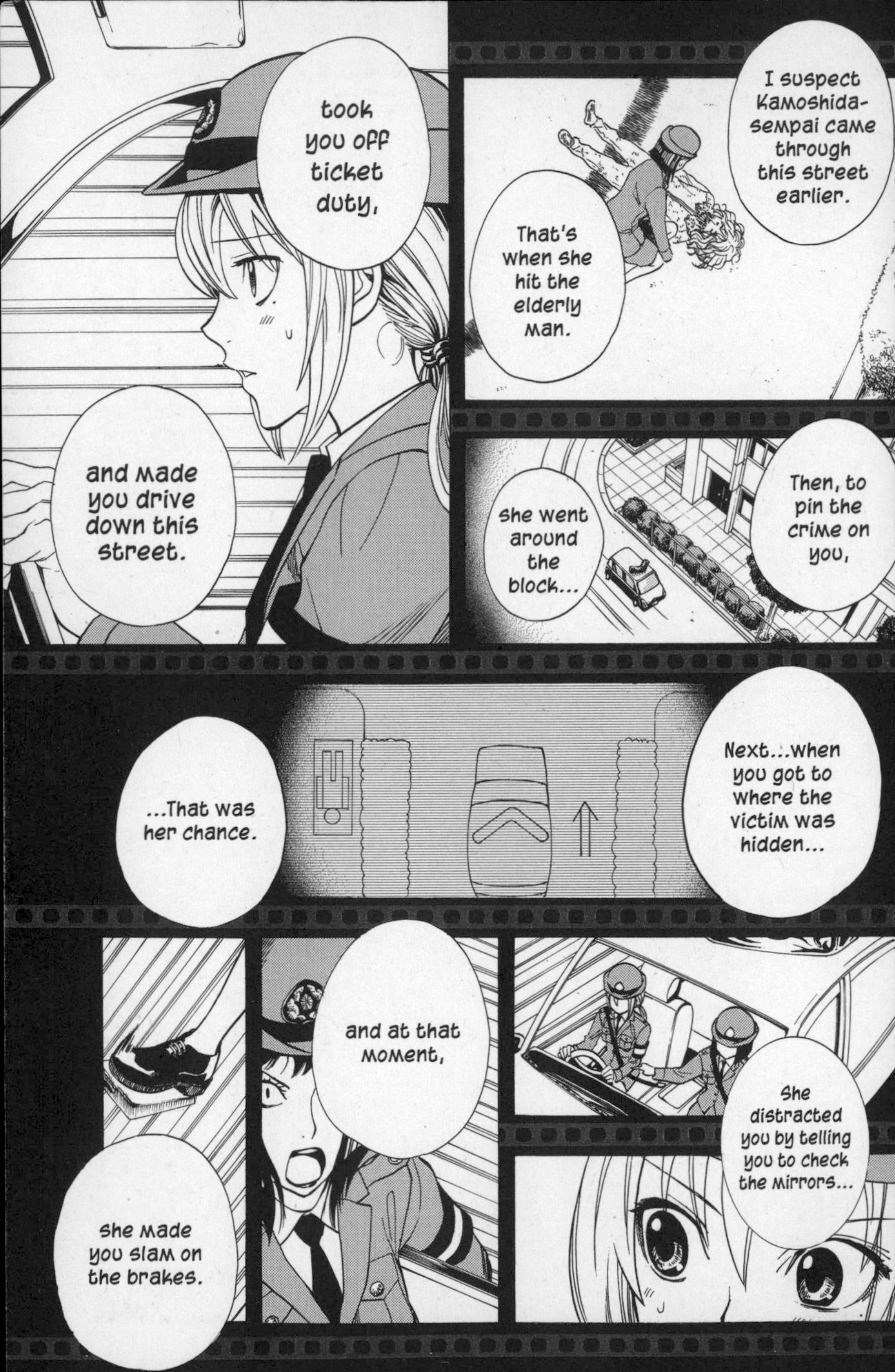
I suspect Kamoshida-sempai came through this street earlier.
That's when she hit the elderly man.
Then, to pin the crime on you,
she went around the block...
took you off ticket duty,
and made you drive down this street.
Next...when you got to where the victim was hidden...
...That was her chance.
She distracted you by telling you to check the mirrors...
and at that moment,
she made you slam on the brakes.

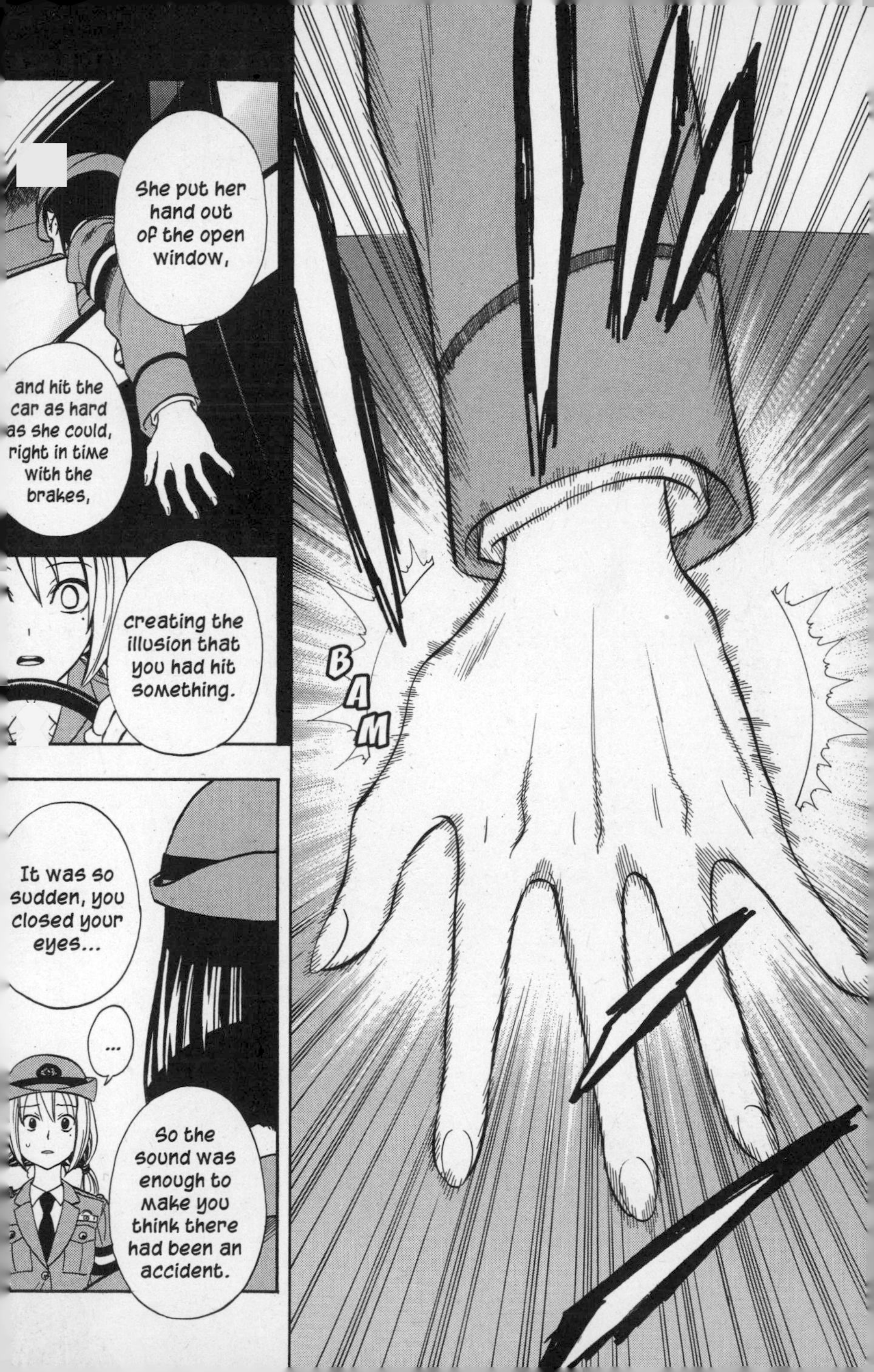
BAM
She put her hand out of the open window,
and hit the car as hard as she could, right in time with the brakes,
creating the illusion that you had hit something.
It was so sudden, you closed your eyes...
...
So the sound was enough to make you think there had been an accident.

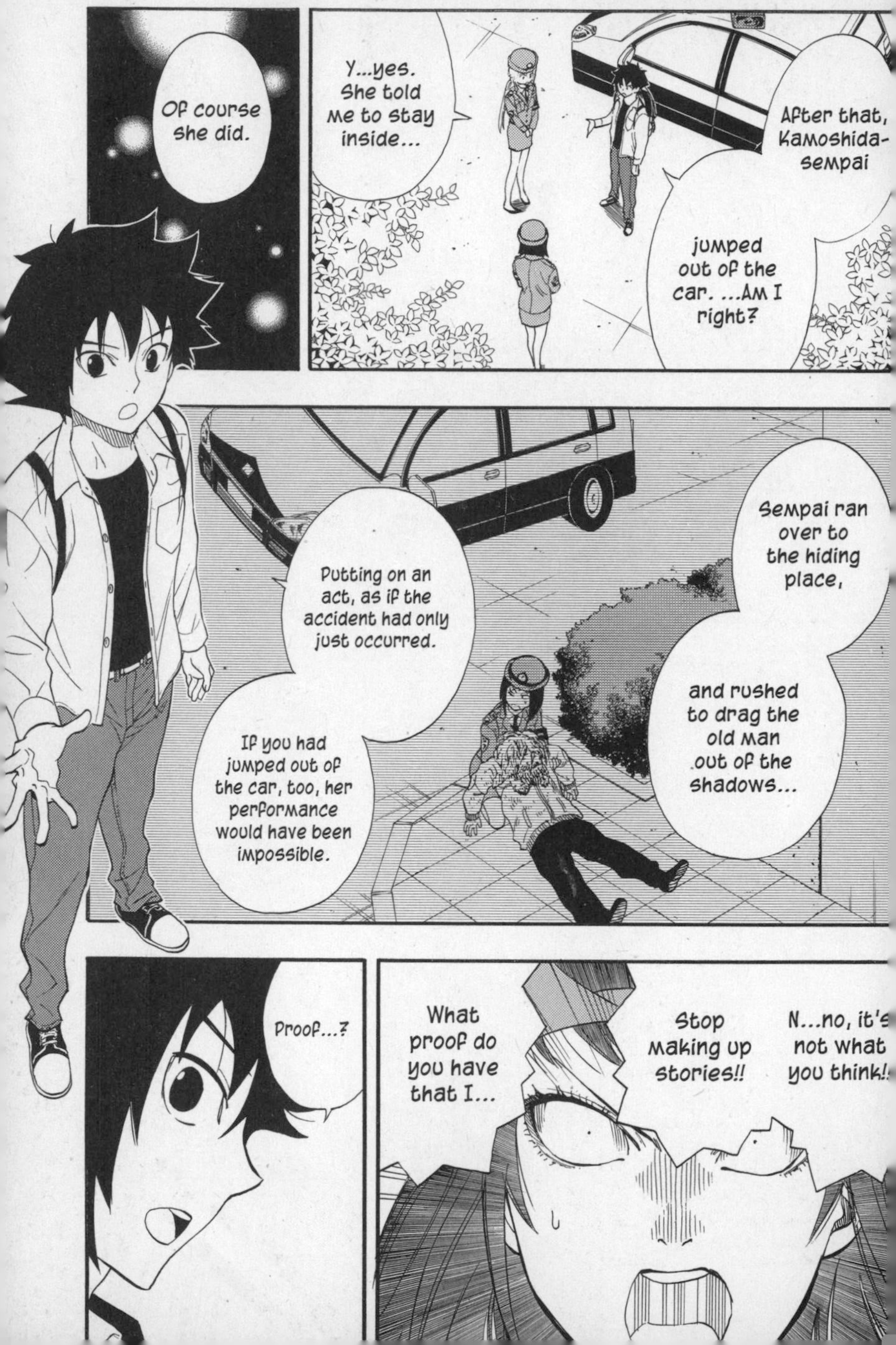
After that, Kamoshida-sempai
jumped out of the car. ...Am I right?
Y...yes. She told me to stay inside...
Of course she did.
Sempai ran over to the hiding place,
and rushed to drag the old man out of the shadows...
Putting on an act, as if the accident had only just occurred.
If you had jumped out of the car, too, her performance would have been impossible.
N...no, it's not what you think!
Stop making up stories!!
What proof do you have that I...
Proof...?

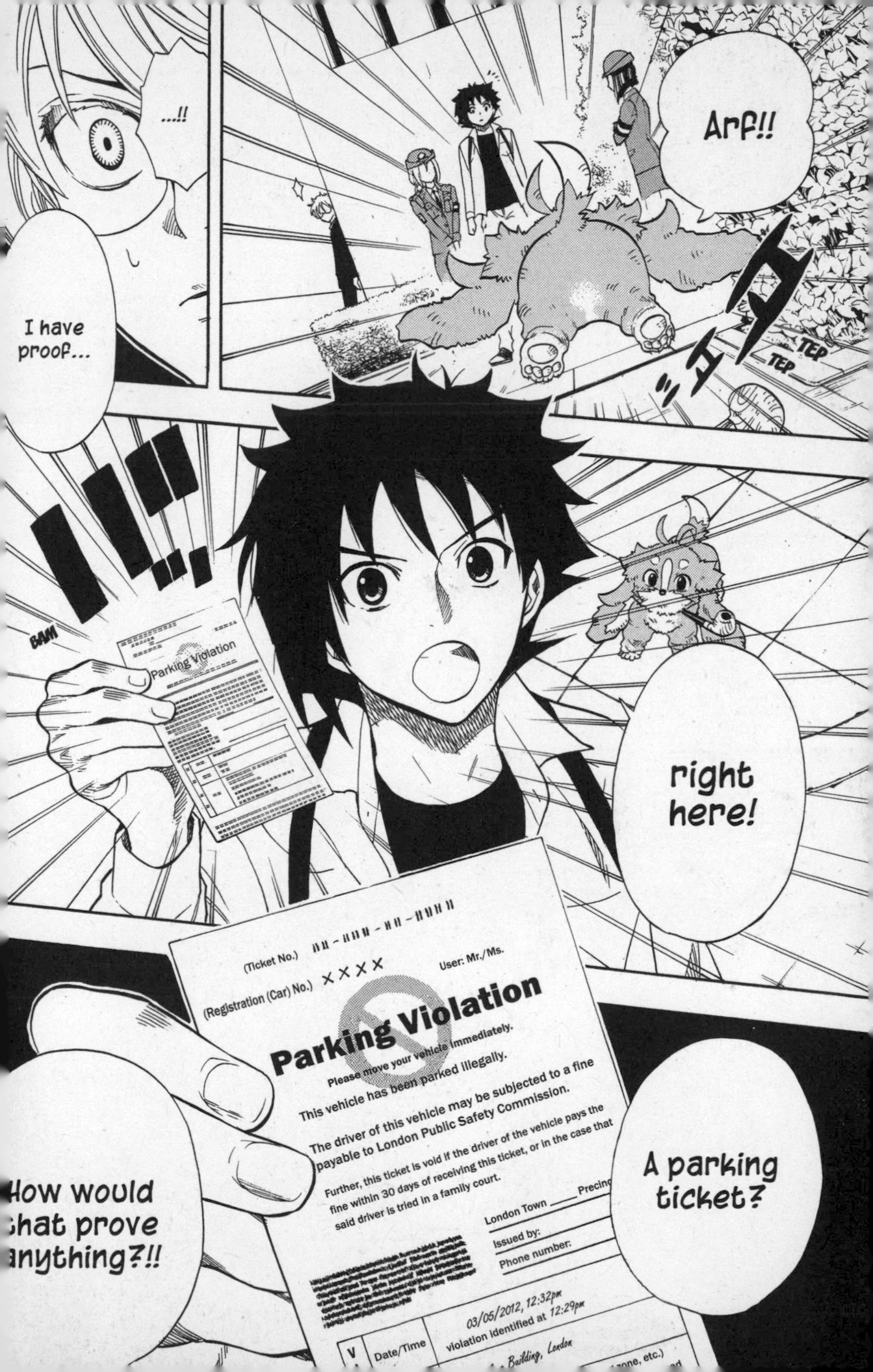
Arf!!
TEP
TEP
...!!
I have proof...
right here!
BAM
Parking Violation
A parking ticket?
How would that prove anything?!!
(Ticket No.)
User: Mr./Ms.
(Registration (Car) No.) XXXX
Parking Violation
Please move your vehicle immediately.
This vehicle has been parked illegally.
The driver of this vehicle may be subjected to a fine payable to London Public Safety Commission.
Further, this ticket is void if the driver of the vehicle pays the fine within 30 days of receiving this ticket, or in the case that said driver is tried in a family court.
London Town ____ Precinc
Issued by:
Phone number:
V
Date/Time
03/05/2012, 12:32pm
violation identified at 12:29pm
Building, London

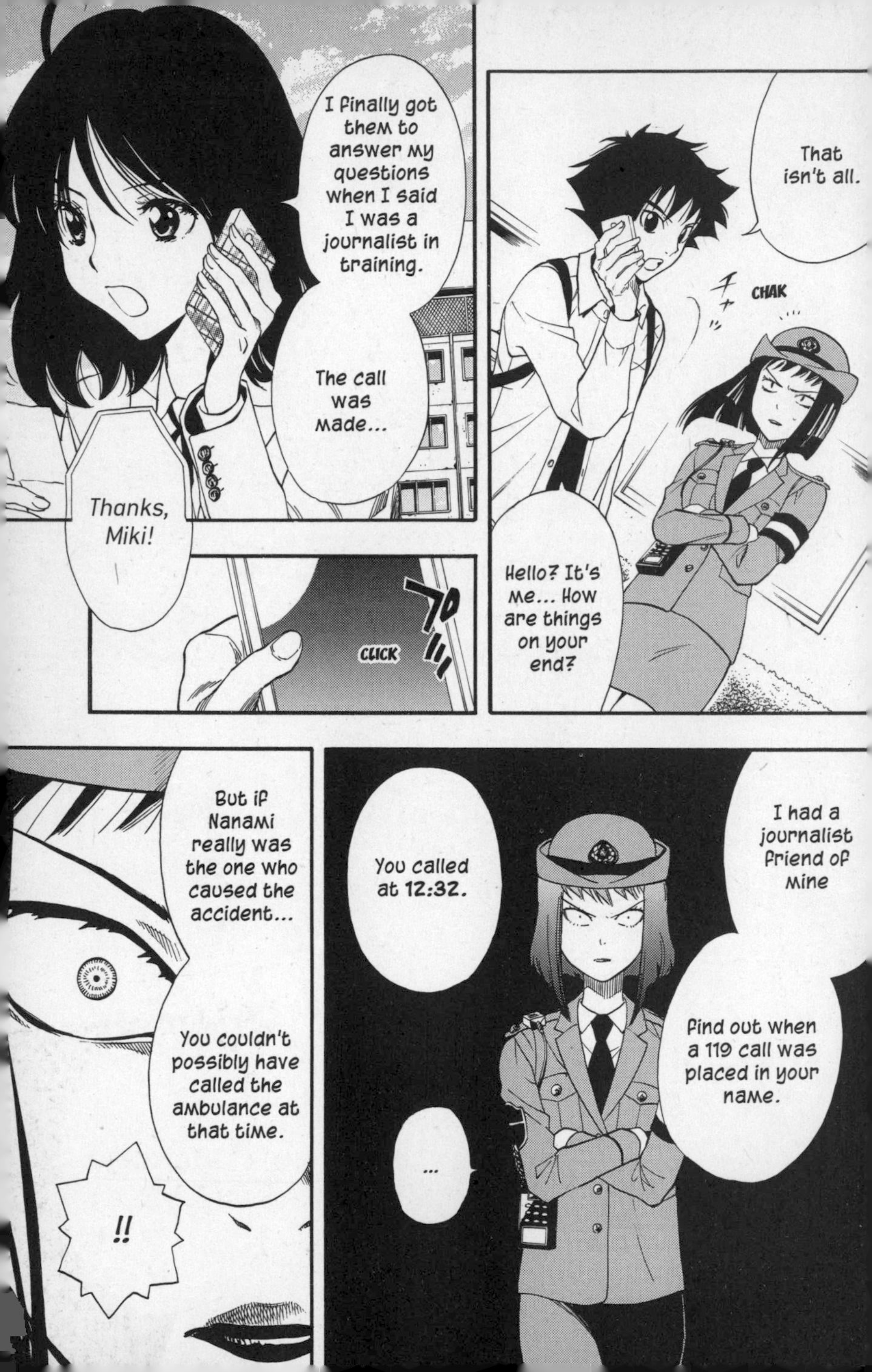
That isn't all.
CHAK
Hello? It's me... How are things on your end?
I finally got them to answer my questions when I said I was a journalist in training.
The call was made...
Thanks, Miki!
CLICK
I had a journalist friend of mine
find out when a 119 call was placed in your name.
You called at 12:32.
...
But if Nanami really was the one who caused the accident...
You couldn't possibly have called the ambulance at that time.
!!

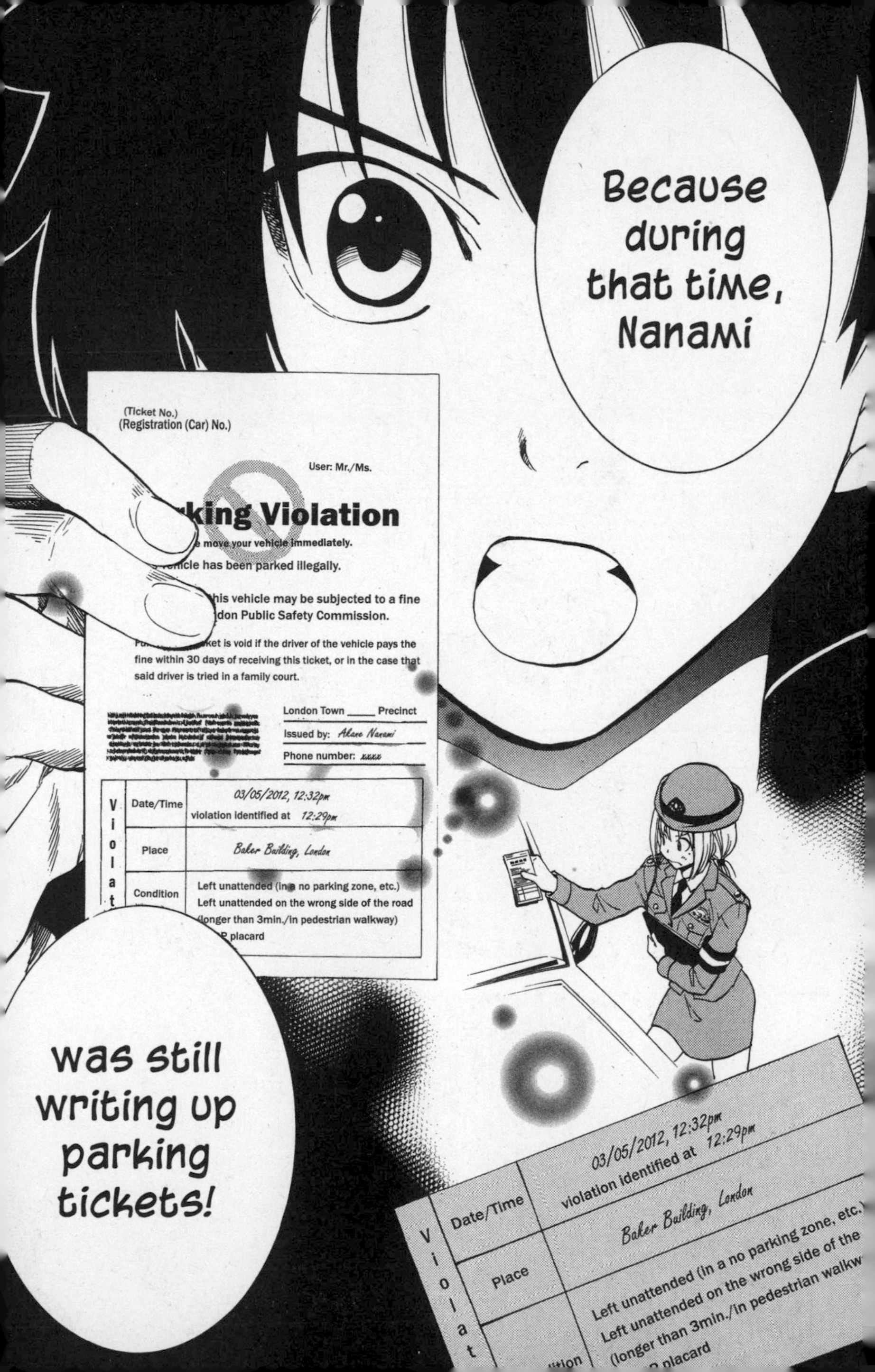
Because during that time, Nanami
(Ticket No.)
(Registration (Car) No.)
User: Mr./Ms.
king Violation
move your vehicle immediately.
vehicle has been parked illegally.
this vehicle may be subjected to a fine
don Public Safety Commission.
ket is void if the driver of the vehicle pays the
fine within 30 days of receiving this ticket, or in the case that
said driver is tried in a family court.
London Town _____ Precinct
Issued by: Akane Nanami
Phone number: xxxx
Date/Time
03/05/2012, 12:32pm
violation identified at 12:29pm
Place
Baker Building, London
Condition
Left unattended (in a no parking zone, etc.)
Left unattended on the wrong side of the road
(longer than 3min./in pedestrian walkway)
placard
was still writing up parking tickets!
Date/Time
03/05/2012, 12:32pm
violation identified at 12:29pm
Place
Baker Building, London
Left unattended (in a no parking zone, etc.)
Left unattended on the wrong side of the
(longer than 3min./in pedestrian walkw
placard

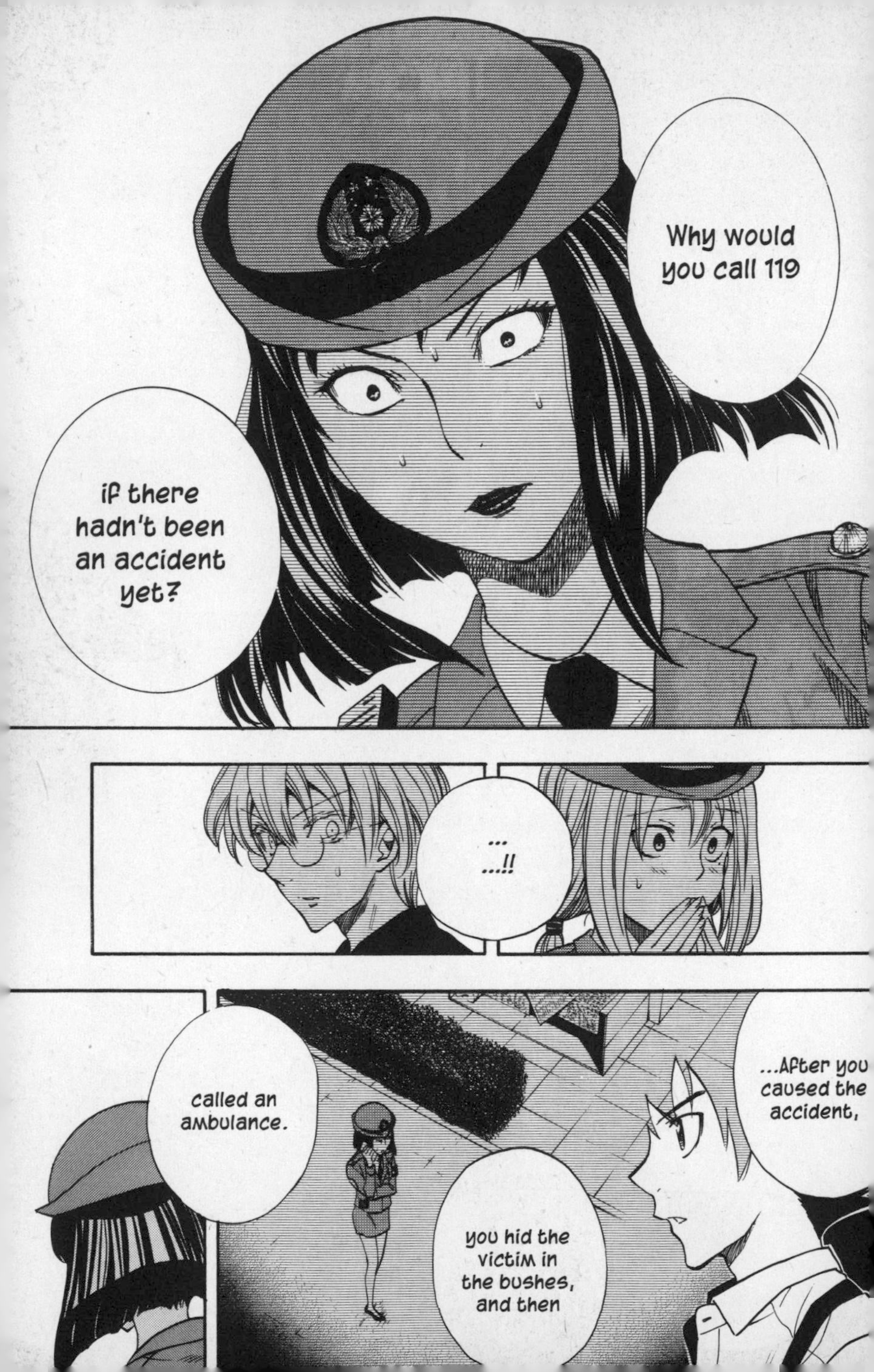
Why would you call 119
if there hadn't been an accident yet?
... ...!!
...After you caused the accident,
you hid the victim in the bushes, and then
called an ambulance.

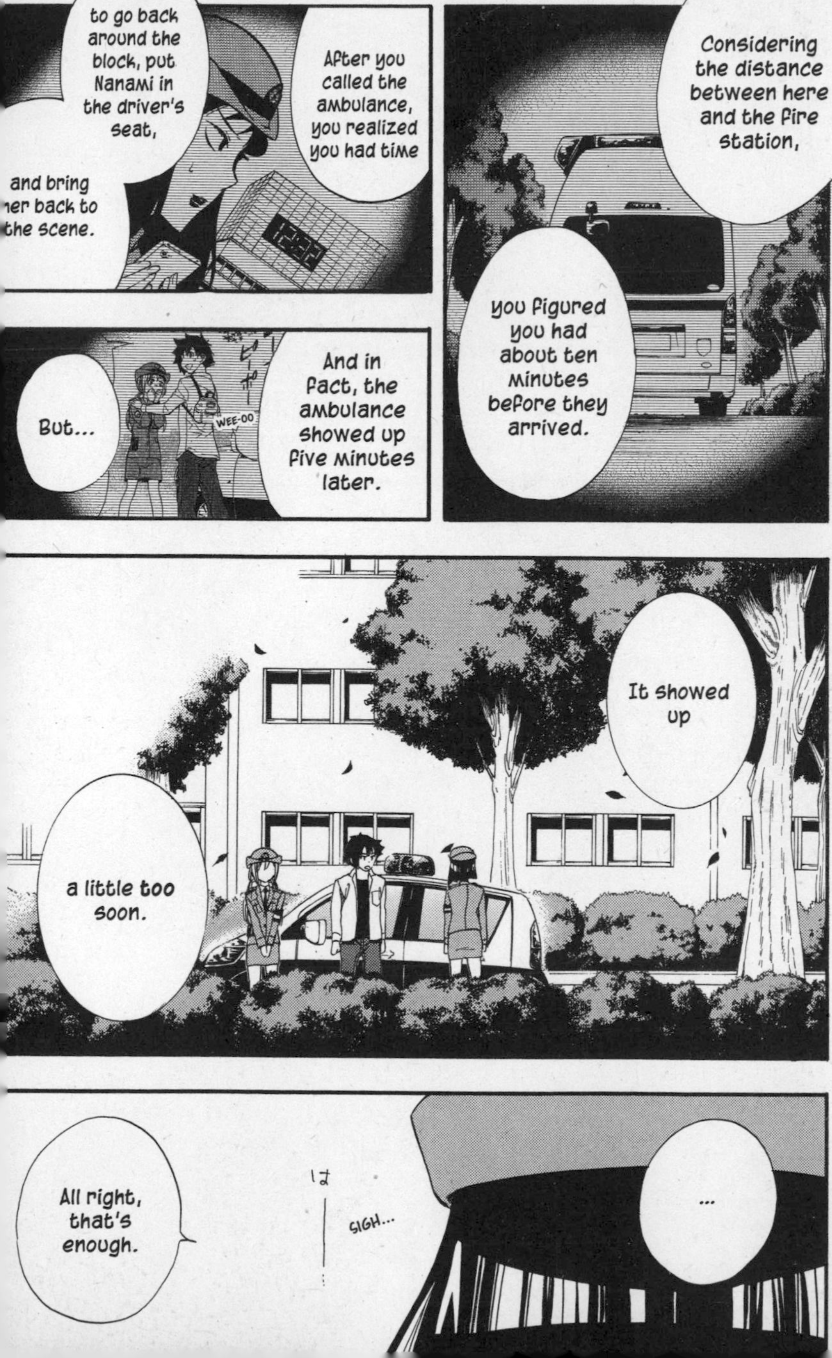
Considering the distance between here and the fire station,
you figured you had about ten minutes before they arrived.
After you called the ambulance, you realized you had time
to go back around the block, put Nanami in the driver's seat,
and bring her back to the scene.
And in fact, the ambulance showed up five minutes later.
WEE-OO
But...
It showed up
a little too soon.
...
SIGH...
All right, that's enough.

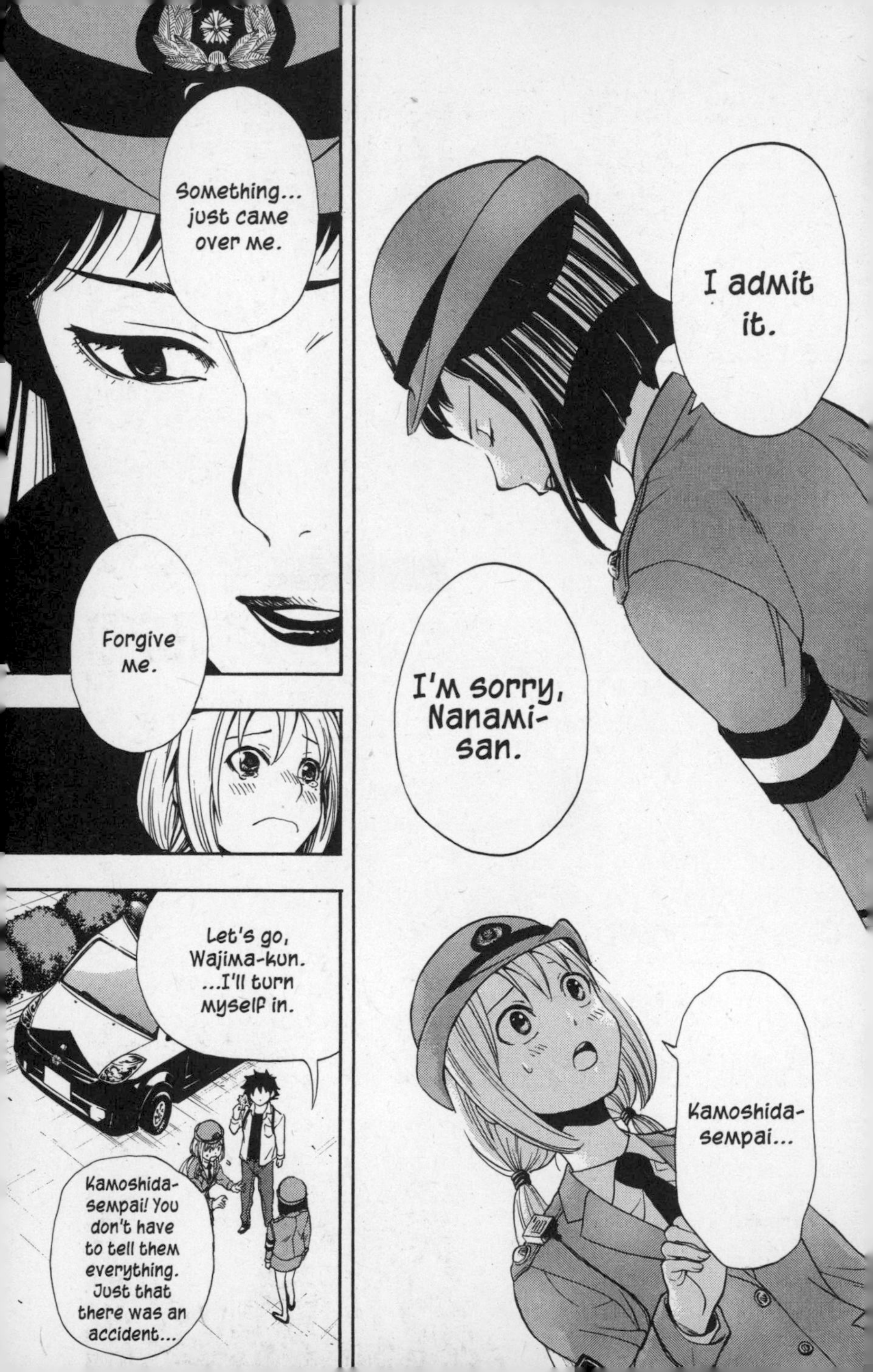
I admit it.
I'm sorry, Nanami-san.
Kamoshida-sempai...
Something... just came over me.
Forgive me.
Let's go, Wajima-kun. ...I'll turn myself in.
Kamoshida-sempai! You don't have to tell them everything. Just that there was an accident...

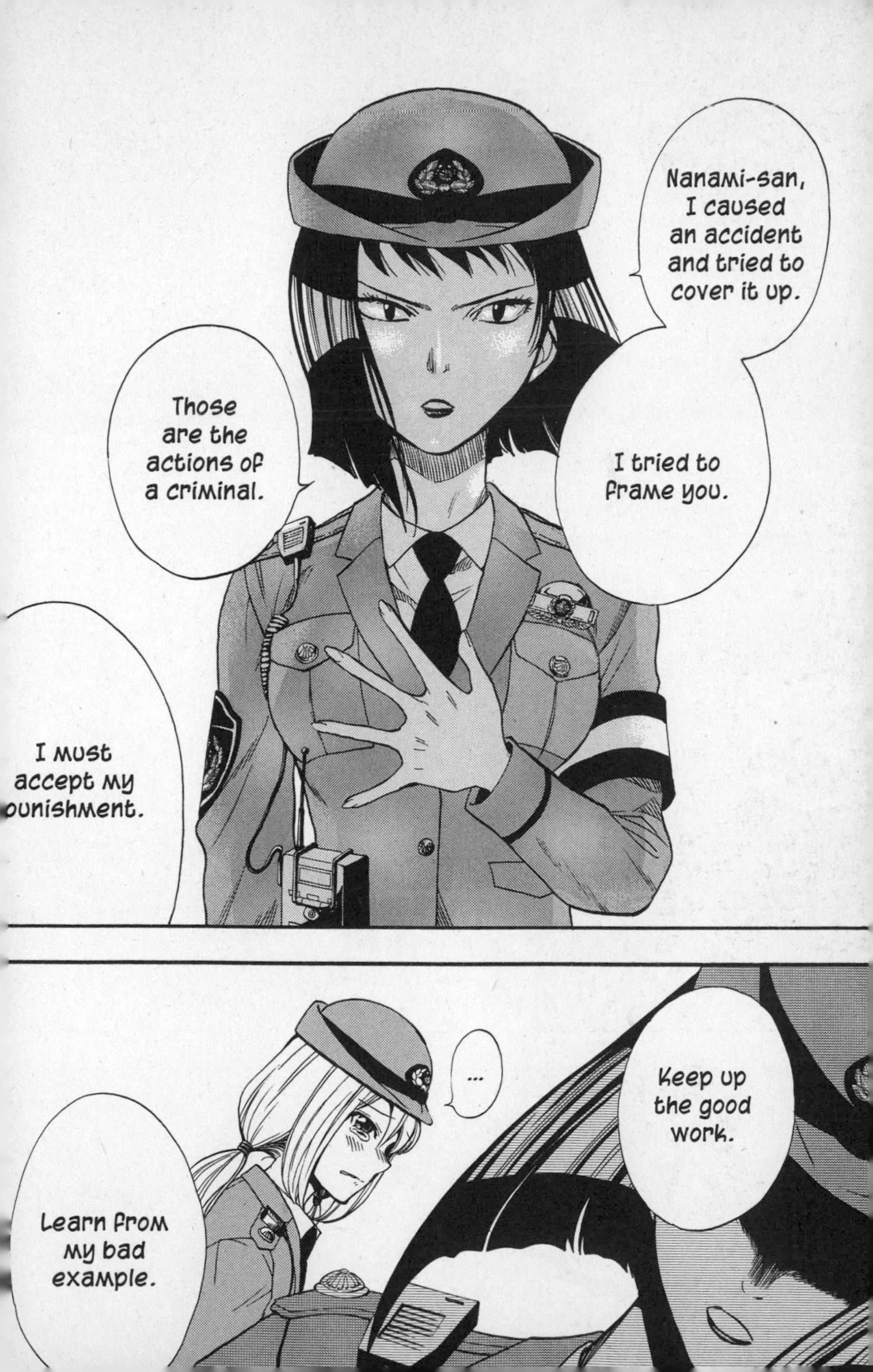
Nanami-san, I caused an accident and tried to cover it up.
I tried to frame you.
Those are the actions of a criminal.
I must accept my punishment.
Keep up the good work.
...
Learn from my bad example.

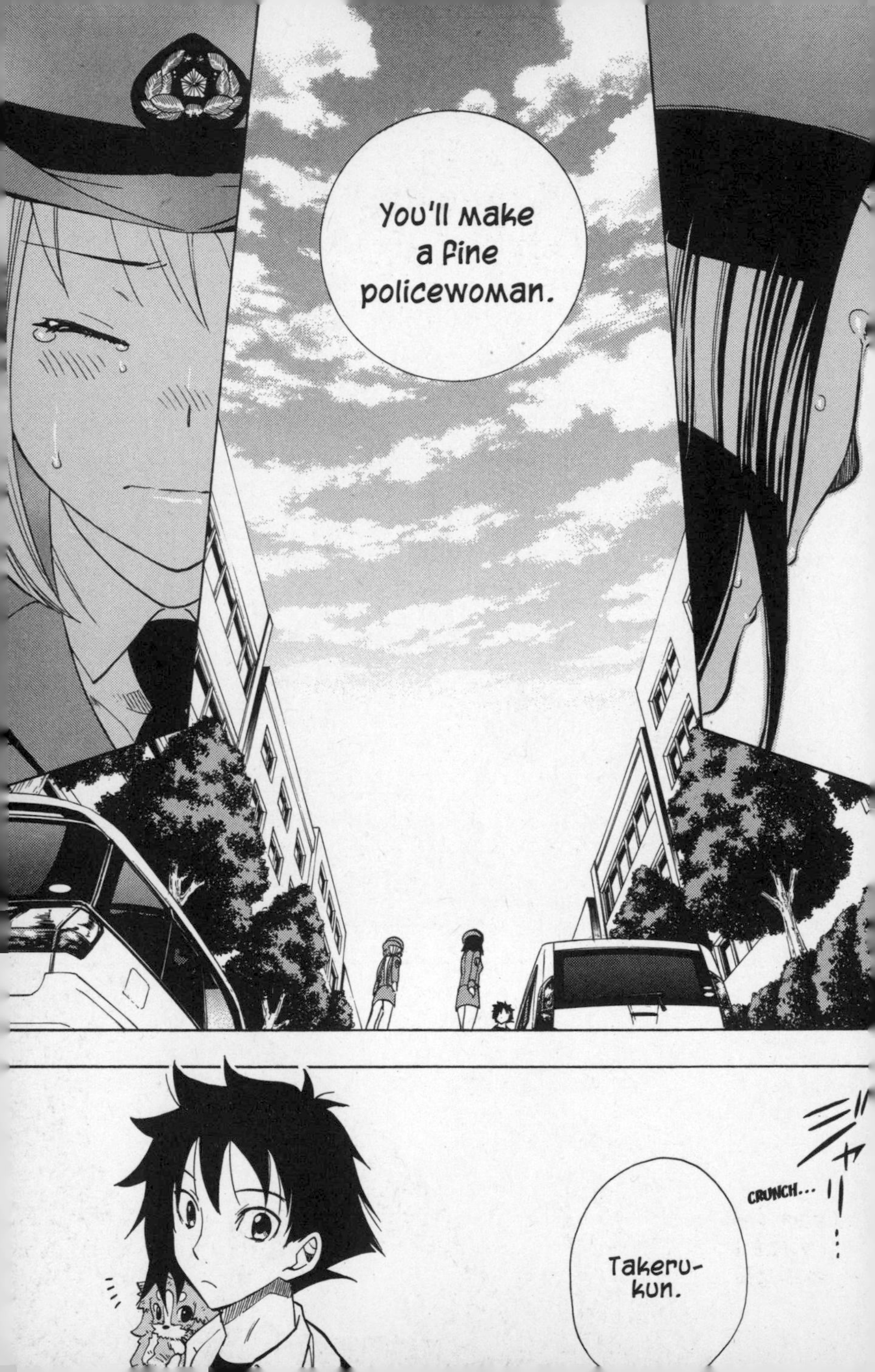
You'll make a fine policewoman.
CRUNCH...
Takeru-kun.

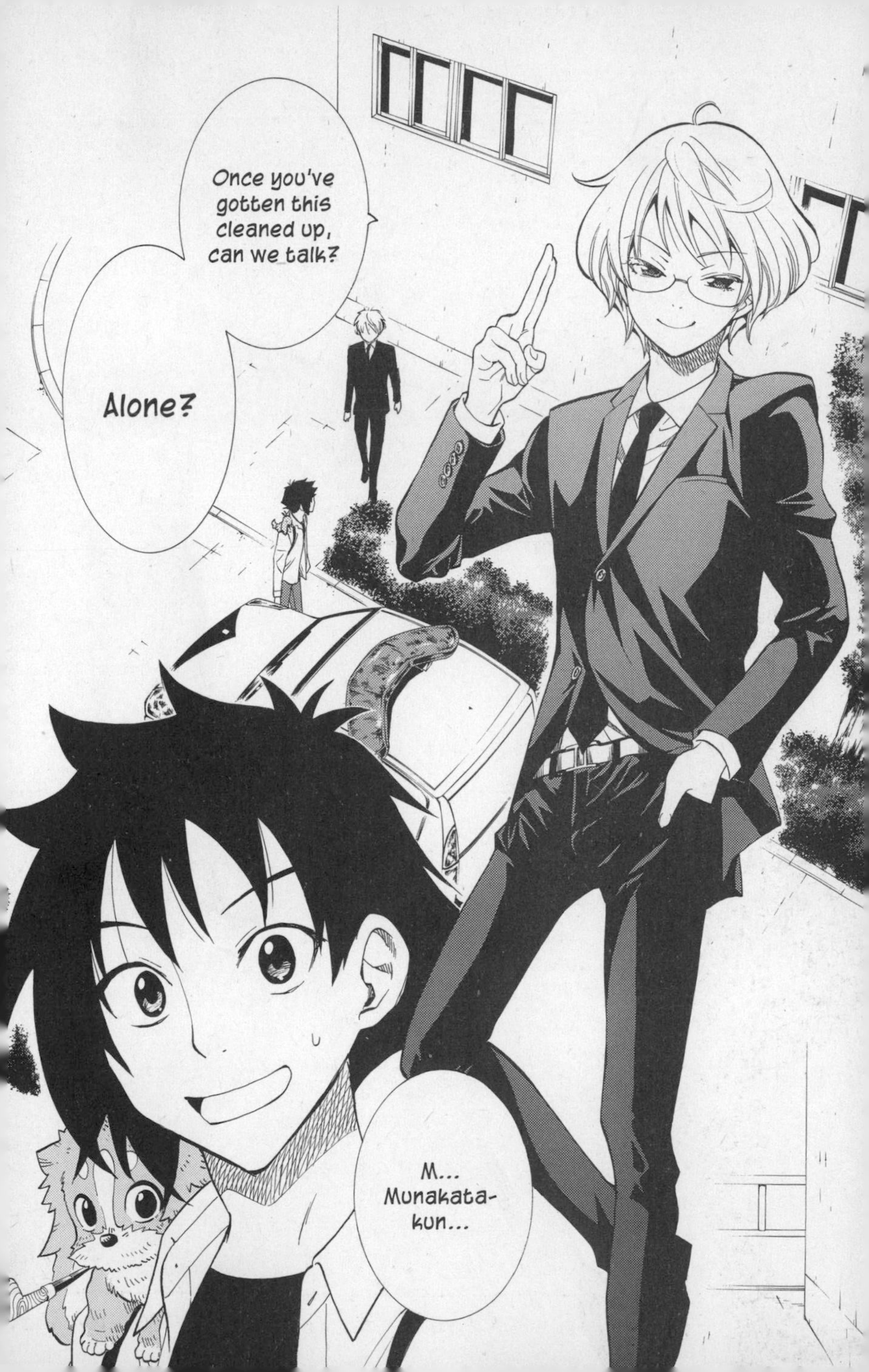
Once you've gotten this cleaned up, can we talk?
Alone?
M... Munakata-kun...

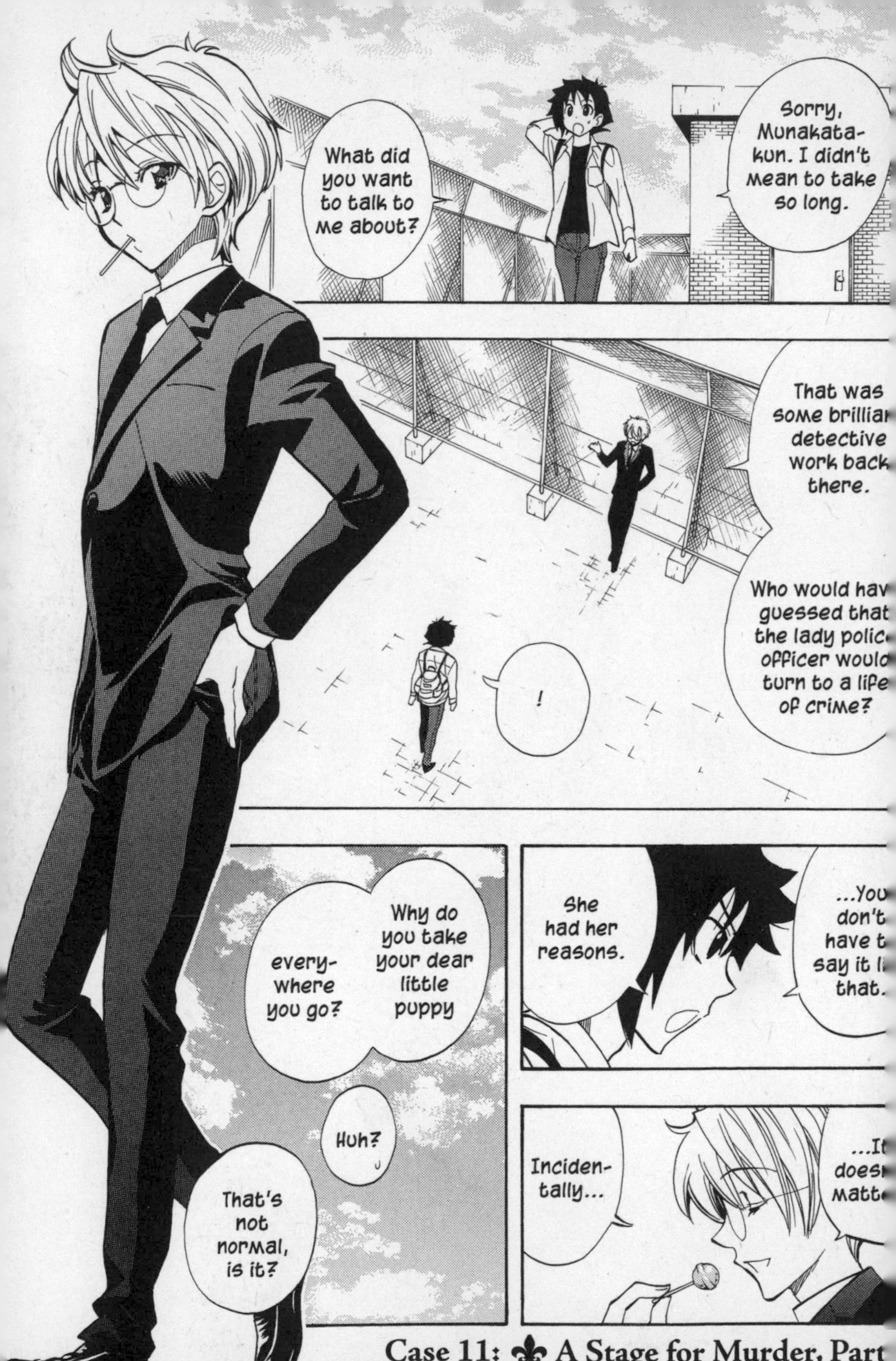
Sorry, Munakata-kun. I didn't mean to take so long.
What did you want to talk to me about?
That was some brillia detective work back there.
Who would hav guessed that the lady polic officer would turn to a life of crime?
!
...You don't have t say it l that.
She had her reasons.
...It doesr matte
Incidentally...
Why do you take your dear little puppy everywhere you go?
Huh?
That's not normal, is it?

Case 11: ⚜ A Stage for Murder, Part

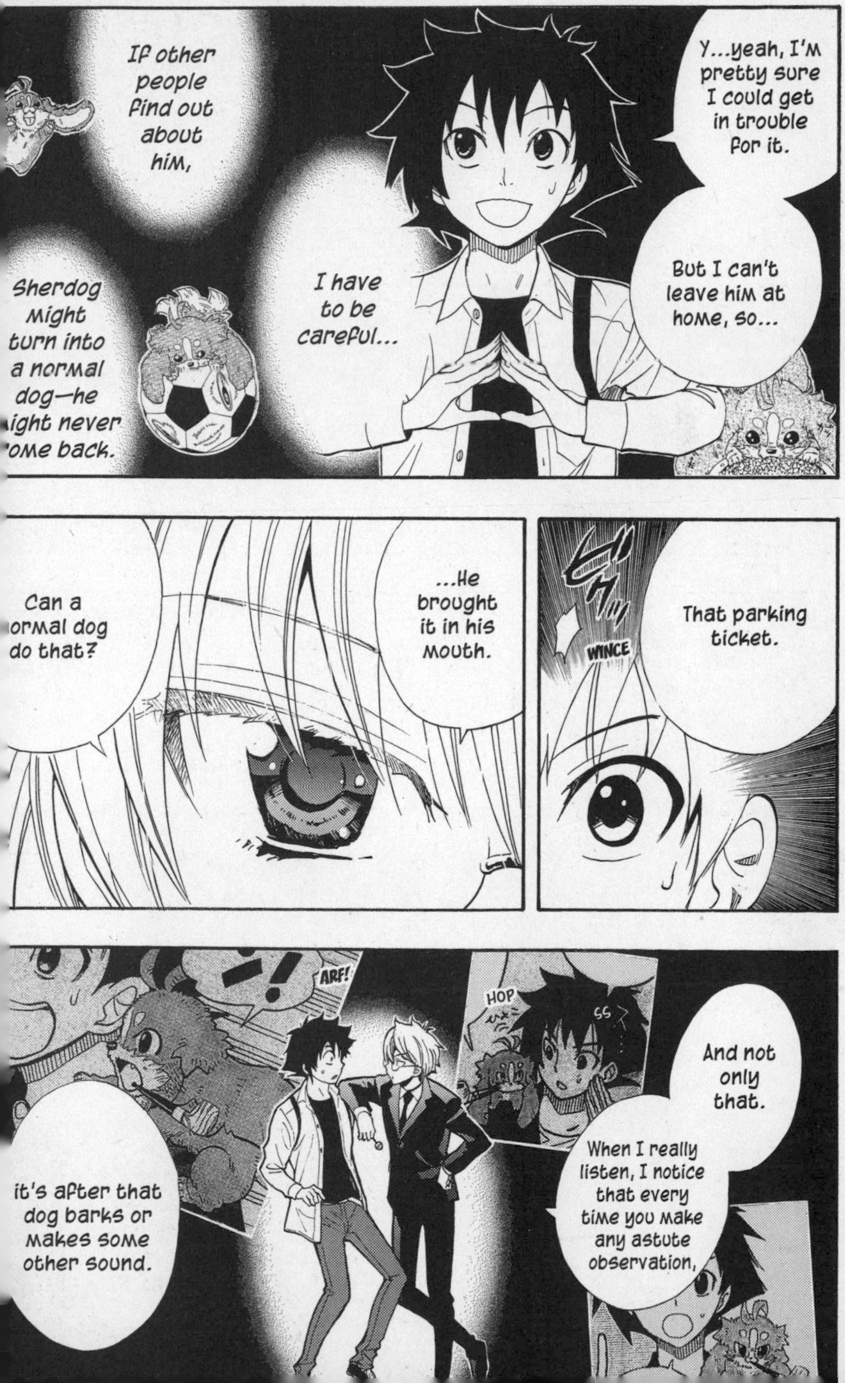
Y...yeah, I'm pretty sure I could get in trouble for it.
But I can't leave him at home, so...
I have to be careful...
If other people find out about him,
Sherdog might turn into a normal dog—he ight never ome back.
That parking ticket.
WINCE
...He brought it in his mouth.
Can a ormal dog do that?
ARF!
HOP
SS
And not only that.
When I really listen, I notice that every time you make any astute observation,
it's after that dog barks or makes some other sound.

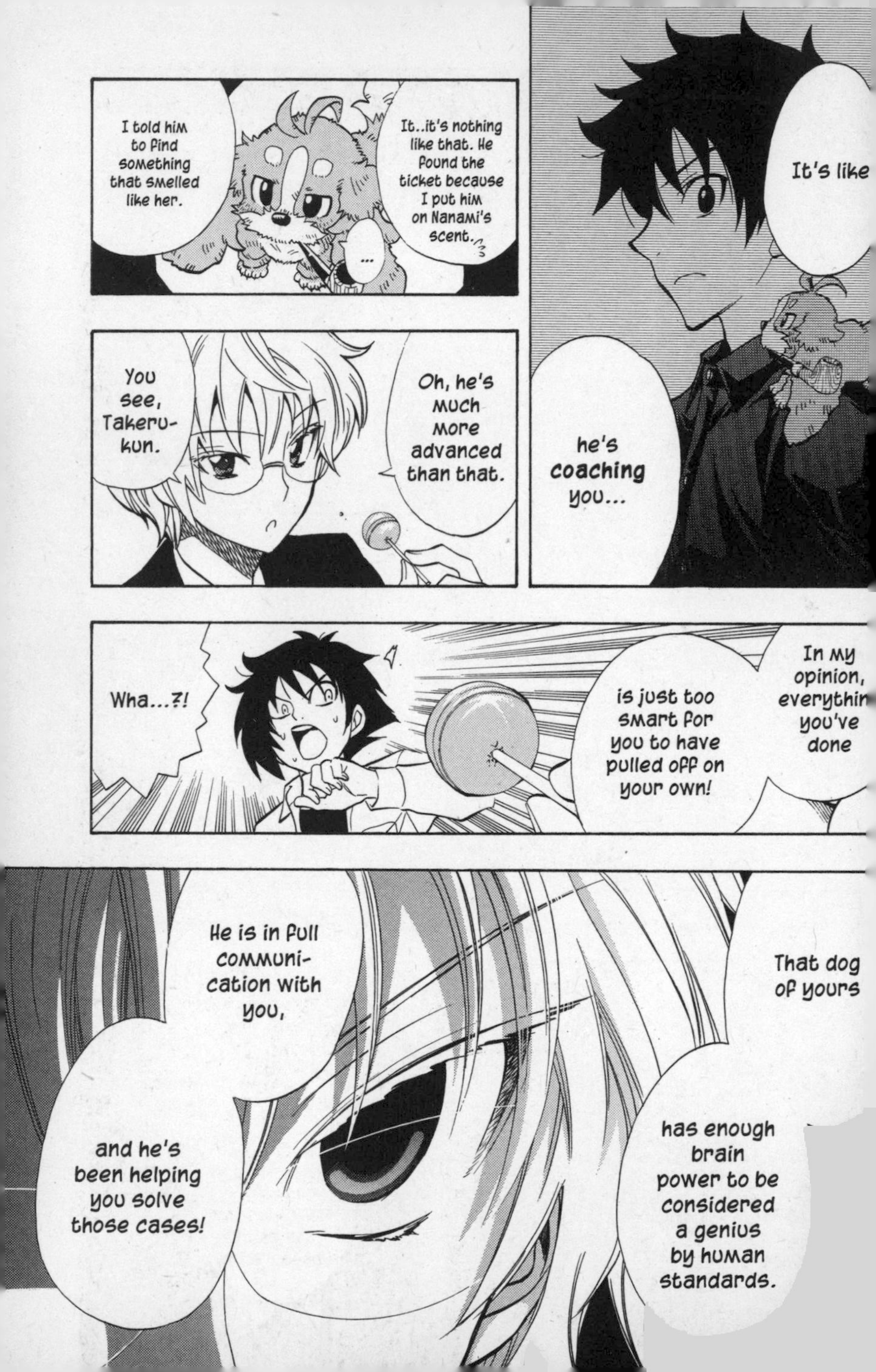
It's like
he's coaching you...
It..it's nothing like that. He found the ticket because I put him on Nanami's scent.
...
I told him to find something that smelled like her.
Oh, he's much more advanced than that.
You see, Takeru-kun.
In my opinion, everythin you've done
is just too smart for you to have pulled off on your own!
Wha...?!
That dog of yours
has enough brain power to be considered a genius by human standards.
He is in full communi-cation with you,
and he's been helping you solve those cases!

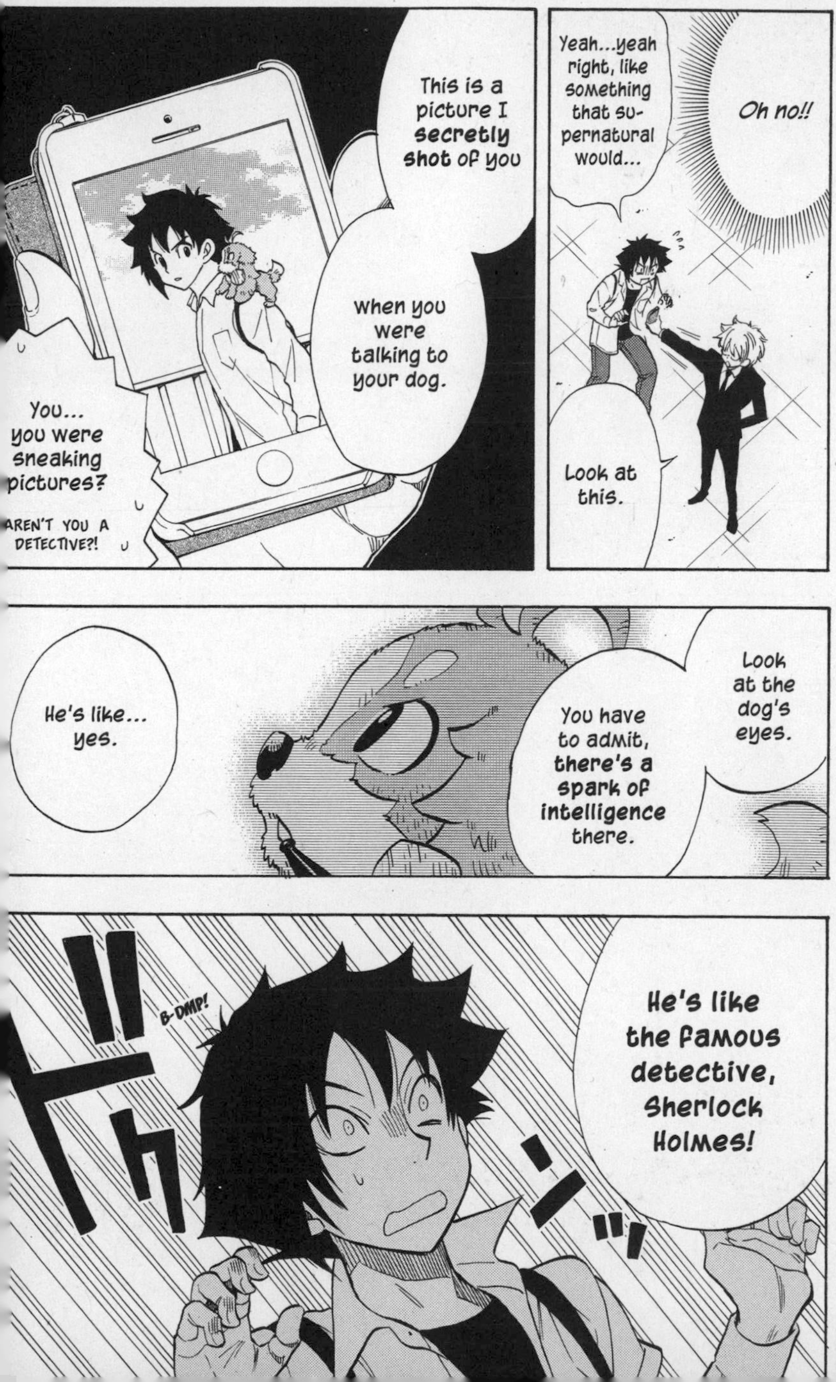
Yeah...yeah right, like something that su-pernatural would...
Oh no!!
Look at this.
This is a picture I **secretly shot** of you
when you were talking to your dog.
You... you were sneaking pictures?
AREN'T YOU A DETECTIVE?!
Look at the dog's eyes.
You have to admit, **there's a spark of intelligence** there.
He's like... yes.
He's like the famous detective, Sherlock Holmes!
B-DMP!

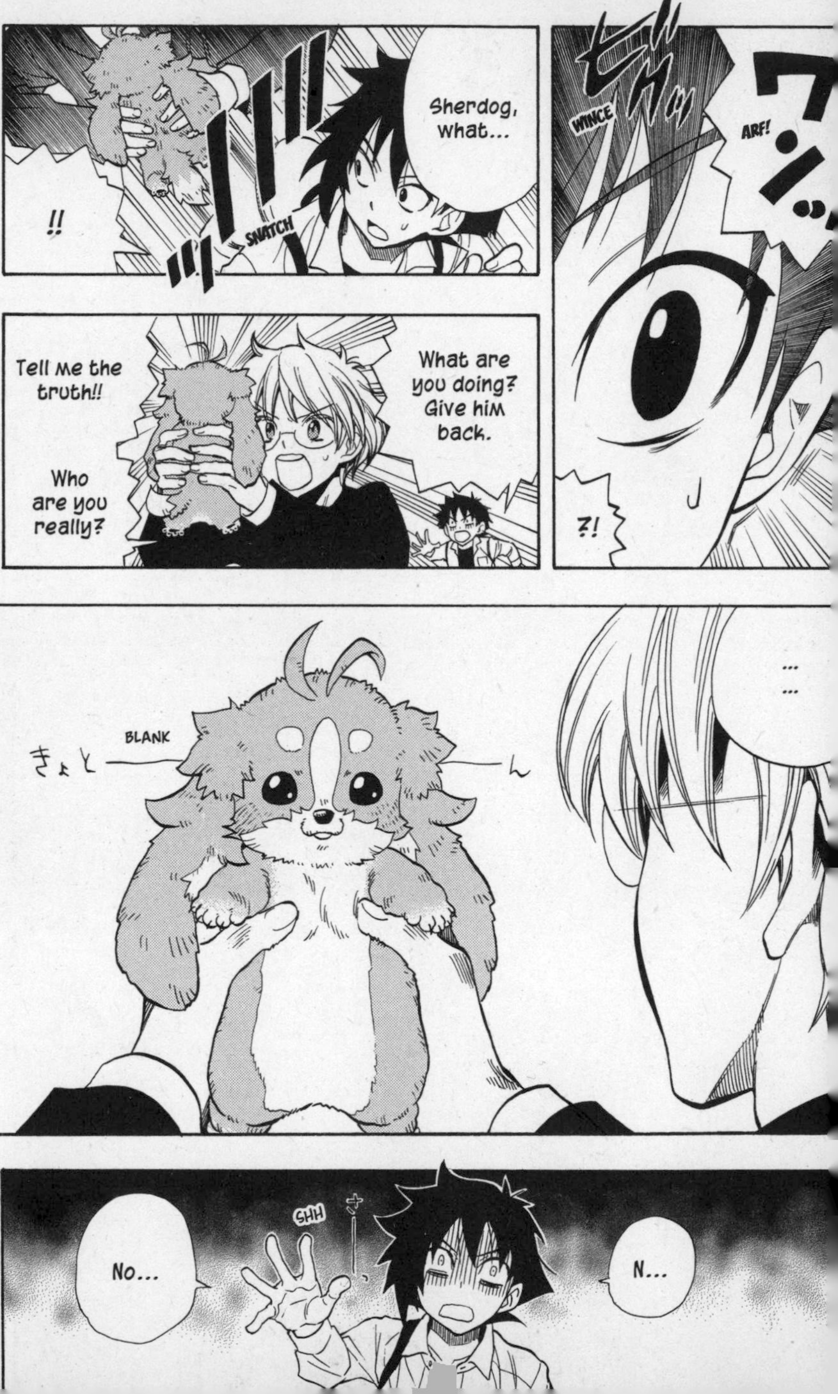WINCE
ARF!
?!
Sherdog, what...
SNATCH
!!
What are you doing? Give him back.
Tell me the truth!!
Who are you really?
...
...
BLANK
きょと
ん
N...
SHH
No...

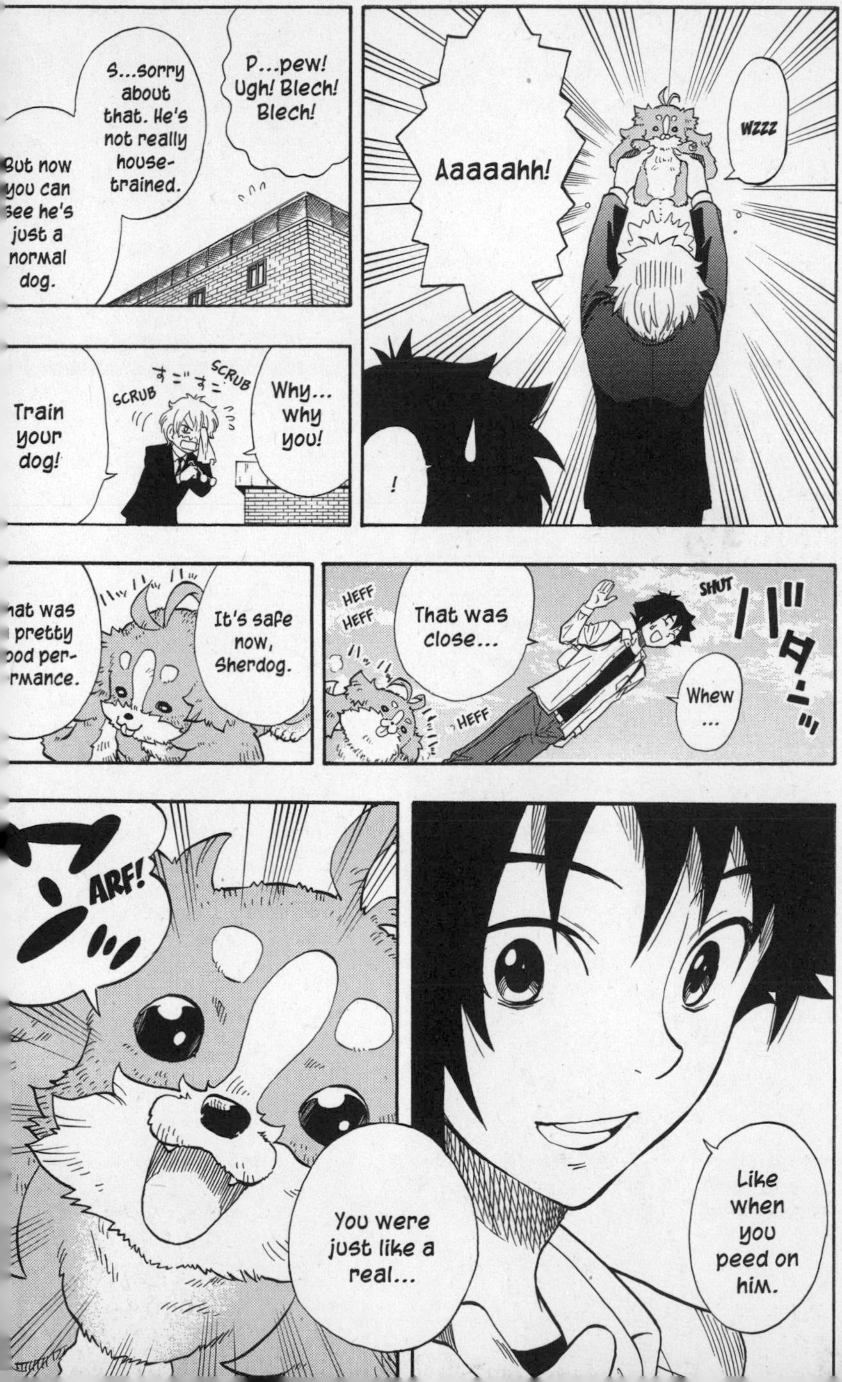
WZZZ
Aaaaahh!
!
P...pew! Ugh! Blech! Blech!
S...sorry about that. He's not really house-trained.
But now you can see he's just a normal dog.
Why... why you!
SCRUB すごすご SCRUB
Train your dog!
SHUT バタ
Whew ...
That was close...
HEFF HEFF
HEFF
It's safe now, Sherdog.
hat was pretty ood per-rmance.
Like when you peed on him.
You were just like a real...
ARF!

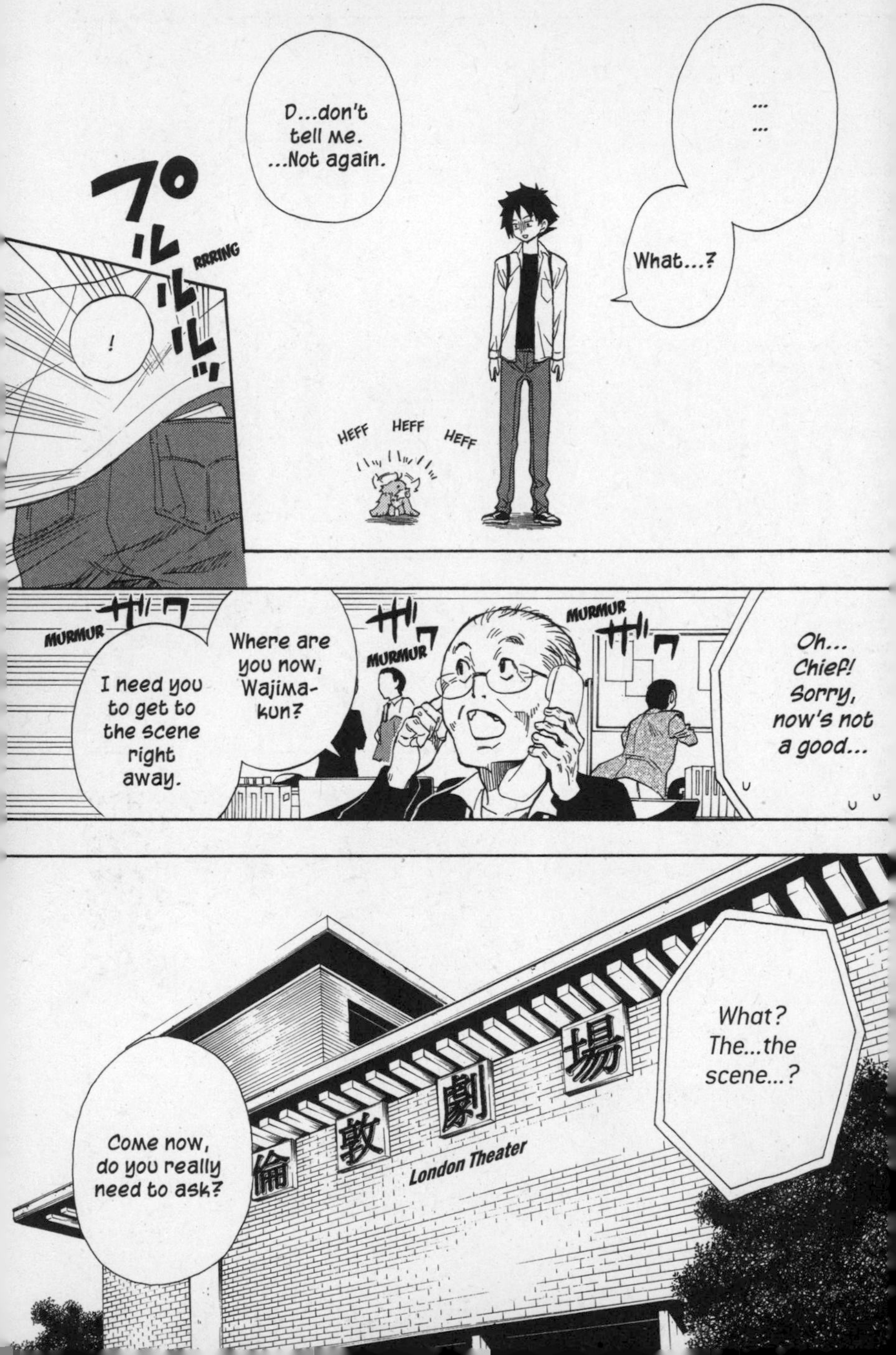

...
...
What...?
D...don't tell me.
...Not again.
HEFF HEFF HEFF
プルルルッ
RRRING
!
Oh... Chief! Sorry, now's not a good...
ザワ
MURMUR
Where are you now, Wajima-kun?
ザワ
MURMUR
I need you to get to the scene right away.
ザワ
MURMUR
What? The...the scene...?
倫敦劇場
London Theater
Come now, do you really need to ask?

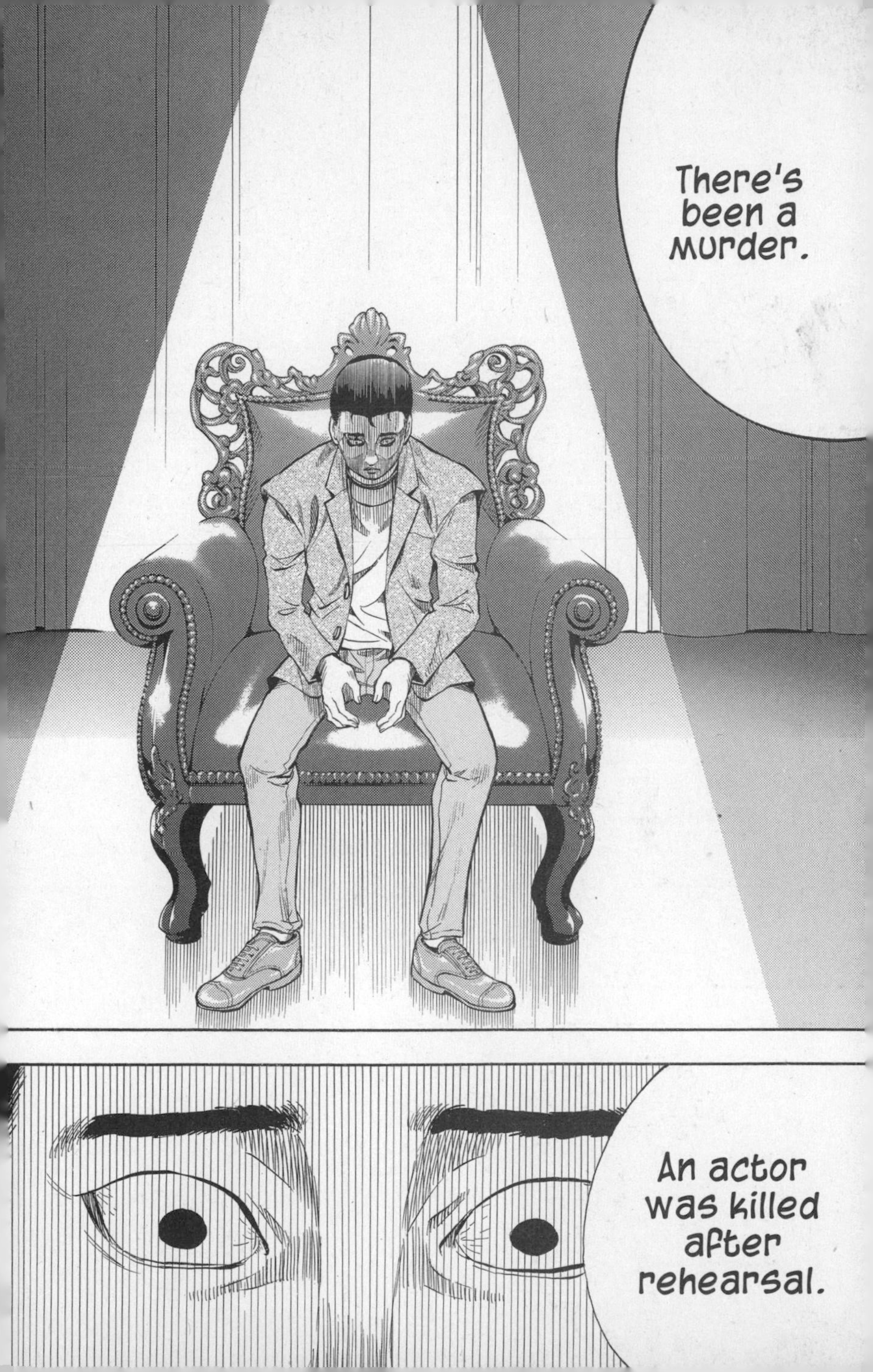
There's been a murder.
An actor was killed after rehearsal.

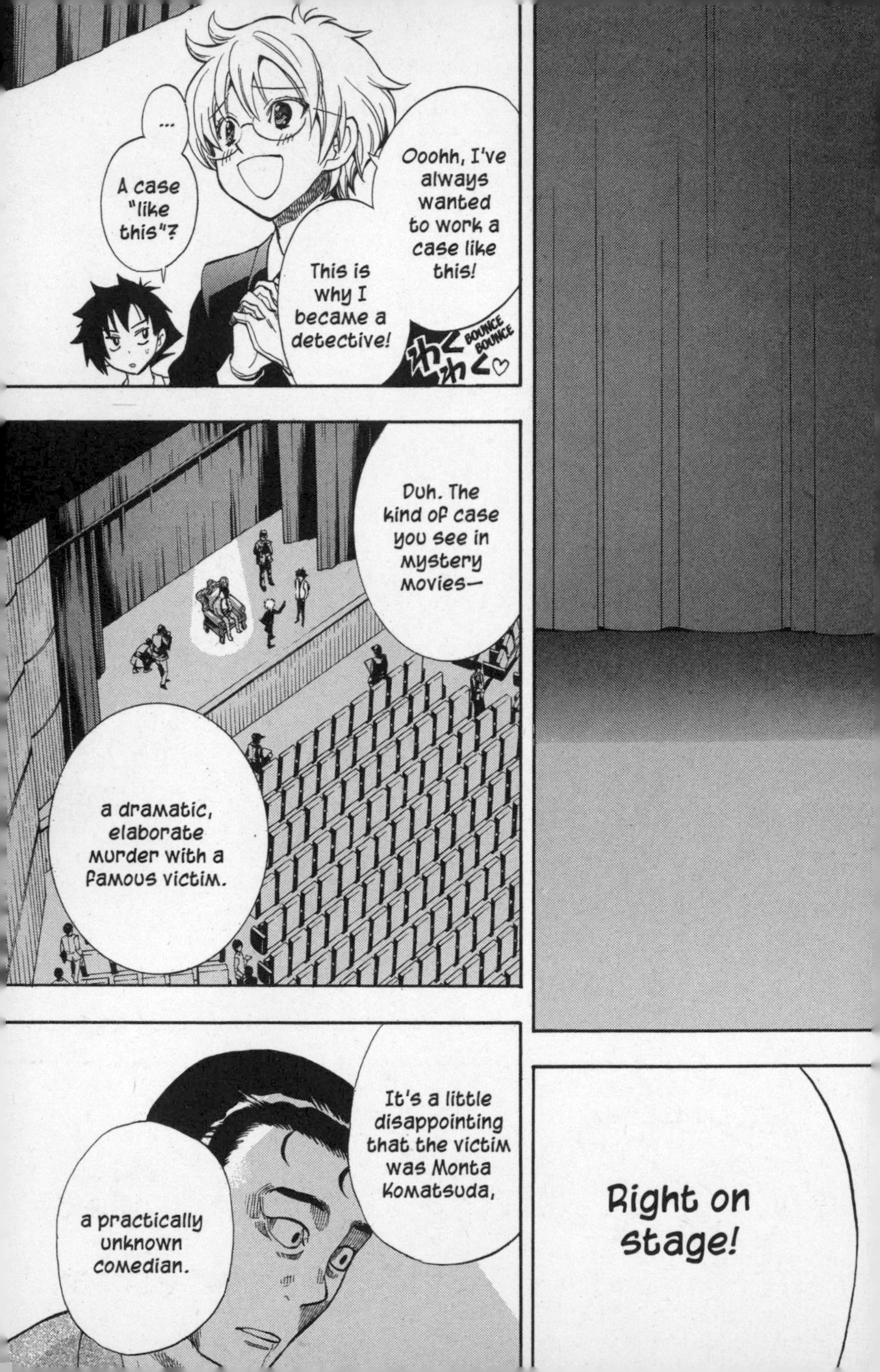
Right on stage!
Ooohh, I've always wanted to work a case like this!
This is why I became a detective!
BOUNCE BOUNCE
...
A case "like this"?
Duh. The kind of case you see in mystery movies—
a dramatic, elaborate murder with a famous victim.
It's a little disappointing that the victim was Monta Komatsuda,
a practically unknown comedian.

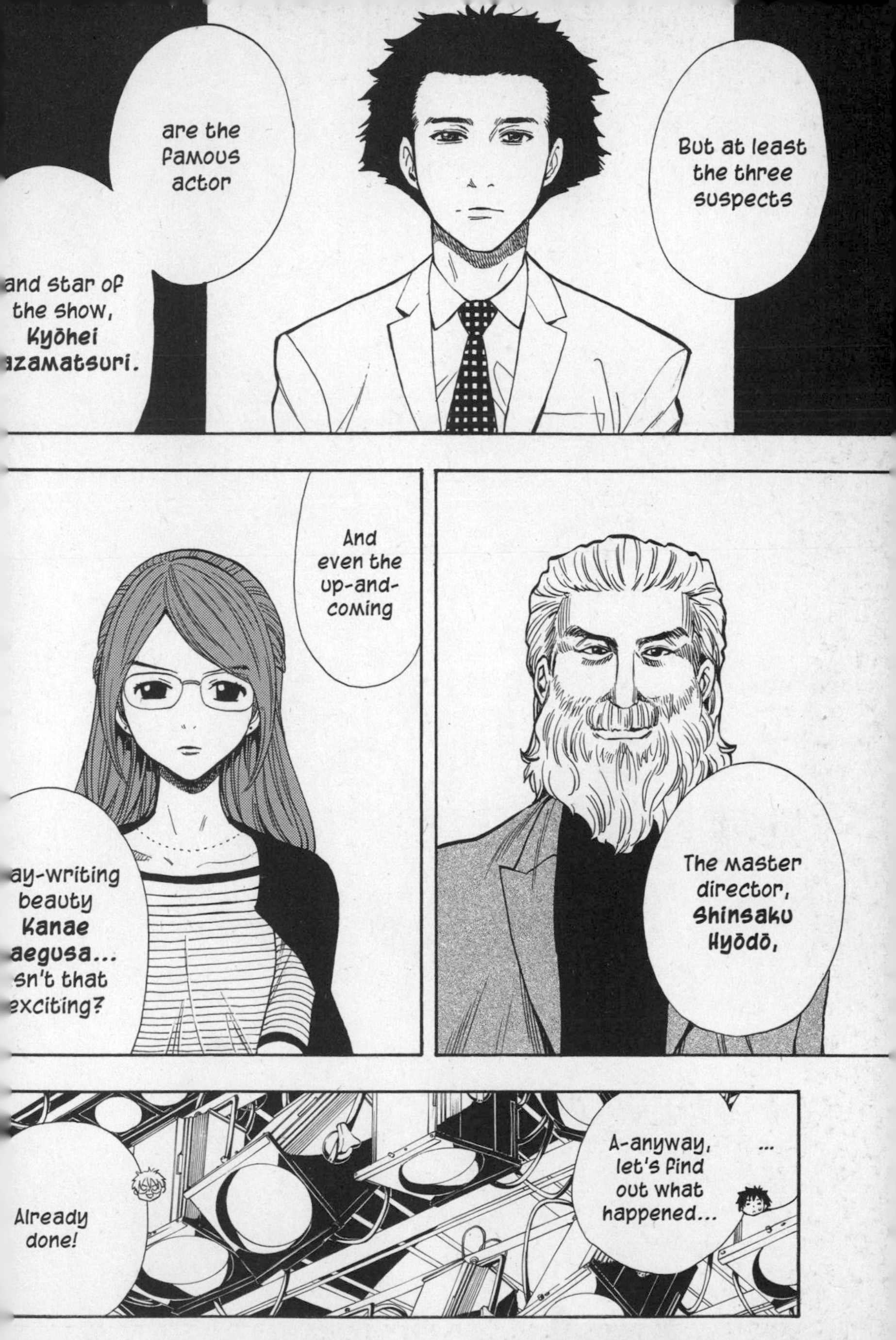
But at least the three suspects
are the famous actor
and star of the show, Kyōhei azamatsuri.
The master director, Shinsaku Hyōdō,
And even the up-and-coming
ay-writing beauty Kanae aegusa... sn't that exciting?
...
A-anyway, let's find out what happened...
Already done!

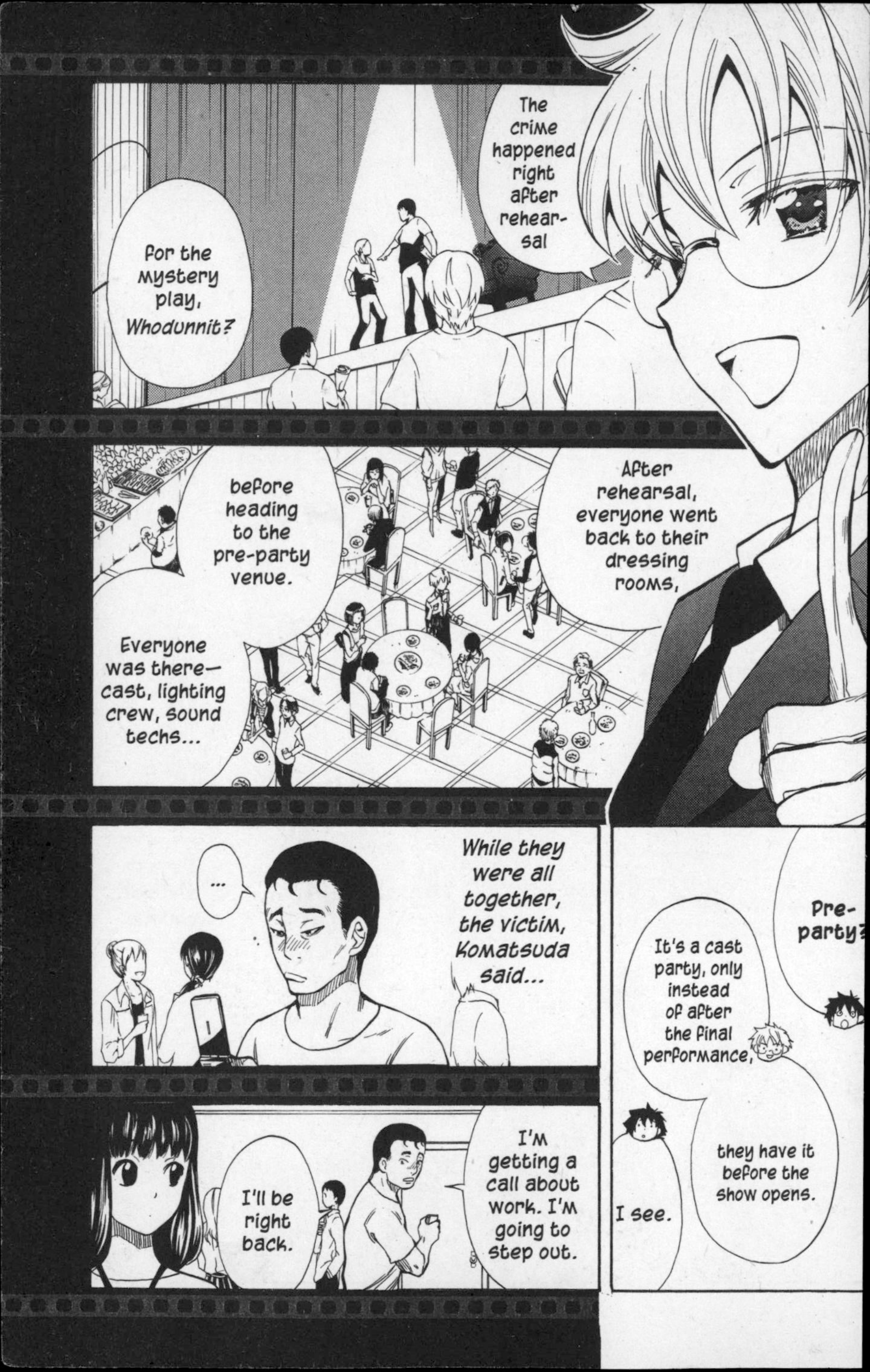
The crime happened right after rehear-sal
for the mystery play, Whodunnit?
After rehearsal, everyone went back to their dressing rooms,
before heading to the pre-party venue.
Everyone was there—cast, lighting crew, sound techs...
Pre-party?
It's a cast party, only instead of after the final performance,
they have it before the show opens.
I see.
While they were all together, the victim, Komatsuda said...
...
I'm getting a call about work. I'm going to step out.
I'll be right back.

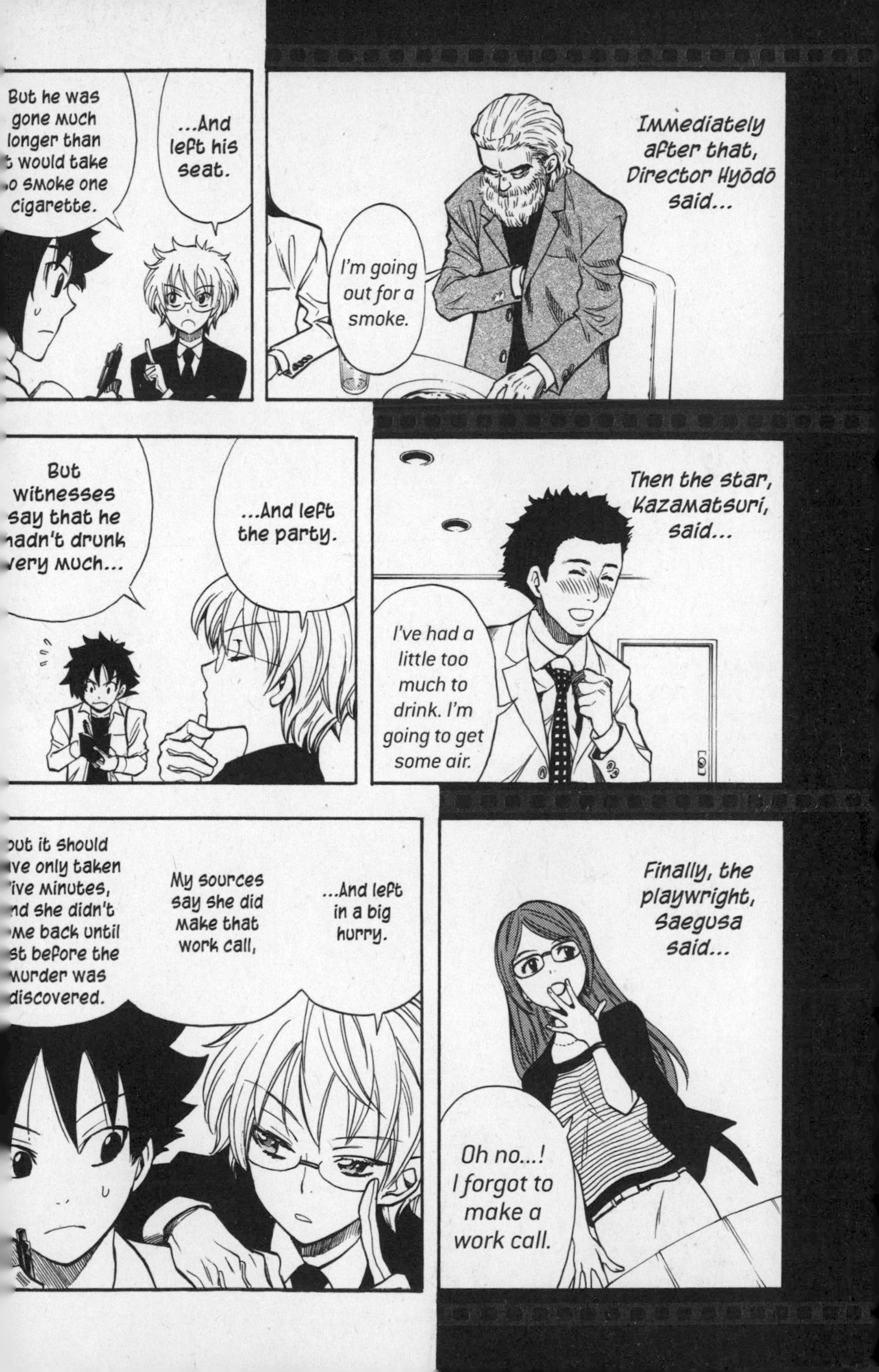
Immediately after that, Director Hyōdō said...
I'm going out for a smoke.
...And left his seat.
But he was gone much longer than t would take o smoke one cigarette.
Then the star, Kazamatsuri, said...
I've had a little too much to drink. I'm going to get some air.
...And left the party.
But witnesses say that he hadn't drunk very much...
Finally, the playwright, Saegusa said...
Oh no...! I forgot to make a work call.
...And left in a big hurry.
My sources say she did make that work call,
out it should ve only taken ive minutes, nd she didn't me back until st before the murder was discovered.

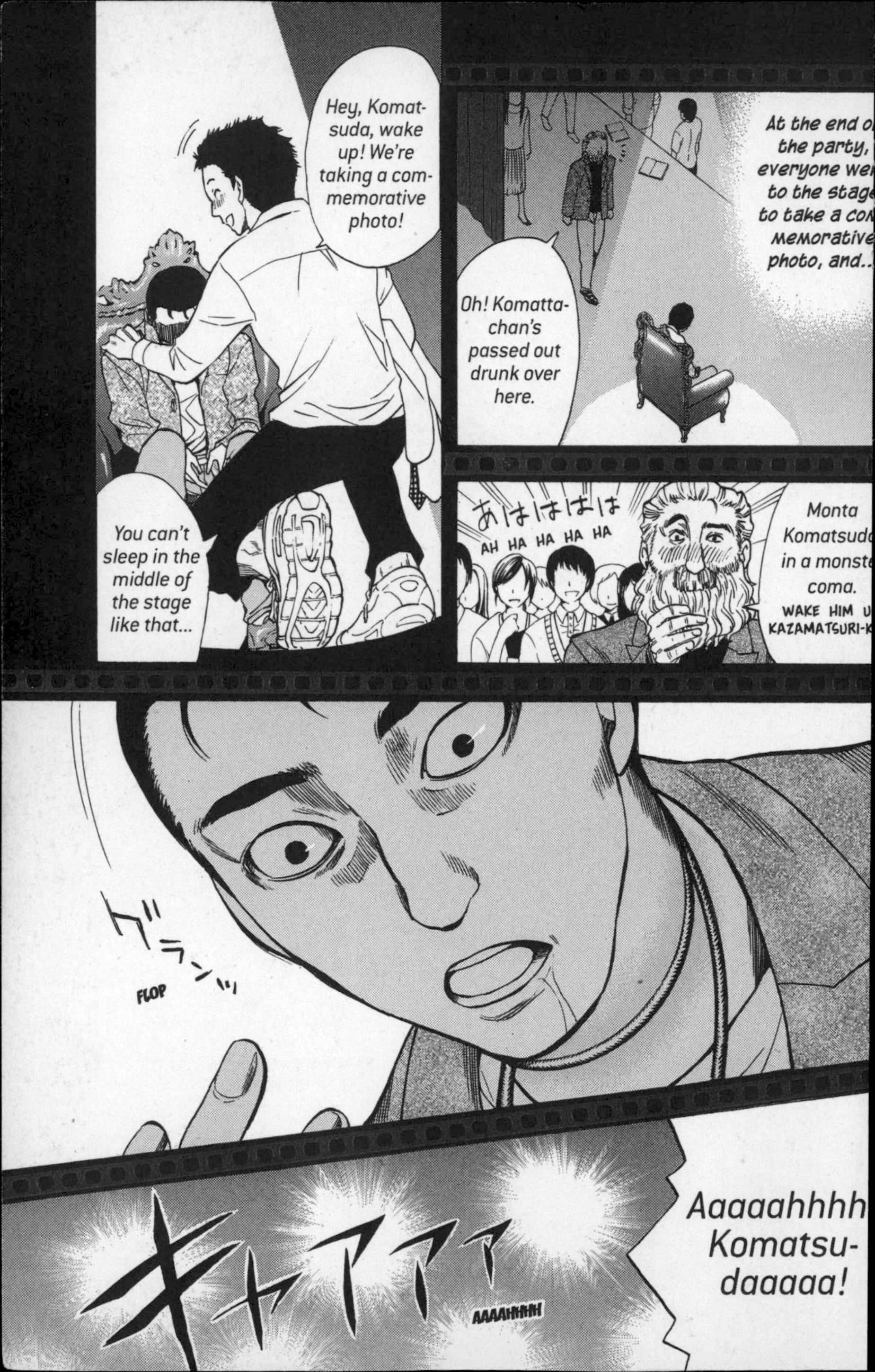
At the end o the party, everyone we to the stag to take a co memorative photo, and..
Oh! Komatta-chan's passed out drunk over here.
あはははは
AH HA HA HA HA
Monta Komatsud in a monst coma.
WAKE HIM U KAZAMATSURI-K
Hey, Komatsuda, wake up! We're taking a commemorative photo!
You can't sleep in the middle of the stage like that...
グランッ
FLOP
Aaaaahhhh Komatsu-daaaaaa!
キャアアア
AAAAHHHH

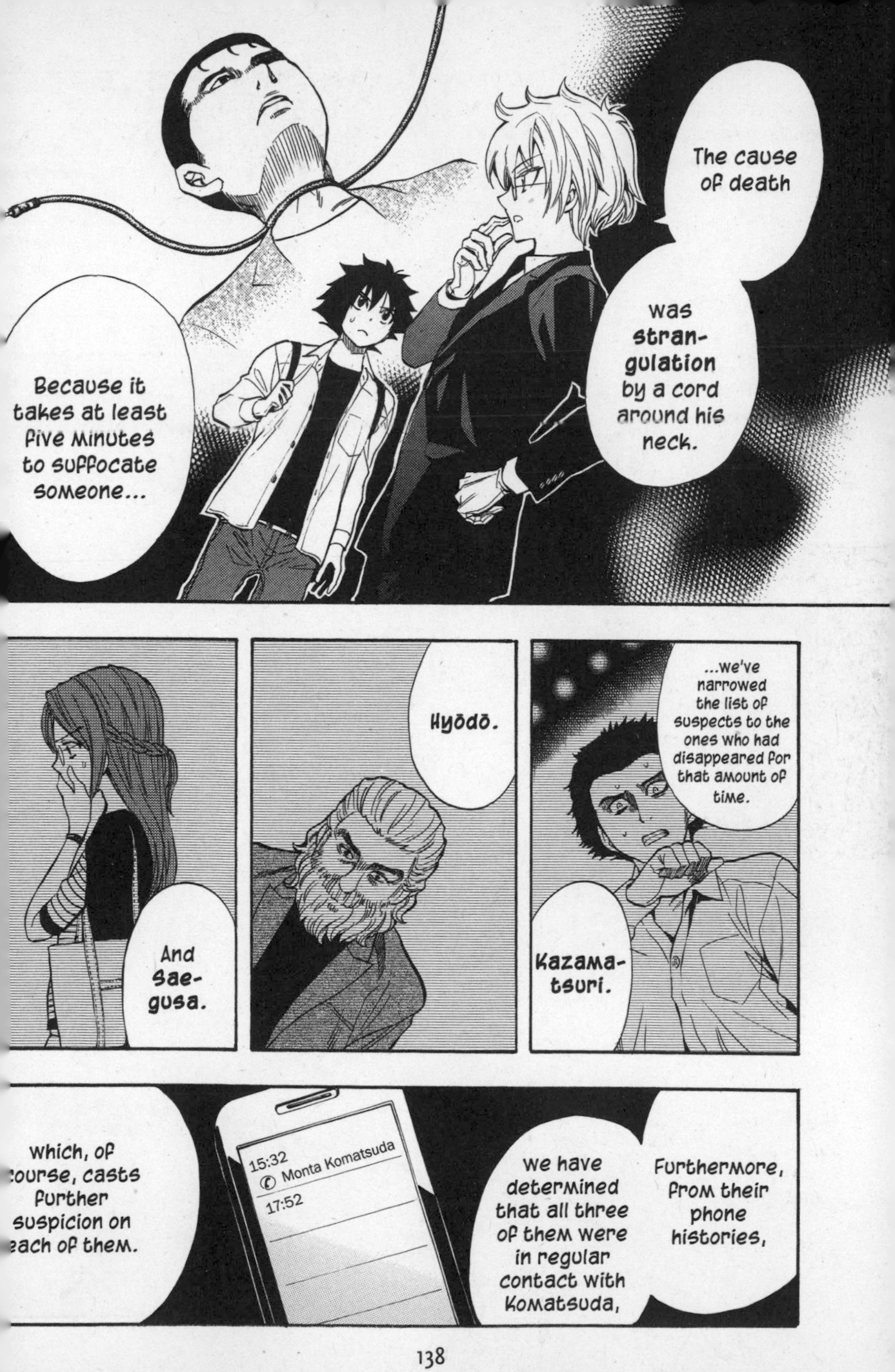
The cause of death
was strangulation by a cord around his neck.
Because it takes at least five minutes to suffocate someone...
...we've narrowed the list of suspects to the ones who had disappeared for that amount of time.
Kazamatsuri.
Hyōdō.
And Saegusa.
Furthermore, from their phone histories,
we have determined that all three of them were in regular contact with Komatsuda,
15:32
Monta Komatsuda
17:52
Which, of course, casts further suspicion on each of them.

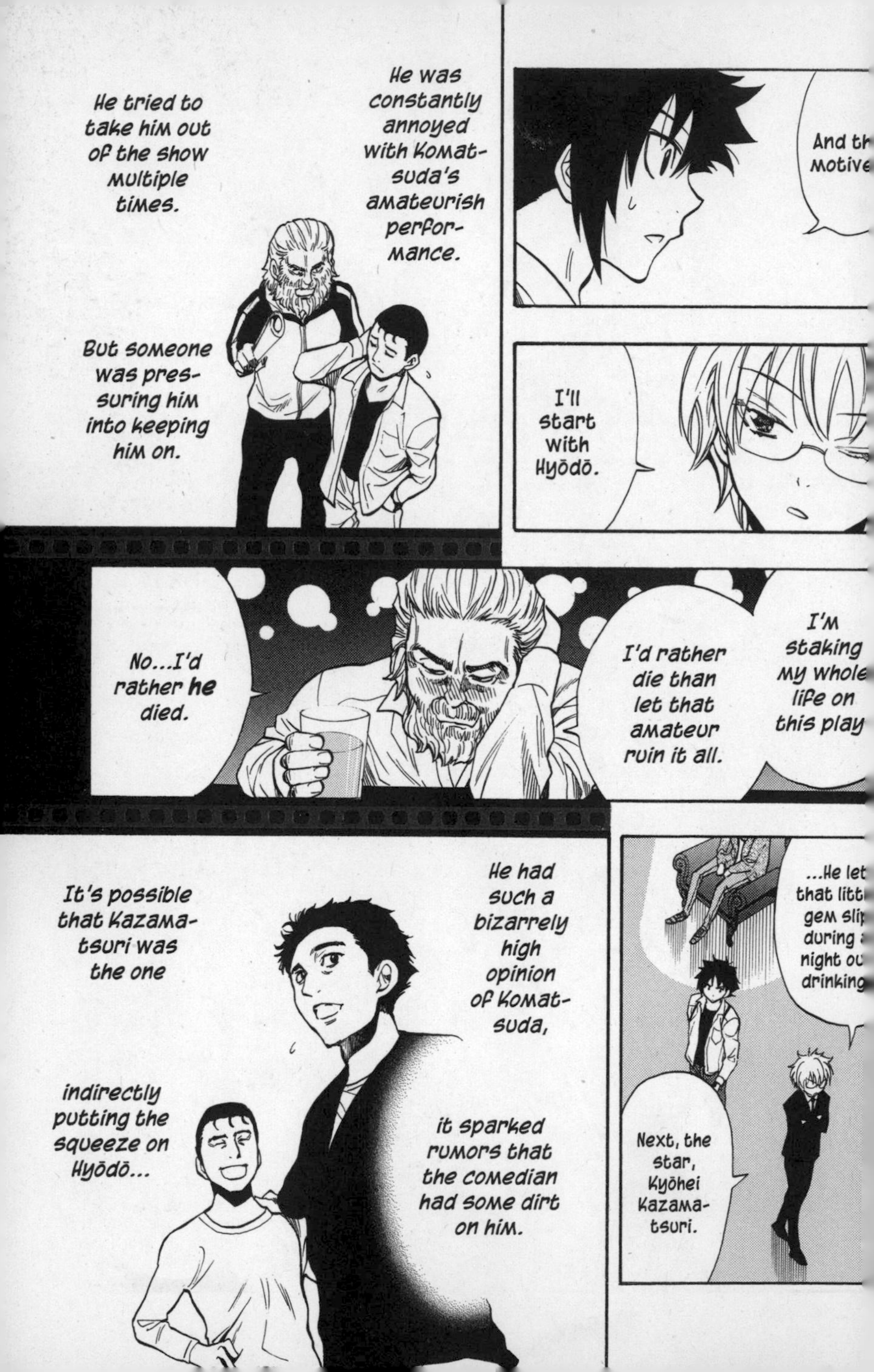
And th
motive
I'll start with Hyōdō.
He was constantly annoyed with Komat-suda's amateurish perfor-mance.
He tried to take him out of the show multiple times.
But someone was pres-suring him into keeping him on.
I'm staking my whole life on this play
I'd rather die than let that amateur ruin it all.
No...I'd rather he died.
...He let that litt gem sli during night ou drinking
Next, the star, Kyōhei Kazama-tsuri.
He had such a bizarrely high opinion of Komat-suda,
It's possible that Kazama-tsuri was the one
it sparked rumors that the comedian had some dirt on him.
indirectly putting the squeeze on Hyōdō...

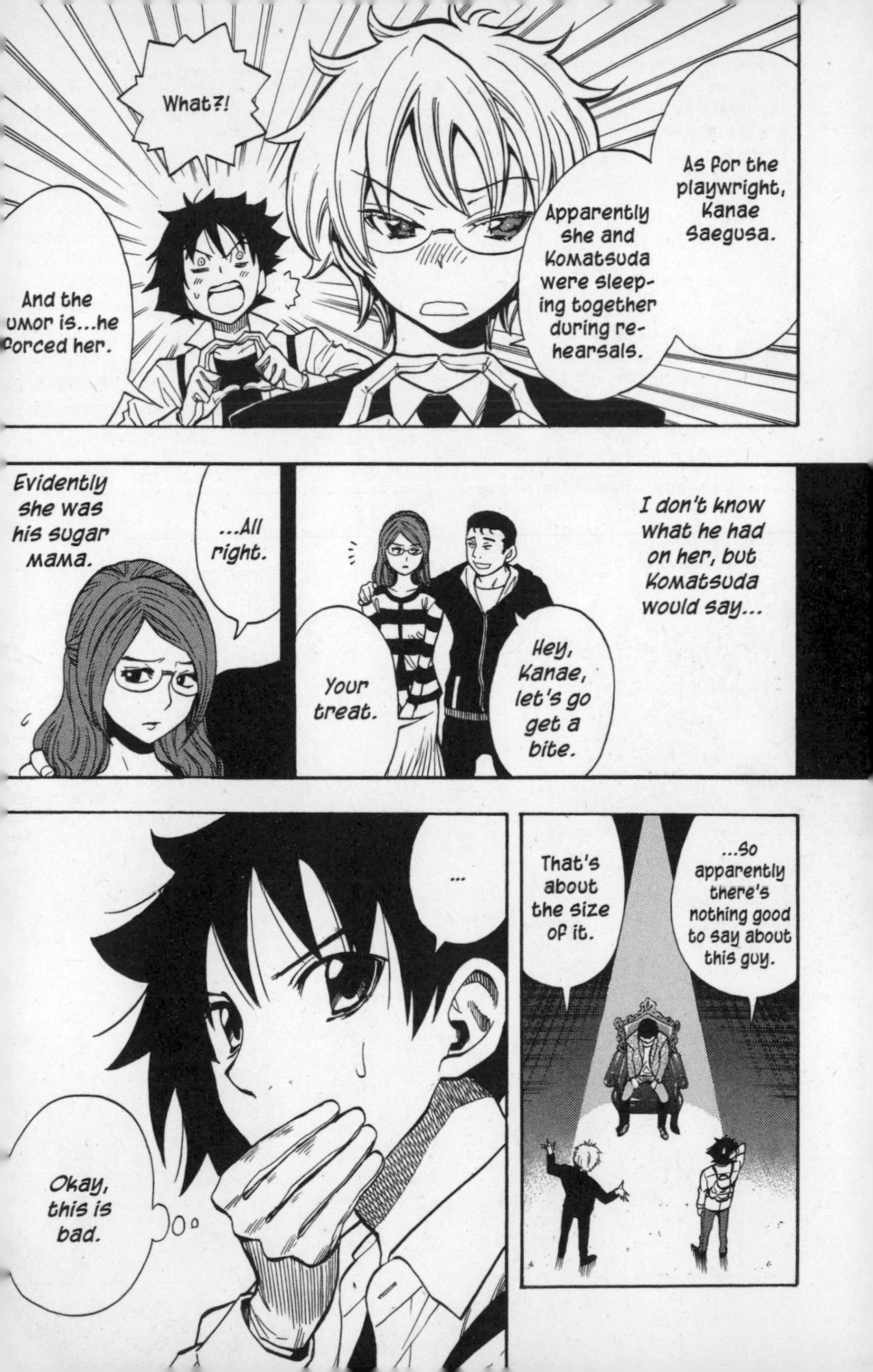
As for the playwright, Kanae Saegusa.
Apparently she and Komatsuda were sleeping together during rehearsals.
What?!
And the umor is...he forced her.
I don't know what he had on her, but Komatsuda would say...
Hey, Kanae, let's go get a bite.
Your treat.
...All right.
Evidently she was his sugar mama.
...So apparently there's nothing good to say about this guy.
That's about the size of it.
...
Okay, this is bad.

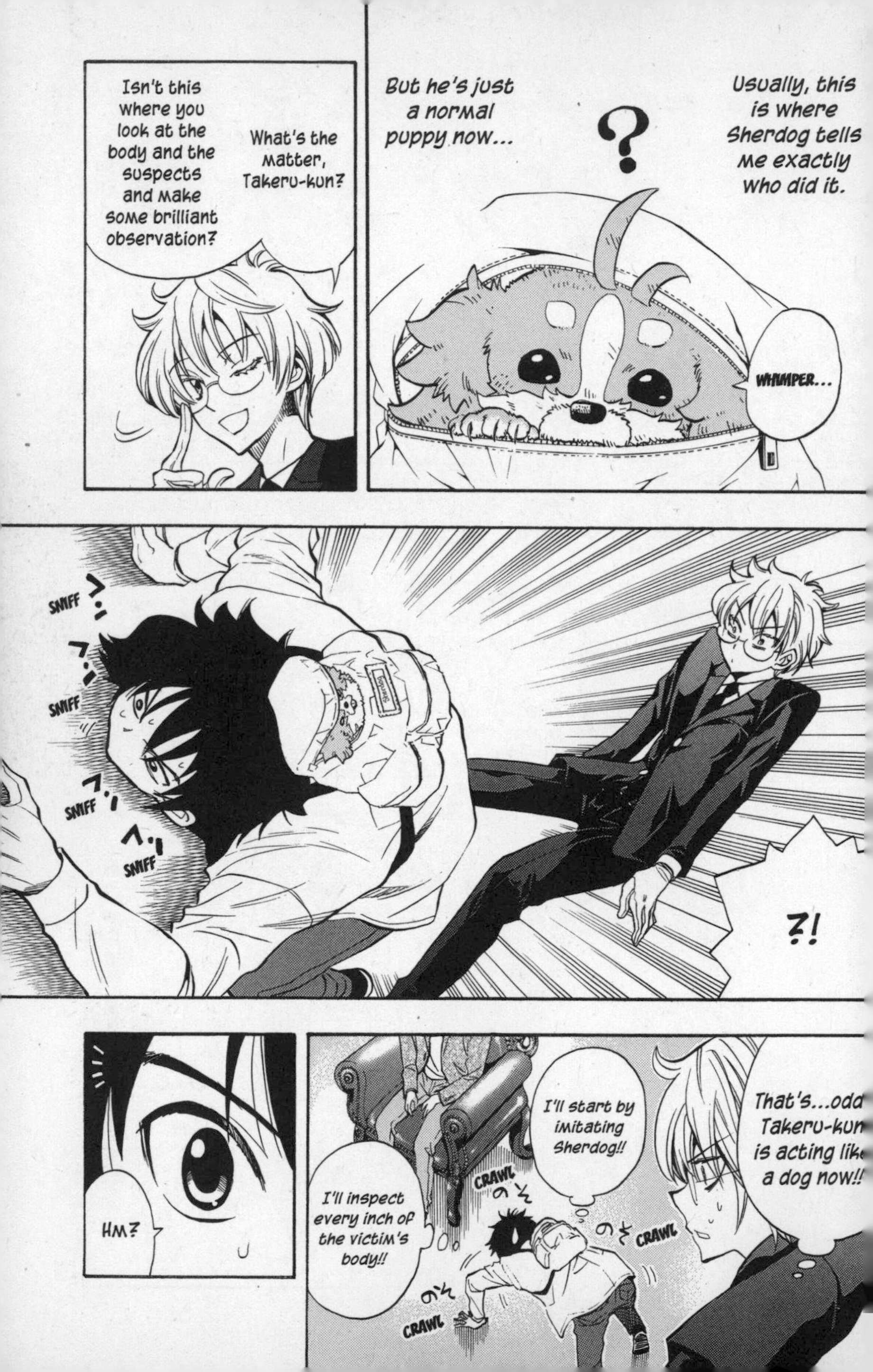
Usually, this is where Sherdog tells me exactly who did it.
But he's just a normal puppy now...
?
WHIMPER...
What's the matter, Takeru-kun?
Isn't this where you look at the body and the suspects and make some brilliant observation?
SNIFF
SNIFF
SNIFF
SNIFF
?!
That's...odd Takeru-kun is acting lik a dog now!!
I'll start by imitating Sherdog!!
CRAWL
CRAWL
I'll inspect every inch of the victim's body!!
CRAWL
HM?

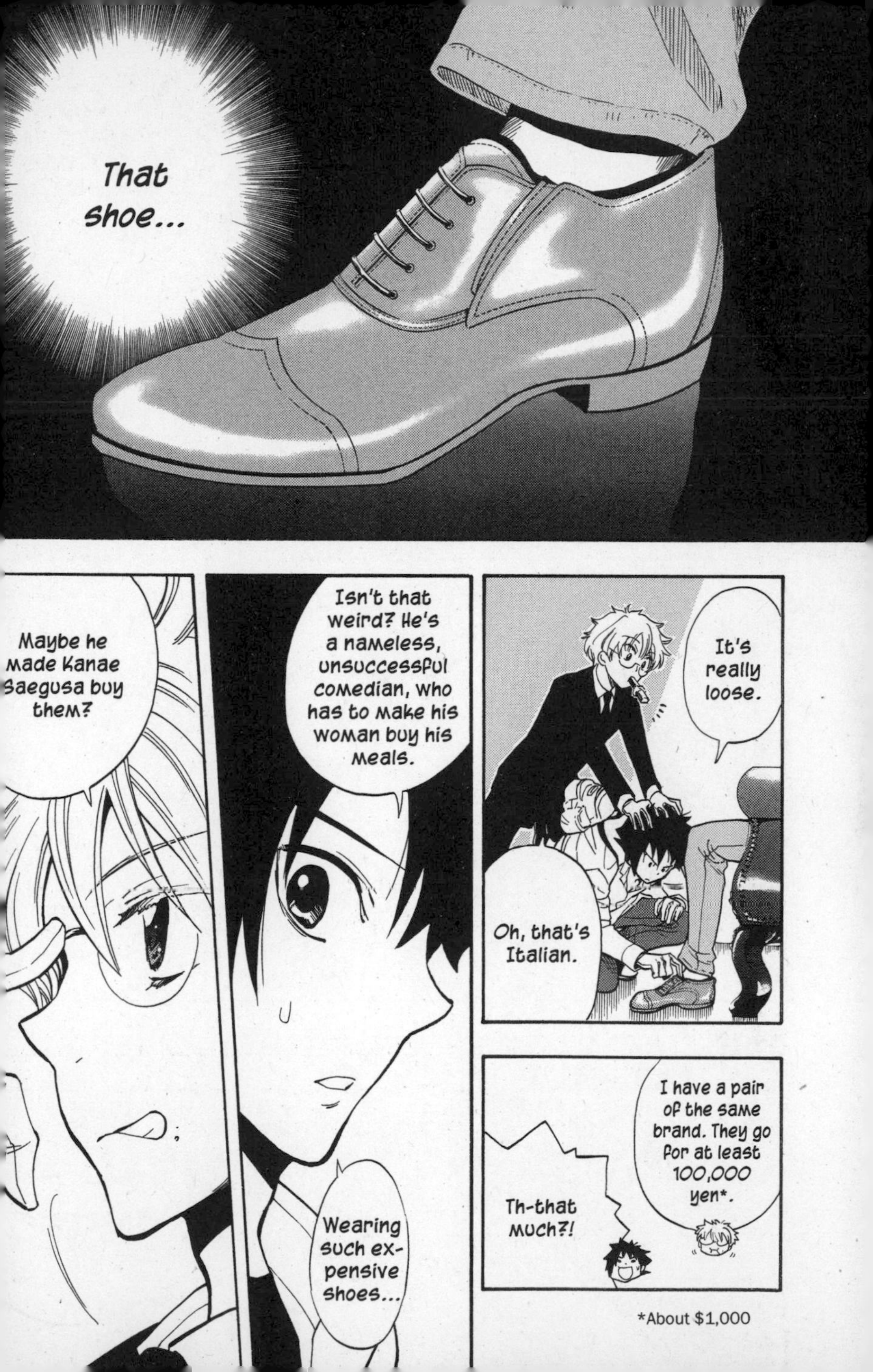
That shoe...
It's really loose.
Oh, that's Italian.
I have a pair of the same brand. They go for at least 100,000 yen*.
Th-that much?!
Isn't that weird? He's a nameless, unsuccessful comedian, who has to make his woman buy his meals.
Wearing such expensive shoes...
Maybe he made Kanae Saegusa buy them?

*About $1,000

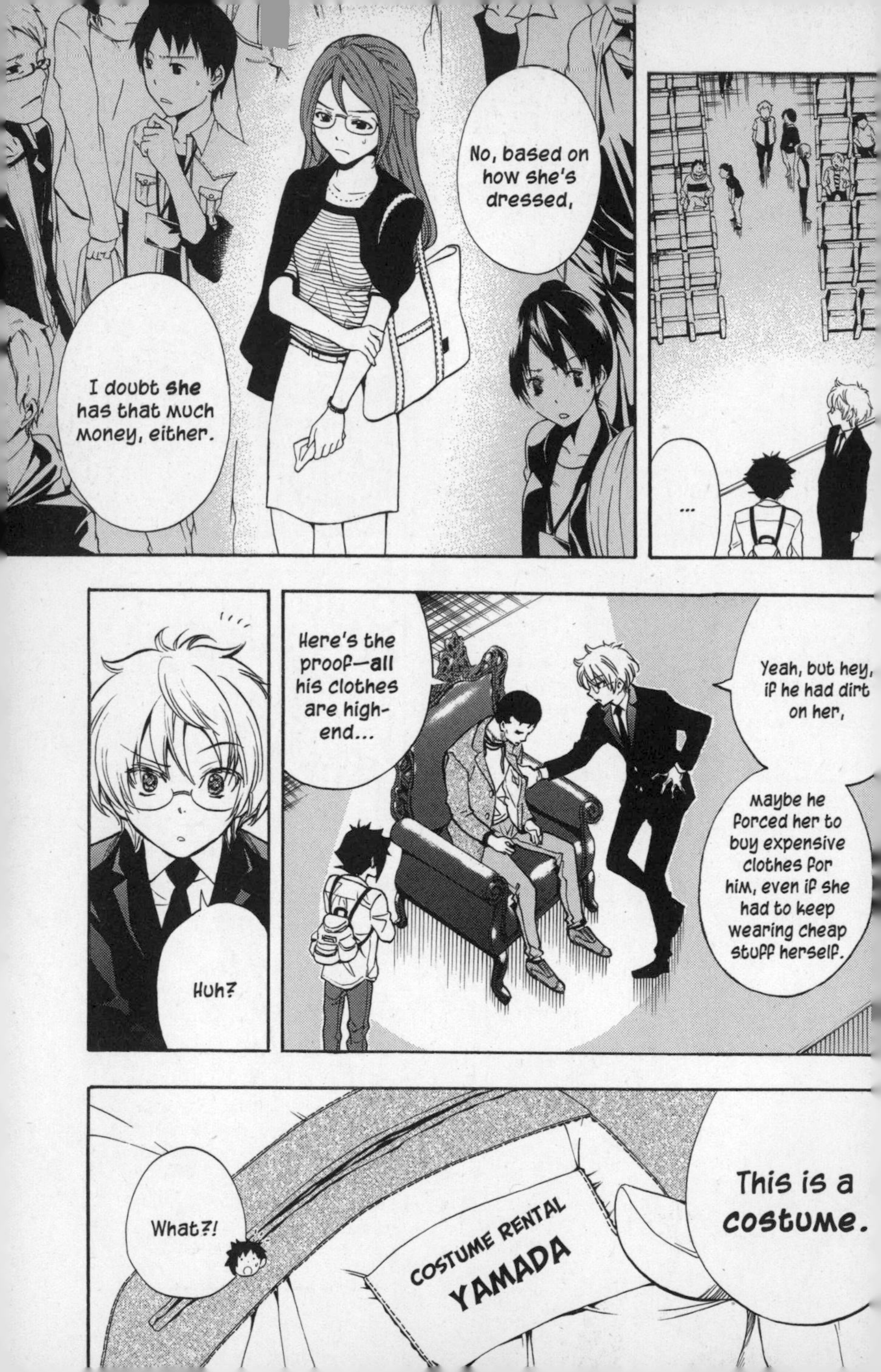
...
No, based on how she's dressed,
I doubt she has that much money, either.
Here's the proof—all his clothes are high-end...
Yeah, but hey, if he had dirt on her,
Maybe he forced her to buy expensive clothes for him, even if she had to keep wearing cheap stuff herself.
Huh?
This is a costume.
COSTUME RENTAL YAMADA
What?!

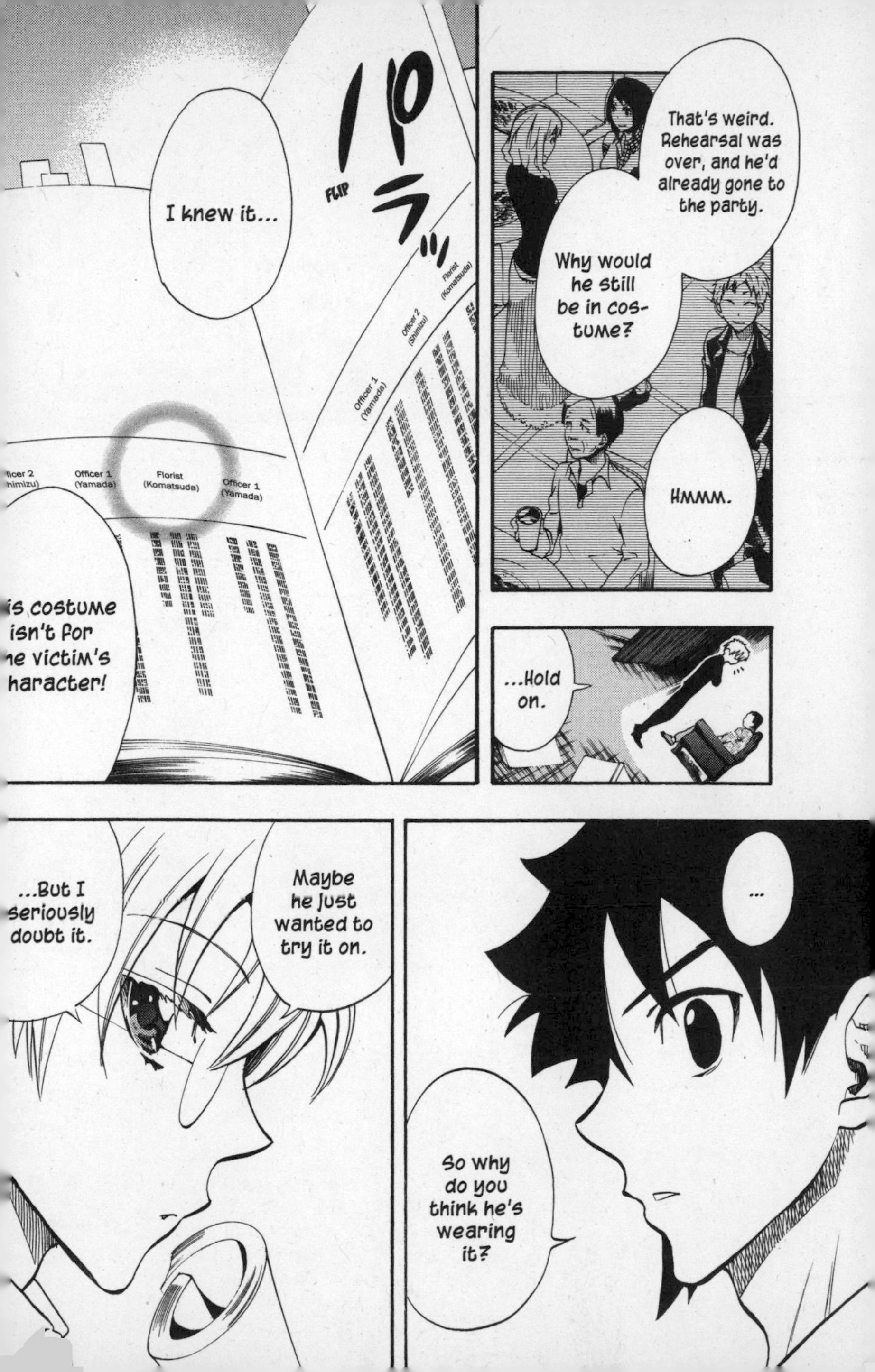
That's weird. Rehearsal was over, and he'd already gone to the party.
Why would he still be in costume?
Hmmm.
...Hold on.
パラッ
FLIP
I knew it...
Florist (Komatsuda)
Officer 2 (Shimizu)
Officer 1 (Yamada)
Officer 1 (Yamada)
Florist (Komatsuda)
Officer 1 (Yamada)
fficer 2 (himizu)
is costume isn't for he victim's haracter!
...
So why do you think he's wearing it?
Maybe he just wanted to try it on.
...But I seriously doubt it.

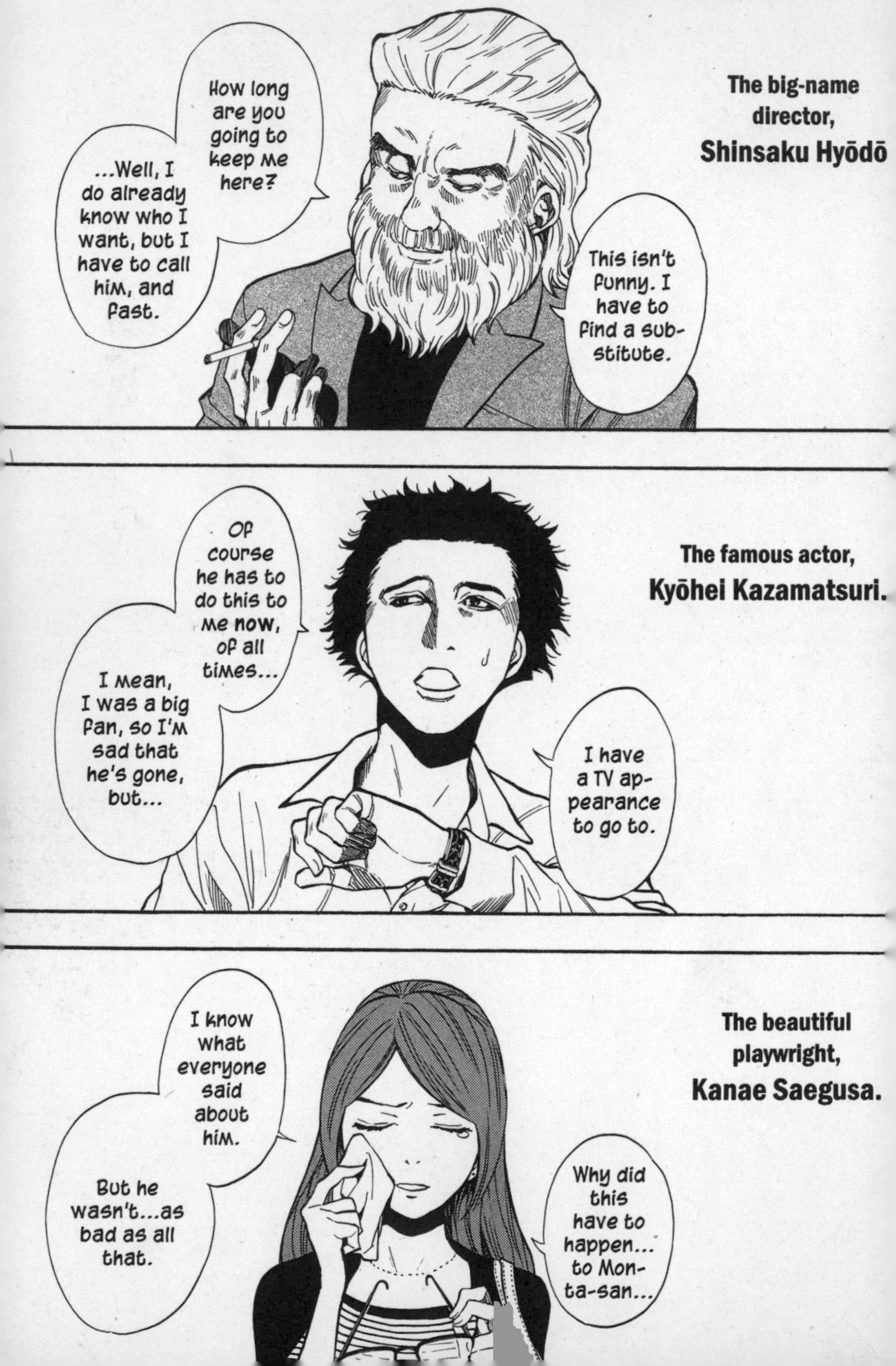
The big-name director, Shinsaku Hyōdō
This isn't funny. I have to find a substitute.
How long are you going to keep me here?
...Well, I do already know who I want, but I have to call him, and fast.
The famous actor, Kyōhei Kazamatsuri.
I have a TV appearance to go to.
Of course he has to do this to me now, of all times...
I mean, I was a big fan, so I'm sad that he's gone, but...
The beautiful playwright, Kanae Saegusa.
Why did this have to happen... to Monta-san...
I know what everyone said about him.
But he wasn't...as bad as all that.

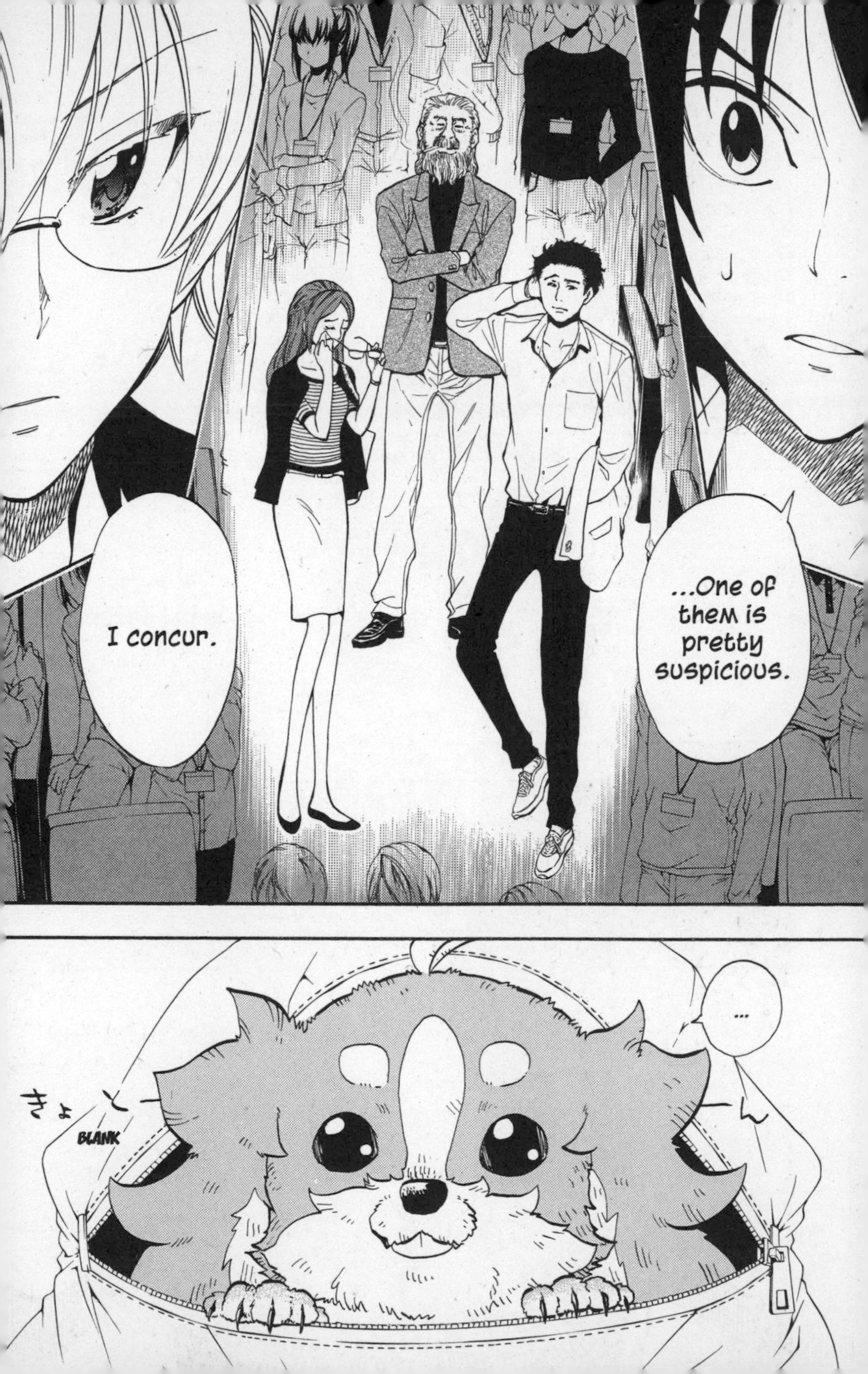
...One of them is pretty suspicious.
I concur.
...
きょとーん
BLANK

Case 11: ⚜ A Stage for Murder, Part 2

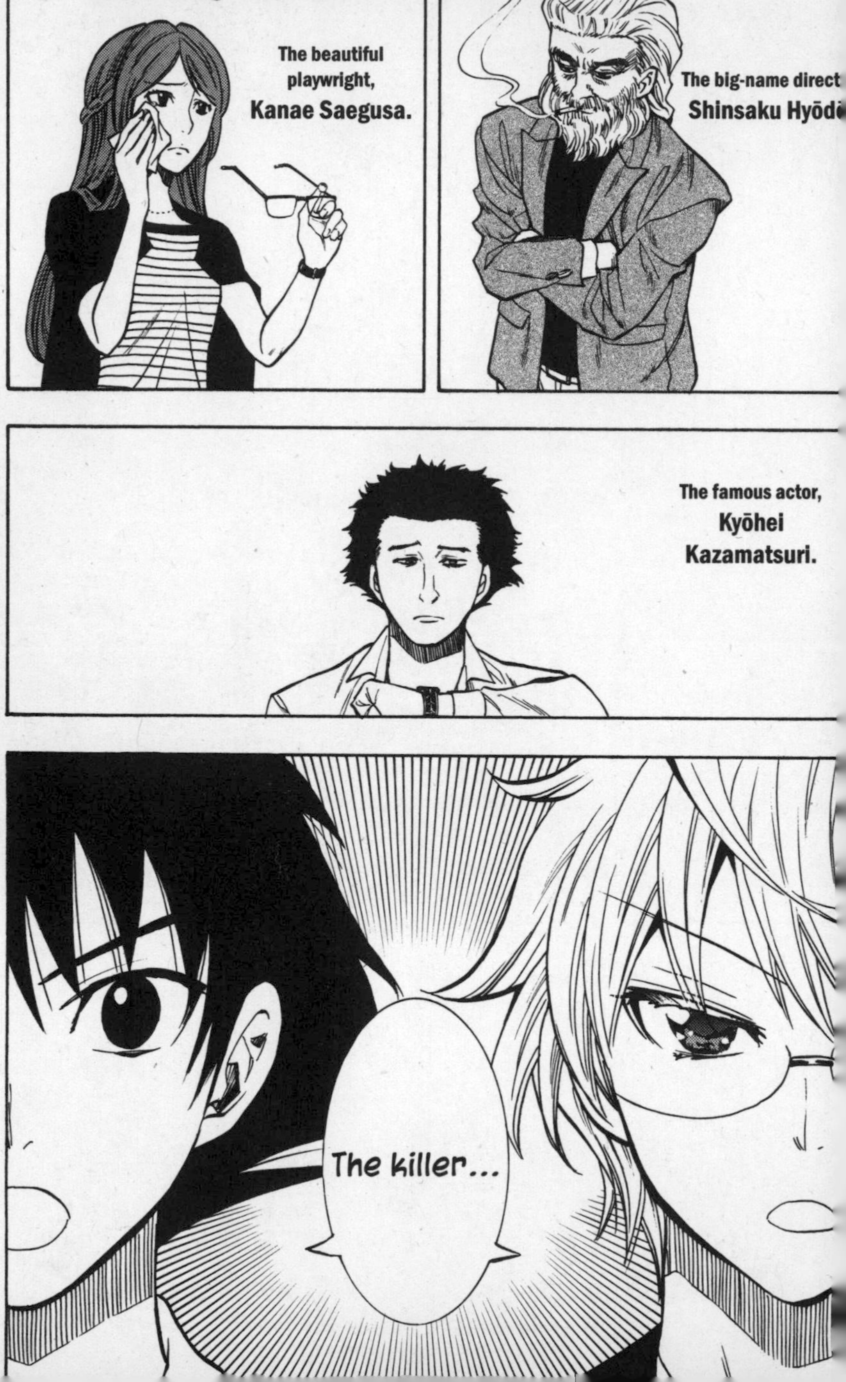

The big-name direct
Shinsaku Hyōd
The beautiful playwright, Kanae Saegusa.
The famous actor, Kyōhei Kazamatsuri.
The killer...

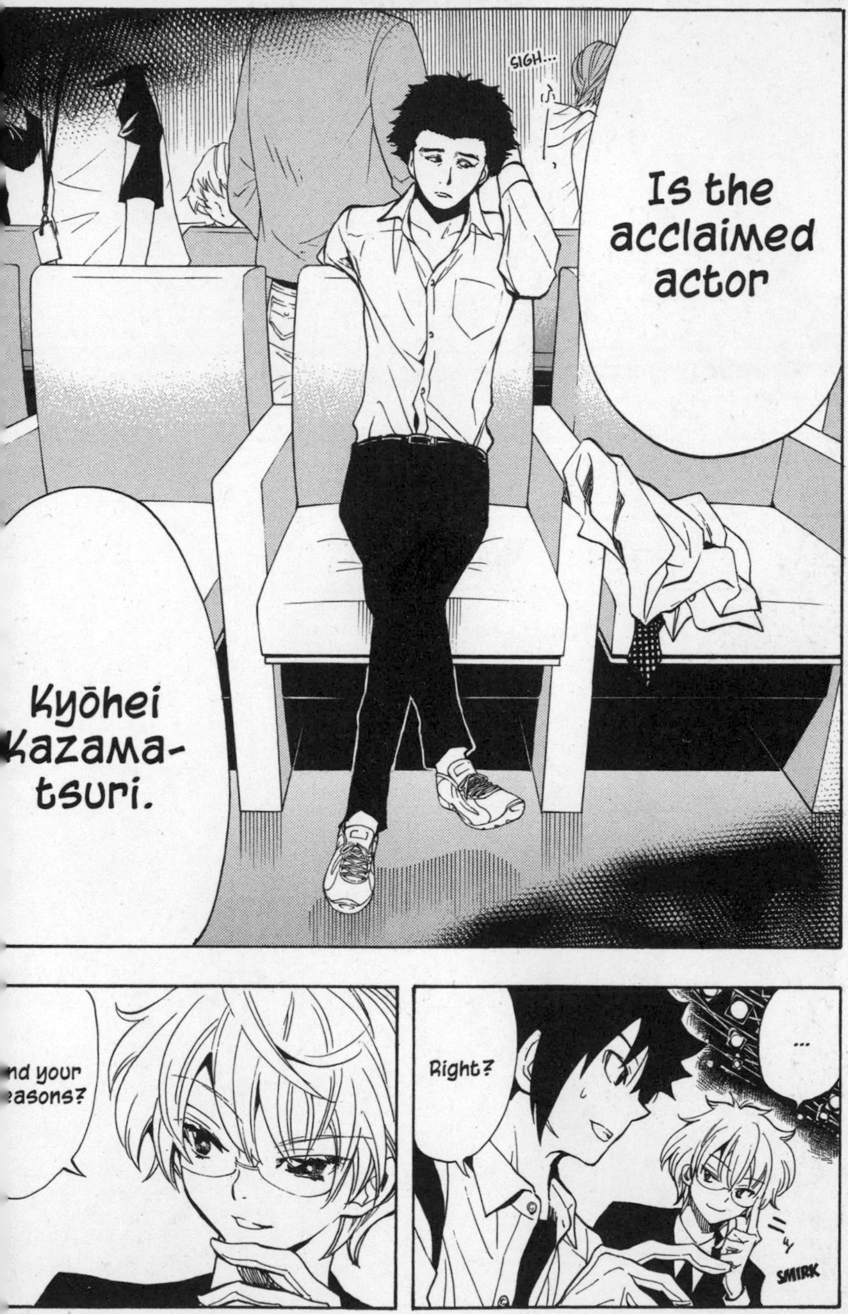
SIGH...
Is the acclaimed actor
Kyōhei Kazama-tsuri.
...
Right?
SMIRK
nd your easons?

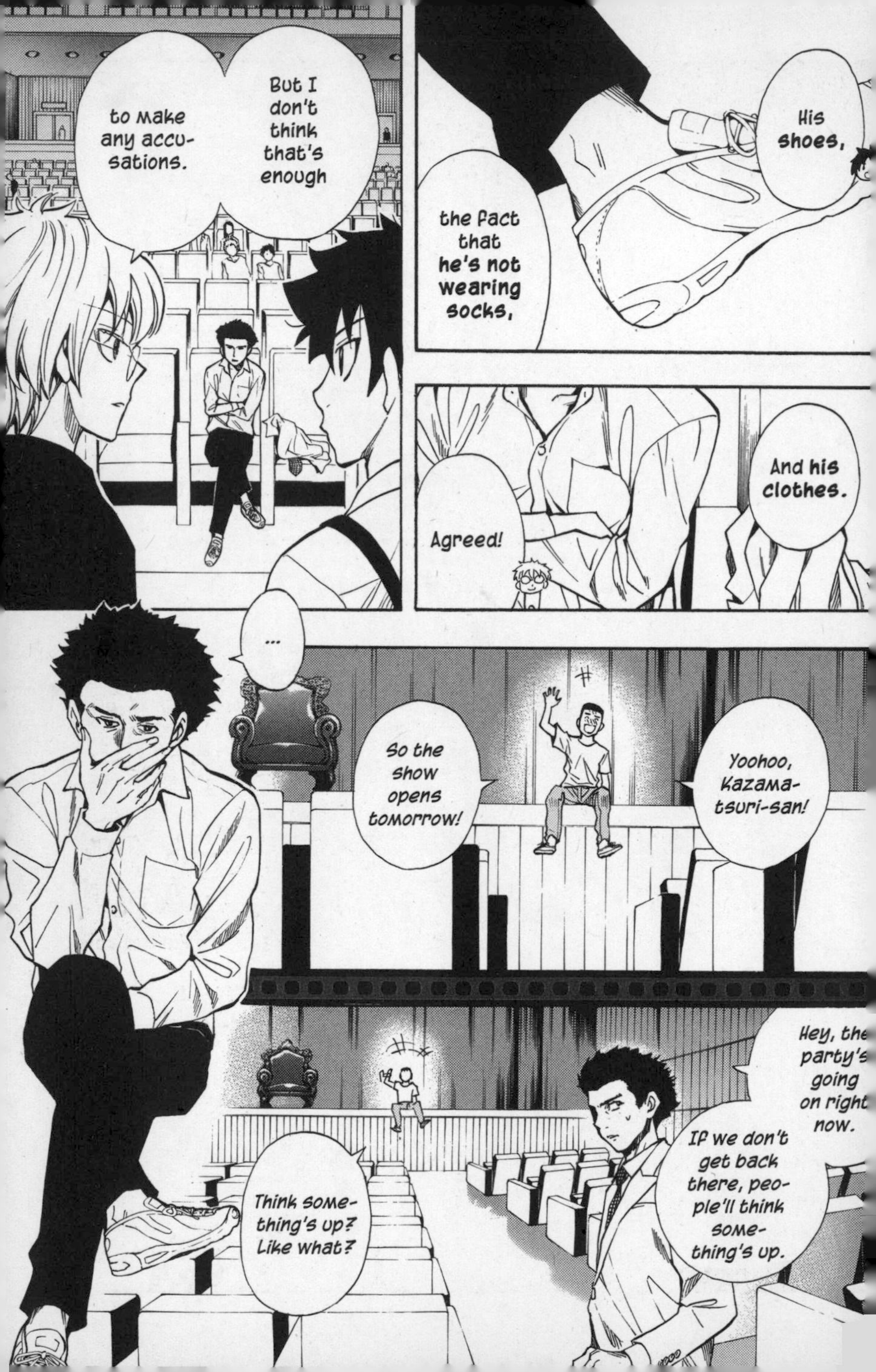
His shoes,
the fact that he's not wearing socks,
And his clothes.
Agreed!
But I don't think that's enough
to make any accusations.
Yoohoo, Kazama-tsuri-san!
So the show opens tomorrow!
...
Hey, the party's going on right now.
If we don't get back there, peo-ple'll think some-thing's up.
Think some-thing's up? Like what?

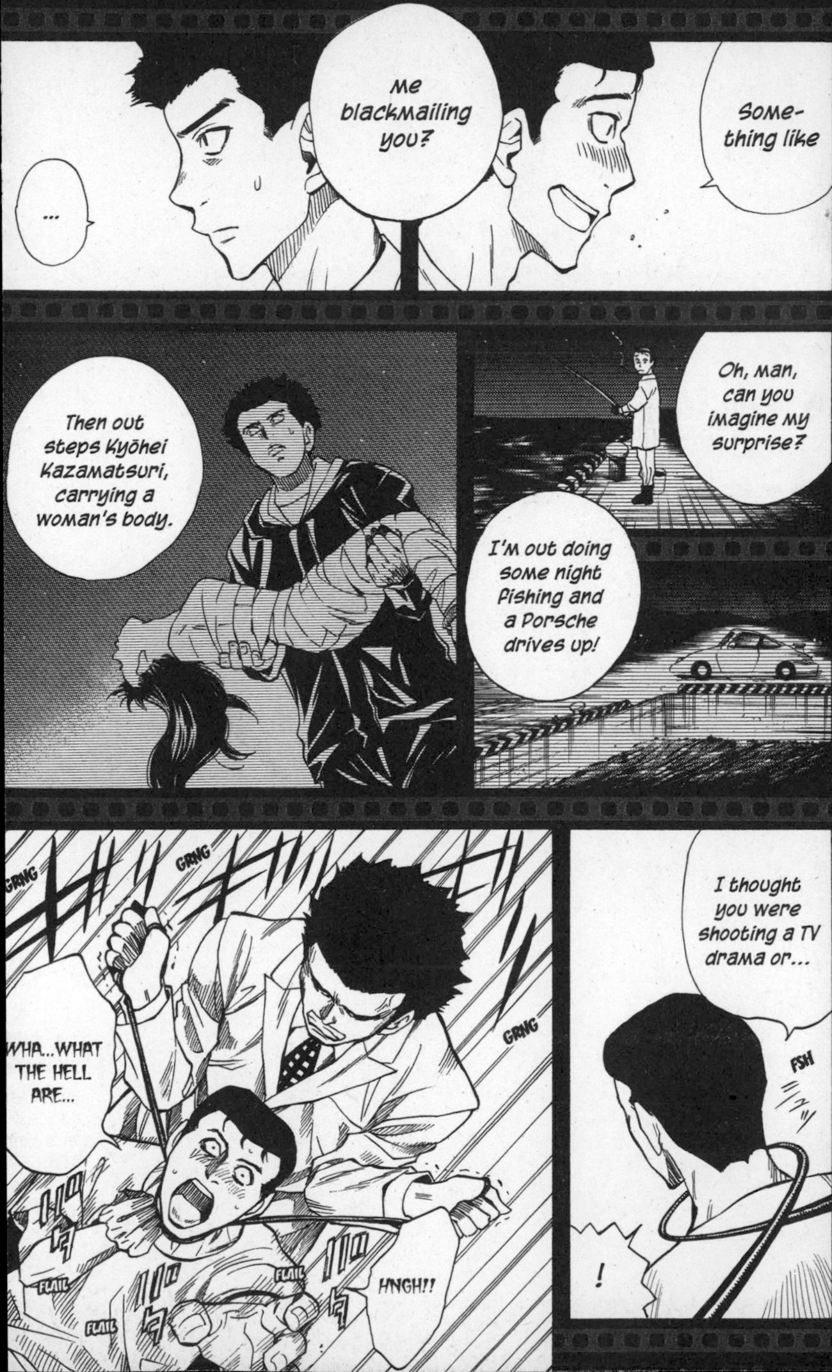
Some-thing like
Me blackmailing you?
...
Oh, man, can you imagine my surprise?
I'm out doing some night fishing and a Porsche drives up!
Then out steps Kyōhei Kazamatsuri, carrying a woman's body.
I thought you were shooting a TV drama or...
FSH
!
GRNG
GRNG
GRNG
WHA...WHAT THE HELL ARE...
FLAIL
FLAIL
FLAIL
HNGH!!

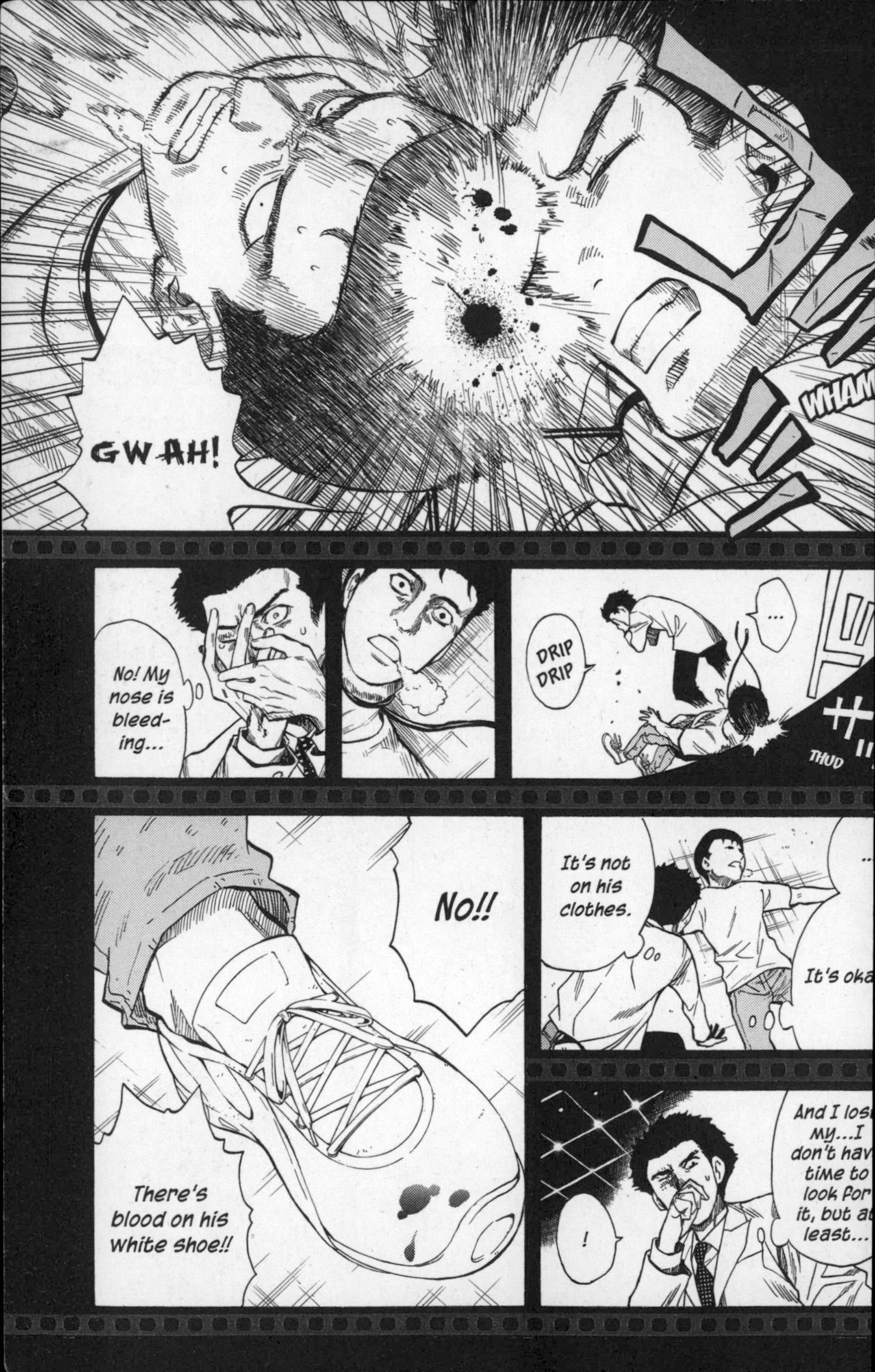
WHAM
GWAH!
...
DRIP DRIP
THUD
No! My nose is bleed-ing...
...
It's not on his clothes.
It's oka
And I los my...I don't hav time to look for it, but a least...
!
No!!
There's blood on his white shoe!!

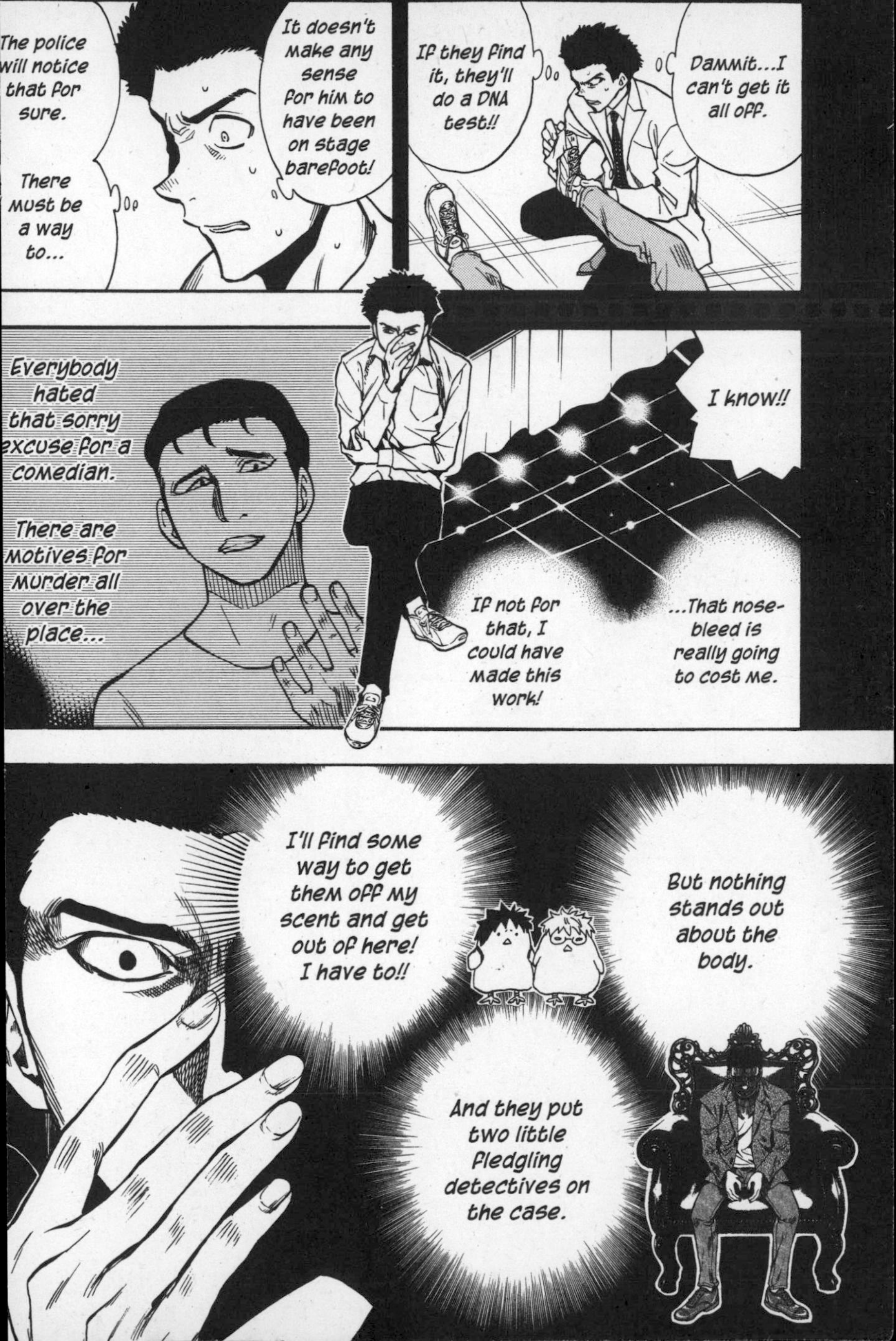
Dammit...I can't get it all off.
If they find it, they'll do a DNA test!!
It doesn't make any sense for him to have been on stage barefoot!
The police will notice that for sure.
There must be a way to...
I know!!
...That nose-bleed is really going to cost me.
If not for that, I could have made this work!
Everybody hated that sorry excuse for a comedian.
There are motives for murder all over the place...
But nothing stands out about the body.
I'll find some way to get them off my scent and get out of here! I have to!!
And they put two little fledgling detectives on the case.

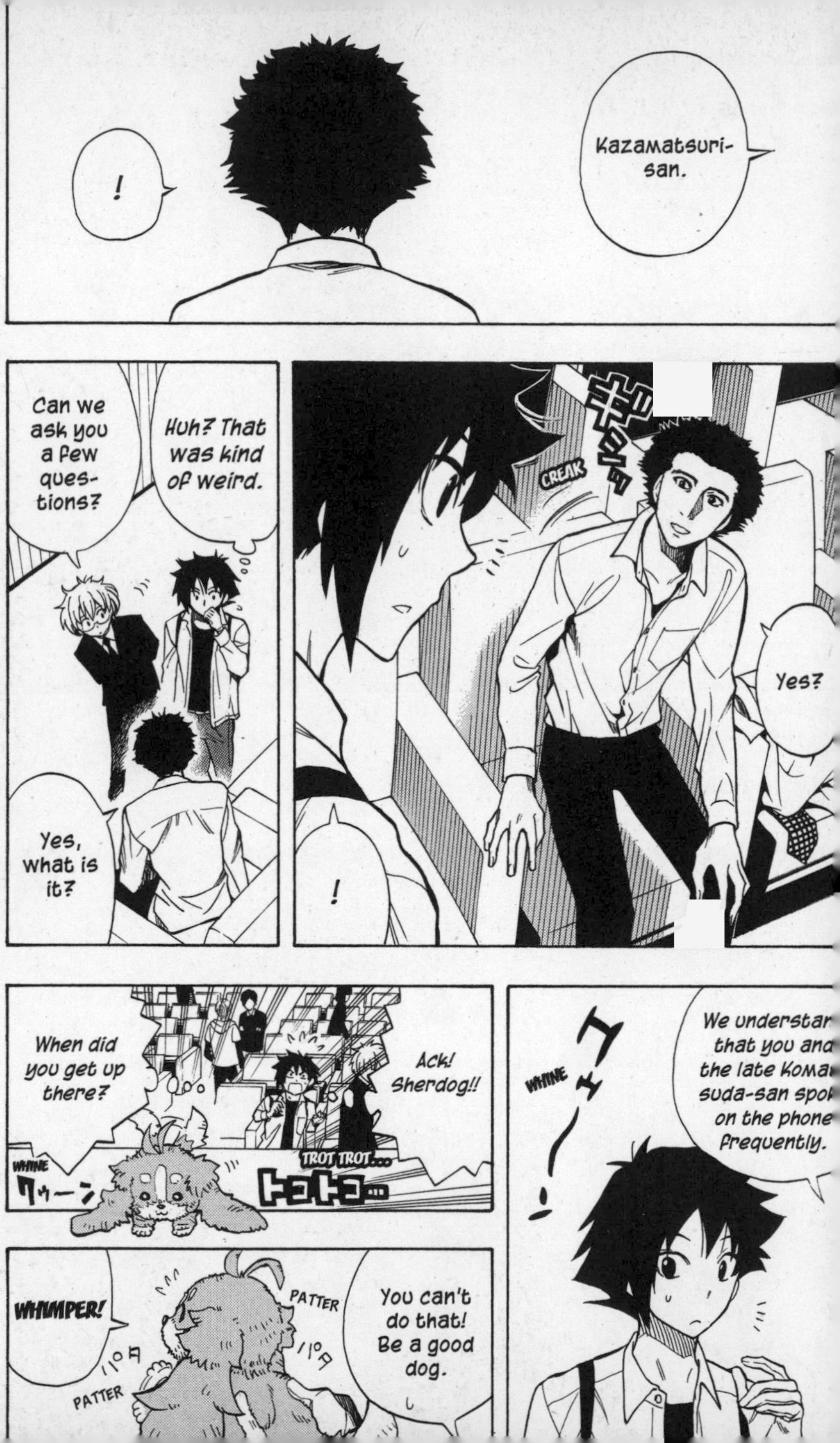
Kazamatsuri-san.
!
CREAK
Yes?
!
Huh? That was kind of weird.
Can we ask you a few ques-tions?
Yes, what is it?
We understar that you and the late Komal suda-san spok on the phone frequently.
WHINE
Ack! Sherdog!!
When did you get up there?
TROT TROT...
WHINE
You can't do that! Be a good dog.
PATTER
PATTER
WHIMPER!

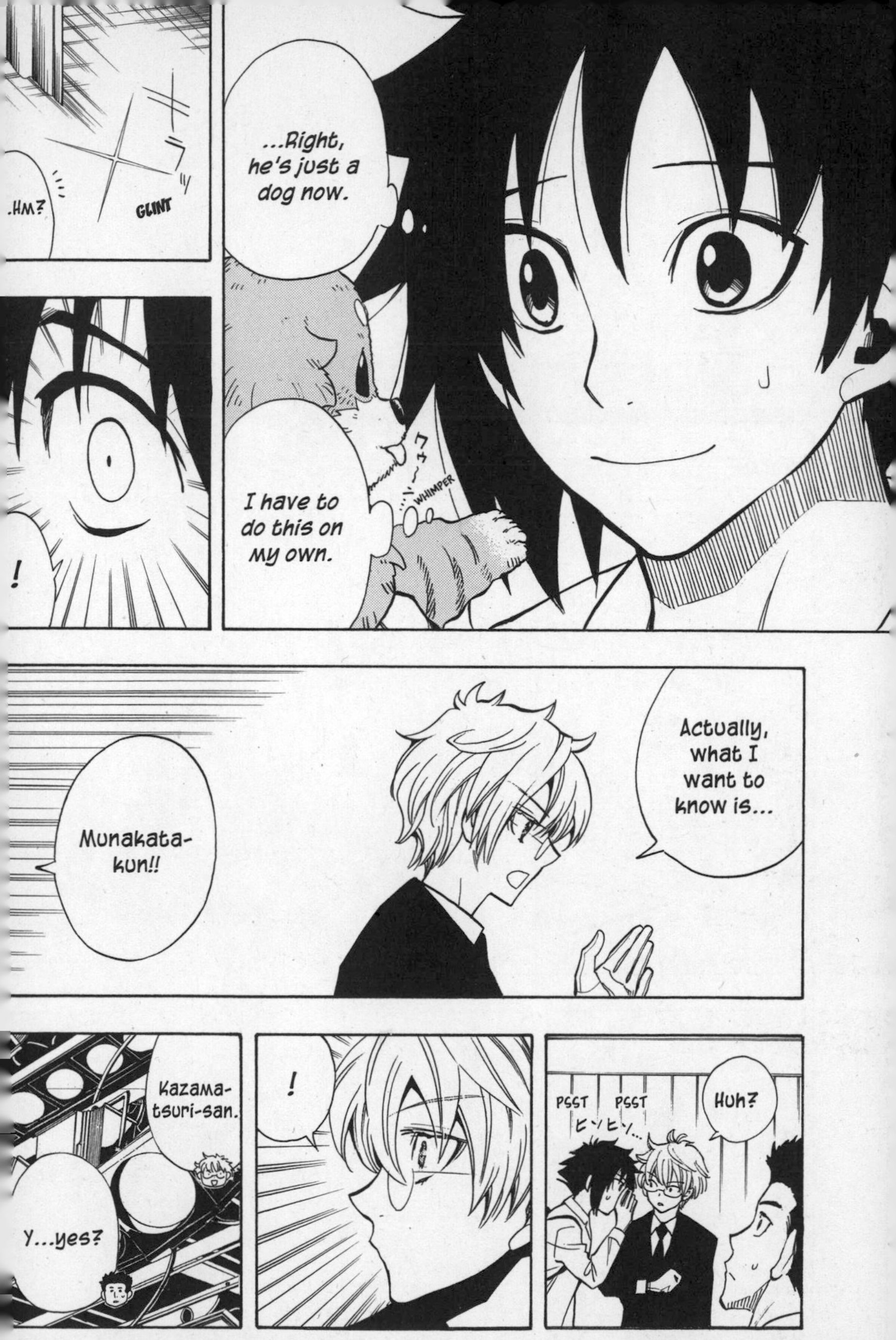
...Right, he's just a dog now.
I have to do this on my own.
WHIMPER
.Hm?
GLINT
!
Actually, what I want to know is...
Munakata-kun!!
Huh?
PSST PSST
ヒソヒソ...
!
Kazama-tsuri-san.
Y...yes?

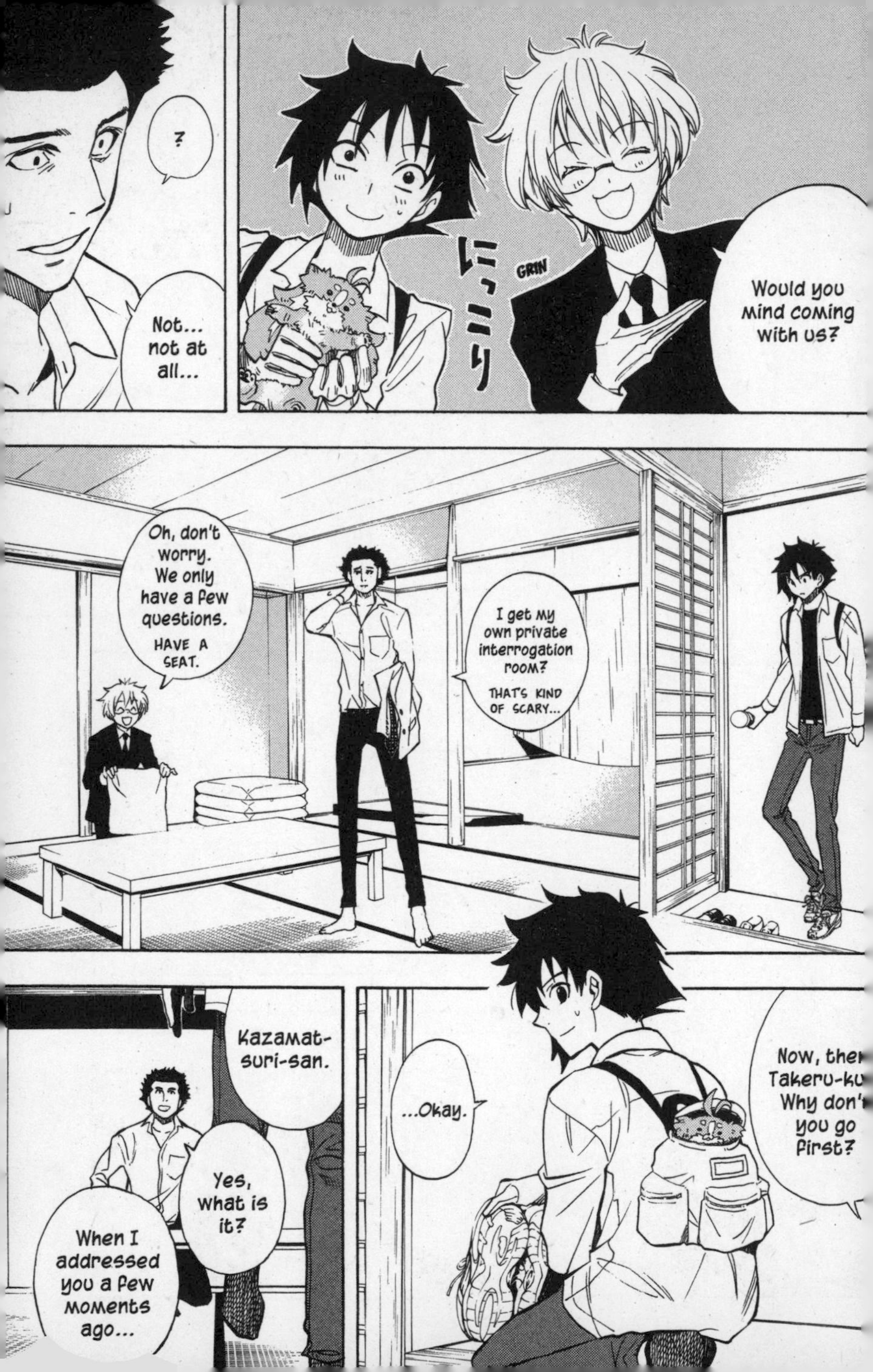
Would you mind coming with us?
にっこり
GRIN
?
Not... not at all...
I get my own private interrogation room?
THAT'S KIND OF SCARY...
Oh, don't worry. We only have a few questions.
HAVE A SEAT.
Now, the
Takeru-ku
Why don'
you go first?
...Okay.
Kazamat-suri-san.
Yes, what is it?
When I addressed you a few moments ago...

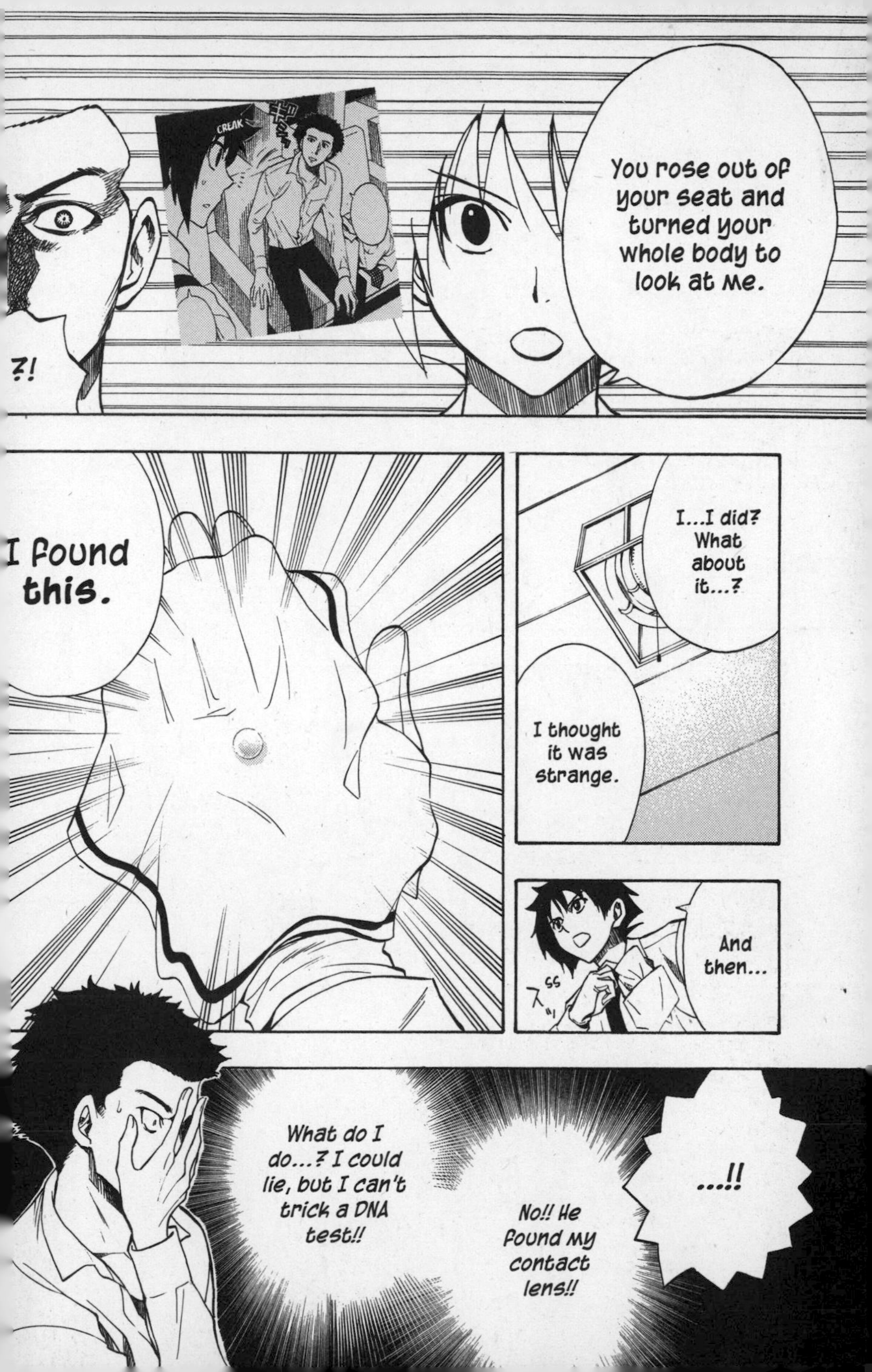
You rose out of your seat and turned your whole body to look at me.
CREAK
?!
I...I did? What about it...?
I thought it was strange.
And then...
SS
I found this.
...!!
No!! He found my contact lens!!
What do I do...? I could lie, but I can't trick a DNA test!!

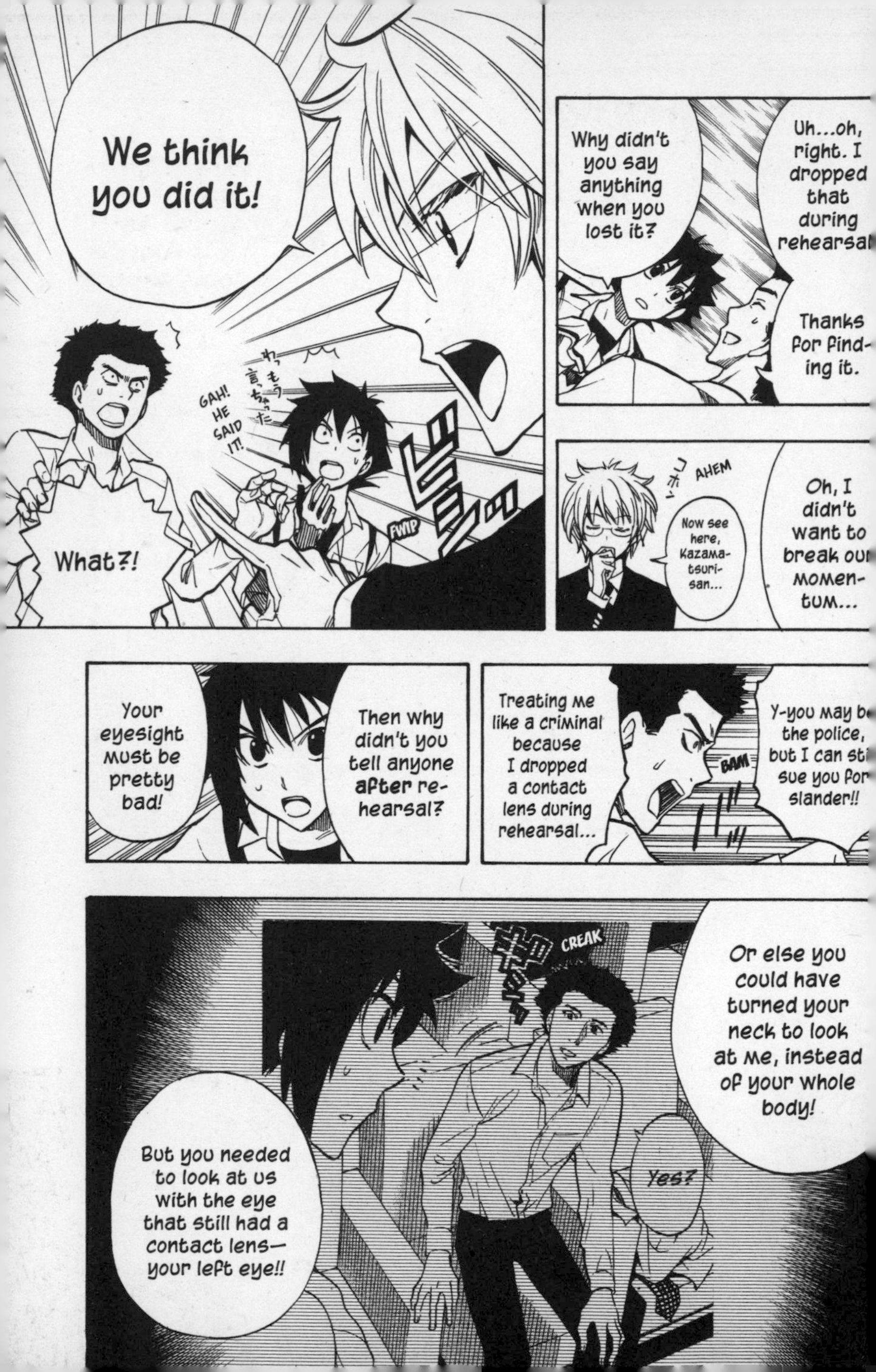
Uh...oh, right. I dropped that during rehearsa
Thanks for finding it.
Why didn't you say anything when you lost it?
Oh, I didn't want to break ou momentum...
コホン
AHEM
Now see here, Kazamatsuri-san...
We think you did it!
わっ もう言っちゃった
GAH! HE SAID IT!
FWIP
What?!
Y-you may b the police, but I can sti sue you for slander!!
BAM
Treating me like a criminal because I dropped a contact lens during rehearsal...
Then why didn't you tell anyone after rehearsal?
Your eyesight must be pretty bad!
Or else you could have turned your neck to look at me, instead of your whole body!
CREAK
Yes?
But you needed to look at us with the eye that still had a contact lens— your left eye!!

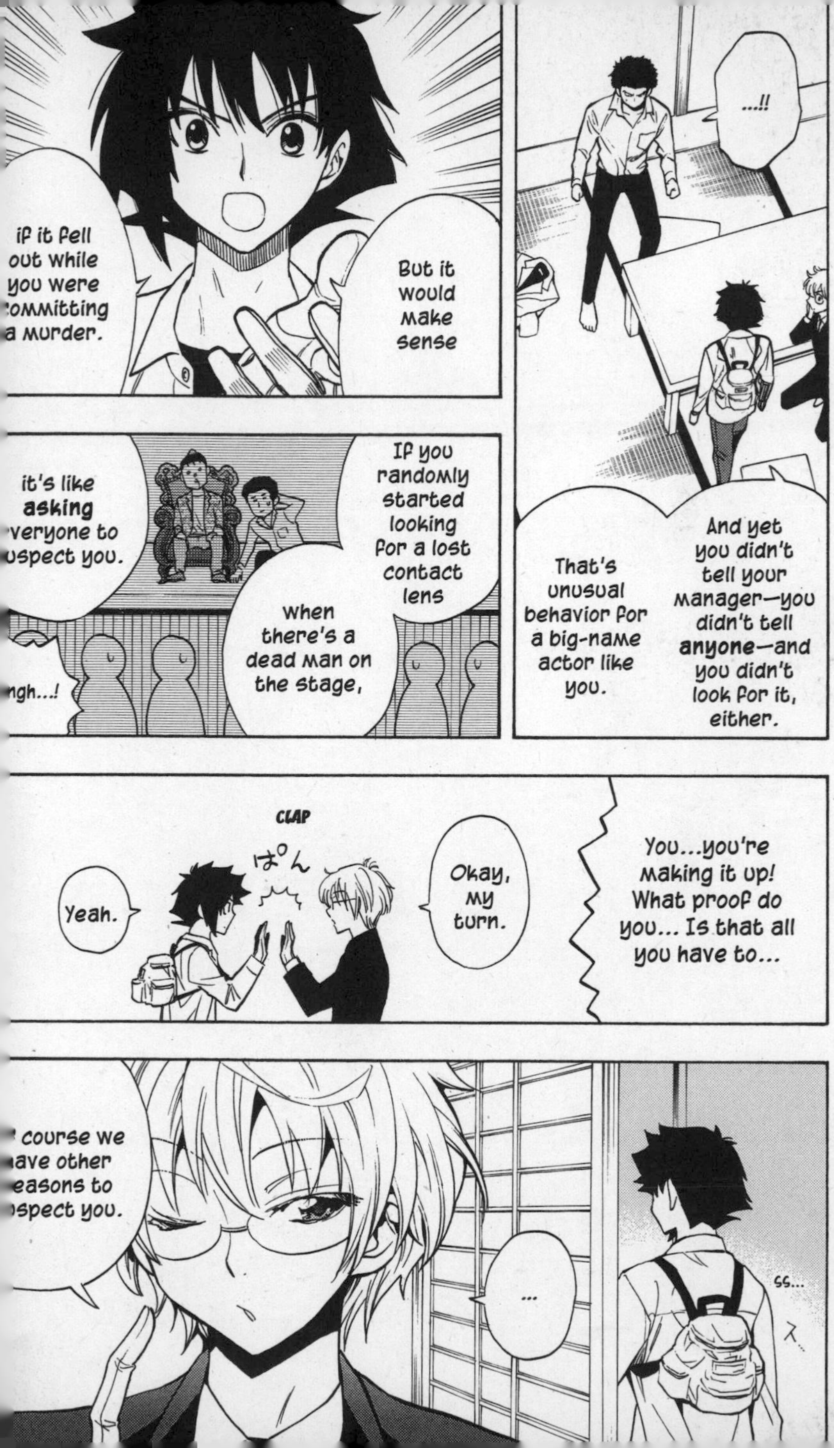

...!!
But it would make sense
if it fell out while you were ommitting a murder.
And yet you didn't tell your manager—you didn't tell anyone—and you didn't look for it, either.
That's unusual behavior for a big-name actor like you.
If you randomly started looking for a lost contact lens
when there's a dead man on the stage,
it's like asking veryone to uspect you.
ngh...!
You...you're making it up! What proof do you... Is that all you have to...
Okay, my turn.
CLAP
ぱん
Yeah.
SS...
ス...
...
course we ave other easons to spect you.

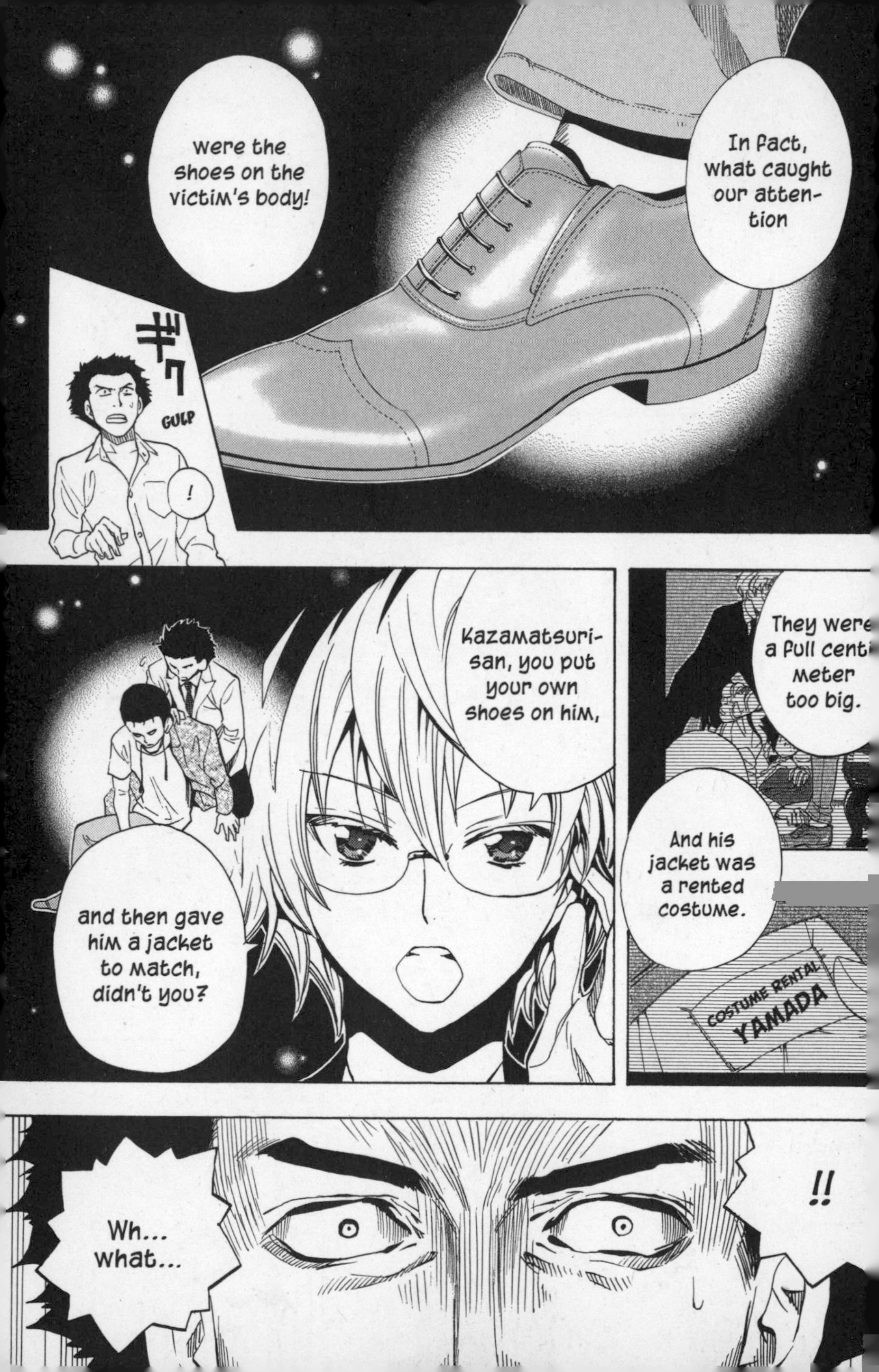
In fact, what caught our attention
were the shoes on the victim's body!
ギク
GULP
!
They were a full centi meter too big.
And his jacket was a rented costume.
COSTUME RENTAL YAMADA
Kazamatsuri-san, you put your own shoes on him,
and then gave him a jacket to match, didn't you?
!!
Wh... what...

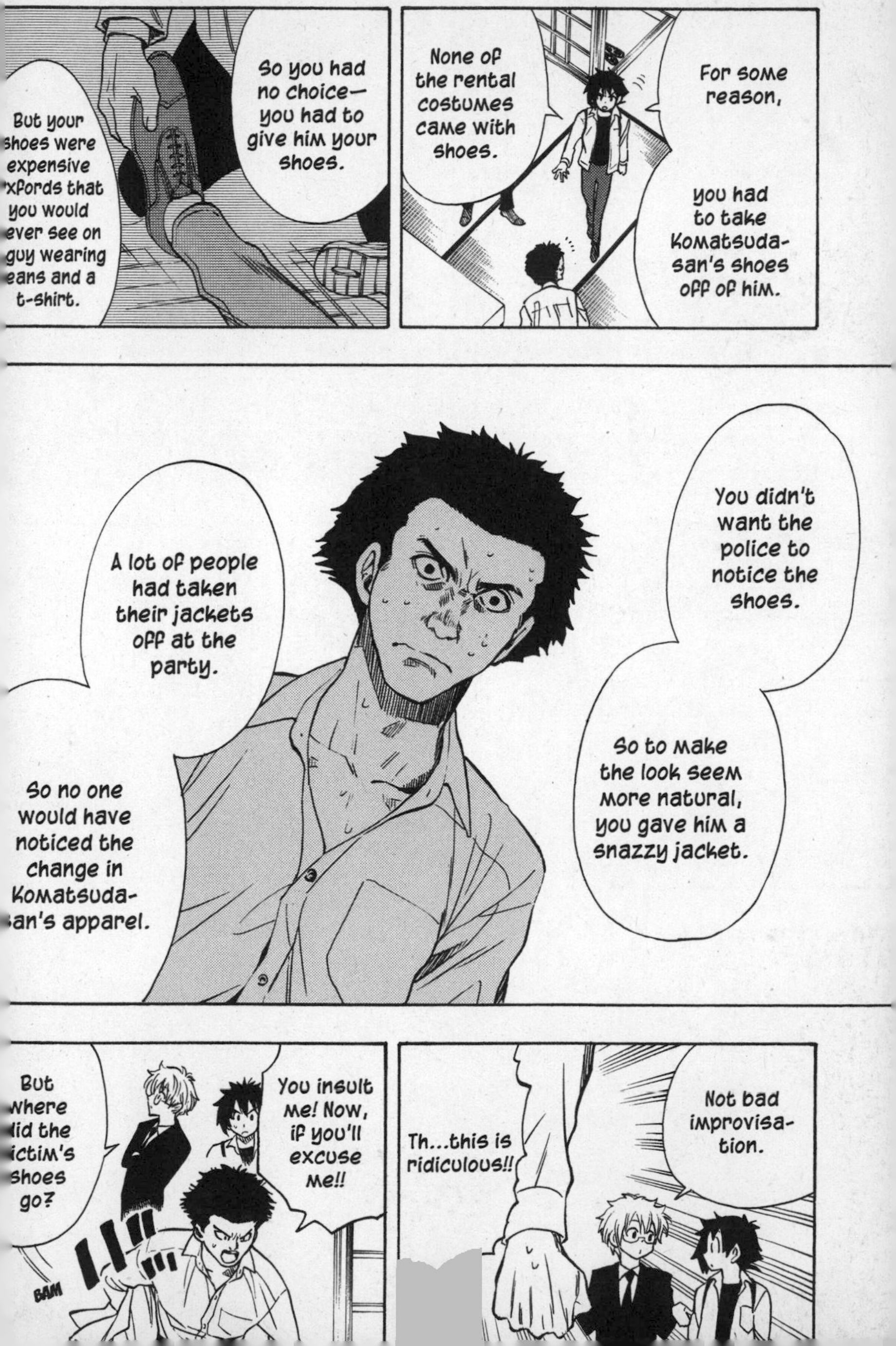
For some reason,
you had to take Komatsuda-san's shoes off of him.
None of the rental costumes came with shoes.
So you had no choice—you had to give him your shoes.
But your shoes were expensive xfords that you would ever see on guy wearing eans and a t-shirt.
You didn't want the police to notice the shoes.
So to make the look seem more natural, you gave him a snazzy jacket.
A lot of people had taken their jackets off at the party.
So no one would have noticed the change in Komatsuda-an's apparel.
Not bad improvisa-tion.
Th...this is ridiculous!!
You insult me! Now, if you'll excuse me!!
But here lid the ictim's shoes go?
BAM

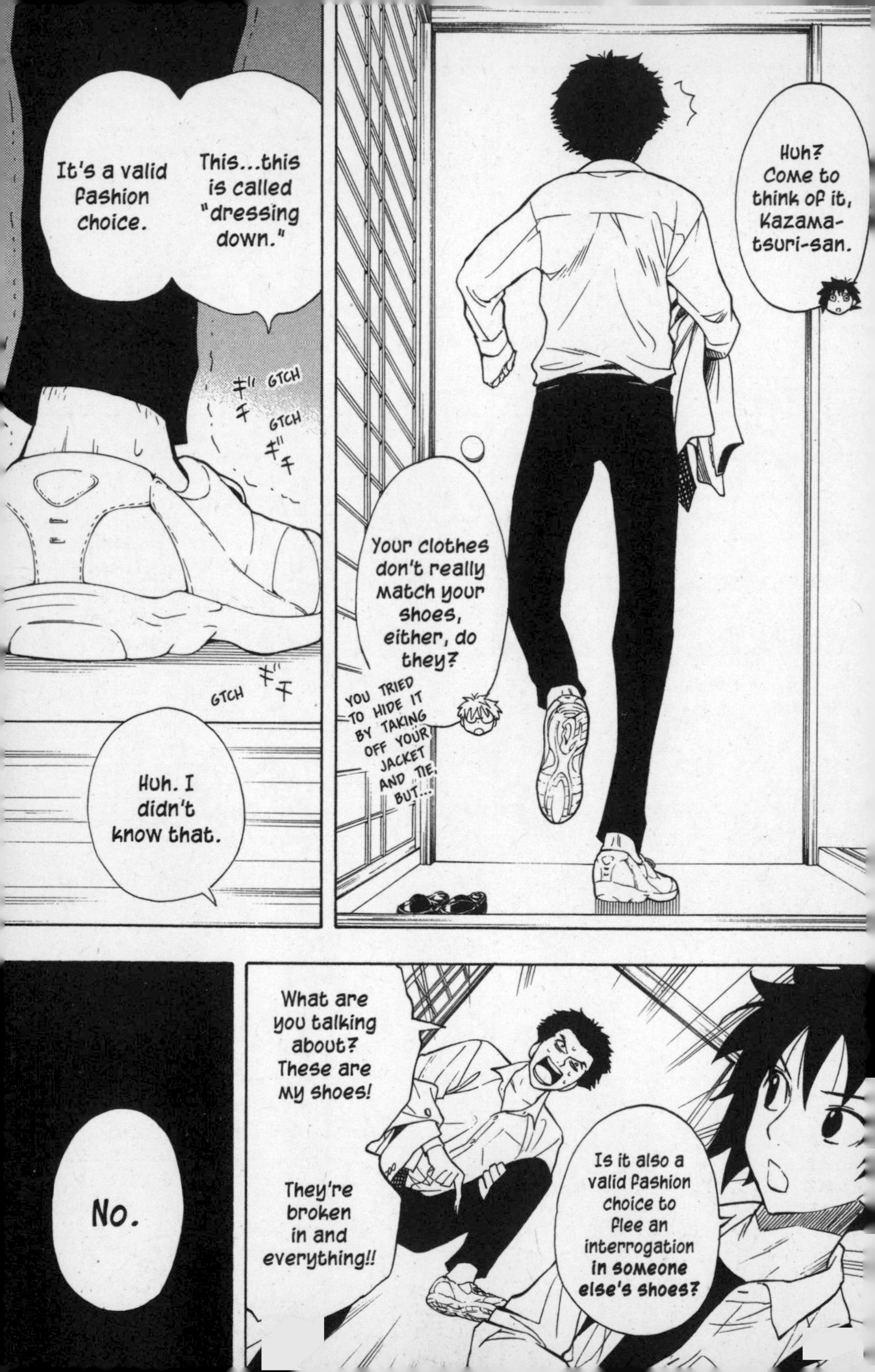
Huh? Come to think of it, Kazamatsuri-san.
Your clothes don't really match your shoes, either, do they?
YOU TRIED TO HIDE IT BY TAKING OFF YOUR JACKET AND TIE, BUT...
This...this is called "dressing down."
It's a valid fashion choice.
ギチ GTCH
ギチ GTCH
ギチ GTCH
Huh. I didn't know that.
Is it also a valid fashion choice to flee an interrogation in someone else's shoes?
What are you talking about? These are my shoes!
They're broken in and everything!!
No.

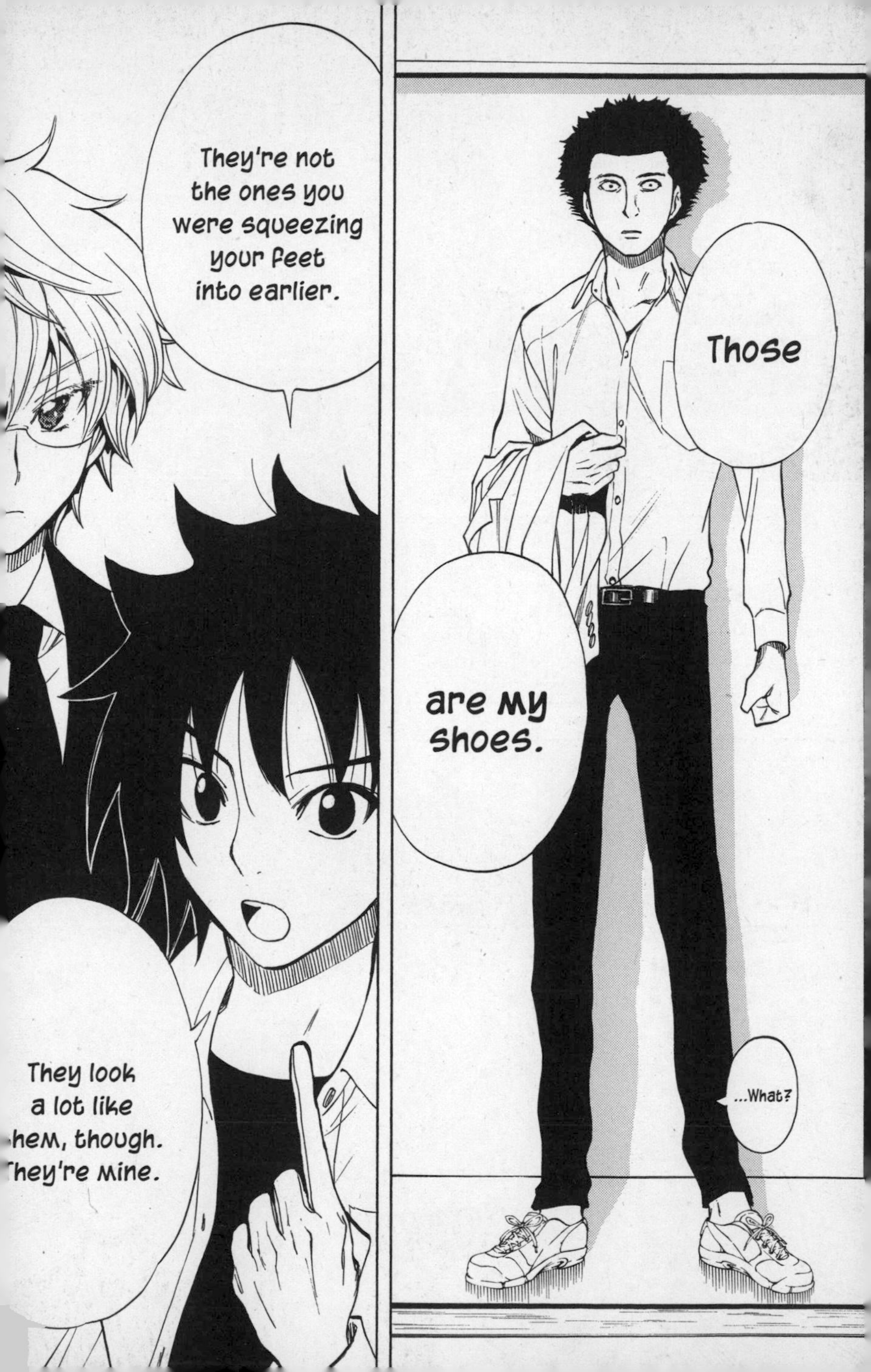
Those
are my shoes.
...What?
They're not the ones you were squeezing your feet into earlier.
They look a lot like
hem, though.
hey're mine.

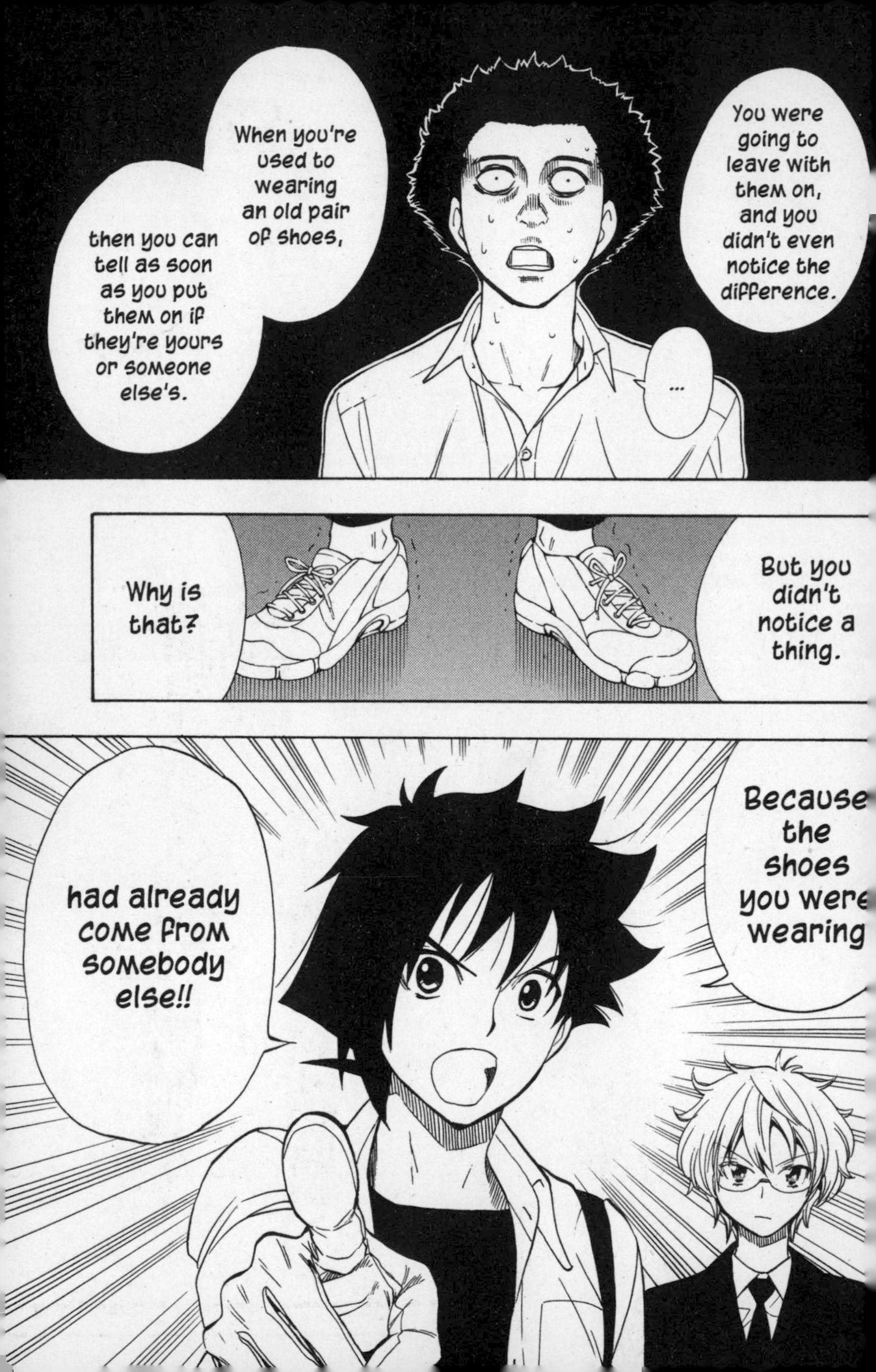
You were going to leave with them on, and you didn't even notice the difference.
When you're used to wearing an old pair of shoes,
then you can tell as soon as you put them on if they're yours or someone else's.
...
But you didn't notice a thing.
Why is that?
Because the shoes you were wearing
had already come from somebody else!!

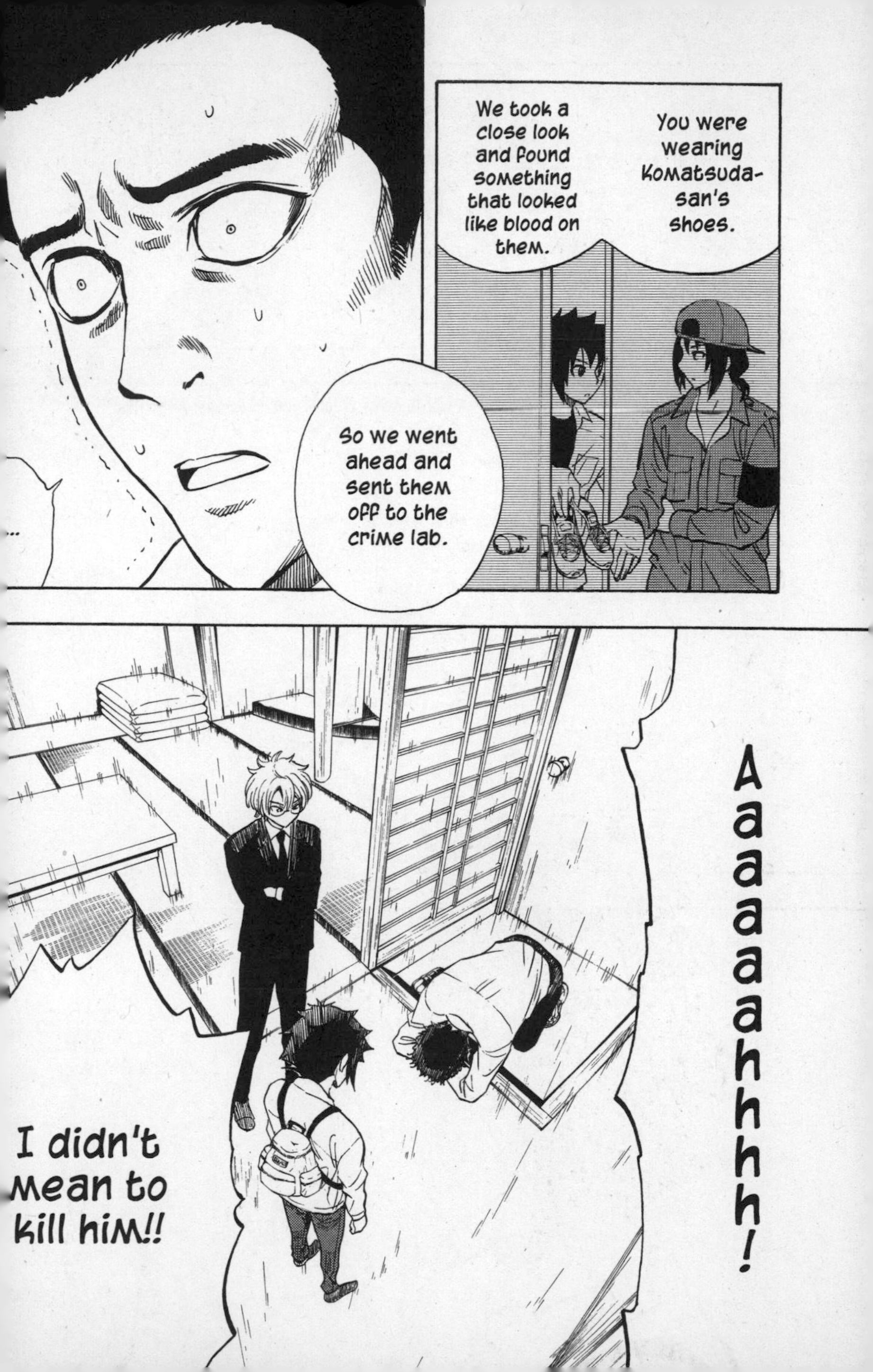

You were wearing Komatsuda-san's shoes.
We took a close look and found something that looked like blood on them.
So we went ahead and sent them off to the crime lab.
...
Aaaaaaahhhh!
I didn't mean to kill him!!

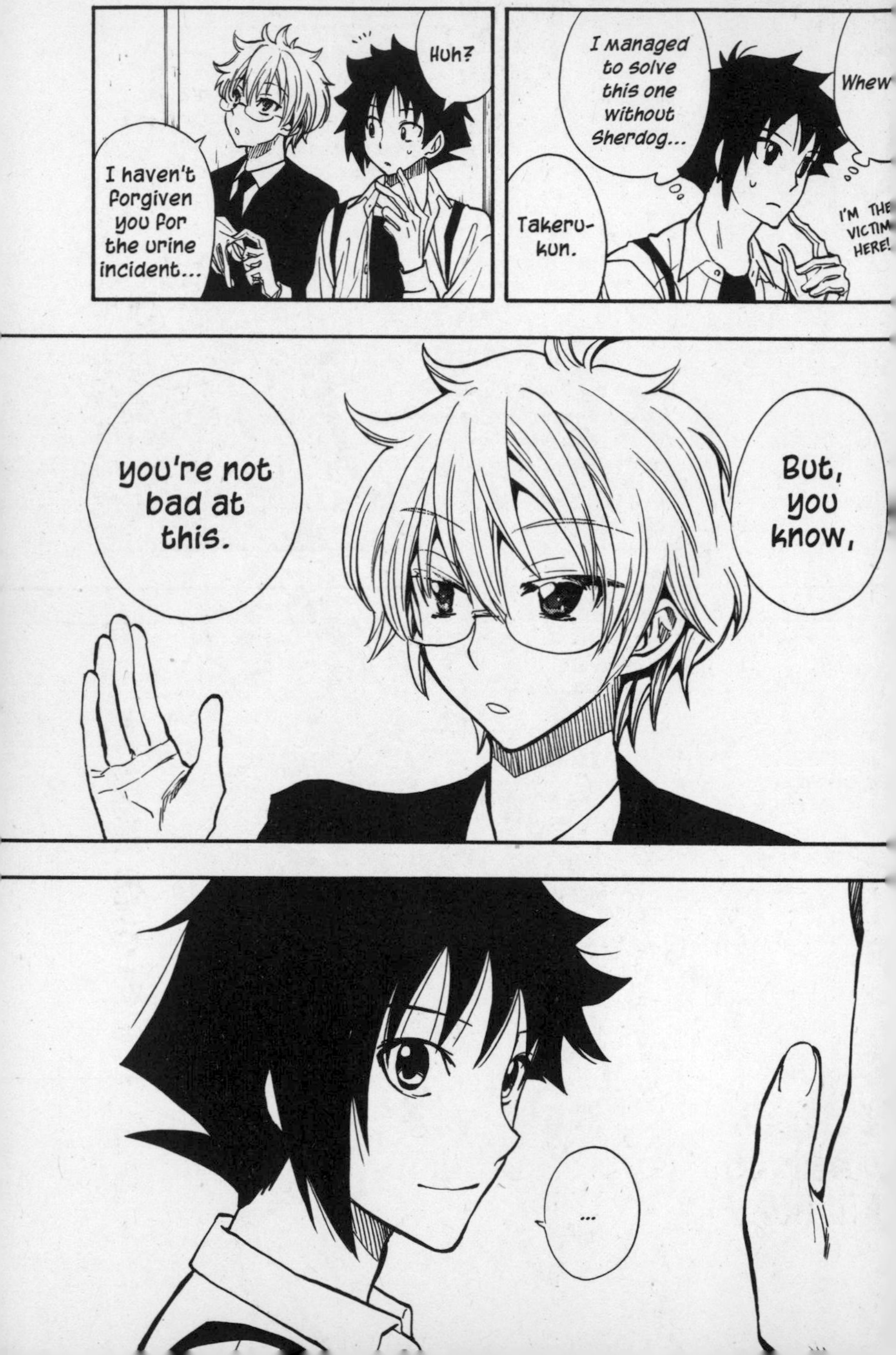
Whew
I managed to solve this one without Sherdog...
I'M THE VICTIM HERE!
Takeru-kun.
Huh?
I haven't forgiven you for the urine incident...
But, you know,
you're not bad at this.
...

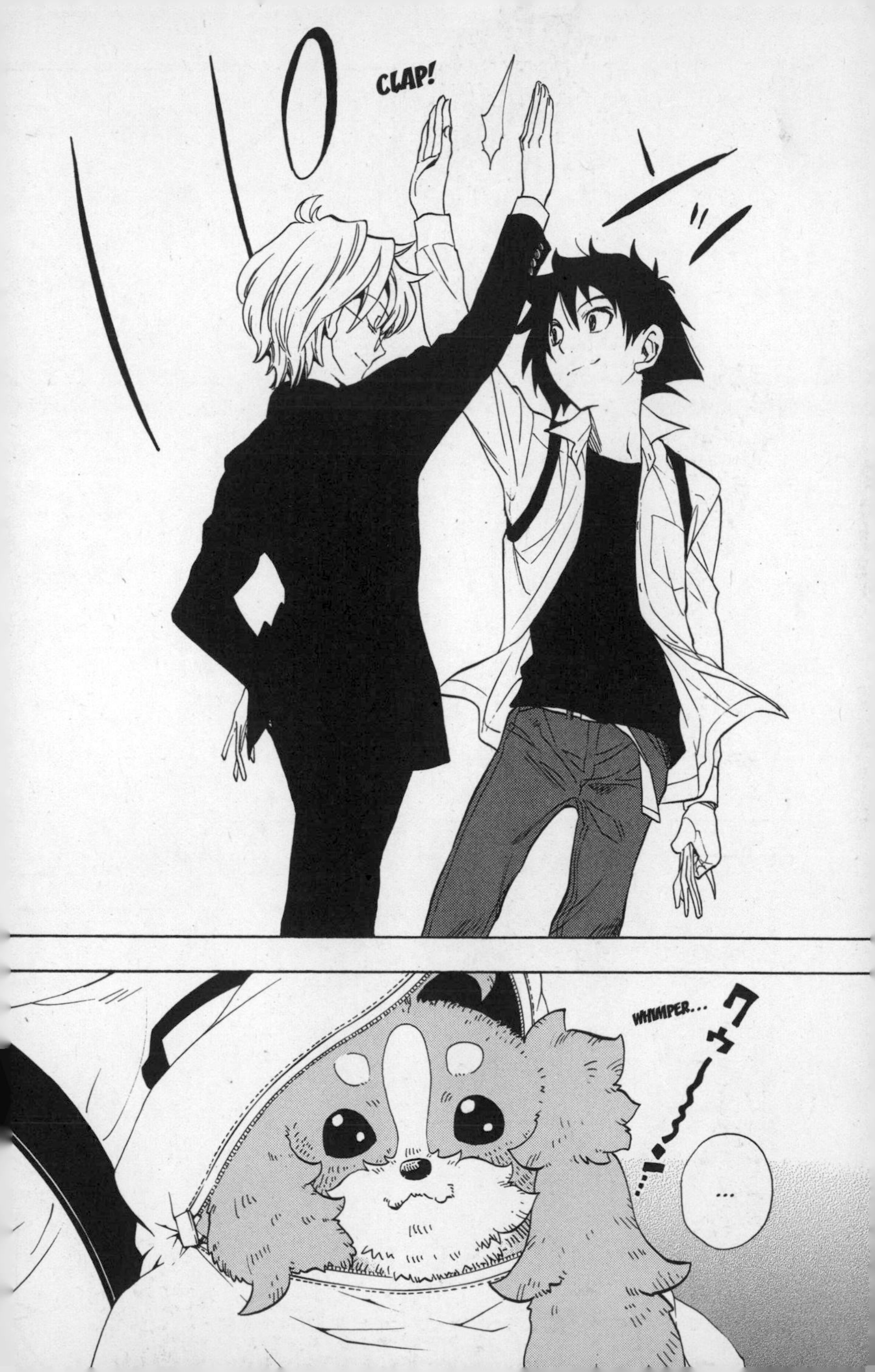
CLAP!
...
クゥー〜〜…!
WHIMPER...

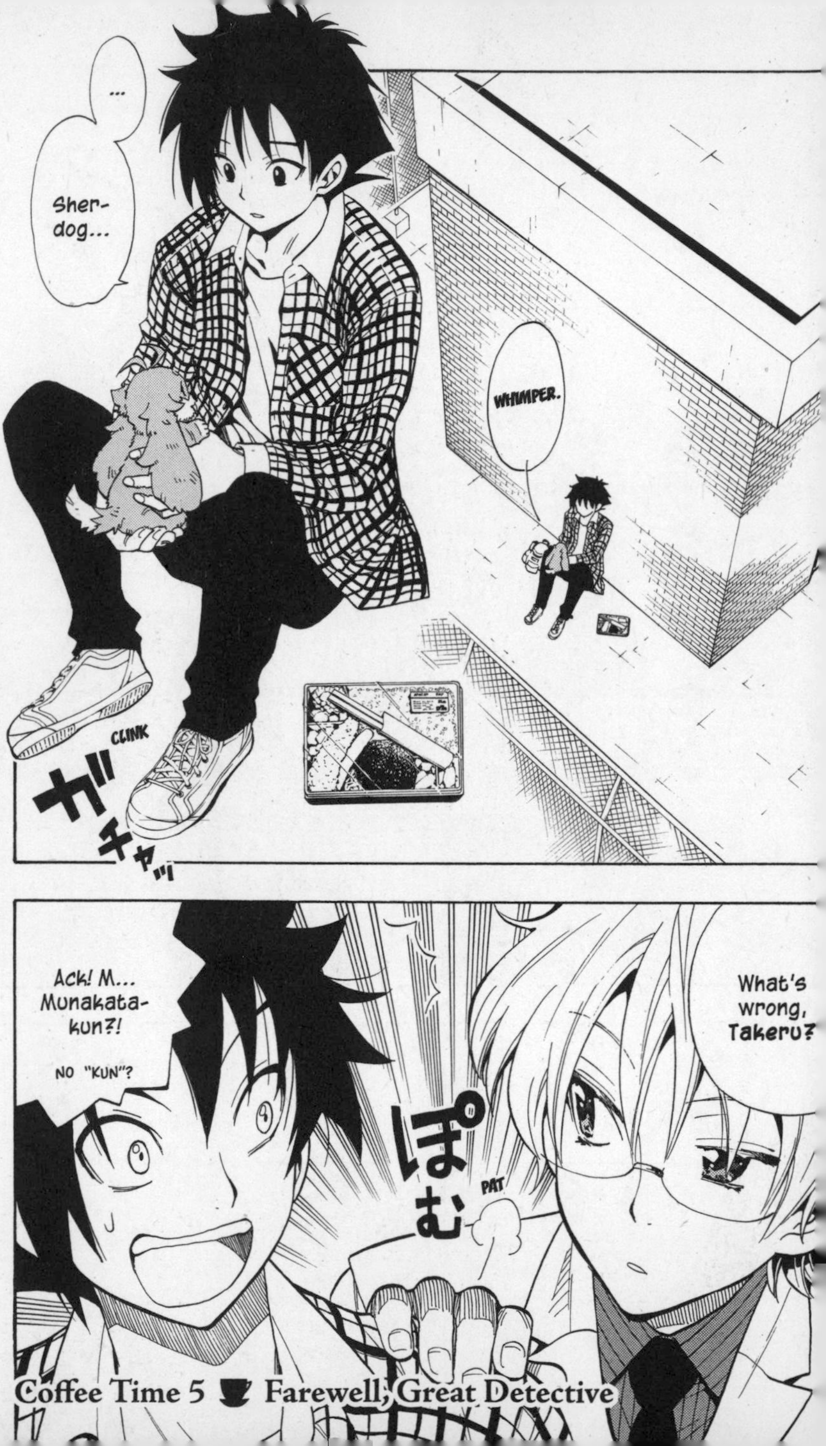
...
Sher-dog...
WHIMPER.
ガチャッ
CLINK
What's wrong, Takeru?
ぽむ
PAT
Ack! M... Munakata-kun?!
NO "KUN"?

Coffee Time 5 Farewell, Great Detective

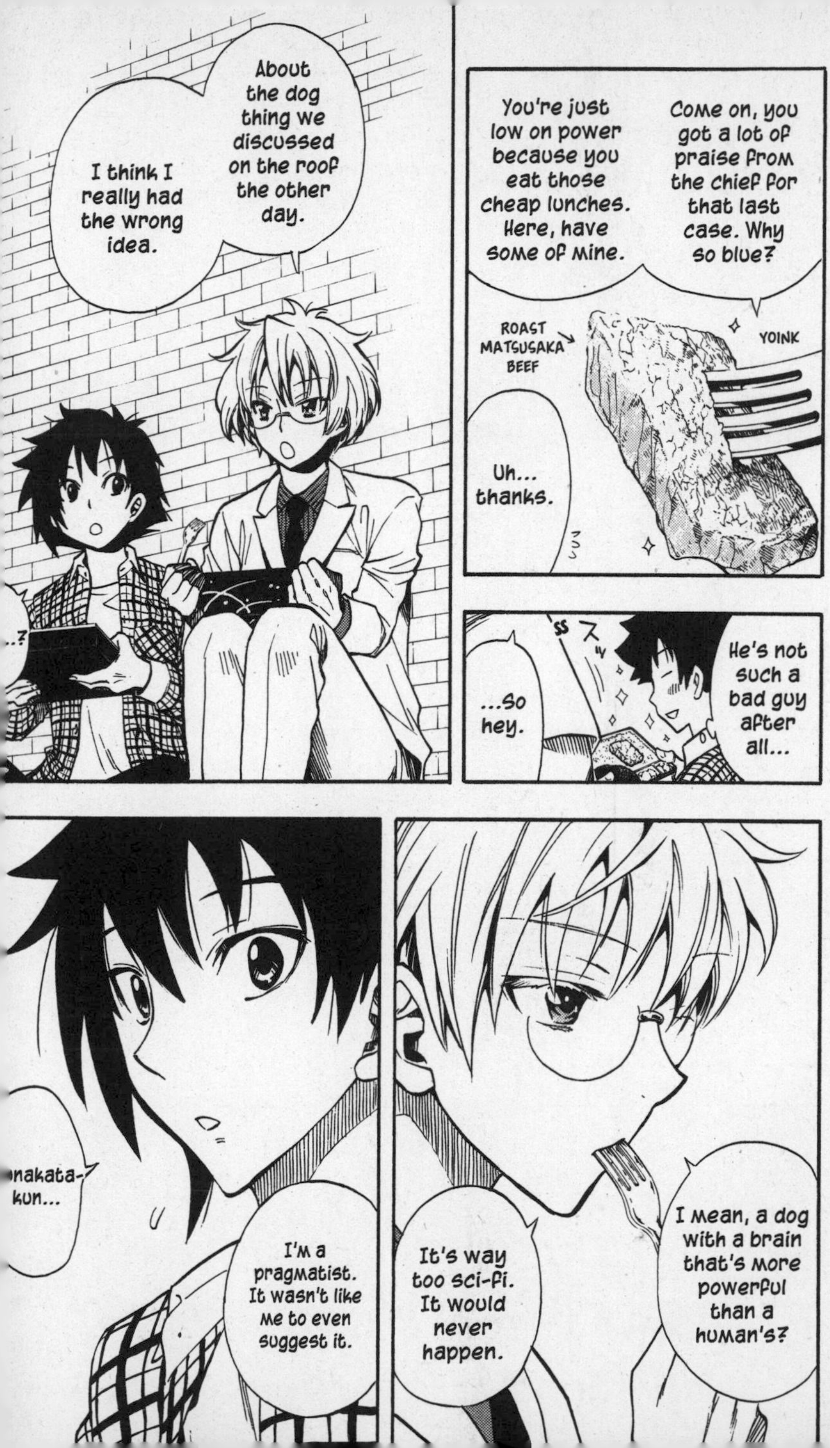
Come on, you got a lot of praise from the chief for that last case. Why so blue?
You're just low on power because you eat those cheap lunches. Here, have some of mine.
YOINK
ROAST MATSUSAKA BEEF
Uh... thanks.
He's not such a bad guy after all...
SS
...So hey.
About the dog thing we discussed on the roof the other day.
I think I really had the wrong idea.
...?
I mean, a dog with a brain that's more powerful than a human's?
It's way too sci-fi. It would never happen.
I'm a pragmatist. It wasn't like me to even suggest it.
nakata-kun...

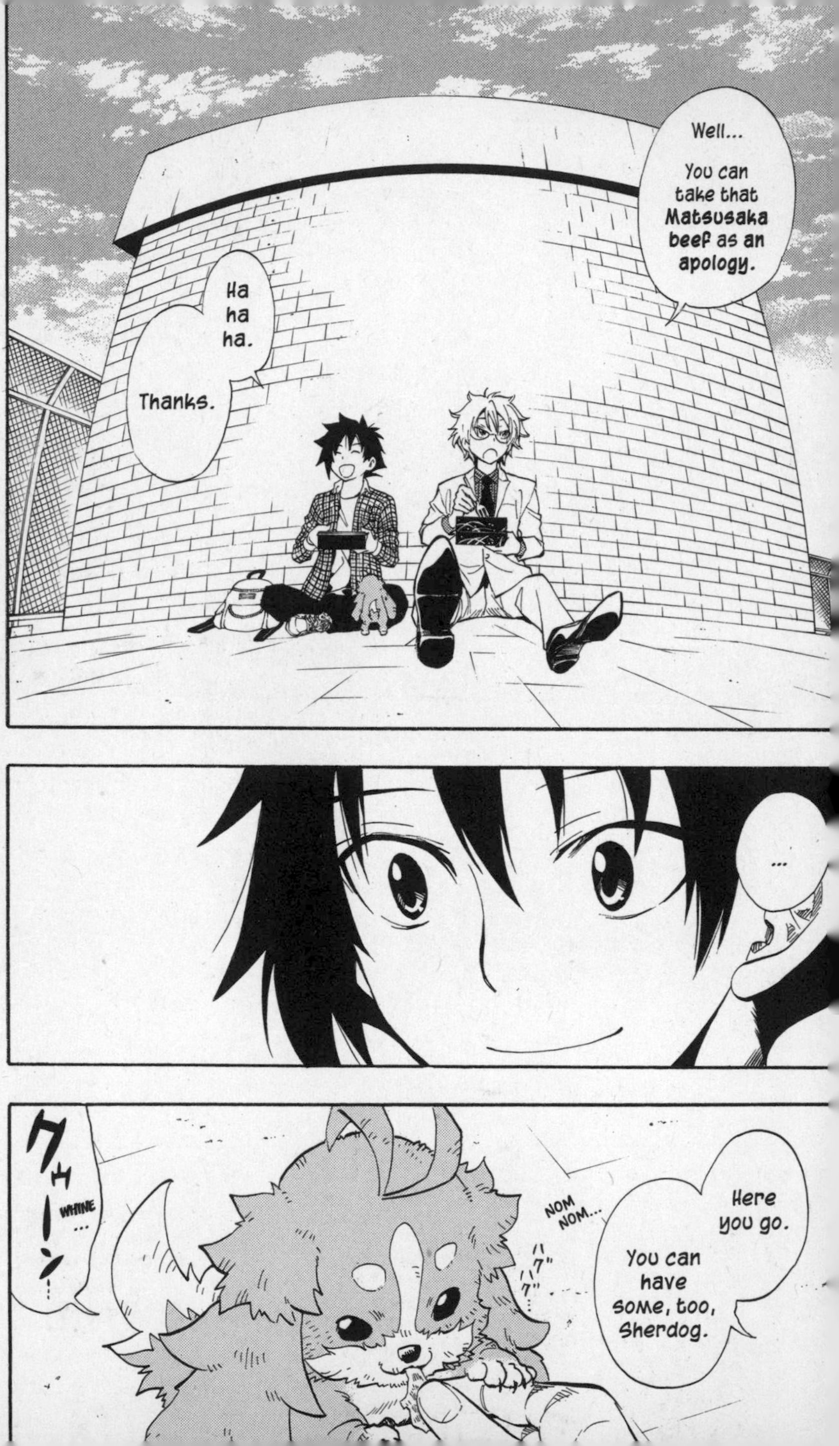

Well... You can take that Matsusaka beef as an apology.
Ha ha ha.
Thanks.
...
Here you go.
You can have some, too, Sherdog.
NOM NOM...
WHINE...

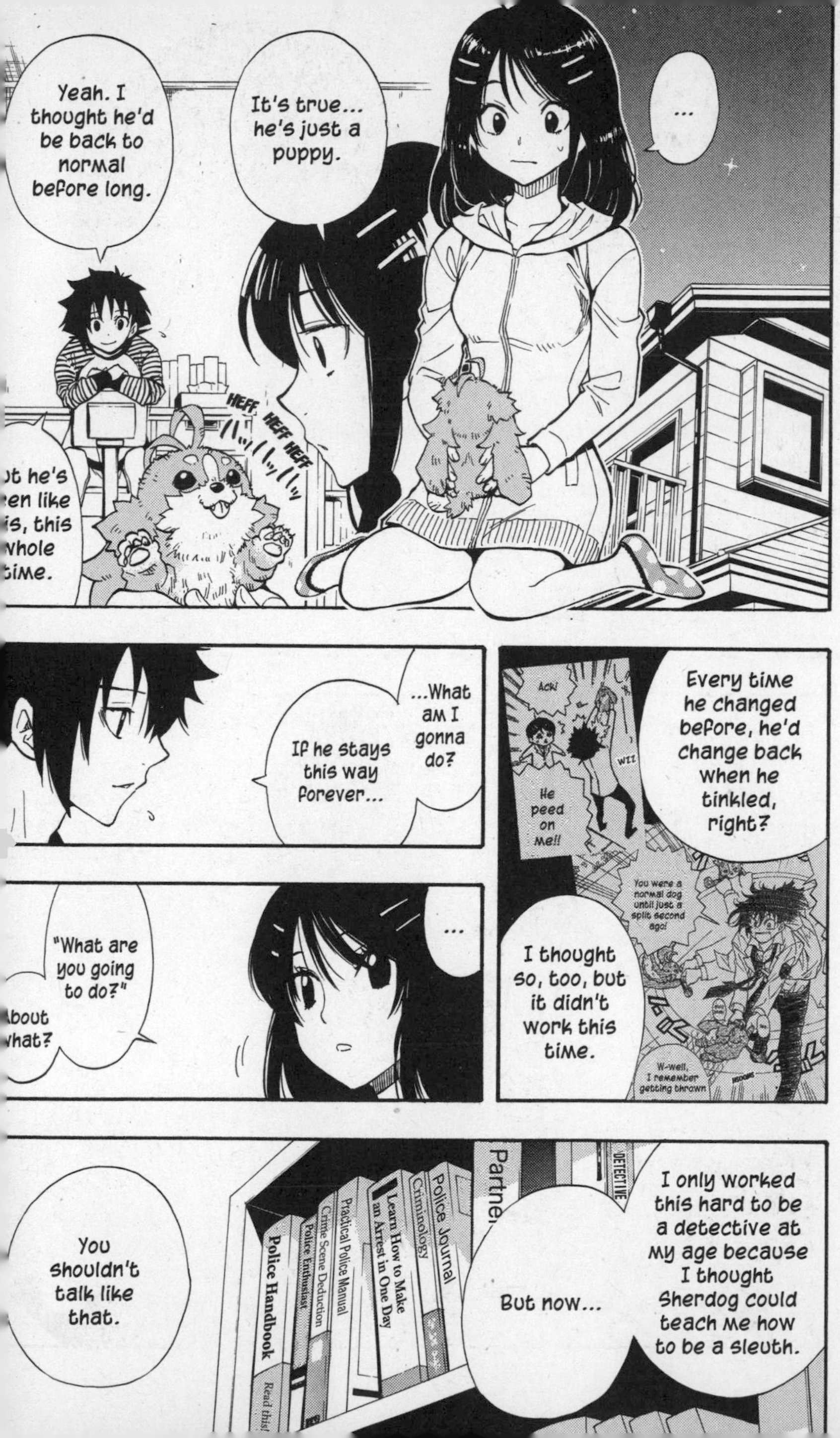
...
It's true... he's just a puppy.
Yeah. I thought he'd be back to normal before long.
HEFF HEFF HEFF
ut he's een like is, this whole time.
Every time he changed before, he'd change back when he tinkled, right?
ACK!
WZZ
He peed on Me!!
You were a normal dog until just a split second ago!
I thought so, too, but it didn't work this time.
W-well, I remember getting thrown
...What am I gonna do?
If he stays this way forever...
...
"What are you going to do?"
About what?
I only worked this hard to be a detective at my age because I thought Sherdog could teach me how to be a sleuth.
But now...
DETECTIVE
Partne
Police Journal
Criminology
Learn How to Make an Arrest in One Day
Practical Police Manual
Crime Scene Deduction
Police Enthusiast
Police Handbook
Read this!
You shouldn't talk like that.

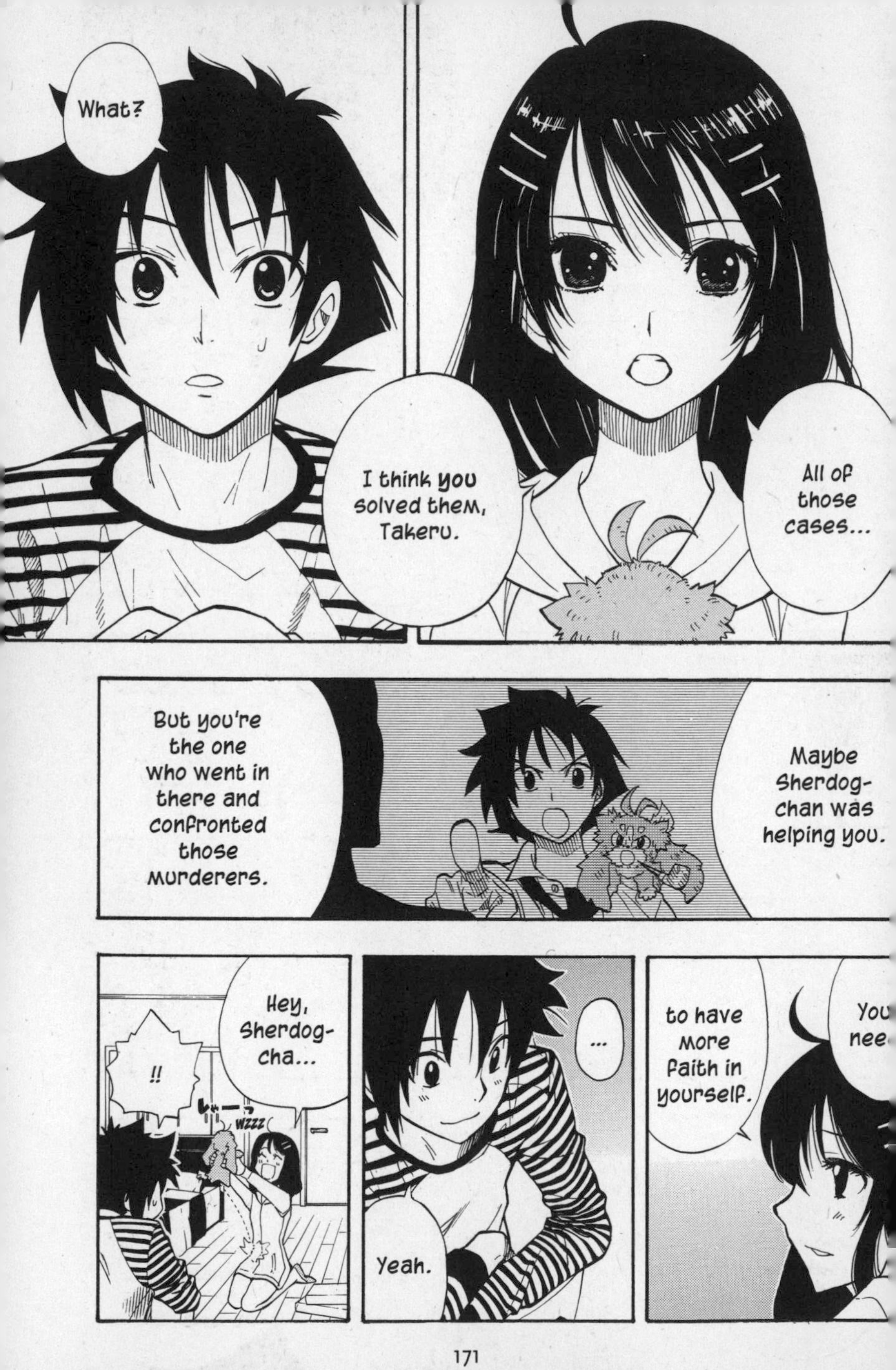
All of those cases...
I think you solved them, Takeru.
What?
Maybe Sherdog-chan was helping you.
But you're the one who went in there and confronted those murderers.
You nee
to have more faith in yourself.
...
Yeah.
Hey, Sherdog-cha...
!!
WZZZ

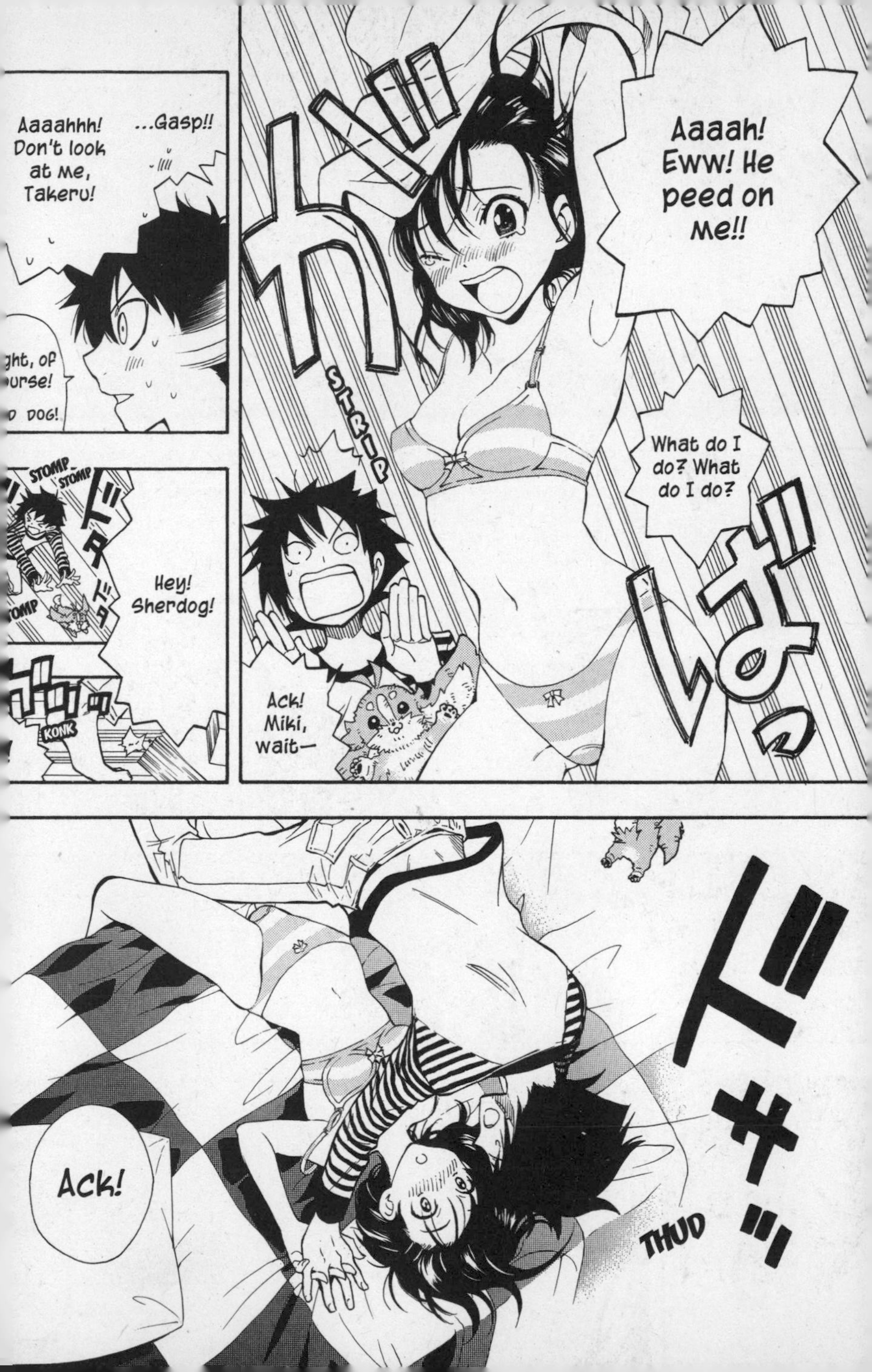
Aaaah! Eww! He peed on me!!
STRIP
What do I do? What do I do?
Ack! Miki, wait—
...Gasp!!
Aaaahhh! Don't look at me, Takeru!
ght, of ourse!
D DOG!
STOMP
STOMP
Hey! Sherdog!
STOMP
KONK
THUD
Ack!

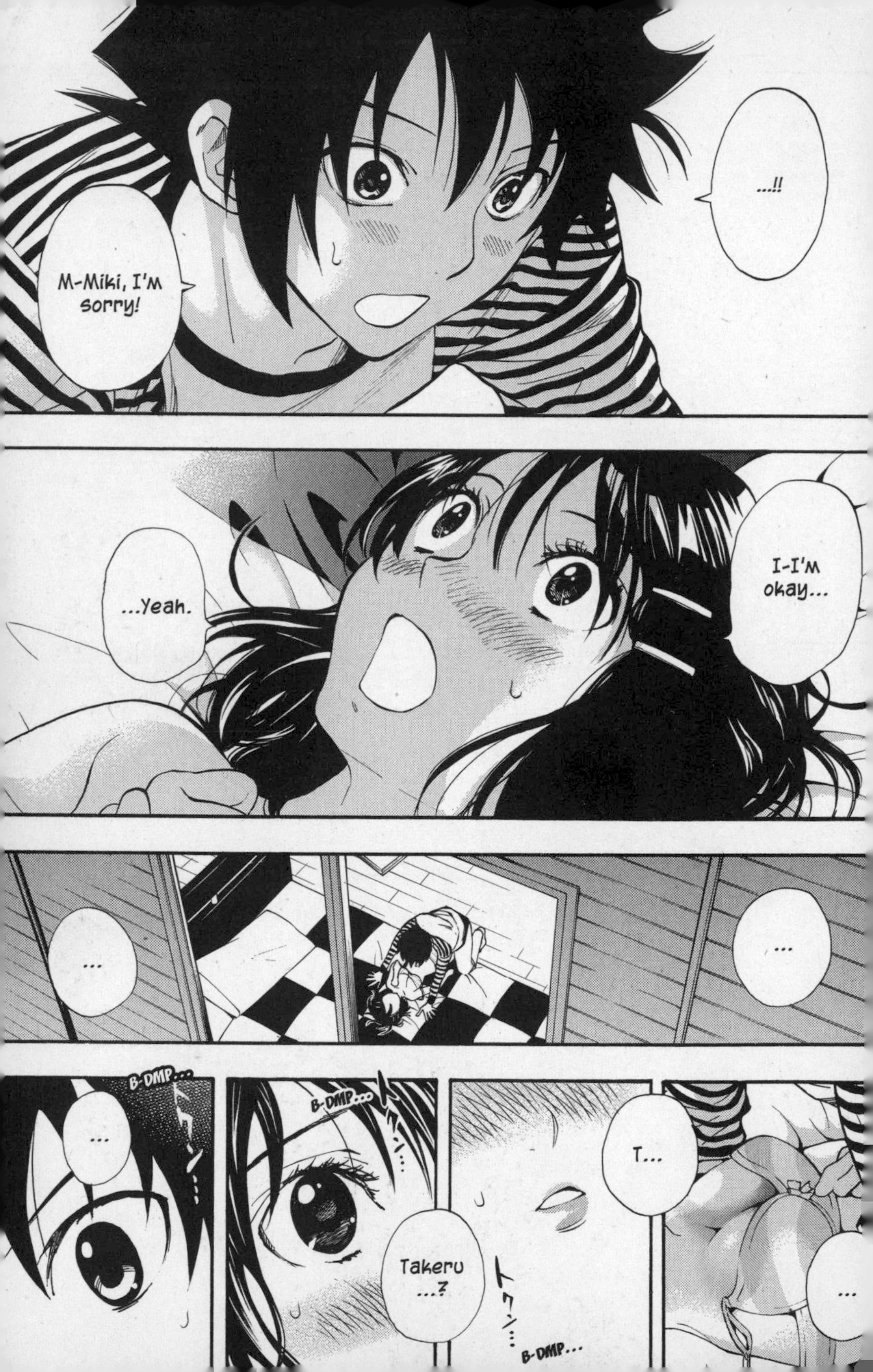

...!!
M-Miki, I'm sorry!
I-I'm okay...
...Yeah.
...
...
...
T...
B-DMP...
Takeru ...?
B-DMP...
B-DMP...
...

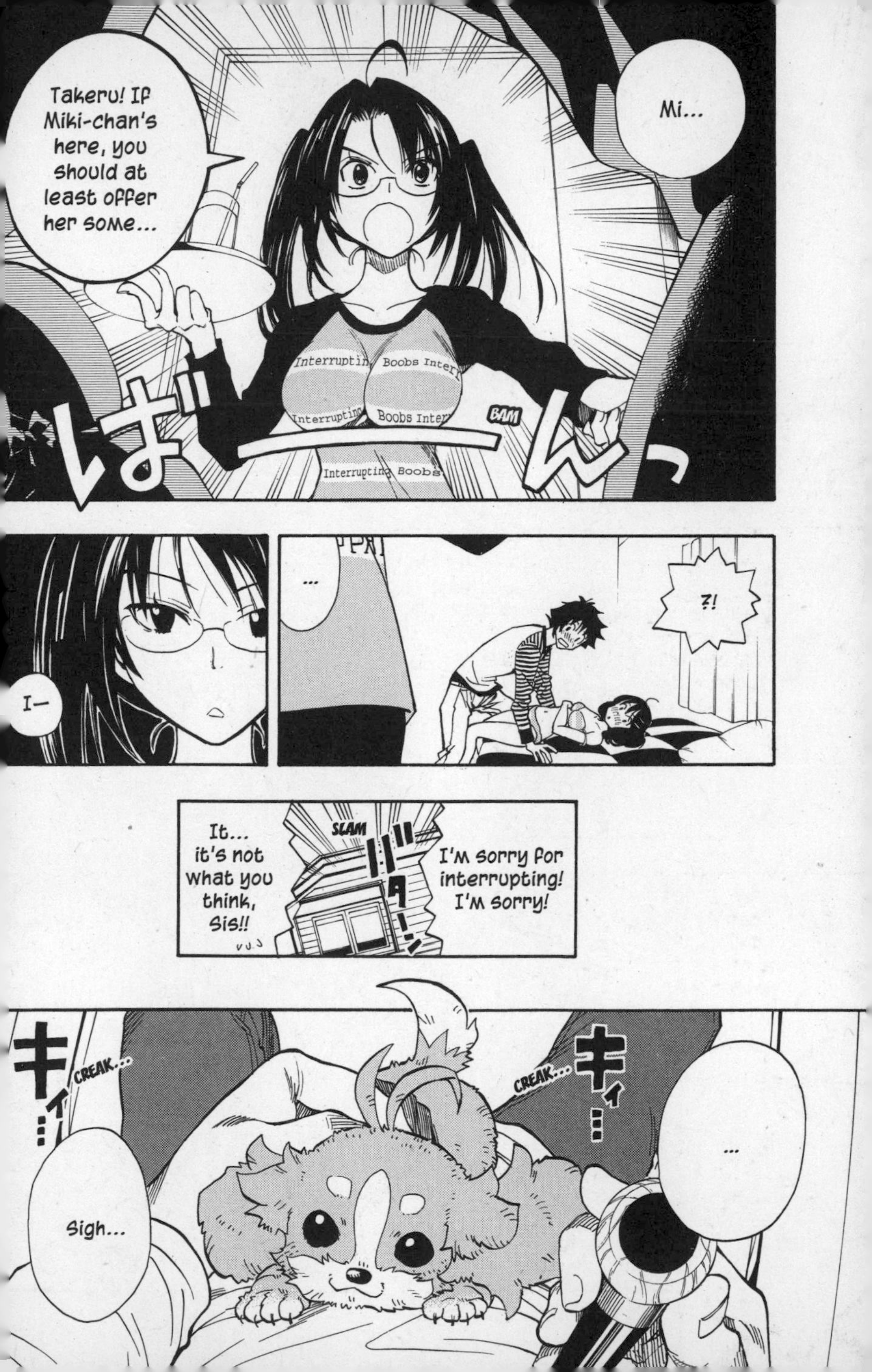
Mi...
Takeru! If Miki-chan's here, you should at least offer her some...
Interrupting Boobs
BAM
?!
...
I—
I'm sorry for interrupting! I'm sorry!
SLAM
It... it's not what you think, Sis!!
CREAK...
...
CREAK...
Sigh...

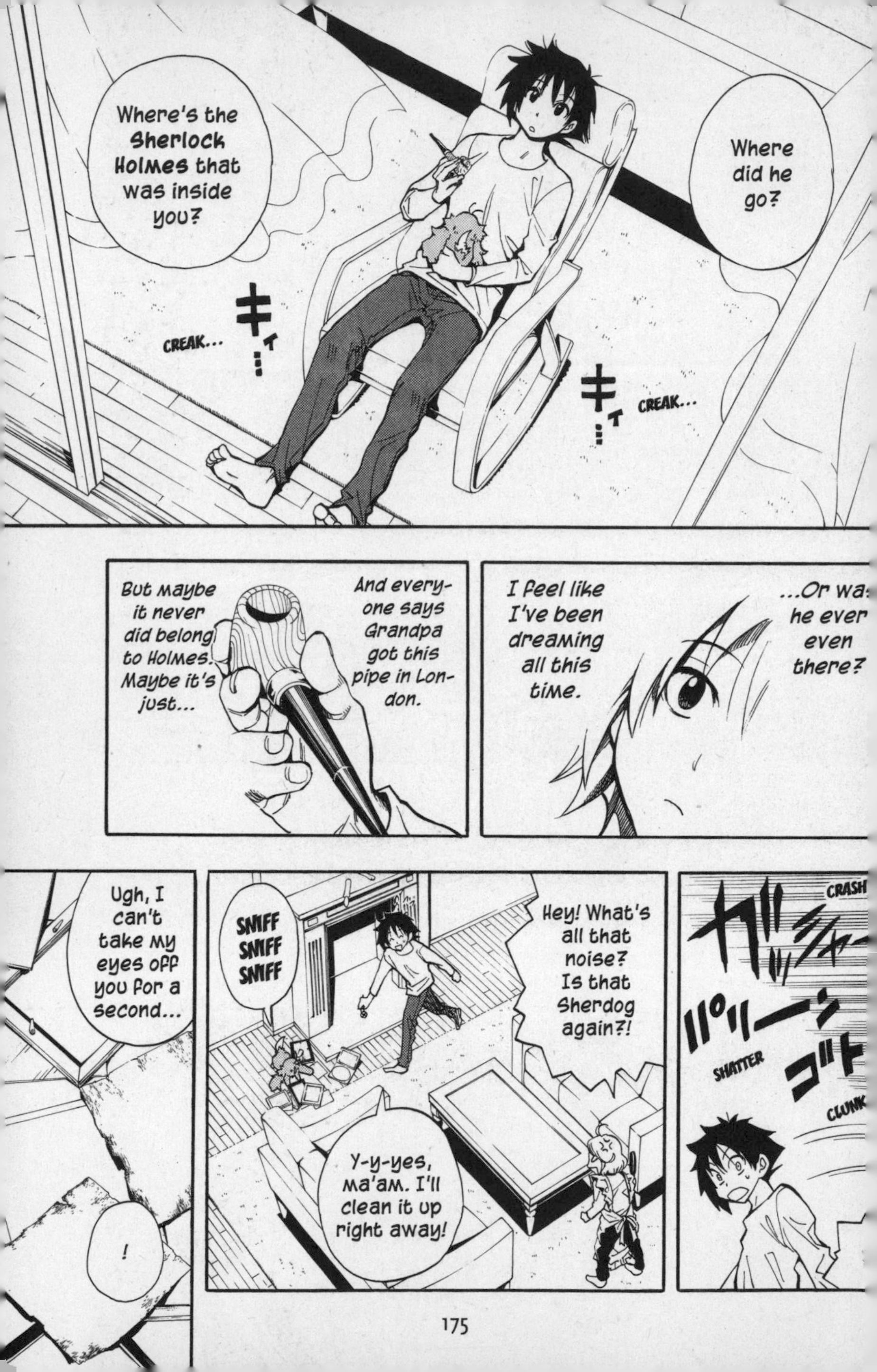
Where did he go?
Where's the Sherlock Holmes that was inside you?
CREAK...
CREAK...
...Or was he ever even there?
I feel like I've been dreaming all this time.
And every-one says Grandpa got this pipe in Lon-don.
But maybe it never did belong to Holmes. Maybe it's just...
CRASH
SHATTER
CLUNK
Hey! What's all that noise? Is that Sherdog again?!
SNIFF SNIFF SNIFF
Y-y-yes, ma'am. I'll clean it up right away!
Ugh, I can't take my eyes off you for a second...
!

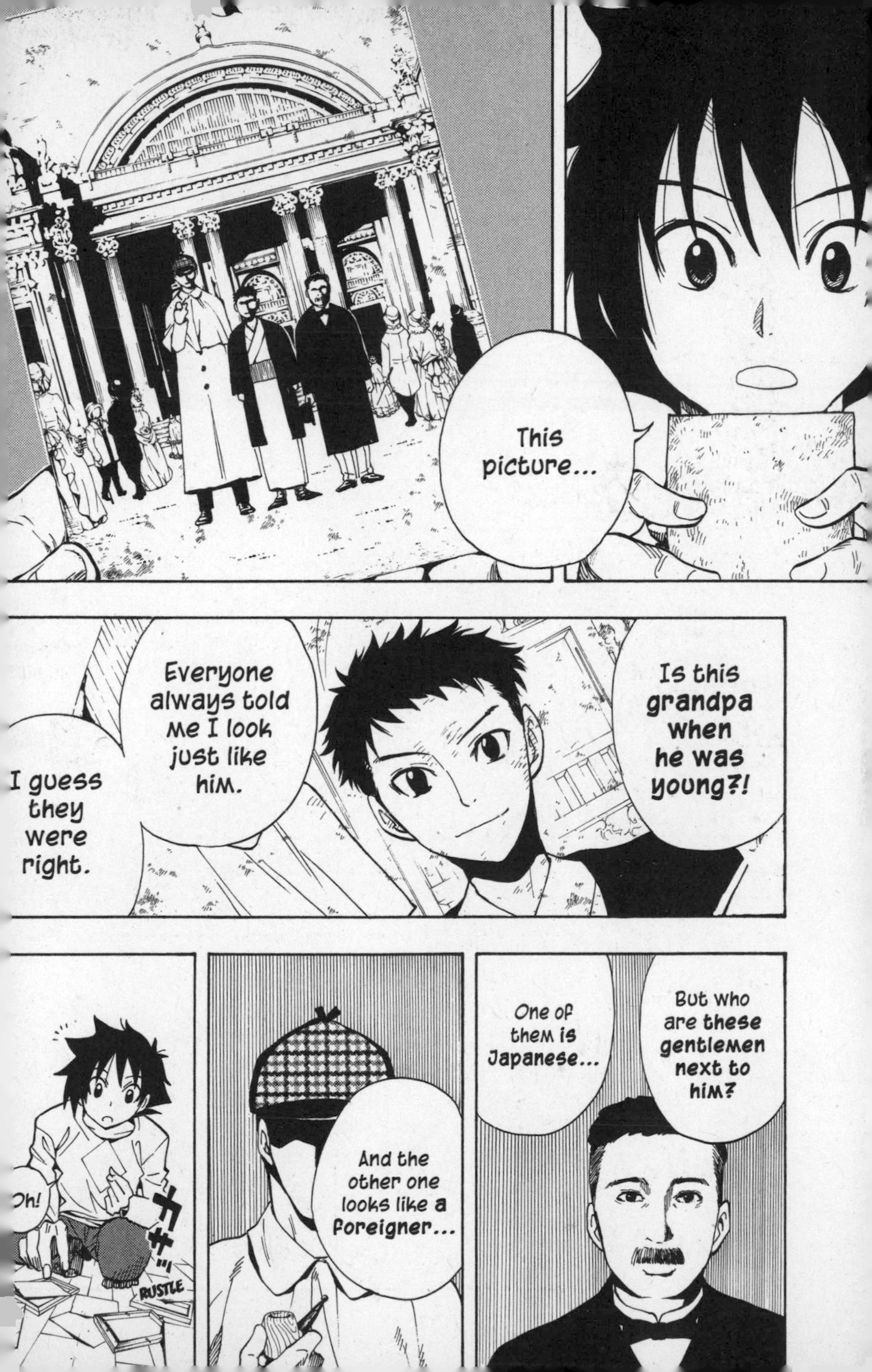

This picture...
Is this grandpa when he was young?!
Everyone always told me I look just like him.
I guess they were right.
But who are these gentlemen next to him?
One of them is Japanese...
And the other one looks like a foreigner...
Oh!
RUSTLE

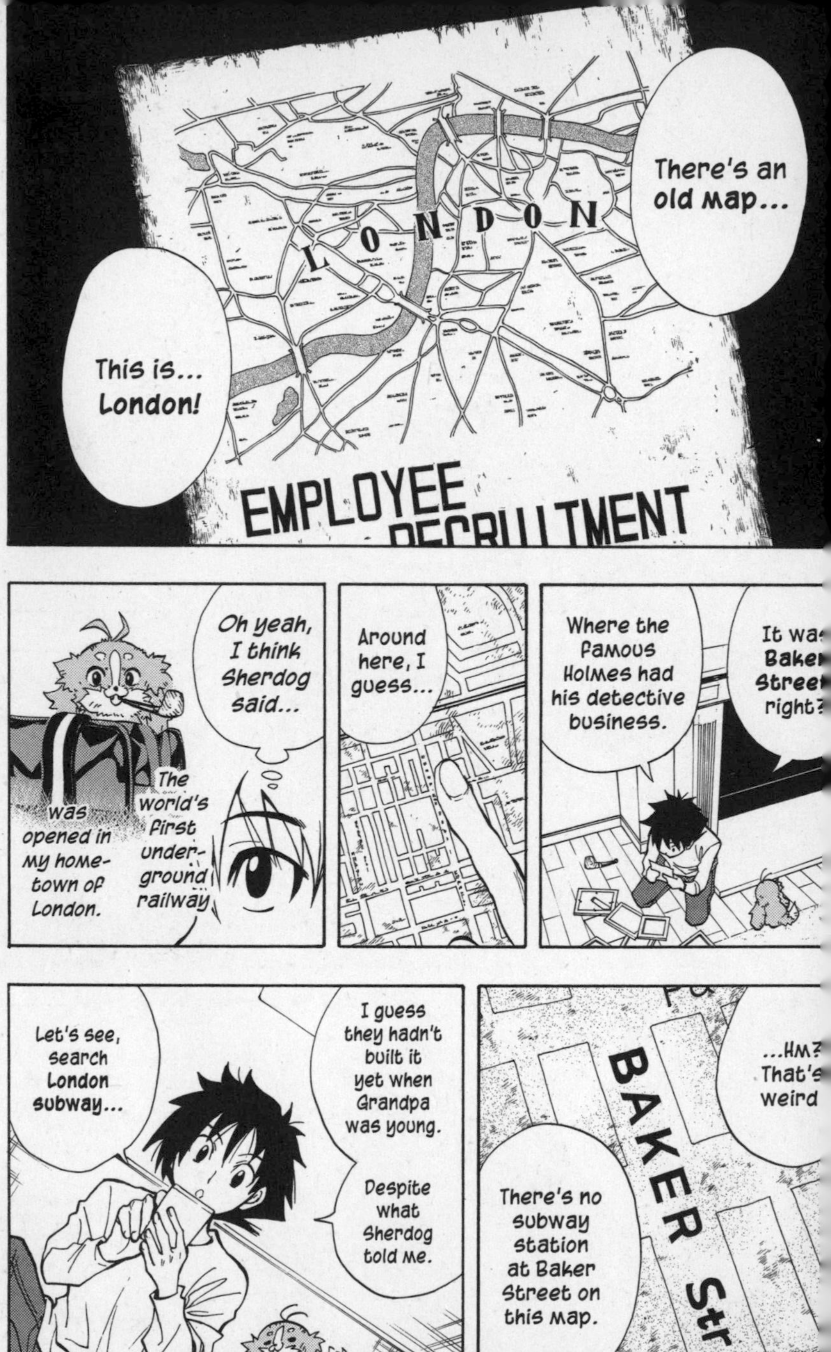
There's an old map...
This is... London!
LONDON
EMPLOYEE
It wa Bake Stree right?
Where the famous Holmes had his detective business.
Around here, I guess...
Oh yeah, I think Sherdog said...
The world's first under-ground railway
was opened in my home-town of London.
...HM? That's weird
There's no subway station at Baker Street on this map.
BAKER Str
Let's see, search London subway...
I guess they hadn't built it yet when Grandpa was young.
Despite what Sherdog told me.

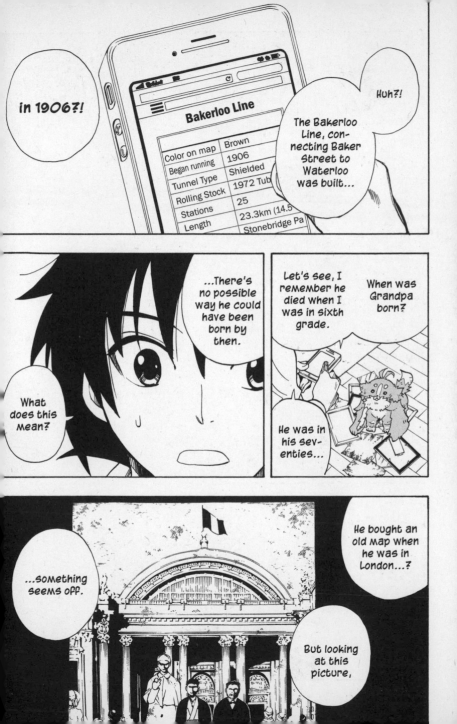

in 1906?!

The Bakerloo Line, connecting Baker Street to Waterloo was built...

Huh?!

Bakerloo Line

Color on map	Brown
Began running	1906
Tunnel Type	Shielded
Rolling Stock	1972 Tub
Stations	25
Length	23.3km (14.5
	Stonebridge Pa

...There's no possible way he could have been born by then.

Let's see, I remember he died when I was in sixth grade.

When was Grandpa born?

What does this mean?

He was in his seventies...

He bought an old map when he was in London...?

...something seems off.

But looking at this picture,

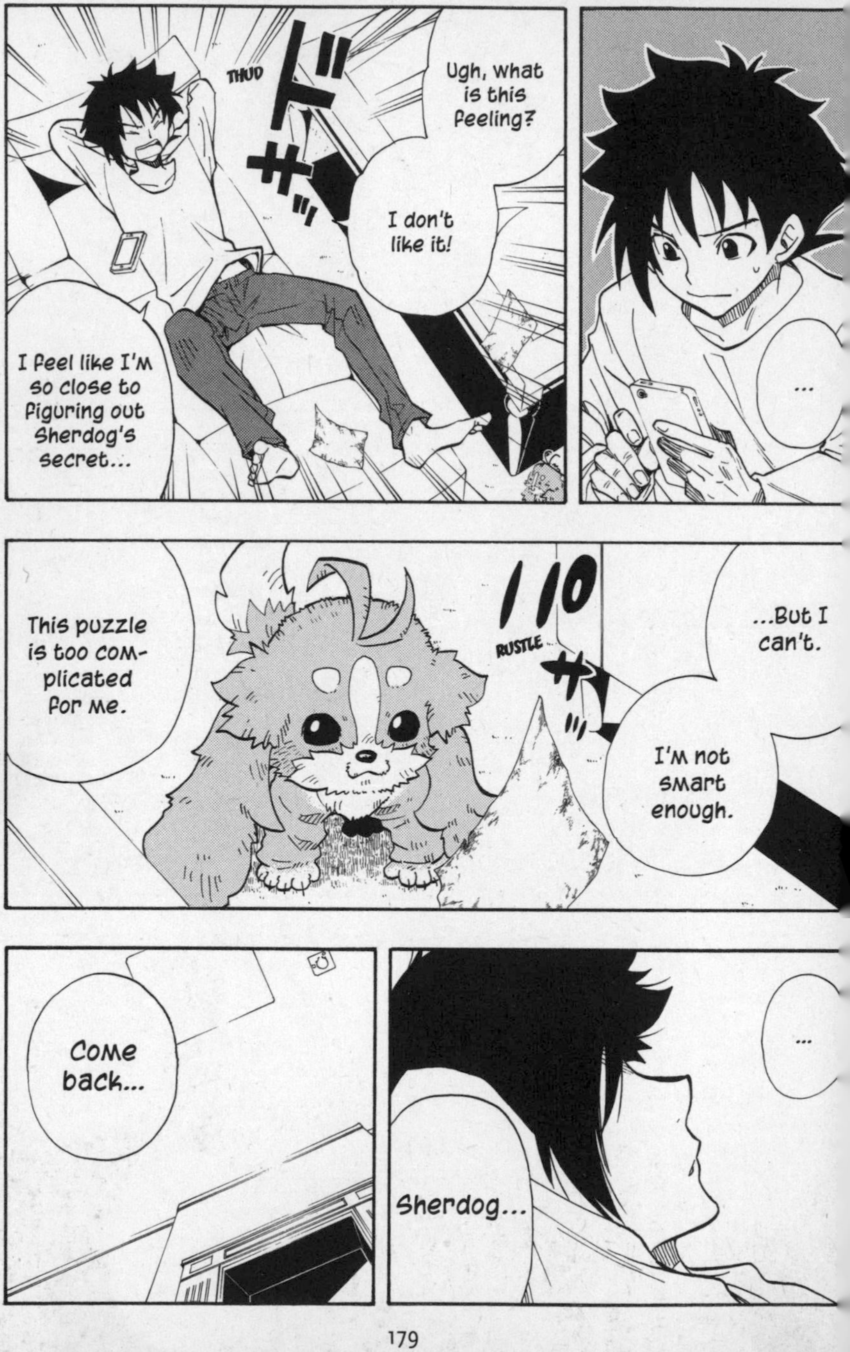
...
THUD
Ugh, what is this feeling?
I don't like it!
I feel like I'm so close to figuring out Sherdog's secret...
...But I can't.
I'm not smart enough.
RUSTLE
This puzzle is too complicated for me.
...
Sherdog...
Come back...

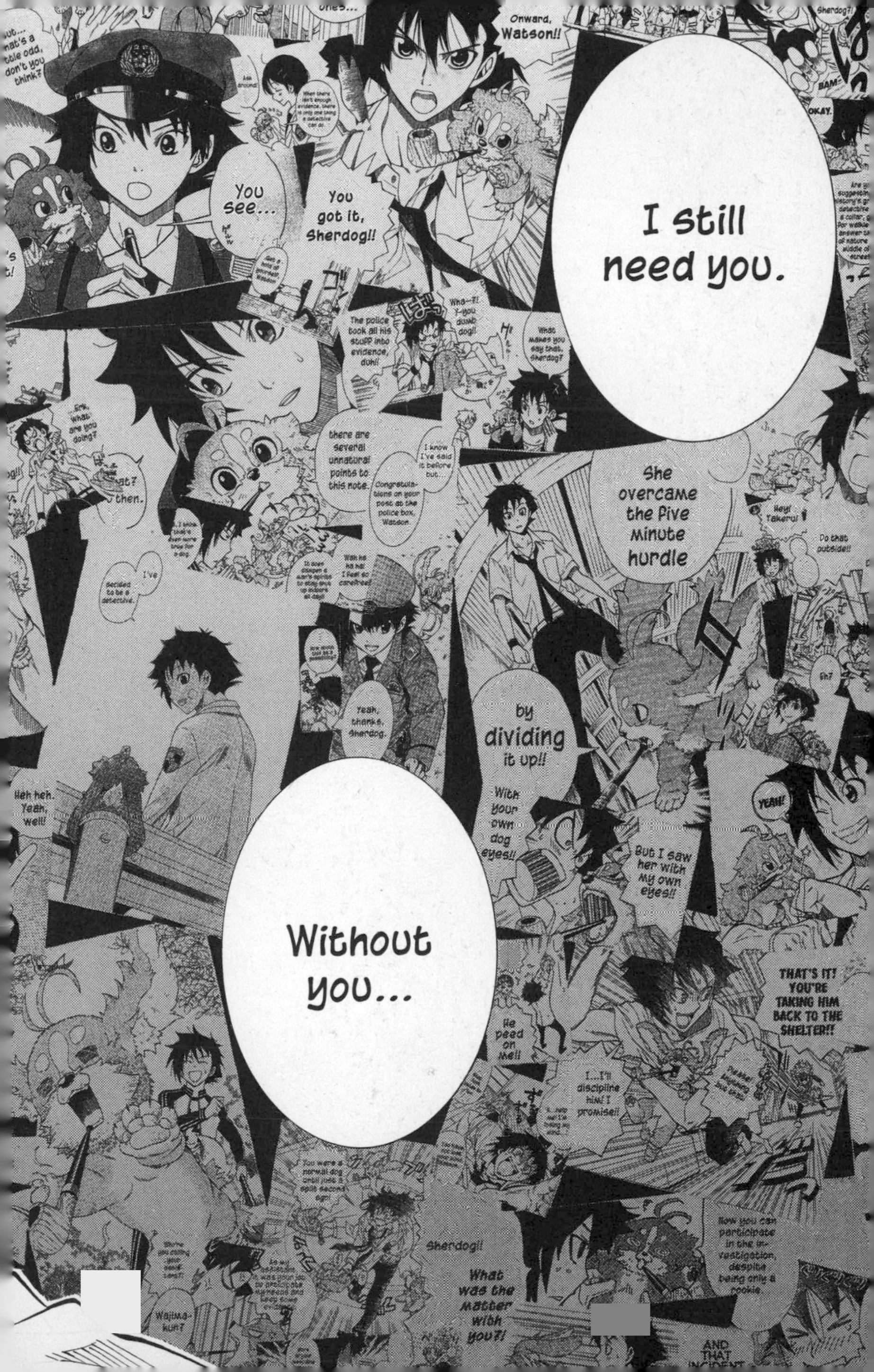
Sherdog!?
OKAY.
Onward, Watson!!
I still need you.
You got it, Sherdog!!
You see...
...that's a little odd, don't you think?
What makes you say that, Sherdog?
Wha--?! Y-you dumb dog!!
The police took all his stuff into evidence, duh!
She overcame the five minute hurdle
I know I've said it before, but...
Congratulations on your post at the police box, Watson.
there are several unnatural points to this note.
Erk, what are you doing?
Hey! Takeru!
Do that outside!!
I've
decided to be a detective.
by dividing it up!!
With your own dog eyes!!
Yeah, thanks, Sherdog.
YEAH!
But I saw her with my own eyes!!
Heh heh. Yeah, well!
Without you...
THAT'S IT! YOU'RE TAKING HIM BACK TO THE SHELTER!!
I...I'll discipline him! I promise!!
He peed on me!!
You were a normal dog until just a split second ago!
Now you can participate in the investigation, despite being only a cookie.
Sherdog!!
What was the matter with you?!
Wajima-kun?

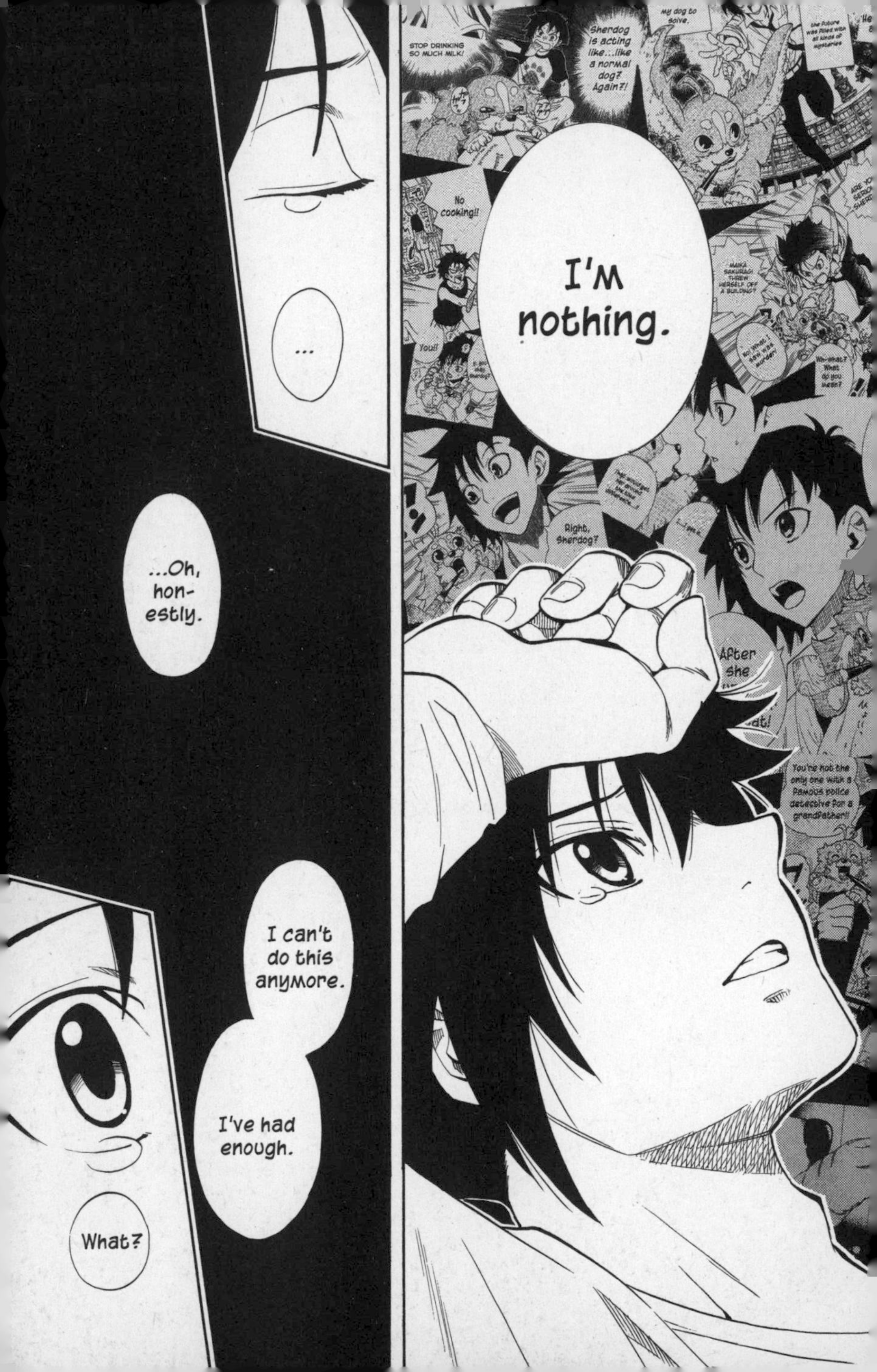
STOP DRINKING SO MUCH MILK!
Sherdog is acting like...like a normal dog? Again?!
No cooking!!
I'M nothing.
Right, Sherdog?
You're not the only one with a famous police detective for a grandfather!!
...
...Oh, honestly.
I can't do this anymore.
I've had enough.
What?

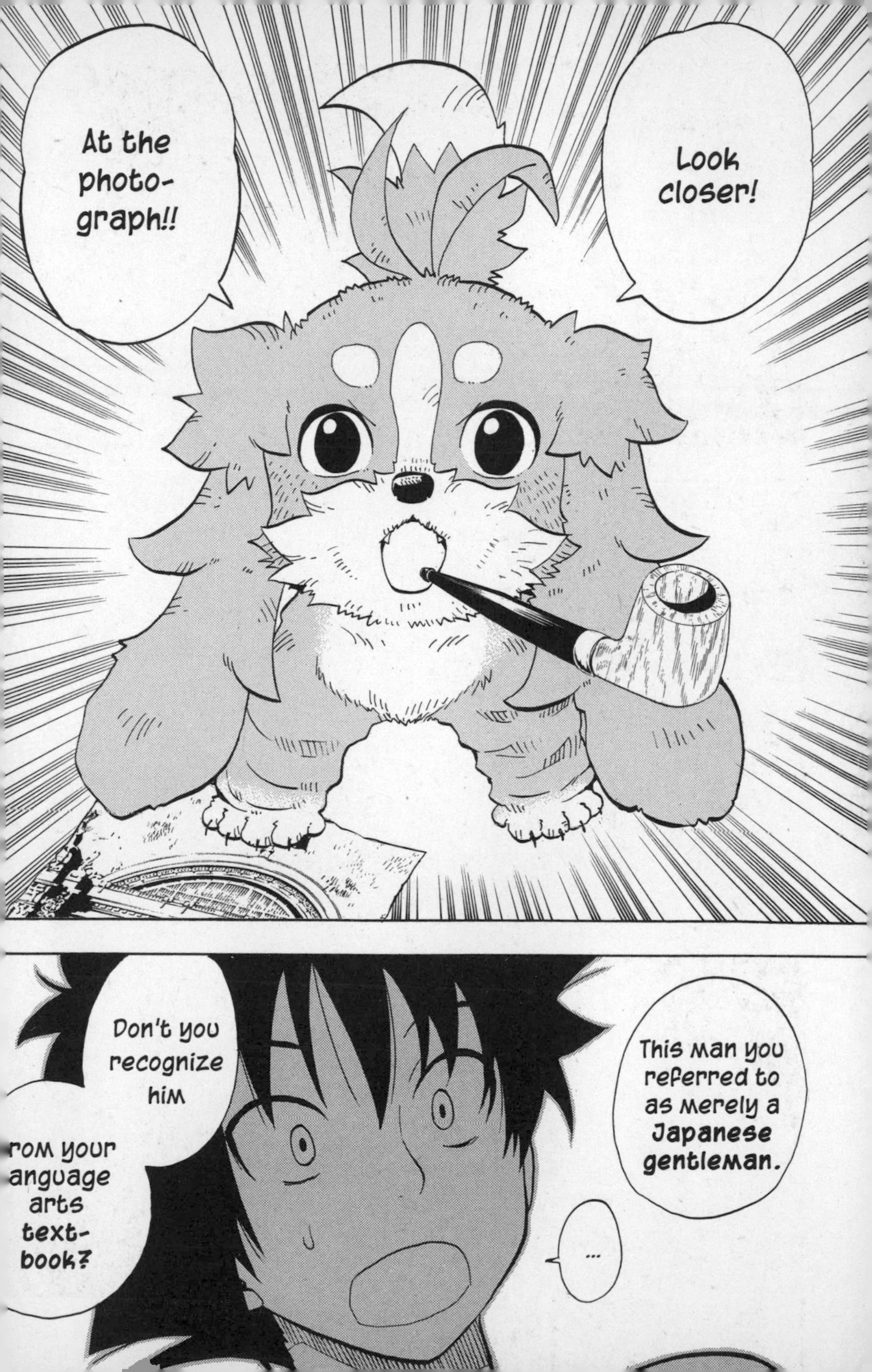
Look closer!
At the photo-graph!!
This man you referred to as merely a Japanese gentleman.
Don't you recognize him rom your anguage arts text-book?
...

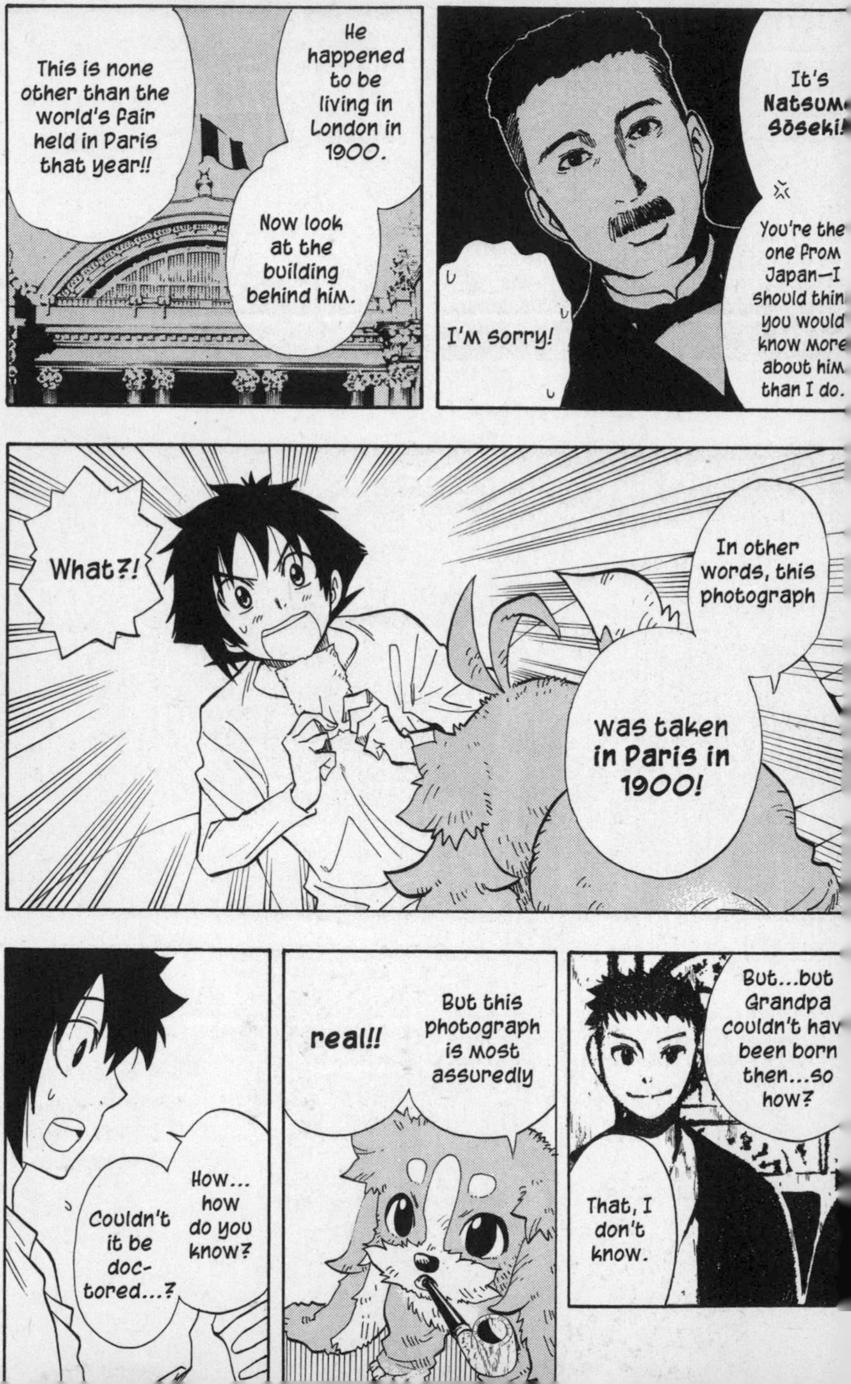
It's Natsume Sōseki!
You're the one from Japan—I should thin you would know more about him than I do.
I'm sorry!
He happened to be living in London in 1900.
This is none other than the world's fair held in Paris that year!!
Now look at the building behind him.
In other words, this photograph
was taken in Paris in 1900!
What?!
But...but Grandpa couldn't hav been born then...so how?
That, I don't know.
But this photograph is most assuredly
real!!
How... how do you know?
Couldn't it be doc-tored...?

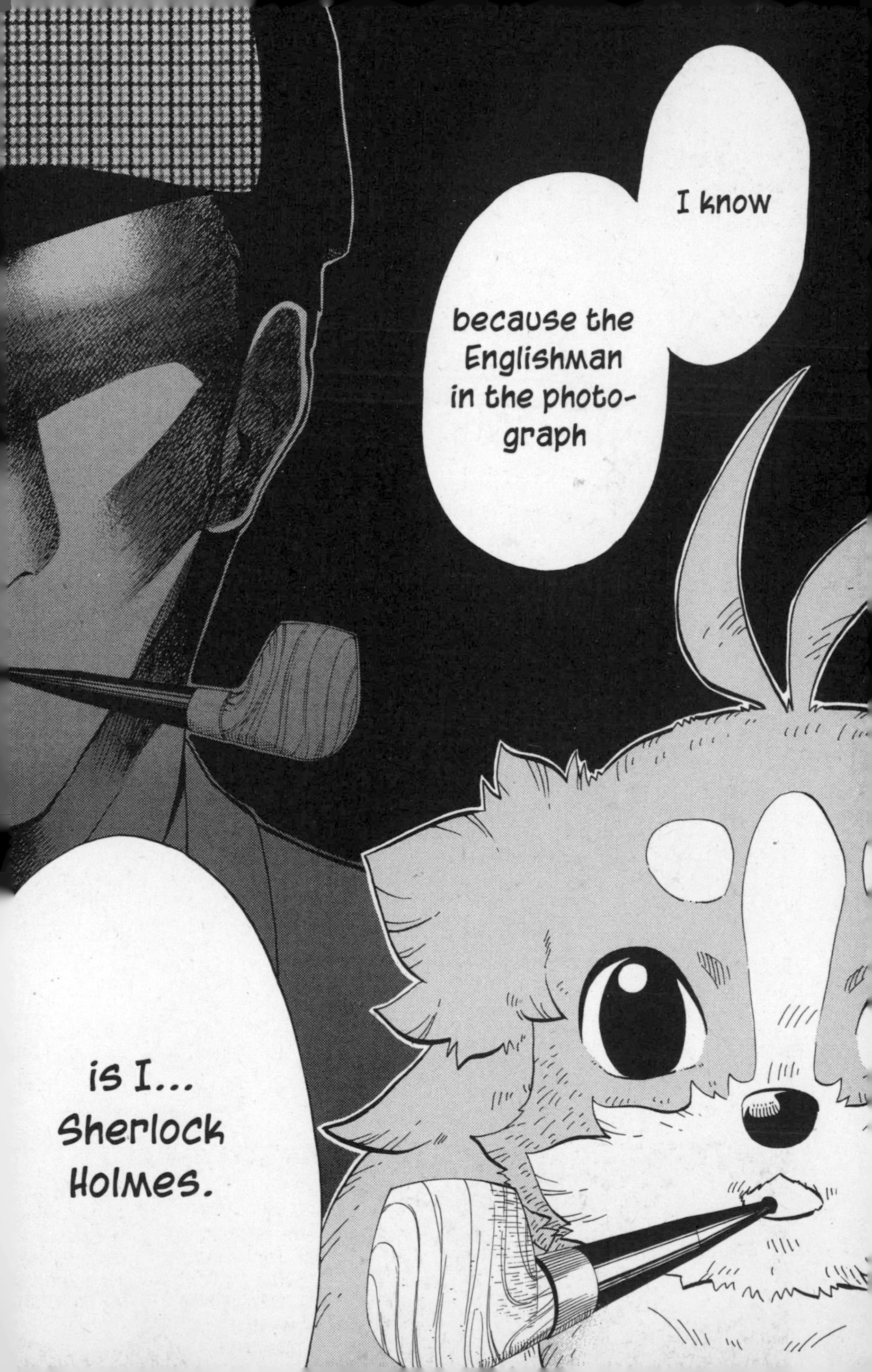
I know
because the Englishman in the photo-graph
is I... Sherlock Holmes.

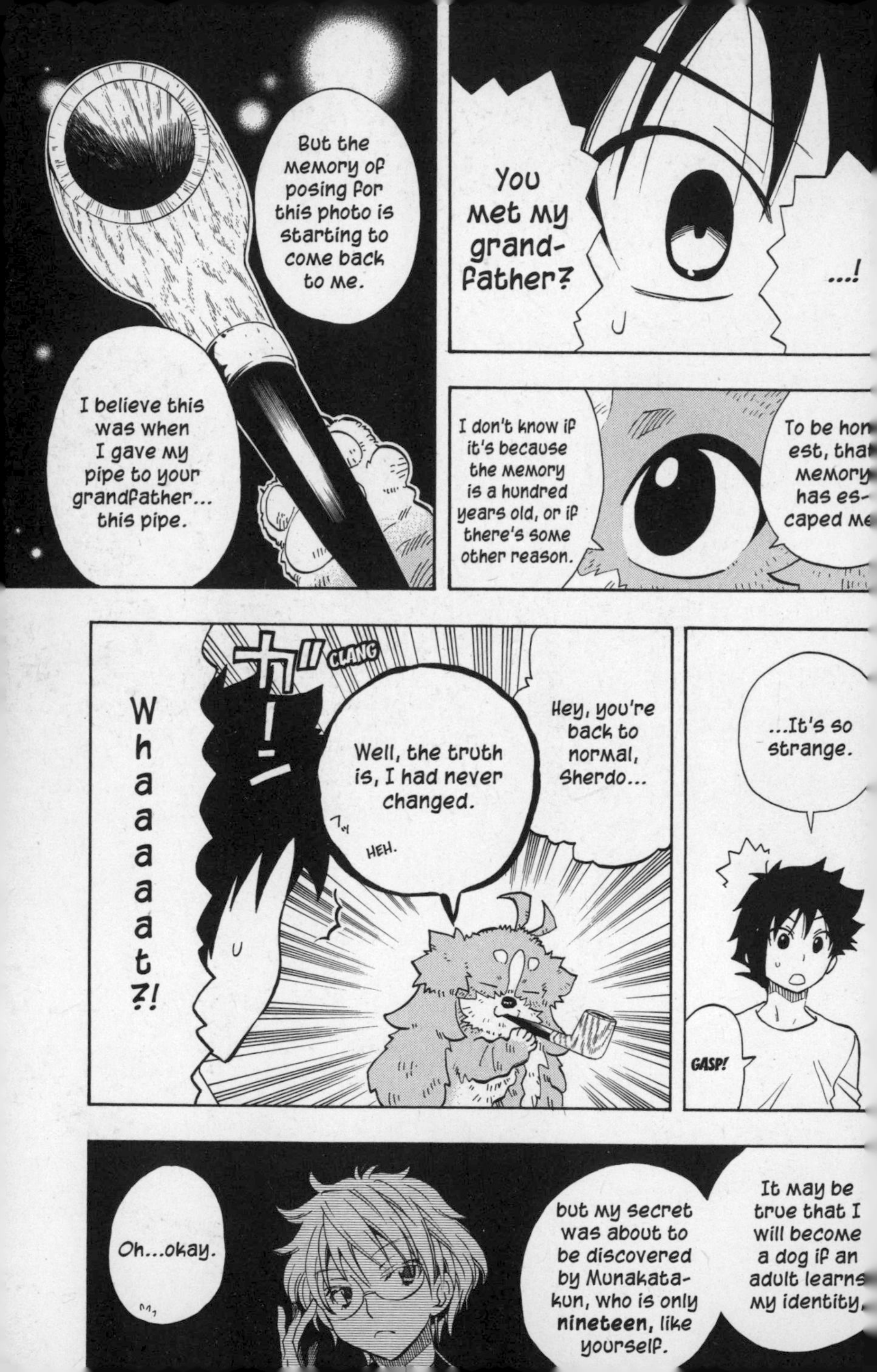
...!
You met my grandfather?
To be honest, that memory has escaped me
I don't know if it's because the memory is a hundred years old, or if there's some other reason.
But the memory of posing for this photo is starting to come back to me.
I believe this was when I gave my pipe to your grandfather... this pipe.
...It's so strange.
GASP!
Hey, you're back to normal, Sherdo...
Well, the truth is, I had never changed.
HEH.
CLANG
Whaaaaaat?!
It may be true that I will become a dog if an adult learns my identity,
but my secret was about to be discovered by Munakata-kun, who is only **nineteen**, like yourself.
Oh...okay.

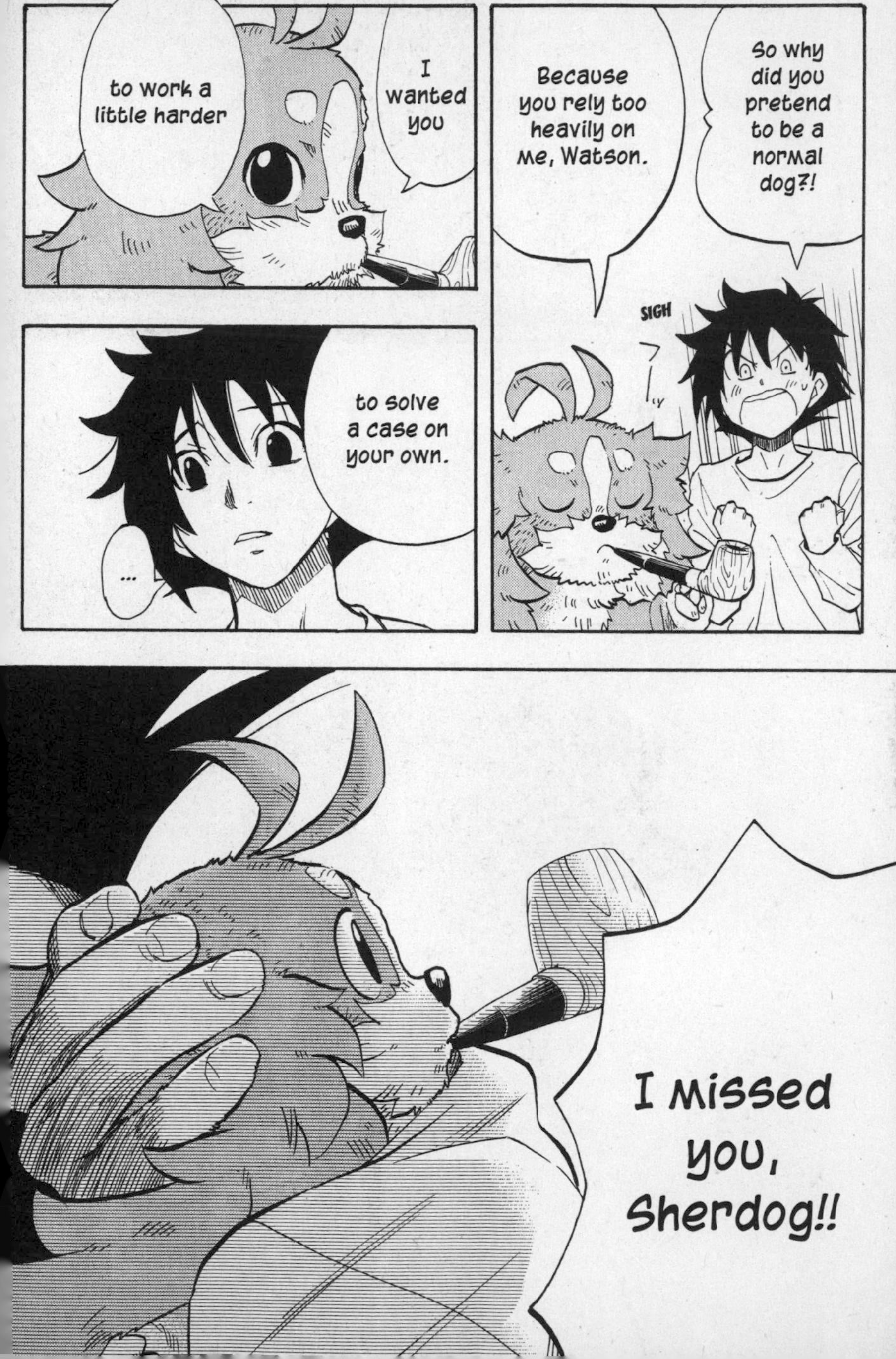
So why did you pretend to be a normal dog?!
Because you rely too heavily on me, Watson.
SIGH
I wanted you
to work a little harder
to solve a case on your own.
...
I missed you, Sherdog!!

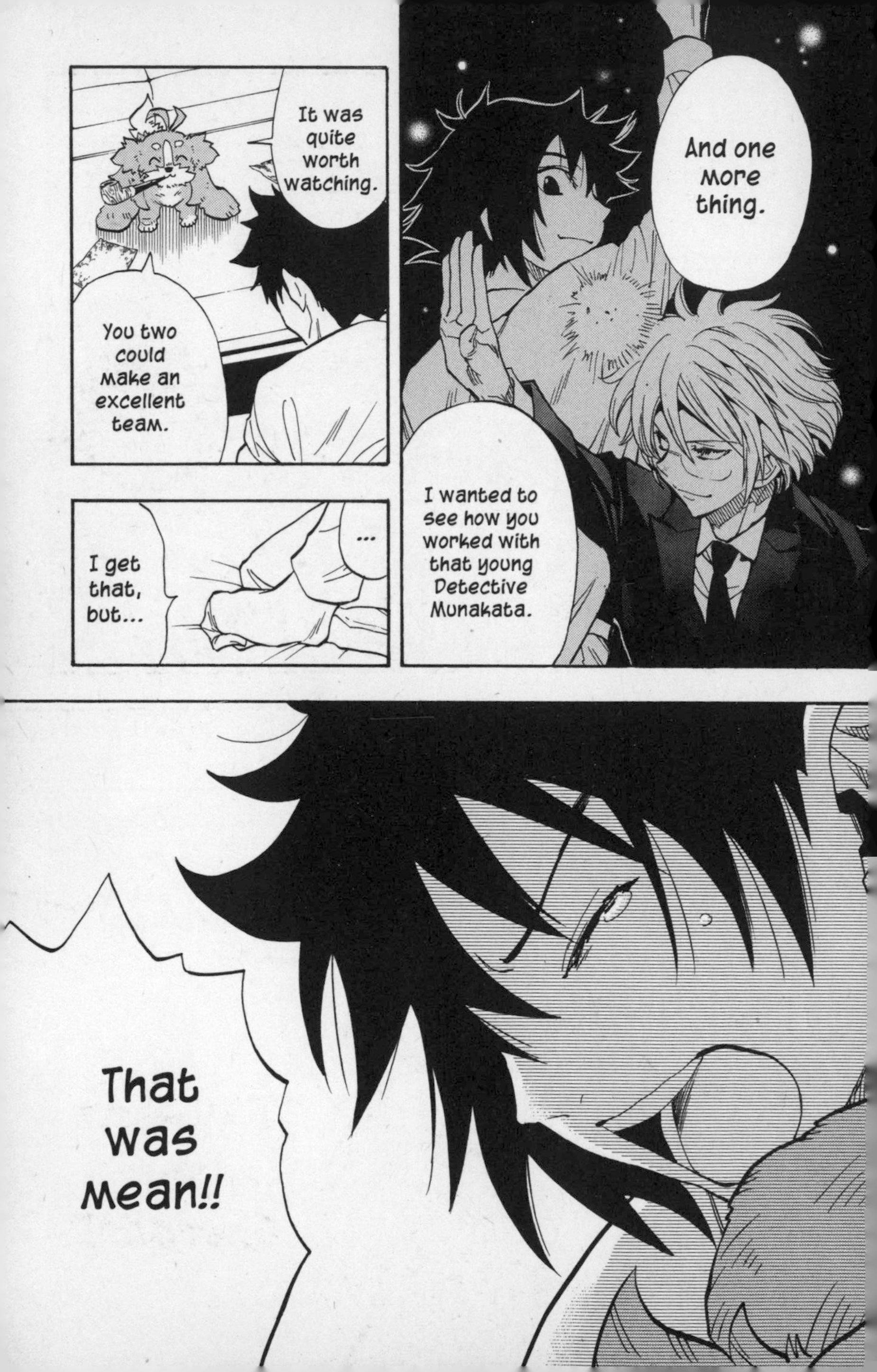
And one more thing.
I wanted to see how you worked with that young Detective Munakata.
It was quite worth watching.
You two could make an excellent team.
...
I get that, but...
That was mean!!

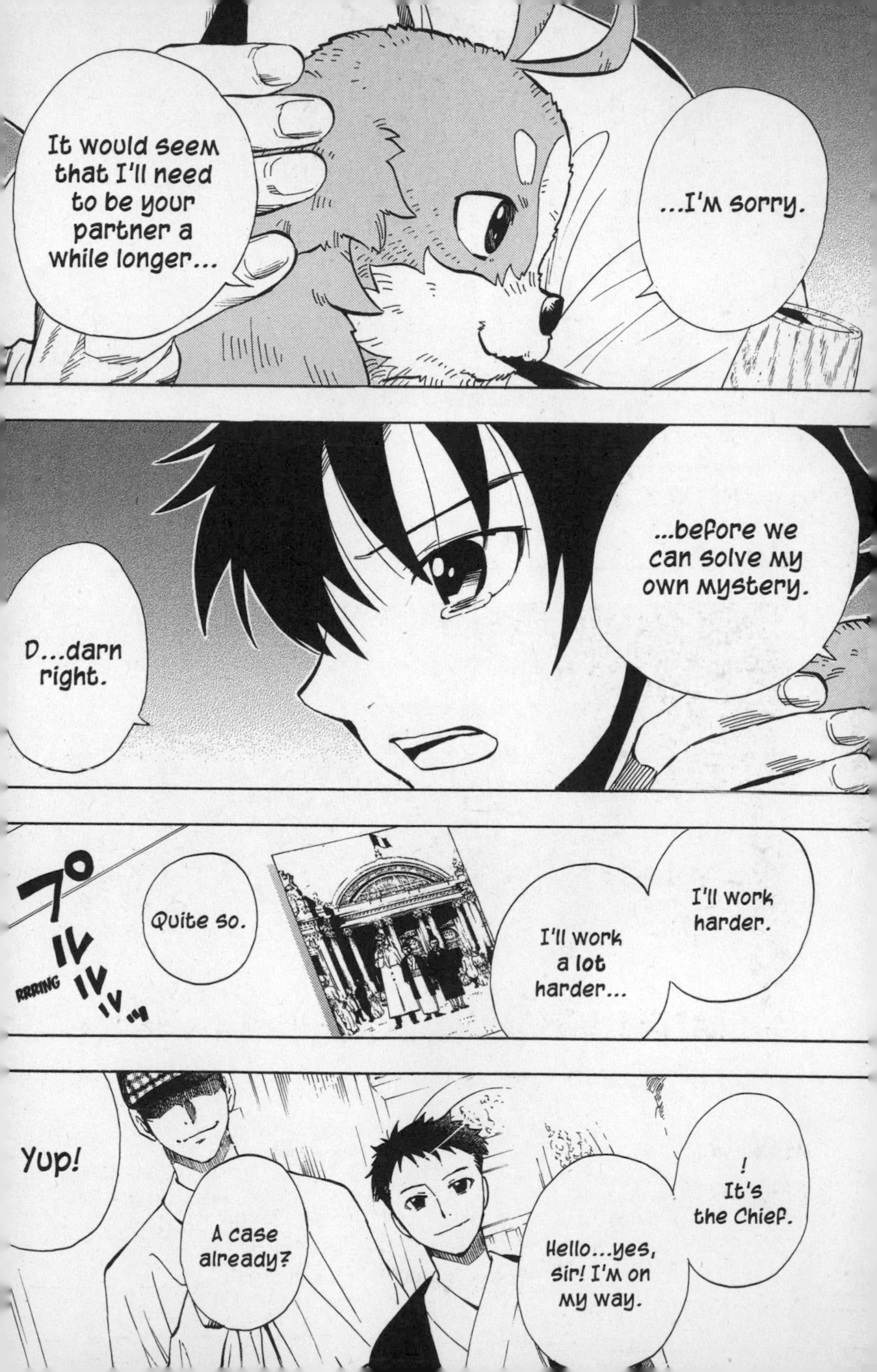
...I'm sorry.
It would seem that I'll need to be your partner a while longer...
...before we can solve my own mystery.
D...darn right.
I'll work harder.
I'll work a lot harder...
Quite so.
RRRING
! It's the Chief.
Hello...yes, sir! I'm on my way.
A case already?
Yup!

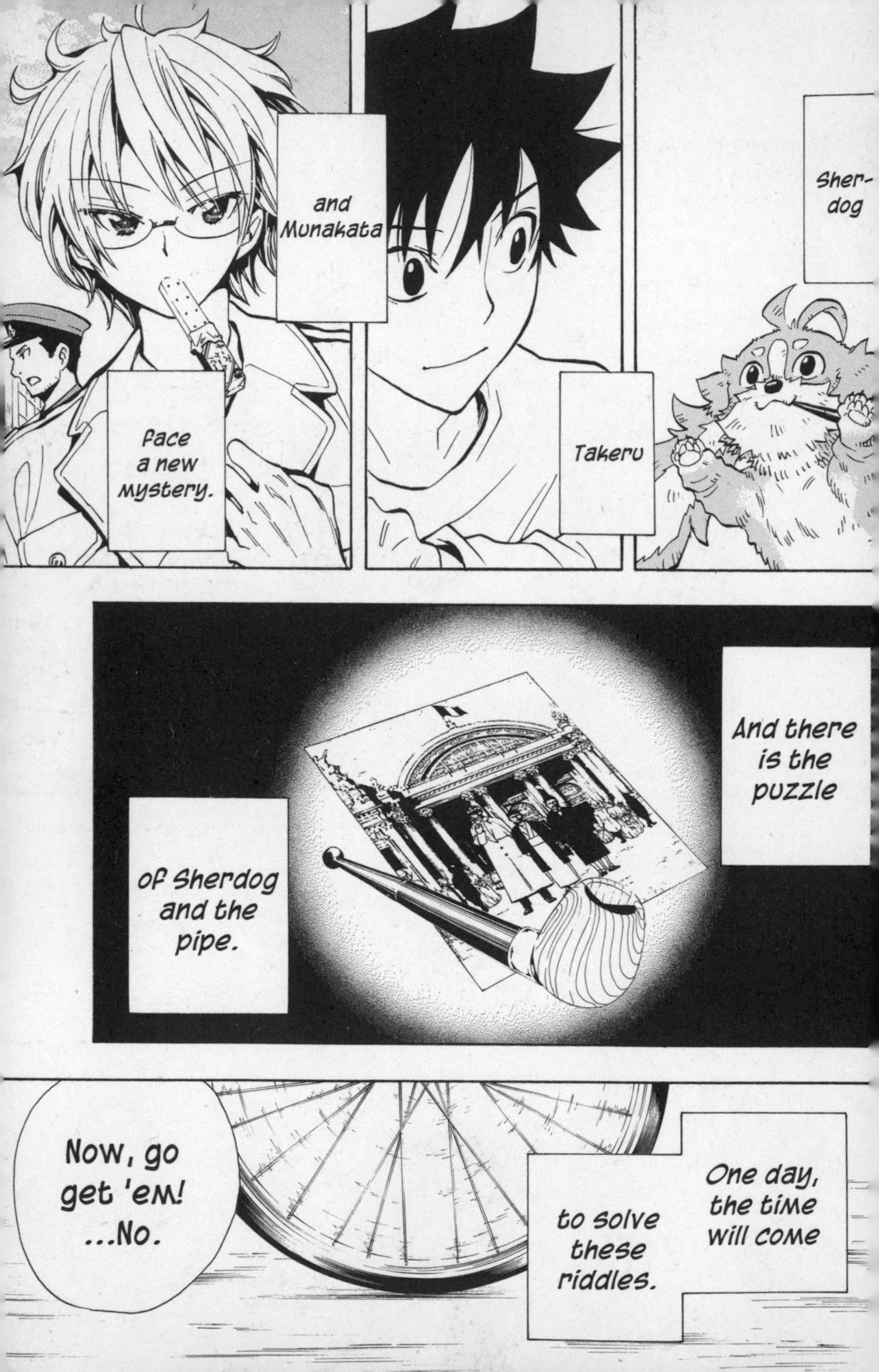
Sher-dog
Takeru
and Munakata
face a new mystery.
And there is the puzzle
of Sherdog and the pipe.
One day, the time will come
to solve these riddles.
Now, go get 'em! ...No.

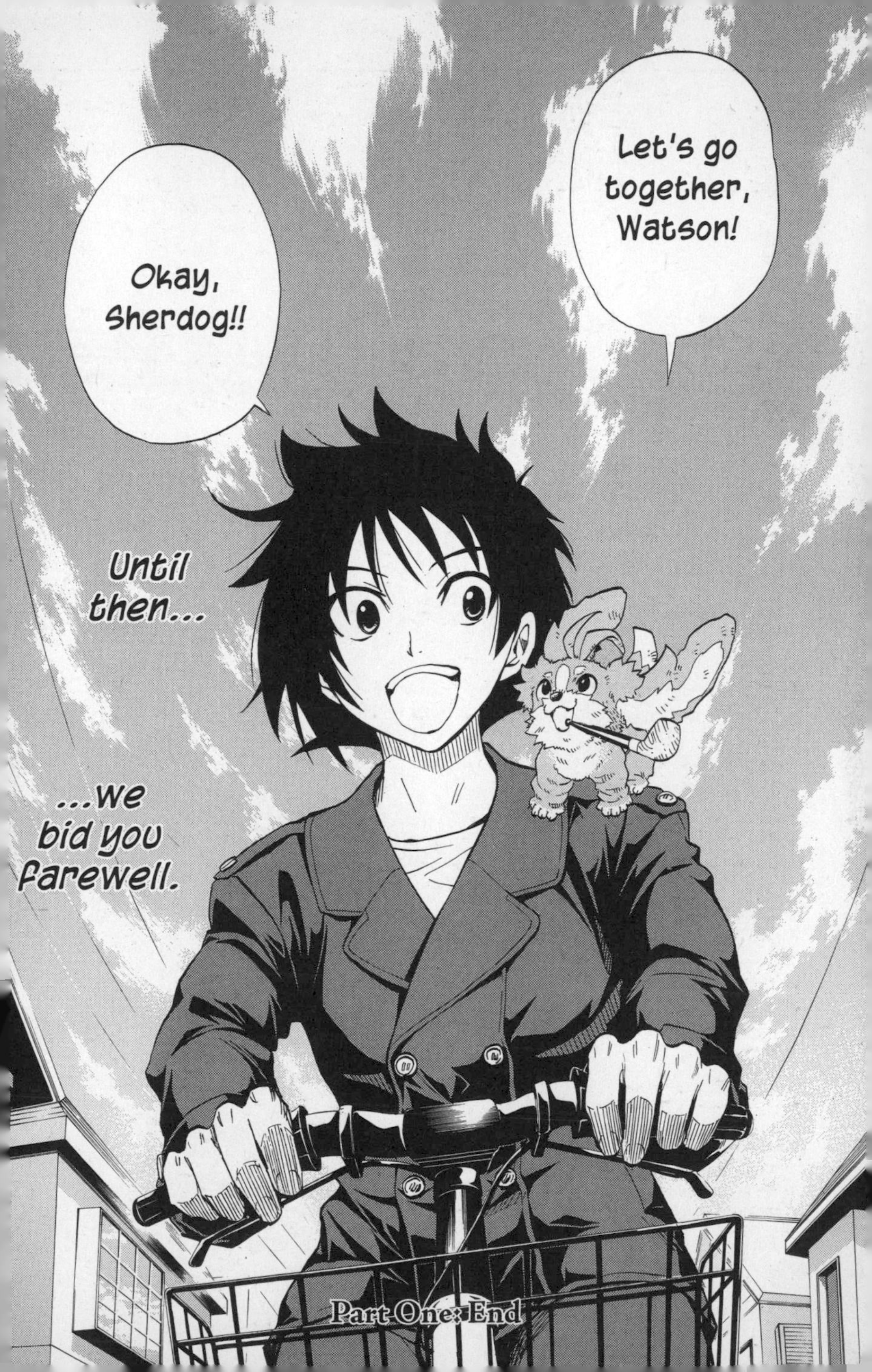
Let's go together, Watson!
Okay, Sherdog!!
Until then...
...we bid you farewell.
Part One: End

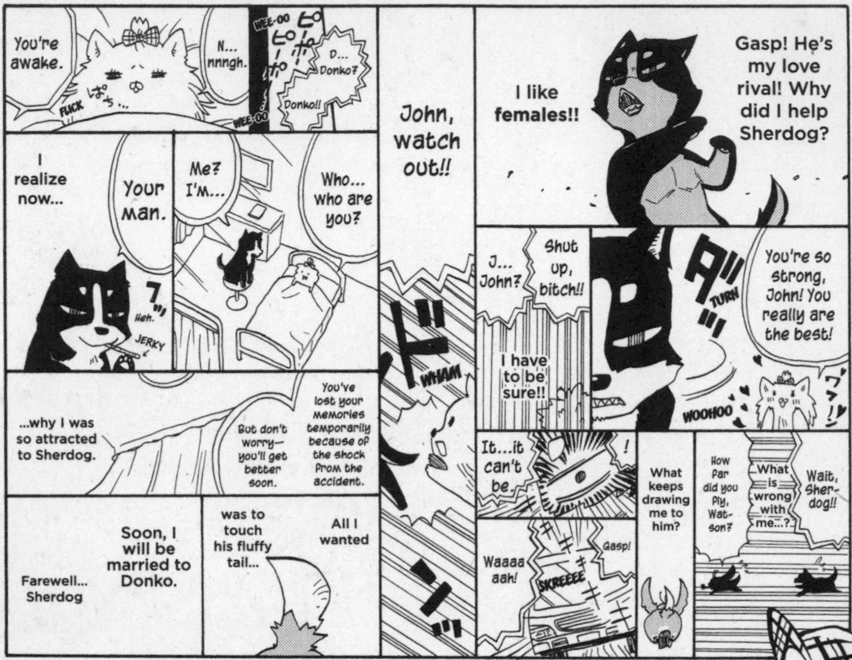
Gasp! He's my love rival! Why did I help Sherdog?
I like females!!
You're so strong, John! You really are the best!
TURN
WOOHOO
Shut up, bitch!!
J... John?
I have to be sure!!
Wait, Sherdog!!
What is wrong with me...?
How far did you fly, Watson?
What keeps drawing me to him?
It...it can't be.
!
Gasp!
Waaaa aah!
SKREEEE
John, watch out!!
WHAM
WEE-OO
D... Donko?
Donko!!
WEE-OO
N... nnngh.
You're awake.
FLICK
Who... who are you?
Me? I'm...
Your man.
I realize now...
Heh.
JERKY
You've lost your memories temporarily because of the shock from the accident.
But don't worry—you'll get better soon.
...why I was so attracted to Sherdog.
All I wanted
was to touch his fluffy tail...
Soon, I will be married to Donko.
Farewell... Sherdog

THANK YOU SO MUCH!!

I'm sorry ☺ I had no idea we would only have one page available for bonus material. ...Who are John and Donko?!

Due to various circumstances, after introducing new characters and the story of the pipe, Sherlock Bones had to get put on hiatus. I'm so sorry! I don't know when there will be a sequel, but Ando-sensei and I are both plenty motivated, so I hope an opportunity will present itself....

Anyway, I really did learn a lot from working on this series. Ando-sensei would improve all the good points of my rough drafts, and he took apart and explained all the bad parts, thoroughly and in a way that made sense. I'm very grateful for the experience! I'm sorry for always drawing the author in such weird caricatures (ha ha).

And I'm always getting so much encouragement from all you readers and your letters, but as usual, I haven't been able to return the favor, and I'm really very sorry. ...I don't think I'll ever change ☺ I hope you won't let that stop you from reading my manga!! Finally, to my editor who I'm always causing trouble for, everyone in marketing, my friends, and family—thank you!! S.

UNTIL WE MEET AGAIN!!

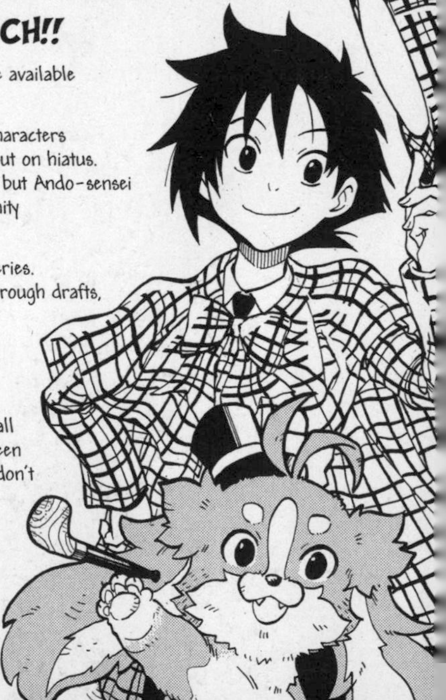

TAKERU & SHERDOG

Translation Notes

Japanese is a tricky language for most Westerners, and translation is often more art than science. For your edification and reading pleasure, here are notes on some of the places where we could have gone in a different direction with our translation of the work, or where a Japanese cultural reference is used.

Spaghetti, Denim, Tex, and His Highness, page 13

All of these are nicknames from Chief Yoshida's favorite detective drama, "Taiyō ni Hoero!", or "Howl at the Sun!" Spaghetti, originally Macaroni Keiji, got his nickname because his style of dress reminded another character of Spaghetti Westerns. Detective Denim got his name for wearing jeans. Tex, or Detective Texas, wears a ten-gallon hat, and His Highness is so-called because of his noble, sophisticated bearing.

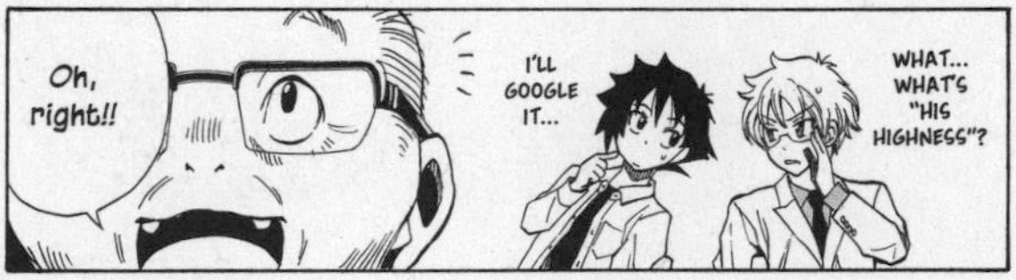
WHAT... WHAT'S "HIS HIGHNESS"?
I'LL GOOGLE IT...
Oh, right!!

You're filthy, Watson, page 30

Since Sherdog is learning all about modern-day Japan during his adventures with Takeru, he learned the term, engacho. The word is usually used by children to identify someone who is infected with dirtiness, such as a friend who stepped in something gross. In this case, he is referring to the tea that Dr. Akane spit all over Takeru's face. Until the engacho is lifted (in this case, by Takeru cleaning his face), the person so identified is to be avoided, so that no one else will catch the dirtiness.

It's a little like cooties.

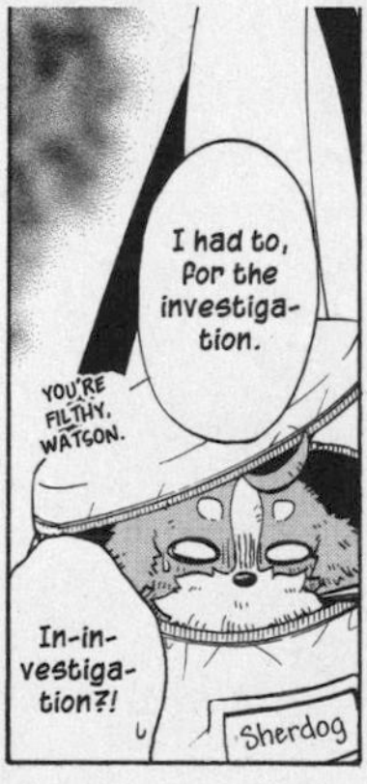
I had to, for the investigation.
YOU'RE FILTHY, WATSON.
In-investigation?!
Sherdog

Deluxe full-course lunch, page 65

Takeru has been sent to buy lunches at a store that specializes in pre-packaged lunches. Kento, in his constant attempt to prove his superiority, asks for the biggest and most expensive lunch on the menu, the deluxe maku-no-uchi lunch. The term maku-no-uchi means "between acts," because such meals were served between the acts of a kabuki play. The lunch has small portions, but of a wide variety of foods, including rice, vegetables, fish, etc.

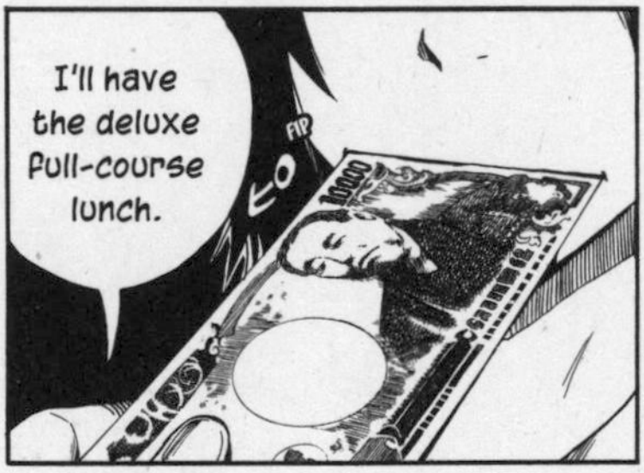
I'll have the deluxe full-course lunch.
FIP

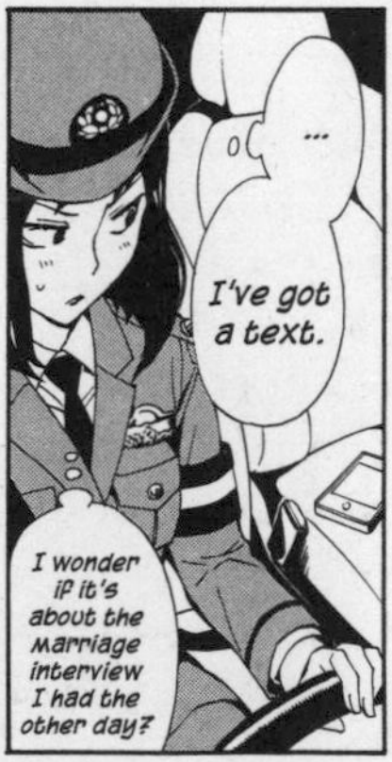
...
I've got a text.
I wonder if it's about the marriage interview I had the other day?

Marriage interview, page 69

Here, Katsuyo is referring to an omiai, which literally means "looking at one another." Basically, an omiai is when a single man and woman meet each other under the understanding that they are looking for a marriage partner.

Monster coma, page 137

The translators would like to apologize for this terrible excuse for a pun. In Japanese, Monta Komatsuda's name lends itself to a pun much more easily. His nickname, as the director calls him, is Komatta, which is a word that basically means "bothersome." Monta sounds like monda, meaning "it is a thing." In Japanese name order, his name is Komatsuda Monta, which easily becomes komatta monda—"it is a bothersome thing," or, "oh, bother."

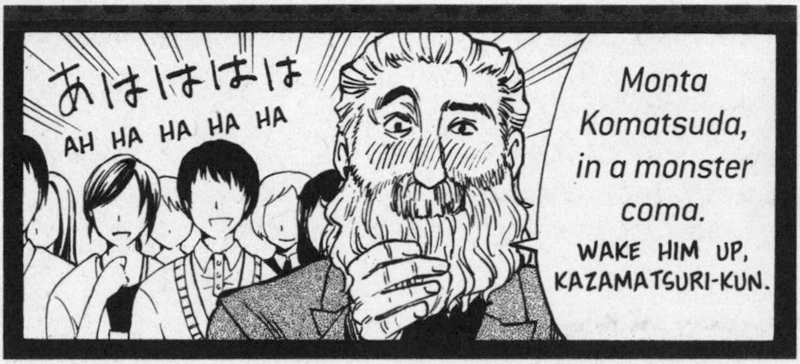

Monta Komatsuda, in a monster coma.
WAKE HIM UP, KAZAMATSURI-KUN.
あははははは
AH HA HA HA HA

Private interrogation room, page 155

As Takeru and Kento have stated, the most suspicious point about Kyōhei Kazamatsuri is his shoes, so they needed a way to get those shoes off of him. In Japan, it is customary to remove one's shoes when inside a building. Many public buildings, like theaters, no longer

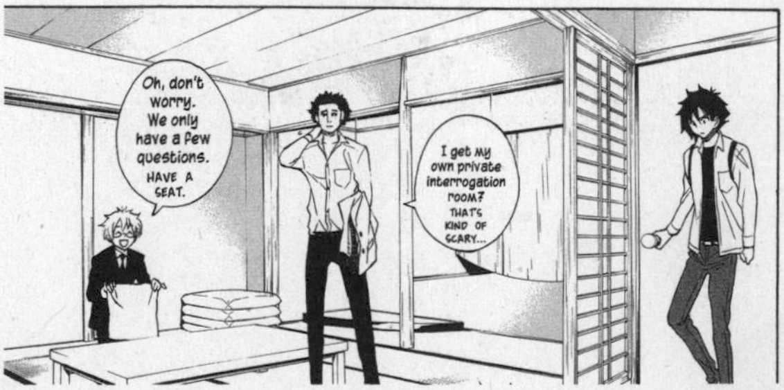

I get my own private interrogation room? THAT'S KIND OF SCARY...
Oh, don't worry. We only have a few questions.
HAVE A SEAT.

require this, but it is still common courtesy in any building to remove one's shoes when entering a room with tatami mat flooring—a room like the one Takeru and Kento use for this interrogation. This is partially because tatami mats were originally used for seating and to sleep on, and it would be rude to get them dirty.

Natsume Sōseki, page 183

Natsume Sōseki is a renowned Japanese author, who wrote several Japanese literary classics, such as Kokoro and Botchan. He also studied abroad in England at the beginning of the 20th century.

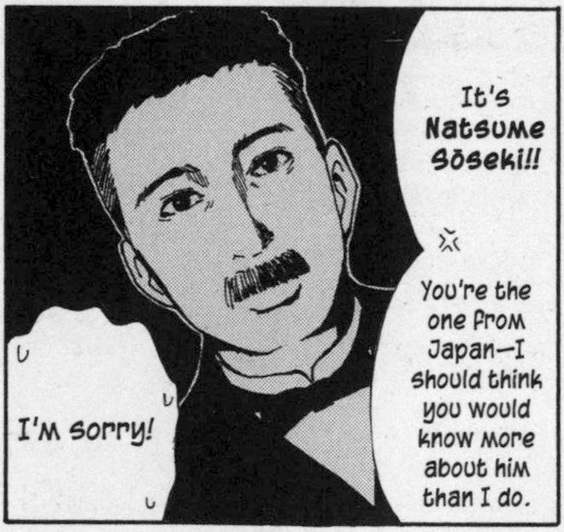
It's Natsume Sōseki!!
You're the one from Japan—I should think you would know more about him than I do.
I'm sorry!

FROM HIRO MASHIMA, CREATOR OF **RAVE MASTER**

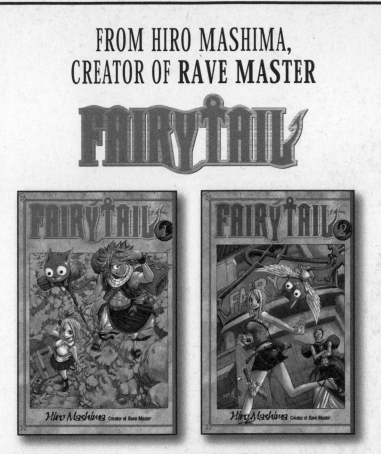

Lucy has always dreamed of joining the Fairy Tail, a club for the most powerful sorcerers in the land. But once she becomes a member, the fun really starts!

Special extras in each volume! Read them all!

RATING T AGES 13+

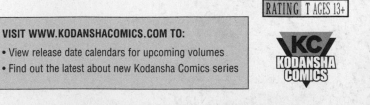

VISIT WWW.KODANSHACOMICS.COM TO:

• View release date calendars for upcoming volumes
• Find out the latest about new Kodansha Comics series

KC KODANSHA COMICS

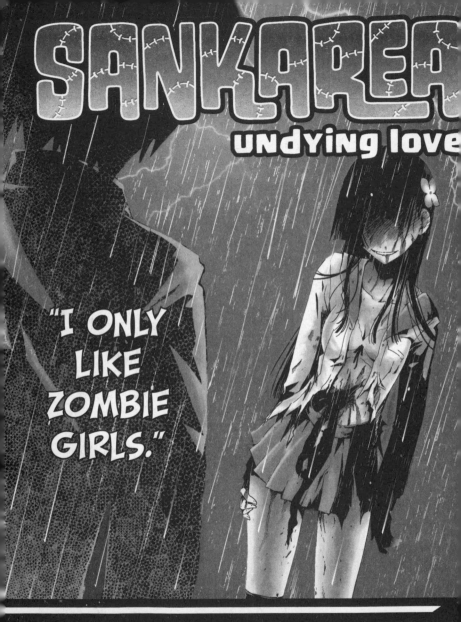

SANKAREA
undying love

"I ONLY LIKE ZOMBIE GIRLS."

Chihiro has an unusual connection to zombie movies. He doesn't feel bad
the survivors – he wants to comfort the undead girls they slaughter! Wher
his pet passes away, he brews a resurrection potion. He's discovered by
local heiress Sanka Rea, and she serves as his first test subject!

KODA
COi

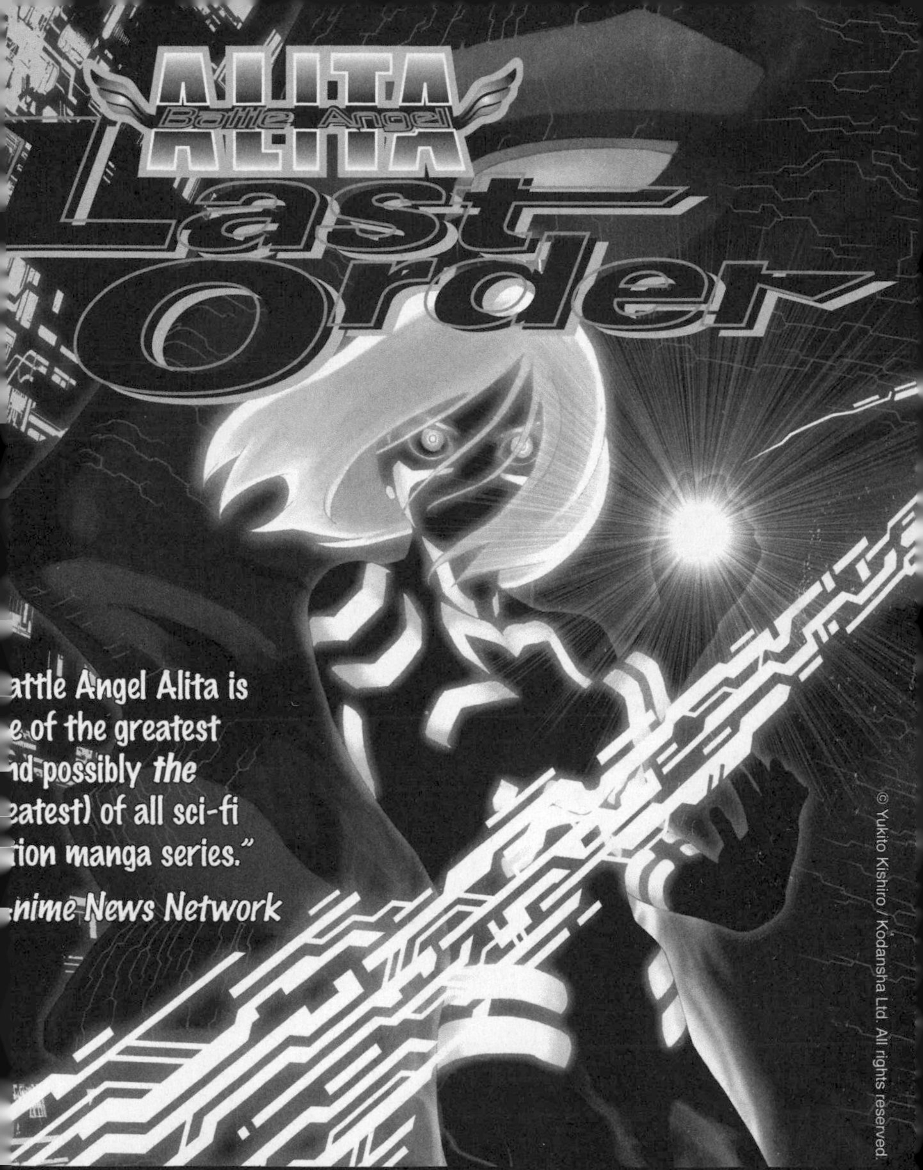

ALITA
Bottle Angel ALITA
Last Order

...he Cyberpunk Legend is Back!

...deluxe omnibus editions of 600+ pages,
...cluding ALL-NEW original stories by
...ta creator Yukito Kishiro!

KC
KODANSHA
COMICS

A Kodansha Comics Trade Paperback Original.

Sherlock Bones volume 7 copyright © 2013 Yuma Ando & Yuki Sato
English translation copyright © 2014 Yuma Ando & Yuki Sato

Published in the United States by Kodansha Comics,
an imprint of Kodansha USA Publishing, LLC, New York.

Publication rights for this English edition arranged through Kodansha Ltd., Tokyo.

First published in Japan in 2013 by Kodansha Ltd., Tokyo, as *Tanteiken Sherdock* volume 7.

ISBN 978-1-61262-582-9

Printed in the United States of America.

www.kodanshacomics.com

9 8 7 6 5 4 3 2 1

Translator: Alethea Nibley and Athena Nibley
Lettering: Kiyoko Shiromasa
Kodansha Comics edition cover design: Phil Balsman

TOMARE! [STOP!]

You are going the wrong way!

Manga is a completely different type of reading experience.

To start at the beginning, go to the end!

That's right! Authentic manga is read the traditional Japanese way—from right to left, exactly the opposite of how American books are read. It's easy to follow: Just go to the other end of the book, and read each page—and each panel—from right side to left side, starting at the top right. Now you're experiencing manga as it was meant to be.